BLACK&DECKER®

THE COMPLETE GUIDE TO
HOME WIRING

*Including Information on Home Electronics
& Wireless Technology*

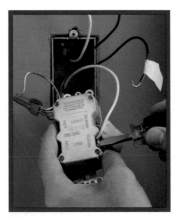

Creative Publishing
international

MINNEAPOLIS, MINNESOTA
www.creativepub.com

Contents

Basic Electrical Repairs

Creative Publishing
international

Copyright © 2005
Creative Publishing international, Inc.
400 First Avenue, Suite 300
Minneapolis, Minnesota 55401
1-800-328-3895
www.creativepub.com
All rights reserved

Printed by R. R. Donnelley
20 19 18 17 16 15 14 13 12 11

President/CEO: Ken Fund

Executive Editor: Bryan Trandem
Creative Director: Tim Himsel

For revised edition:
Editor: Andrew Karre
Contributing Editor: Jodie Carter
Project Manager: Tracy Stanley
Art Director: Jon Simpson
Photographer: Andrea Rugg
Scene Shop Carpenter: Randy Austin
Production Manager: Laura Hokkanen

THE COMPLETE GUIDE TO HOME WIRING
Created by: The Editors of Creative Publishing international, Inc., in cooperation with Black & Decker. Black & Decker® is a trademark of The Black & Decker Corporation and is used under license.

Library of Congress
Cataloging-in-Publication Data

The complete guide to home wiring : includes information on home electronics & wireless technology / editor, Andrew Karre.-- Rev. ed.
   p. cm.
   Includes index.
   ISBN 1-58923-213-5 (soft cover)
   1. Electric wiring, Interior--Amateurs' manuals.
2. Dwellings--Maintenance and repair--Amateurs' manuals. 3. Dwellings--Electric equipment--Amateurs' manuals.
I. Karre, Andrew. II. Creative Publishing International III. Title.

TK3285.C68 2006
621.319'24--dc22
                              2005015825

Advanced Wiring Projects

Portions of *The Complete Guide to Home Wiring* are taken from the Black & Decker® books *Basic Wiring & Electrical Repairs* and *Advanced Home Wiring*. Other books in the Black & Decker® Home Improvement Library™ include:

Complete Guide to Easy Woodworking Projects
Complete Guide to Building Decks
Complete Guide to Painting & Decorating
Complete Guide to Windows & Doors
Complete Guide to Creative Landscapes

Complete Guide to Home Storage
Complete Guide to Bathrooms
Complete Guide to Ceramic & Stone Tile
Complete Guide to Flooring
Complete Guide to Home Masonry
Complete Guide to Roofing & Siding
Complete Guide to Kitchens

Introduction

In everything from food preparation to climate control, from entertainment to work, electricity plays a critical role in our lives. Knowing about your electrical system and how it works will allow you to make smart, money-saving decisions to improve your home's functionality, convenience, and safety—and it will allow you to make use of the latest technology.

This newly updated and revised edition of the top-selling *The Complete Guide to Home Wiring* is a comprehensive tour through the sometimes intimidating subject of electricity. With easy-to-understand definitions, step-by-step instructions, and clear color photos, you will recognize that most electrical work around your home, from basic repairs to advanced wiring projects, is work you yourself can easily accomplish.

Even if you hire professionals to replace fixtures or install new circuits, understanding how wiring works and what is required to complete a job will make you a more savvy consumer and help you make the best use of your money.

What You'll Find In This Book

The first section of the book covers basic electrical repairs. Each major component of your home's electrical system is clearly defined and thoroughly covered. Definitions for and discussions about all types of wires and cables, fuse boxes and breaker panels, switches, and receptacles will help you identify and work with the existing materials and fixtures in your home. You will learn how to troubleshoot and fix virtually any switch, receptacle, lamp, light fixture, doorbell, or thermostat as problems arise. All the tools and materials necessary for performing the repairs are shown, as well as professional techniques for using them. You'll see how mapping your home's electrical system makes it much simpler and safer to do work. There is also a review of the problems that an electrical inspector would point out and the instructions to fix them.

The second section of the book presents complete wiring projects for your home and yard. Whether you are remodeling and working in new construction or making changes within the existing structure, these detailed projects can easily be adapted to your home's particular needs. You will learn each step to planning a successful major wiring project, from understanding electrical code requirements to designing a layout that best suits your needs. There are also 31 up-to-code, full-color circuit maps designed to simplify wiring layouts.

Of course, wiring isn't limited to your home's interior. In this book, you'll find techniques for outdoor wiring, including how to add lights to your house, deck, and landscaping.

Finally, *The Complete Guide to Home Wiring* features information and projects for the fastest-growing areas of home wiring: automation and networking. You'll find a helpful overview of home automation technology, as well as simple automation projects. Also included are complete instructions for installing a low-voltage structured wiring system to meet the rapidly expanding needs of new data, video, and telecommunication technologies. This system ensures optimum performance today and a solid foundation for future upgrades.

Whether your wiring project involves fixing a light switch or completing a kitchen, bathroom, basement, or attic remodel, all the information you need is right here. This newly revised edition of *The Complete Guide to Home Wiring* will be a time- and money-saving asset for all your wiring repairs and improvements.

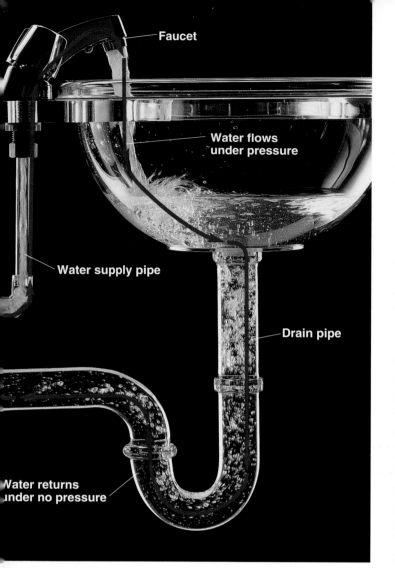

Faucet

Water flows under pressure

Water supply pipe

Drain pipe

Water returns under no pressure

Understanding Electricity

A household electrical system can be compared with a home's plumbing system. Electrical current flows in wires in much the same way that water flows inside pipes. Both electricity and water enter the home, are distributed throughout the house, do their "work," and exit.

In plumbing, water first flows through the pressurized water supply system. In electricity, current first flows along hot wires. Current flowing along hot wires also is pressurized. The pressure of electrical current is called **voltage**.

Large supply pipes can carry a greater volume of water than small pipes. Likewise, large electrical wires carry more current than small wires. This current-carrying capacity of wires is called **amperage**.

Water is made available for use through the faucets, spigots, and showerheads in a home. Electricity is made available through receptacles, switches, and fixtures.

Water finally leaves the home through a drain system, which is not pressurized. Similarly, electrical current flows back through neutral wires. The current in neutral wires is not pressurized and is said to be at zero voltage.

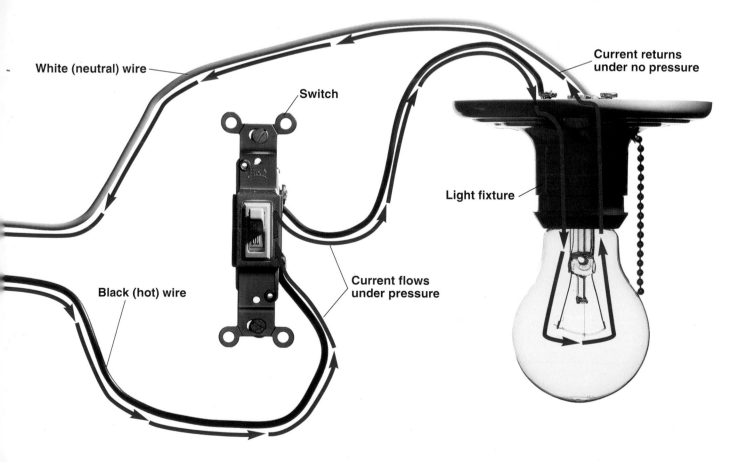

White (neutral) wire

Switch

Current returns under no pressure

Light fixture

Black (hot) wire

Current flows under pressure

Glossary of Electrical Terms

ampere (or **amp**): Refers to the rate at which electrical power flows to a light, tool, or appliance.

armored cable: Two or more wires that are grouped together and protected by a flexible metal covering.

box: A device used to contain wiring connections.

BX: See **armored cable.**

cable: Two or more wires that are grouped together and protected by a covering or sheath.

circuit: A continuous loop of electrical current flowing along wires or cables.

circuit breaker: A safety device that interrupts an electrical circuit in the event of an overload or short circuit.

conductor: Any material that allows electrical current to flow through it. Copper wire is an especially good conductor.

conduit: A metal or plastic tube used to protect wires.

continuity: An uninterrupted electrical pathway through a circuit or electrical fixture.

current: The movement of electrons along a conductor.

duplex receptacle: A receptacle that provides connections for two plugs.

feed wire: A conductor that carries 120-volt current uninterrupted from the service panel.

fuse: A safety device, usually found in older homes, that interrupts electrical circuits during an overload or short circuit.

Greenfield: See **armored cable.**

grounded wire: See **neutral wire.**

grounding wire: A wire used in an electrical circuit to conduct current to the earth in the event of a short circuit. The grounding wire often is a bare copper wire.

hot wire: Any wire that carries voltage. In an electrical circuit, the hot wire usually is covered with black or red insulation.

insulator: Any material, such as plastic or rubber, that resists the flow of electrical current. Insulating materials protect wires and cables.

junction box: See **box.**

meter: A device used to measure the amount of electrical power being used.

neutral wire: A wire that returns current at zero voltage to the source of electrical power. Usually covered with white or light gray insulation. Also called the grounded wire.

outlet: See **receptacle.**

overload: A demand for more current than the circuit wires or electrical device was designed to carry. Usually causes a fuse to blow or a circuit breaker to trip.

pigtail: A short wire used to connect two or more circuit wires to a single screw terminal.

polarized receptacle: A receptacle designed to keep hot current flowing along black or red wires, and neutral current flowing along white or gray wires.

power: The result of hot current flowing for a period of time. Use of power makes heat, motion, or light.

receptacle: A device that provides plug-in access to electrical power.

Romex: A brand name of plastic-sheathed electrical cable that is commonly used for indoor wiring.

screw terminal: A place where a wire connects to a receptacle, switch, or fixture.

service panel: A metal box usually near the site where electrical power enters the house. In the service panel, electrical current is split into individual circuits. The service panel has circuit breakers or fuses to protect each circuit.

short circuit: An accidental and improper contact between two current-carrying wires, or between a current-carrying wire and a grounding conductor.

switch: A device that controls electrical current passing through hot circuit wires. Used to turn lights and appliances on and off.

UL: An abbreviation for Underwriters Laboratories, an organization that tests electrical devices and manufactured products for safety.

voltage (or **volts**): A measurement of electricity in terms of pressure.

wattage (or **watt**): A measurement of electrical power in terms of total energy consumed. Watts can be calculated by multiplying the voltage times the amps.

wire connector: A device used to connect two or more wires together. Also called a wire nut.

Electricity & Safety

Safety should be the primary concern of anyone working with electricity. Although most household electrical repairs are simple and straightforward, always use caution and good judgment when working with electrical wiring or devices. Common sense can prevent accidents.

The basic rule of electrical safety is: **Always turn off power to the area or device you are working on.** At the main service panel, remove the fuse or shut off the circuit breaker that controls the circuit you are servicing. Then check to make sure the power is off by testing for power with a neon circuit tester (page 18). Restore power only when the repair or replacement project is complete.

Follow the safety tips shown on these pages. Never attempt an electrical project beyond your skill or confidence level. Never attempt to repair or replace your main service panel or service entrance head (pages 12 to 13). These are jobs for a qualified electrician and require that the power company shuts off power to your house.

Shut off power to the proper circuit at the fuse box or main service panel before beginning work.

Make a map of your household electrical circuits (pages 30 to 33) to help you turn the proper circuits on and off for electrical repairs.

Close service panel door and post a warning sign to prevent others from turning on power while you are working on electrical projects.

Keep a flashlight near your main service panel. Check flashlight batteries regularly.

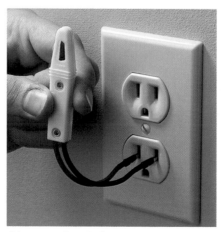

Always check for power at the fixture you are servicing before you begin any work.

Use only UL approved electrical parts or devices. These devices have been tested for safety by Underwriters Laboratories.

Wear rubber-soled shoes while working on electrical projects. On damp floors, stand on a rubber mat or dry wooden boards.

Use fiberglass or wood ladders when making routine household repairs near the service head.

Use GFCI receptacles (ground-fault circuit-interrupters) where specified by local electrical codes (pages 74 to 77).

Protect children with receptacle caps or childproof receptacle covers (page 69).

Use extension cords only for temporary connections. Never place them underneath rugs or fasten them to walls, baseboards, or other surfaces.

Use correct fuses or breakers in the main service panel (pages 28 to 29). Never install a fuse or breaker that has a higher amperage rating than the circuit wires.

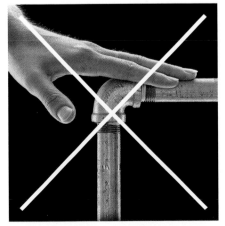

Do not touch metal pipes, faucets, or fixtures while working with electricity. The metal may provide a grounding path, allowing electrical current to flow through your body.

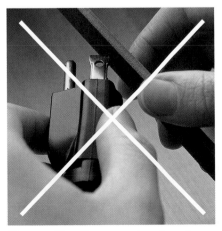

Never alter the prongs of a plug to fit a receptacle. If possible, install a new grounded receptacle.

Do not drill walls or ceilings without first shutting off electrical power to the circuits that may be hidden. Use double-insulated tools.

Your Electrical System

Electrical power that enters the home is produced by large **power plants.** Power plants are located in all parts of the country and generate electricity with turbines that are turned by water, wind, or steam. From these plants electricity enters large "step-up" transformers that increase voltage to half a million volts or more.

Electricity flows easily at these large voltages and travels through high-voltage transmission lines to communities that can be hundreds of miles from the power plants. "Step-down" transformers located at **substations** then reduce the voltage for distribution along street lines. On **utility power poles,** smaller transformers further reduce the voltage to ordinary 120-volt current for household use.

Lines carrying current to the house either run underground or are strung overhead and attached to a post called a **service head.** Most homes built after 1950 have three wires running to the service head: two power lines, each carrying 120 volts of current, and a grounded neutral wire. Power from the two 120-volt lines may be combined at the **service panel** to supply current to large, 240-volt appliances like clothes dryers or electric water heaters.

Many older homes have only two wires running to the service head, with one 120-volt line and a grounded neutral wire. This older two-wire service is inadequate for today's homes. Contact an electrical contractor and your local power utility company to upgrade to a three-wire service.

Incoming power passes through an **electric meter** that measures power consumption. Power then enters the service panel, where it is distributed to circuits that run throughout the house. The service panel also contains fuses or circuit breakers that shut off power to the individual circuits in the event of a short circuit or an overload. Certain high-wattage appliances, like microwave ovens, are usually plugged into their own individual circuits to prevent overloads.

Voltage ratings determined by power companies and manufacturers have changed over the years. Current rated at 110 volts changed to 115 volts, then 120 volts. Current rated at 220 volts changed to 230 volts, then 240 volts. Similarly, ratings for receptacles, tools, light fixtures, and appliances have changed from 115 volts to 125 volts. These changes will not affect the performance of new devices connected to older wiring. For making electrical calculations, such as the ones shown in "Evaluating Circuits for Safe Capacity" (pages 34 to 35), use a rating of 120 volts or 240 volts for your circuits.

Power plants supply electricity to thousands of homes and businesses. Step-up transformers increase the voltage produced at the plant, making the power flow more easily along high-voltage transmission lines.

Substations are located near the communities they serve. A typical substation takes current from high-voltage transmission lines and reduces it for distribution along street lines.

Utility pole transformers reduce the high-voltage current that flows through power lines along neighborhood streets. A utility pole transformer reduces voltage from 10,000 volts to the normal 120-volt current used in households.

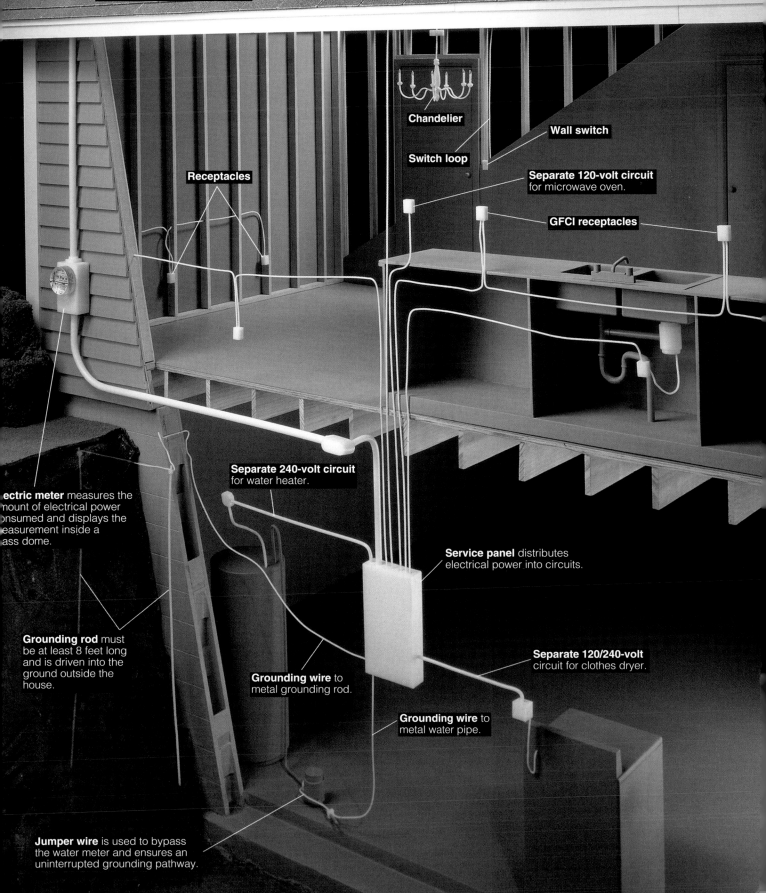

Service head or weather head anchors the service wires and prevents moisture from entering the house.

Service wires supply electricity to the house from the utility company's power lines.

Chandelier

Switch loop

Wall switch

Separate 120-volt circuit for microwave oven.

Receptacles

GFCI receptacles

Separate 240-volt circuit for water heater.

Service panel distributes electrical power into circuits.

ectric meter measures the mount of electrical power onsumed and displays the easurement inside a ass dome.

Grounding rod must be at least 8 feet long and is driven into the ground outside the house.

Grounding wire to metal grounding rod.

Separate 120/240-volt circuit for clothes dryer.

Grounding wire to metal water pipe.

Jumper wire is used to bypass the water meter and ensures an uninterrupted grounding pathway.

Parts of the Electrical System

The service head, sometimes called the weather head, anchors the service wires to the home. Three wires provide the standard 240-volt service necessary for the average home. Older homes may have two-wire service that provides only 120 volts of power. Two-wire service should be upgraded to three-wire service by an electrical contractor.

The electric meter measures the amount of electrical power consumed. It is usually attached to the side of the house, and connects to the service head. A thin metal disc inside the meter rotates when power is used. The electric meter belongs to your local power utility company. If you suspect the meter is not functioning properly, contact the power company.

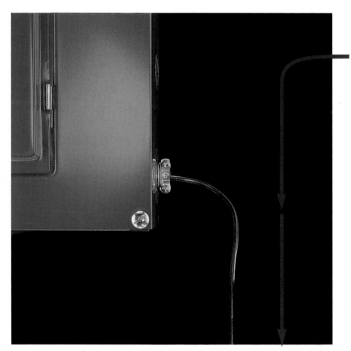

Grounding wire connects the electrical system to the earth through grounding rods or, in older systems, through a cold water pipe. In the event of an overload or short circuit, the grounding wire allows excess electrical power to find its way harmlessly to the earth.

Light fixtures attach directly to a household electrical system. They are usually controlled with wall switches. The two common types of light fixtures are **incandescent** (page 78) and **fluorescent** (page 92).

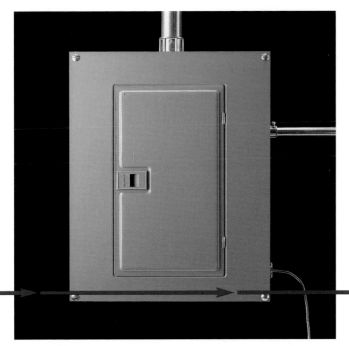

The main service panel, sometimes called a **fuse box** or **breaker box,** distributes power to individual circuits. Fuses or circuit breakers protect each circuit from short circuits and overloads. Fuses and circuit breakers also are used to shut off power to individual circuits while repairs are made.

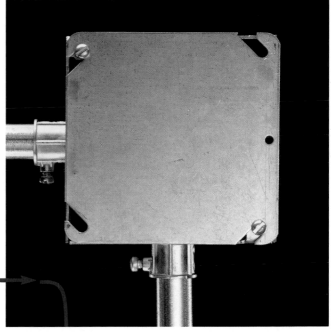

Electrical boxes enclose wire connections. According to the National Electrical Code, all wire splices or connections must be contained entirely in a plastic or metal electrical box.

Switches control electrical current passing through hot circuit wires. Switches can be wired to control light fixtures, ceiling fans, appliances, and receptacles.

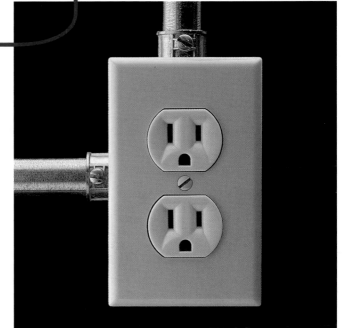

Receptacles, sometimes called **outlets,** provide plug-in access to electrical power. A 125-volt, 15-amp receptacle with a grounding hole is the most typical receptacle in wiring systems installed after 1965. Most receptacles have two plug-in locations and are called **duplex receptacles.**

Understanding Circuits

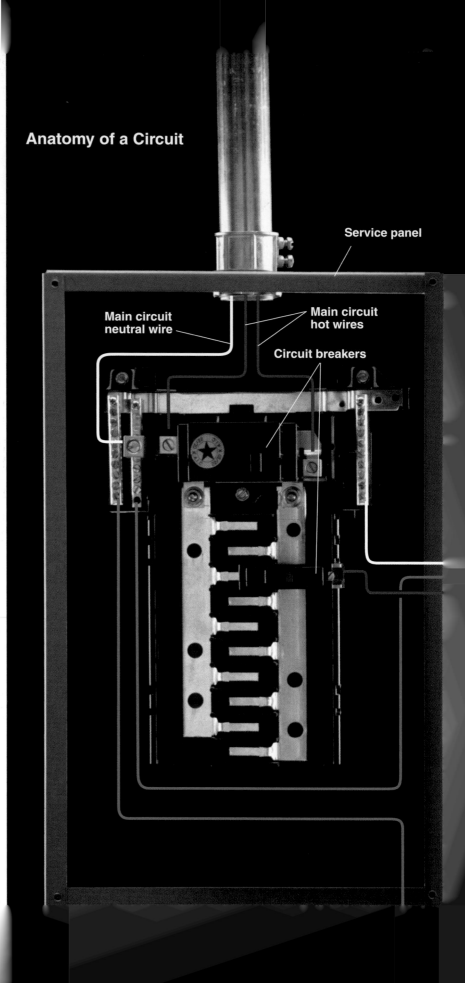

Anatomy of a Circuit

Service panel

Main circuit neutral wire

Main circuit hot wires

Circuit breakers

An electrical circuit is a continuous loop. Household circuits carry power from the main service panel, throughout the house, and back to the main service panel. Several switches, receptacles, light fixtures, or appliances may be connected to a single circuit.

Current enters a circuit loop on hot wires and returns along neutral wires. These wires are color coded for easy identification. Hot wires are black or red, and neutral wires are white or light gray. For safety, most circuits include a bare copper or green insulated grounding wire. The grounding wire conducts current in the event of a short circuit or overload, and helps reduce the chance of severe electrical shock. The service panel also has a grounding wire connected to a metal water pipe and metal grounding rod buried underground (pages 16 to 17).

If a circuit carries too much power, it can overload. A fuse or a circuit breaker protects each circuit in case of overloads (pages 28 to 29). To calculate how much power any circuit can carry, see "Evaluating Circuits for Safe Capacity" (pages 34 to 35).

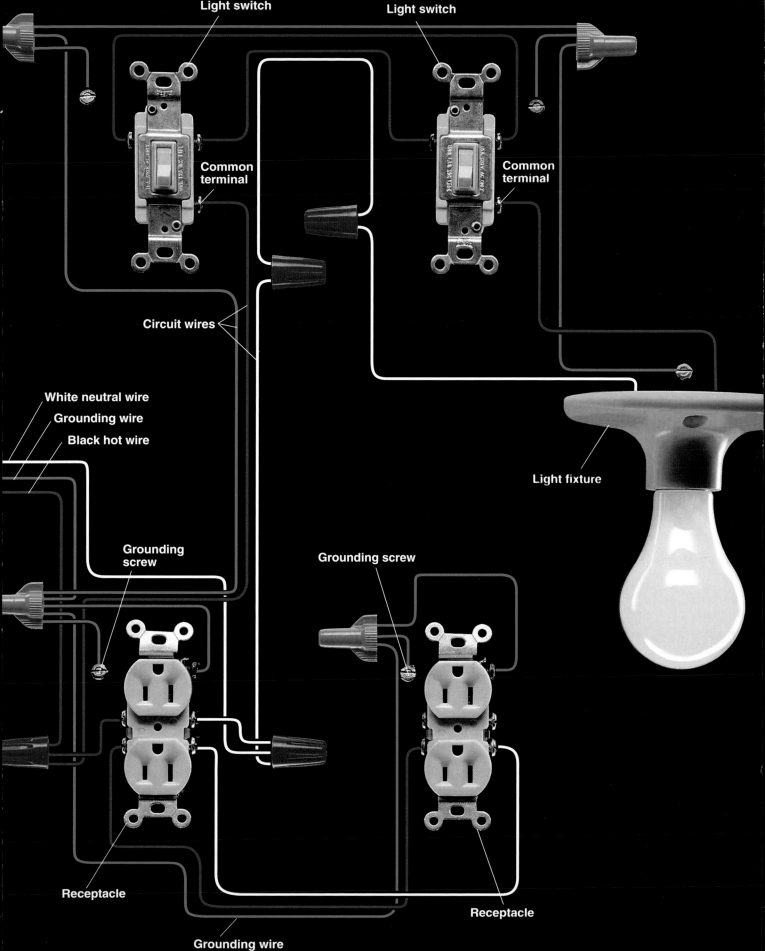

Light switch

Light switch

Common terminal

Common terminal

Circuit wires

White neutral wire

Grounding wire

Black hot wire

Grounding screw

Grounding screw

Light fixture

Receptacle

Receptacle

Grounding wire

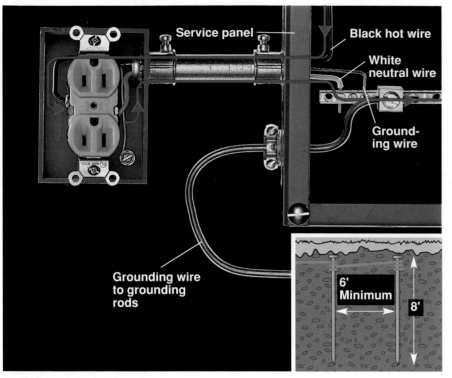

Normal current flow: Current enters the electrical box along a black hot wire, then returns to the service panel along a white neutral wire. Any excess current passes into the earth via a grounding wire attached to grounding rods or a metal water pipe.

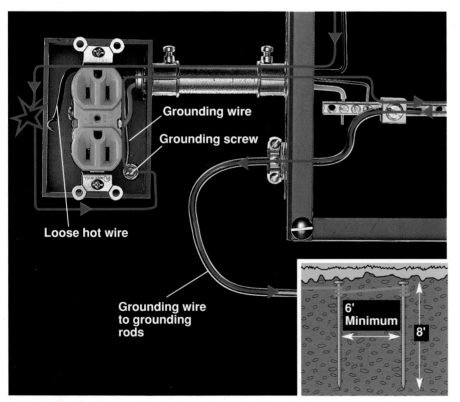

Short circuit: Current is detoured by a loose wire in contact with the metal box. The grounding wire picks it up and channels it safely back to the main service panel. There, it returns to its source along a neutral service cable or enters the earth via the grounding system.

Grounding & Polarization

Electricity always seeks to return to its source and complete a continuous circuit. In a household wiring system, this return path is provided by white neutral wires that return current to the main service panel. From the service panel, current returns along a neutral service wire to a power pole transformer.

A **grounding wire** provides an additional return path for electrical current. The grounding wire is a safety feature. It is designed to conduct electricity if current seeks to return to the service panel along a path other than the neutral wire, a condition known as a **short circuit**.

A short circuit is a potentially dangerous situation. If an electrical box, tool, or appliance becomes short circuited and is touched by a person, the electrical current may attempt to return to its source by passing through that person's body.

However, electrical current always seeks to move along the easiest path. A grounding wire provides a safe, easy path for current to follow back to its source. If a person touches an electrical box, tool, or appliance that has a properly installed grounding wire, any chance of receiving a severe electrical shock is greatly reduced.

In addition, household wiring systems are required to be connected directly to the earth. The earth has a unique ability to absorb the electrons of electrical current. In the event of a short circuit or overload, any excess electricity will find its way along the grounding wire to the earth, where it becomes harmless.

This additional grounding is completed by wiring the household electrical system to a metal cold water pipe and metal grounding rods that are buried in the earth.

After 1920, most American homes included receptacles that accepted **polarized plugs**. While not a true grounding method, the two-slot polarized plug and receptacle was designed to keep hot current flowing along black or red wires, and neutral current flowing along white or gray wires.

Armored cable and metal conduit, widely installed in homes during the 1940s, provided a true grounding path. When connected to metal junction boxes, it provided a metal pathway back to the service panel.

Modern cable includes a green insulated or bare copper wire that serves as the grounding path. This grounding wire is connected to all three-slot receptacles and metal boxes to provide a continuous pathway for any short-circuited current. By plugging a three-prong plug into a grounded three-slot receptacle, appliances and tools are protected from short circuits.

Use a receptacle adapter to plug three-prong plugs into two-slot receptacles, but use it only if the receptacle connects to a grounding wire or grounded electrical box. Adapters have short grounding wires or wire loops that attach to the receptacle's coverplate mounting screw. The mounting screw connects the adapter to the grounded metal electrical box.

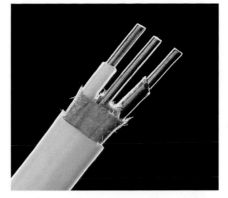

Modern NM (nonmetallic) cable, found in most wiring systems installed after 1965, contains a bare copper wire that provides grounding for receptacle and switch boxes.

Armored cable, sometimes called BX or Greenfield cable, has a metal sheath that serves as the grounding pathway. Short-circuited current flows through the metal sheath back to the service panel.

Polarized receptacles have a long slot and a short slot. Used with a polarized plug, the polarized receptacle keeps electrical current directed for safety.

Three-slot receptacles are required by code for new homes. They are usually connected to a standard two-wire cable with ground.

Receptacle adapter allows three-prong plugs to be inserted into two-slot receptacles. The adapter can be used only with grounded receptacles, and the grounding loop or wire of the adapter must be attached to the coverplate mounting screw of the receptacle.

Double-insulated tools have non-conductive plastic bodies to prevent shocks caused by short circuits. Because of these features, double-insulated tools can be used safely with ungrounded receptacles.

Combination tool is essential for home wiring projects. It cuts cables and individual wires, measures wire gauges, and strips the insulation from wires. It has insulated handles.

Needlenose pliers bends and shapes wires for making screw terminal connections. Some needlenose pliers also have cutting jaws for clipping wires.

Continuity tester is used to check switches, lighting fixtures, and other devices for faults. It has a battery that generates current and a loop of wire for creating an electrical circuit (page 52).

Cordless screwdriver drives a wide variety of screws and fasteners. They are particularly handy for quickly removing coverplates, switches, and receptacles.

Neon circuit tester is used to check circuit wires for power. Testing for power is an essential safety step in any electrical repair project.

Insulated screwdrivers have rubber-coated handles that reduce the risk of shock if the screwdriver should accidentally touch live wires.

Fuse puller is used to remove cartridge-type fuses from the fuse blocks usually found in older main service panels.

Plug-in tester can be used to identify hot and neutral slots on a standard three-slot receptacle, and to test for grounding.

Cable ripper fits over NM (nonmetallic) cable. A small cutting point rips the outer plastic vinyl sheath on NM cable so the sheath can be removed without damaging wires.

Tools for Electrical Repairs

Home electrical repairs require only a few inexpensive tools. As with any tool purchase, invest in quality when buying tools for electrical repairs.

Keep tools clean and dry, and store them securely. Tools with cutting jaws, like needlenose pliers and combination tools, should be resharpened or discarded if the cutting edges become dull.

Several testing tools are used in electrical repair projects. Neon circuit testers (page 70), continuity testers (page 52), and multimeters (below) should be checked periodically to make sure they are operating properly. Continuity testers and multimeters have batteries that should be replaced regularly.

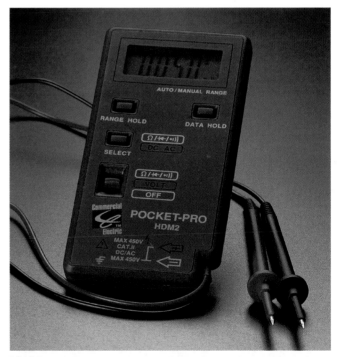

Multimeters are versatile, battery-operated tools frequently used to measure electrical voltages and to test for live wires (pages 70 to 71). They also are used to test for continuity in switches, light fixtures, and other electrical devices. An adjustable control makes it possible to measure current ranging from 1 to 1,000 volts. A multimeter is an essential tool for measuring current in low-voltage transformers, like those used to power doorbell and thermostat systems (pages 102 to 113).

Flexible armored cable, sometimes called "Greenfield" or "BX," was used extensively from the 1920s to the 1940s. It was an improvement over knob and tube wiring because it provided a shield for the wires. Armored cable is grounded through the metal coils of the cable itself: there is no separate ground wire.

Metal conduit protects wires and was installed from the 1940s until 1970. Individual wires are inserted into a rigid tubing. The metal walls of the conduit provide the grounding path: no separate grounding wire is present. Conduit is still recommended by codes for some installations, like exposed wiring in a basement or garage.

Early NM (nonmetallic) cable was used from 1930 until about 1965. It features a flexible rubberized fabric sheathing that protects the individual wires. NM cable greatly simplified wiring installations because separate wires no longer had to be pulled by hand through a metal conduit or armored cable. Early NM cable had no separate grounding wire.

Knob and tube wiring, so called because of the shape of its porcelain insulating brackets, was common in wiring systems installed before 1940. Wires are covered with a layer of rubberized cloth fabric, called "loom," but have no sheath for additional protection.

Modern NM (nonmetallic) cable came into use in 1965. It includes a bare copper grounding wire. Wire insulation and outer sheathing are both made of plastic vinyl, which is more durable and moisture-resistant than the rubber materials used in older NM cable. Modern NM cable is inexpensive and easy to install, and is preferred for most installations.

UF (underground feeder) cable has wires that are embedded in a solid-core plastic vinyl sheathing and includes a bare copper grounding wire. It is designed for installations in damp conditions, such as buried circuits that supply power to a detached garage, shed, or yard light.

Wires & Cables

Wires are made of copper, aluminum, or aluminum covered with a thin layer of copper. Solid copper wires are the best conductors of electricity and are the most widely used. Aluminum and copper-covered aluminum wires require special installation techniques. They are discussed on page 124.

A group of two or more wires enclosed in a metal, rubber, or plastic sheath is called a **cable** (photo, page opposite). The sheath protects the wires from damage. Metal conduit also protects wires, but it is not considered a cable.

Individual wires are covered with rubber or plastic vinyl insulation. An exception is a bare copper grounding wire, which does not need an insulation cover. The insulation is color coded (chart, right) to identify the wire as a hot wire, a neutral wire, or a grounding wire.

In most wiring systems installed after 1965, the wires and cables are insulated with plastic vinyl. This type of insulation is very durable and can last as long as the house itself.

Before 1965, wires and cables were insulated with rubber. Rubber insulation has a life expectancy of about 25 years (see Evaluating Old Wiring, pages 136 to 139). Old insulation that is cracked or damaged can be reinforced temporarily by wrapping the wire with plastic electrical tape. However, old wiring with cracked or damaged insulation should be inspected by a qualified electrician to make sure it is safe.

Wires must be large enough for the amperage rating of the circuit (chart, right). A wire that is too small can become dangerously hot. Wire sizes are categorized according to the American Wire Gauge (AWG) system. To check the size of a wire, use the wire stripper openings of a combination tool (page 18) as a guide.

Everything You Need

Tools: Cable ripper, combination tool, screwdriver, needlenose pliers.

Materials: Wire connectors, pigtail wires (if needed).

See Inspector's Notebook:

• Common Cable Problems (pages 125 to 127).
• Checking Wire Connections (pages 128 to 129).
• Electrical Box Inspection (pages 129 to 131).

Wire Color Chart

Wire color	Function
White	Neutral wire carrying current at zero voltage.
Black	Hot wire carrying current at full voltage.
Red	Hot wire carrying current at full voltage.
White, black markings	Hot wire carrying current at full voltage.
Green	Serves as a grounding pathway.
Bare copper	Serves as a grounding pathway.

Individual wires are color coded to identify their function. In some circuit installations, the white wire serves as a hot wire that carries voltage. If so, this white wire may be labeled with black tape or paint to identify it as a hot wire.

Wire Size Chart

Wire gauge	Wire capacity & use
#6	60 amps, 240 volts; central air conditioner, electric furnace.
#8	40 amps, 240 volts; electric range, central air conditioner.
#10	30 amps, 240 volts; window air conditioner, clothes dryer.
#12	20 amps, 120 volts; light fixtures, receptacles, microwave oven.
#14	15 amps, 120 volts; light fixtures, receptacles.
#16	Light-duty extension cords.
#18 to 22	Thermostats, doorbells, security systems.

Wire sizes (shown actual size) are categorized by the American Wire Gauge system. The larger the wire size, the smaller the AWG number.

Reading NM (Nonmetallic) Cable

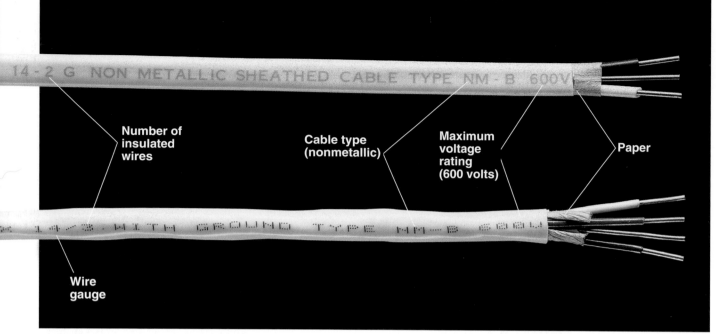

Number of insulated wires

Cable type (nonmetallic)

Maximum voltage rating (600 volts)

Paper

Wire gauge

NM (nonmetallic) cable is labeled with the number of insulated wires it contains. The bare grounding wire is not counted. For example, a cable marked 14/2 G (or 14/2 WITH GROUND) contains two insulated 14-gauge wires, plus a bare copper grounding wire.

Cable marked 14/3 WITH GROUND has three 14-gauge wires plus a grounding wire. A strip of paper inside the cable protects the individual wires. NM cable also is stamped with a maximum voltage rating, as determined by Underwriters Laboratories (UL).

Reading Unsheathed, Individual Wire

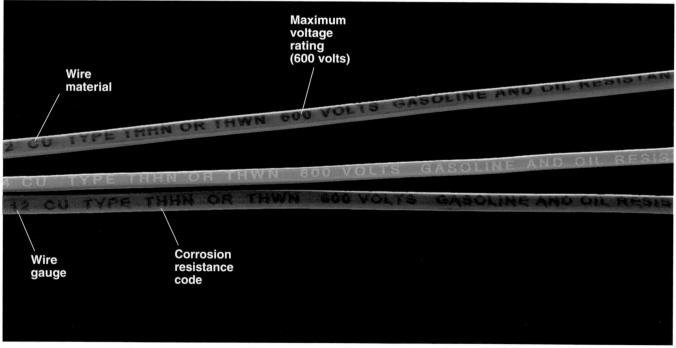

Maximum voltage rating (600 volts)

Wire material

Wire gauge

Corrosion resistance code

Unsheathed, individual wires are used for conduit and raceway installations. Wire insulation is coded with letters to indicate resistance to moisture, heat, and gas or oil. Code requires certain letter combinations for certain applications. *T* indicates thermoplas-

tic insulation. *H* stands for heat resistance and two *H*s indicate high resistance up to 194° F. *W* denotes wire suitable for wet locations. Wire coded with an *N* is impervious to damage from oil or gas.

How to Strip NM (Nonmetallic) Cable & Wires

Cutting point

1 Measure and mark the cable 8" to 10" from end. Slide the cable ripper onto the cable, and squeeze tool firmly to force cutting point through plastic sheathing.

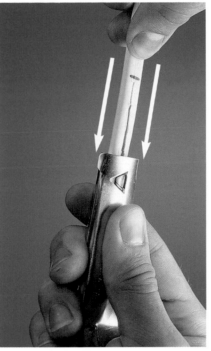

2 Grip the cable tightly with one hand, and pull the cable ripper toward the end of the cable to cut open the plastic sheathing.

3 Peel back the plastic sheathing and the paper wrapping from the individual wires.

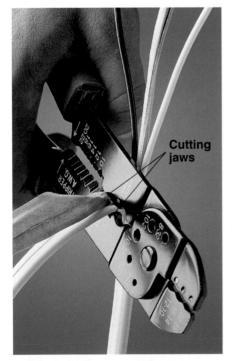

Cutting jaws

4 Cut away the excess plastic sheathing and paper wrapping, using the cutting jaws of a combination tool.

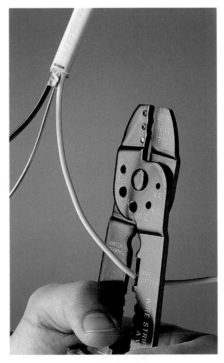

5 Cut the individual wires, if necessary, using the cutting jaws of the combination tool.

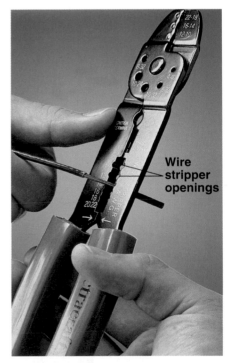

Wire stripper openings

6 Strip insulation for each wire, using the stripper openings. Choose the opening that matches the gauge of the wire, and take care not to nick or scratch the ends of the wires.

How to Connect Wires to Screw Terminals

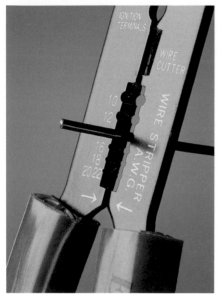

1 Strip about ¾" of insulation from each wire, using a combination tool. Choose the stripper opening that matches the gauge of the wire, then clamp wire in tool. Pull the wire firmly to remove plastic insulation.

2 Form a C-shaped loop in the end of each wire, using a needlenose pliers. The wire should have no scratches or nicks.

3 Hook each wire around the screw terminal so it forms a clockwise loop. Tighten screw firmly. Insulation should just touch head of screw. Never place the ends of two wires under a single screw terminal. Instead, use a pigtail wire (page opposite).

How to Connect Wires to Switches and Receptacles with Push-in Fittings

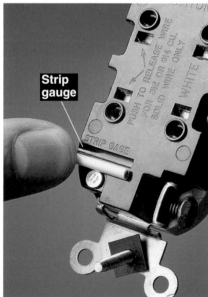

1 Mark the amount of insulation to be stripped from each wire, using the strip gauge on the back of the switch or receptacle. Strip the wires using a combination tool (step 1, above). Never use push-in fittings with aluminum wiring.

2 Insert the bare copper wires firmly into the push-in fittings on the back of the switch or receptacle. When inserted, wires should have no bare copper exposed. NOTE: Although push-in fittings are convenient, most experts believe screw terminal connections (above) are more dependable.

Remove a wire from a push-in fitting by inserting a small nail or screwdriver in the release opening next to the wire. Wire will pull out easily.

How to Connect Two or More Wires with a Wire Connector

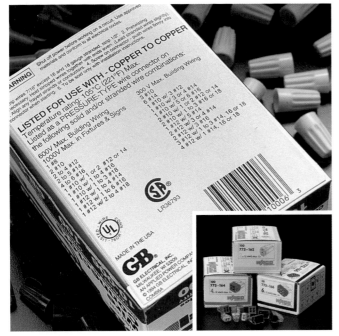

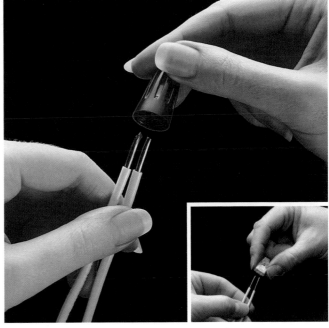

1 Select a twist-on or push-in (inset) wire connector rated for the size and number of wires you are connecting. Wire connectors are color-coded by size, but the coding scheme varies by manufacturer. Green is generally reserved for grounds. Strip about ¾" of insulation off each wire to be connected.

2 Hold the wires together, slide a wire connector down onto them, and twist clockwise until wires are snug. For push-in connectors (inset), simply slide the bare wire ends into the holes. Tug gently to make sure the wires are secure. In a proper connection, no bare wire should be exposed.

How to Pigtail Two or More Wires

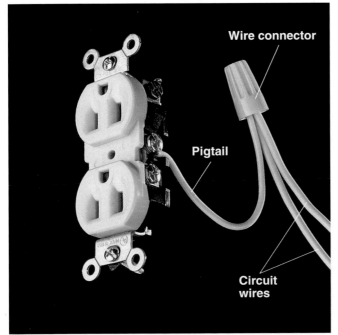

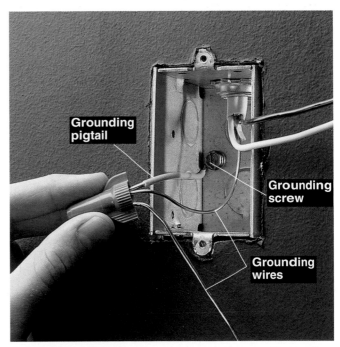

Connect two or more wires to a single screw terminal with a pigtail. A pigtail is a short piece of wire. One end of the pigtail connects to a screw terminal, and the other end connects to circuit wires, using a wire connector. A pigtail also can be used to lengthen circuit wires that are too short (page 130).

Grounding pigtail has green insulation and is available with a preattached grounding screw. This grounding screw connects to the grounded metal electrical box. The end of the pigtail wire connects to the bare copper grounding wires with a wire connector.

Service Panels

Every home has a main service panel that distributes electrical current to the individual circuits. The main service panel usually is found in the basement, garage, or utility area, and can be identified by its metal casing. Before making any repair to your electrical system, you must shut off power to the correct circuit at the main service panel. The service panel should be indexed (pages 30 to 33) so circuits can be identified easily.

Service panels vary in appearance, depending on the age of the system. Very old wiring may operate on 30-amp service that has only two circuits. New homes can have 200-amp service with 30 or more circuits. Find the size of the service by reading the amperage rating printed on the main fuse block or main circuit breaker.

Regardless of age, all service panels have **fuses** or **circuit breakers** (pages 28 to 29) that control each circuit and protect them from overloads. In general, older service panels use fuses, while newer service panels use circuit breakers.

In addition to the main service panel, your electrical system may have a subpanel that controls some of the circuits in the home. A subpanel has its own circuit breakers or fuses, and is installed to control circuits that have been added to an existing wiring system.

The subpanel resembles the main service panel but is usually smaller. It may be located near the main panel, or it may be found near the areas served by the new circuits. Garages and attics that have been updated often have their own subpanels. If your home has a subpanel, make sure that its circuits are indexed correctly.

When handling fuses or circuit breakers, make sure the area around the service panel is dry. Never remove the protective cover on the service panel. After turning off a circuit to make electrical repairs, remember to always test the circuit for power before touching any wires.

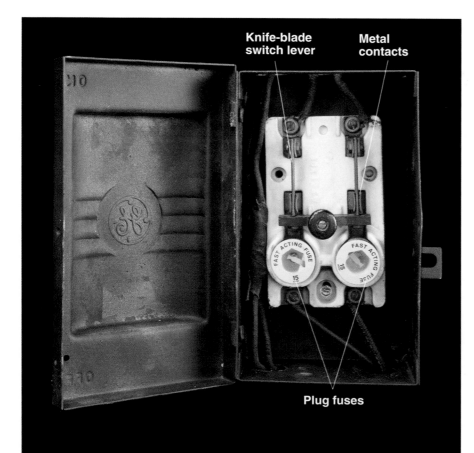

Knife-blade switch lever

Metal contacts

Plug fuses

A 30-amp service panel, common in systems installed before 1950, is identified by a ceramic fuse holder containing two plug fuses and a "knife-blade" switch lever. The fuse holder sometimes is contained in a black metal box mounted in an entryway or basement. This 30-amp service panel provides only 120 volts of power and now is considered inadequate. For example, most home loan programs, like the FHA (Federal Housing Administration), require that 30-amp service be updated to 100 amps or more before a home can qualify for mortgage financing.

To shut off power to individual circuits in a 30-amp panel, carefully unscrew the plug fuses, touching only the insulated rim of the fuse. To shut off power to the entire house, open the knife-blade switch. Be careful not to touch the metal contacts on the switch.

A 60-amp fuse panel often is found in wiring systems installed between 1950 and 1965. It usually is housed in a gray metal cabinet that contains four individual plug fuses, plus one or two pull-out fuse blocks that hold cartridge fuses. This type of panel is regarded as adequate for a small, 1,100-square-foot house that has no more than one 240-volt appliance. Many homeowners update 60-amp service to 100 amps or more so that additional lighting and appliance circuits can be added to the system. Home loan programs also may require that 60-amp service be updated before a home can qualify for financing.

To shut off power to a circuit, carefully unscrew the plug fuse, touching only its insulated rim. To shut off power to the entire house, hold the handle of the main fuse block and pull sharply to remove it. Major appliance circuits are controlled with another cartridge fuse block. Shut off the appliance circuit by pulling out this fuse block.

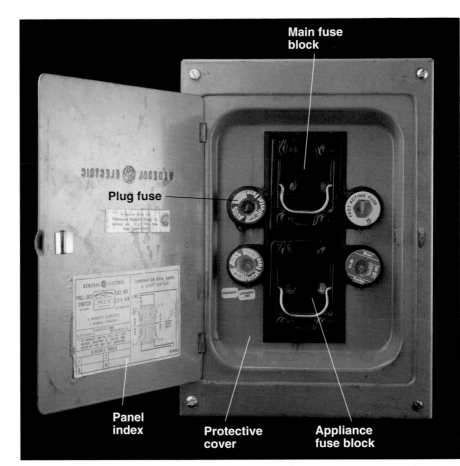

Main fuse block

Plug fuse

Panel index

Protective cover

Appliance fuse block

A circuit breaker panel providing 100 amps or more of power is common in wiring systems installed during the 1960s and later. A circuit breaker panel is housed in a gray metal cabinet that contains two rows of individual circuit breakers. The size of the service can be identified by reading the amperage rating of the main circuit breaker, which is located at the top of the main service panel.

A 100-amp service panel is now the minimum standard for most new housing. It is considered adequate for a medium-sized house with no more than three major electric appliances. However, larger houses with more electrical appliances require a service panel that provides 150 amps or more.

To shut off power to individual circuits in a circuit breaker panel, flip the lever on the appropriate circuit breaker to the OFF position. To shut off the power to the entire house, turn the main circuit breaker to the OFF position.

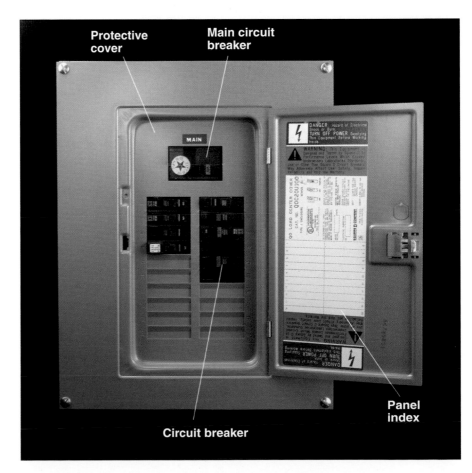

Protective cover

Main circuit breaker

Circuit breaker

Panel index

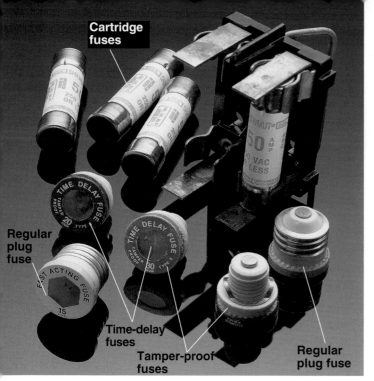

Cartridge fuses

Time-delay fuses

Regular plug fuse

Tamper-proof fuses

Time-delay fuses

Regular plug fuse

Fuses are used in older service panels. Plug fuses usually control 120-volt circuits rated for 15, 20, or 30 amps. Tamper-proof plug fuses have threads that fit only matching sockets, making it impossible to install a wrong-sized fuse. Time-delay fuses absorb temporary heavy power loads without blowing. Cartridge fuses control 240-volt circuits and range from 30 to 100 amps.

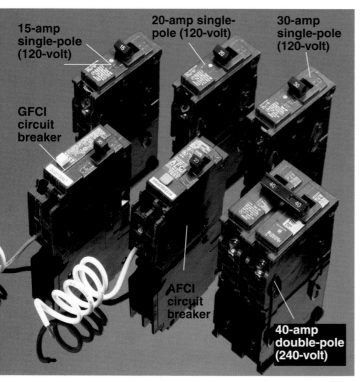

15-amp single-pole (120-volt)

20-amp single-pole (120-volt)

30-amp single-pole (120-volt)

GFCI circuit breaker

AFCI circuit breaker

40-amp double-pole (240-volt)

Circuit breakers are found in the majority of panels installed since the 1940s. Single-pole breakers control 120-volt circuits. Double-pole breakers rated for 20 to 60 amps control 240-volt circuits. Ground-fault circuit interrupter (GFCI) and arc-fault circuit interrupter (AFCI) breakers provide protection from shocks and fire-causing arcs for the entire circuit.

Fuses & Circuit Breakers

Fuses and circuit breakers are safety devices designed to protect the electrical system from short circuits and overloads. Fuses and circuit breakers are located in the main service panel.

Most service panels installed before 1965 rely on fuses to control and protect individual circuits. Screw-in plug fuses protect 120-volt circuits that power lights and receptacles. Cartridge fuses protect 240-volt appliance circuits and the main shut-off of the service panel.

Inside each fuse is a current-carrying metal alloy ribbon. If a circuit is overloaded, the metal ribbon melts and stops the flow of power. A fuse must match the amperage rating of the circuit. Never replace a fuse with one that has a larger amperage rating.

In most service panels installed after 1965, circuit breakers protect and control individual circuits. Single-pole circuit breakers protect 120-volt circuits, and double-pole circuit breakers protect 240-volt circuits. Amperage ratings for circuit breakers range from 15 to 100 amps.

Each circuit breaker has a permanent metal strip that heats up and bends when voltage passes through it. If a circuit is overloaded, the metal strip inside the breaker bends enough to "trip" the switch and stop the flow of power. If a circuit breaker trips frequently even though the power demand is small, the mechanism inside the breaker may be worn out. Worn circuit breakers should be replaced by an electrician.

When a fuse blows or a circuit breaker trips, it is usually because there are too many light fixtures and plug-in appliances drawing power through the circuit. Move some of the plug-in appliances to another circuit, then replace the fuse or reset the breaker. If the fuse blows or the breaker trips again immediately, there may be a short circuit in the system. Call a licensed electrician if you suspect a short circuit.

Everything You Need

Tools: Fuse puller and continuity tester (for cartridge fuses only).

Materials: Replacement fuse.

How to Identify & Replace a Blown Plug Fuse

1 Go to the main service panel and locate the blown fuse. If the metal ribbon inside fuse is cleanly melted (right), the circuit was overloaded. If window in fuse is discolored (left), there was a short circuit in the system.

2 Unscrew the fuse, being careful to touch only the insulated rim of the fuse. Replace it with a fuse that has the same amperage rating.

How to Remove, Test & Replace a Cartridge Fuse

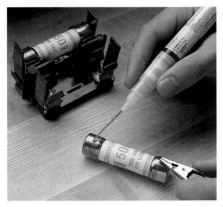

1 Remove cartridge fuses by gripping the handle of the fuse block and pulling sharply.

2 Remove the individual cartridge fuses from the block, using a fuse puller.

3 Test each fuse, using a continuity tester. If the tester glows, the fuse is good. If the tester does not glow, replace the fuse with one that has the same amperage rating.

How to Reset a Circuit Breaker

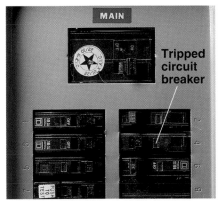

1 Open the service panel and locate the tripped breaker. The lever on the tripped breaker will be either in the OFF position, or in a position between ON and OFF.

2 Reset the tripped circuit breaker by pressing the circuit breaker lever all the way to the OFF position, then pressing it to the ON position.

Test AFCI and GFCI circuit breakers by pushing the TEST button. Breaker should trip to the OFF position. If not, the breaker is faulty and must be replaced by an electrician.

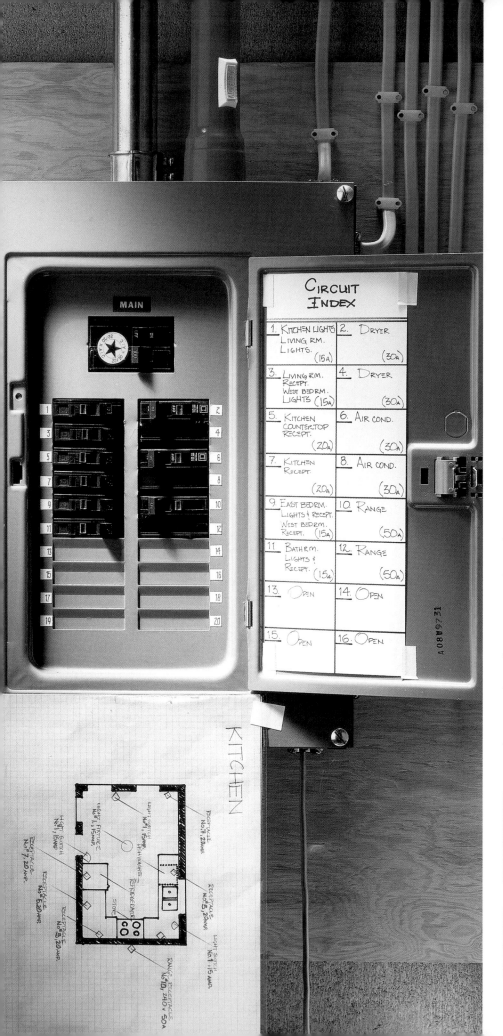

Mapping Circuits & Indexing the Service Panel

Making repairs to an electrical system is easier and safer if you have an accurate, up-to-date map of your home's electrical circuits. A circuit map shows all lights, appliances, switches, and receptacles connected to each circuit. The map allows you to index the main service panel so that the correct circuit can be shut off when repairs are needed.

Mapping all the circuits and indexing the main service panel requires four to six hours. If your service panel was indexed by a previous owner, it is a good idea to make your own circuit map to make sure the old index is accurate. If circuits have been added or changed, the old index will be outdated.

The easiest way to map circuits is to turn on one circuit at a time and check to see which light fixtures, receptacles, and appliances are powered by the circuit. All electrical devices must be in good working condition before you begin.

A circuit map also will help you evaluate the electrical demands on each circuit (pages 34 to 35). This information can help you determine if your wiring system needs to be updated.

Everything You Need
Tools: Pens, circuit tester.
Materials: Graph paper, masking tape.

See Inspector's Notebook:
• Service Panel Inspection (pages 123 to 124).

How to Map Circuits & Index a Service Panel

1 Make a sketch of each room in the house on graph paper. Include the hallways, basement and attic, and all utility areas. Or use a blueprint of your house.

2 Make a sketch of the outside of the house, the garage, and any other separate structures that are wired for electricity.

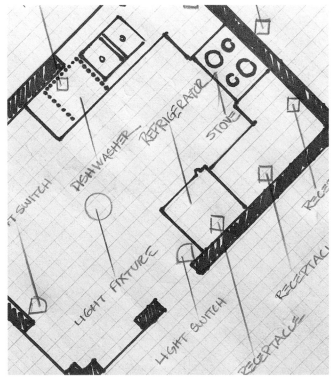

3 On each sketch, indicate the location of all receptacles, light fixtures, switches, appliances, doorbells, thermostats, heaters, fans, and air conditioners.

4 At the main service panel, number each circuit breaker or fuse. Turn off all the circuit breakers or loosen all the fuses, but leave the main shutoff in the ON position.

(continued next page)

5 Turn on one circuit at a time by flipping the circuit breaker lever or tightening the correct fuse. Note the amperage rating printed on the circuit breaker lever or on the rim of the fuse (page 28).

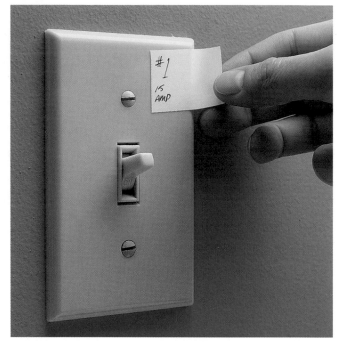

6 Turn on switches, lights, and appliances throughout the house, and identify those that are powered by the circuit. Write the circuit number and amperage rating on a piece of masking tape. The tape makes a handy temporary reference.

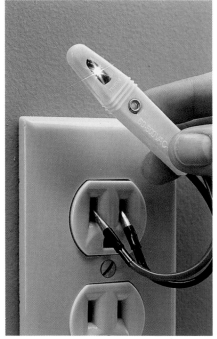

7 Test receptacles for power, using a neon circuit tester. Make sure to check both halves of the receptacle.

8 Indicate which circuit supplies power to each receptacle. Although uncommon, remember that receptacles can be wired so that each half of the receptacle is powered by a different circuit.

9 To check the furnace for power, set thermostat to highest temperature setting. Furnaces and their low-voltage thermostats are on the same circuit. If the circuit is hot, the furnace will begin running. The lowest temperature setting will turn on the central air conditioner.

10 Check the electric water heater for power by setting its thermostat to highest temperature setting. Water heater will begin to heat if it is powered by the circuit.

11 Check the doorbell system for power by ringing all of the doorbells.

12 On the circuit maps, indicate the circuit number, the voltage, and the amperage rating of each receptacle, switch, light fixture, and appliance.

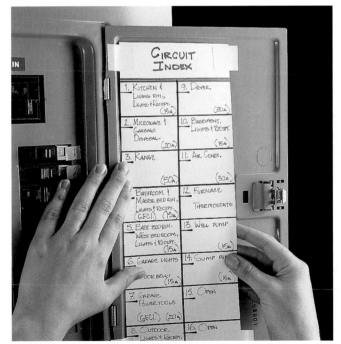

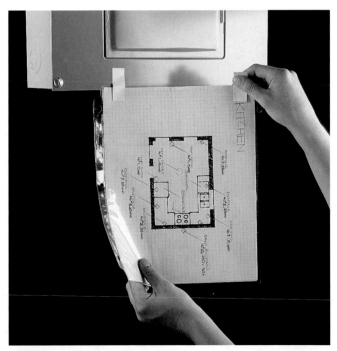

13 On the door of the main service panel, tape an index that provides a brief summary of all the fixtures, receptacles, and appliances that are powered by each circuit.

14 Attach the completed circuit maps to the main service panel, and make sure the power is turned on for all the circuits.

Evaluating Circuits for Safe Capacity

Every electrical circuit in a home has a "safe capacity." Safe capacity is the total amount of power the circuit wires can carry without tripping circuit breakers or blowing fuses. According to the National Electrical Code, the power used by light fixtures, lamps, tools, and appliances, called the "demand," must not exceed the safe capacity of the circuit.

Finding the safe capacity and the demand of a circuit is easy. Make these simple calculations to reduce the chances of tripped circuit breakers or blown fuses, or to help plan the location of new appliances or plug-in lamps.

First, determine the amperage and voltage rating of the circuit. If you have an up-to-date circuit map (pages 30 to 33) these ratings should be indicated on the map. If not, open the service panel door and read the amperage rating printed on the circuit breaker or on the rim of the fuse. The type of circuit breaker or fuse (page 28) indicates the voltage of the circuit.

Use the amperage and voltage ratings to find the safe capacity of the circuit. Safe capacities of the most common household circuits are given in the table at right.

Safe capacities can be calculated by multiplying the amperage rating by voltage. The answer is the total capacity, expressed in watts, a unit of electrical measurement. To find the safe capacity, reduce the total capacity by 20%.

Next, compare the safe capacity of the circuit to the total power demand. To find the demand, add the wattage ratings for all light fixtures, lamps, and appliances on the circuit. For lights, use the wattage rating printed on the light bulbs. Wattage ratings for appliances often are printed on the manufacturer's label. Approximate wattage ratings for many common household items are given in the table on the opposite page. If you are unsure about the wattage rating for a tool or appliance, use the highest number shown in the table to make calculations.

Compare the power demand to the safe capacity. The power demand should not exceed the safe capacity of the circuit. If it does, you must move lamps or appliances to another circuit. Or make sure that the power demand of the lamps and appliances turned on at the same time does not exceed the safe capacity of the circuit.

Amps × Volts	Total capacity	Safe capacity
15 A × 120 V =	1800 watts	1440 watts
20 A × 120 V =	2400 watts	1920 watts
25 A × 120 V =	3000 watts	2400 watts
30 A × 120 V =	3600 watts	2880 watts
20 A × 240 V =	4800 watts	3840 watts
30 A × 240 V =	7200 watts	5760 watts

How to Find Wattage & Amperage Ratings

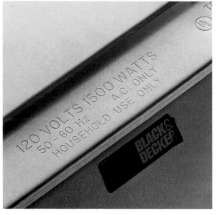

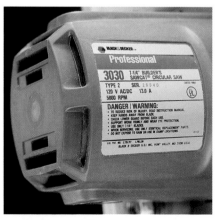

Light bulb wattage ratings are printed on the top of the bulb. If a light fixture has more than one bulb, remember to add the wattages of all the bulbs to find the total wattage of the fixture.

Appliance wattage ratings are often listed on the manufacturer's label. Or use the table of typical wattage ratings on the opposite page.

Amperage rating can be used to find the wattage of an appliance. Multiply the amperage by the voltage of the circuit. For example, a 13-amp, 120-volt circular saw is rated for 1560 watts.

Sample Circuit Evaluation

Circuit #__6__ Amps _20_ Volts _120_ Total capacity _2400_ (watts) Safe capacity _1920_ (watts)

Appliance or fixture	Notes	Wattage rating
Refrigerator	Constant use	480
Ceiling light	3 - 60 watt bulbs	180
Microwave oven		625
Electric can opener	Occasional use	144
Stereo	Portable boom box	300
Ceiling light (hallway)	2 60 watt bulbs	120
	Total demand:	1849 (watts)

Photocopy this sample circuit evaluation to keep a record of the power demand of each circuit. The words and numbers printed in blue will not reproduce on photocopies. In this sample kitchen circuit, the demand on the circuit is very close to the safe capacity. Adding another appliance, such as an electric frying pan, could overload the circuit and cause a fuse to blow or a circuit breaker to trip.

Typical Wattage Ratings (120-volt Circuit Except Where Noted)

Appliance	Amps	Watts	Appliance	Amps	Watts
Air conditioner (central)	13 to 36 (240-v)	3120 to 8640	Garbage disposer	3.5 to 7.5	420 to 900
Air conditioner (window)	6 to 13	720 to 1560	Hair dryer	5 to 10	600 to 1200
Blender	2 to 4	240 to 480	Heater (portable)	7 to 12	840 to 1440
Broiler	12.5	1500	Microwave oven	4 to 10	480 to 1200
Can opener	1.2	144	Range (oven/stove)	5.5 to 10.8 (240-v)	1320 to 2600
Circular saw	10 to 12	1200 to 1440	Refrigerator	2 to 4	240 to 600
Coffee maker	4 to 8	480 to 960	Router	8	960
Clothes dryer	16.5 to 34 (240-v)	3960 to 8160	Sander (portable)	2 to 5	240 to 600
Clothes iron	9	1080	Saw (table)	7 to 10	840 to 1200
Computer	4 to 7	480 to 840	Sewing machine	1	120
Dishwasher	8.5 to 12.5	1020 to 1500	Stereo	2.5 to 4	300 to 480
Drill (portable)	2 to 4	240 to 480	Television (color)	2.5	300
DVD player	2.5 to 4	300 to 480	Toaster	9	1080
Fan (ceiling)	3.5	420	Trash compactor	4 to 8	480 to 960
Fan (portable)	2	240	Vacuum cleaner	6 to 11	720 to 1320
Freezer	2 to 4	240 to 600	Waffle iron	7.5	900
Frying pan	9	1080	Washing machine	12.5	1500
Furnace, forced-air gas	6.5 to 13	780 to 1560	Water heater	15.8 to 21 (240-v)	3800 to 5040

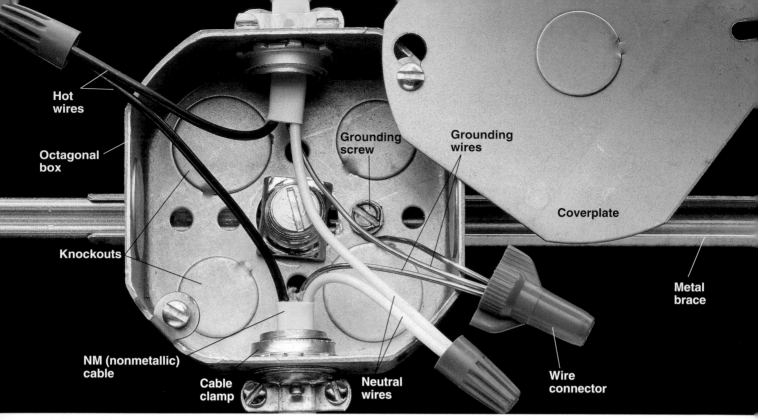

Hot wires

Octagonal box

Knockouts

NM (nonmetallic) cable

Cable clamp

Grounding screw

Grounding wires

Coverplate

Metal brace

Neutral wires

Wire connector

Octagonal boxes usually contain wire connections for ceiling fixtures. Cables are inserted into the box through knockout openings and are held with cable clamps. Because the ceiling fixture attaches directly to the box, the box should be anchored firmly to a framing member. Often, it is nailed directly to a ceiling joist. However, metal braces are available that allow a box to be mounted between joists or studs. A properly installed octagonal box can support a ceiling fixture weighing up to 35 pounds. Any box must be covered with a tightly fitting coverplate, and the box must not have open knockouts.

Electrical Boxes

The National Electrical Code requires that wire connections or cable splices be contained inside an approved metal or plastic box. This shields framing members and other flammable materials from electrical sparks. If you have exposed wire connections or cable splices, protect your home by installing electrical boxes.

Electrical boxes come in several shapes. Rectangular and square boxes are used for switches and receptacles. Rectangular (2" × 3") boxes are used for single switches or duplex receptacles. Square (4" × 4") boxes are used any time it is convenient for two switches or receptacles to be wired or "ganged" in one box, an arrangement common in kitchens or entry hallways. Octagonal electrical boxes contain wire connections for ceiling fixtures.

All electrical boxes are available in different depths. A box must be deep enough so a switch or receptacle can be removed or installed easily without crimping and damaging the circuit wires. Replace an undersized box with a larger box, using the Electrical Box Chart (right) as a guide. The NEC also says that all electrical boxes must

remain accessible. Never cover an electrical box with drywall, paneling, or wallcoverings.

> **See Inspector's Notebook:**
> * Electrical Box Inspection (pages 129 to 131).
> * Common Cable Problems (pages 125 to 127).

Electrical Box Chart

Box shape		Maximum number of individual wires in box*	
		14-gauge	12-gauge
2" × 3" rectangular	2½" deep	3	3
	3½" deep	5	4
4" × 4" square	1½" deep	6	5
	2⅛" deep	9	7
Octagonal	1½" deep	4	3
	2⅛" deep	7	6

*Do not count pigtail wires or grounding wires.

Common Electrical Boxes

Detachable side

Adapter cover

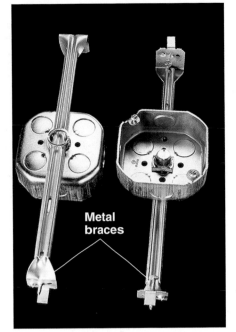

Metal braces

Rectangular boxes are used with wall switches and duplex receptacles. Single-size rectangular boxes (shown above) may have detachable sides that allow them to be ganged together to form double-size boxes.

Square 4" × 4" boxes are large enough for most wiring applications. They are used for cable splices and ganged receptacles or switches. To install one switch or receptacle in a square box, use an adapter cover.

Braced octagonal boxes fit between ceiling joists. The metal braces extend to fit any joist spacing and are nailed or screwed to framing members.

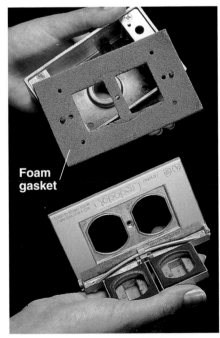

Foam gasket

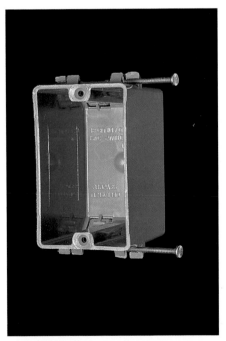

Outdoor boxes have sealed seams and foam gaskets to guard a switch or receptacle against moisture. Corrosion-resistant coatings protect all metal parts.

Retrofit boxes upgrade older boxes to larger sizes. One type (above) has built-in clamps that tighten against the inside of a wall and hold the box in place. A retrofit box with flexible brackets is shown on page 41.

Plastic boxes are common in new construction. They can be used only with NM (nonmetallic) cable. Box may include preattached nails for anchoring the box to framing members. Wall switches must have grounding screws if installed in plastic boxes.

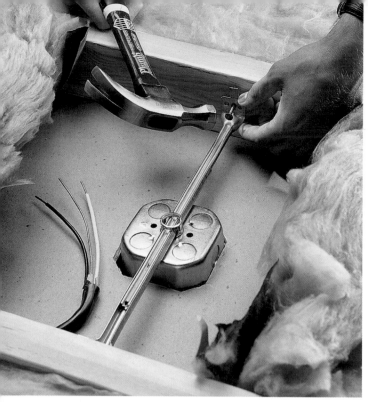

Installing an Electrical Box

Install an electrical box any time you find exposed wire connections or cable splices. Exposed connections sometimes can be found in older homes, where wires attach to light fixtures. Exposed splices (page 127) can be found in areas where NM (nonmetallic) cable runs through uncovered joists or wall studs, such as in an unfinished basement or utility room.

When installing an electrical box, make sure there is enough cable to provide about 8" of wire inside the box. If the wires are too short, you can add pigtails to lengthen them (page 130). If the electrical box is metal, make sure the circuit grounding wires are pigtailed to the box.

Electrical boxes are required for all wire connections. The box protects wood and other flammable materials from electrical sparks (arcing). Electrical boxes should always be anchored to joists or studs.

Everything You Need

Tools: Circuit tester, screwdriver, hammer.

Materials: Screws or nails, electrical box, cable clamps, locknuts, pigtail wire, wire connectors.

How to Install an Electrical Box for Cable Splices

1 Turn off power to circuit wires at the main service panel. Carefully remove any tape or wire connectors from the exposed splice. Avoid contact with the bare wire ends until the wires have been tested for power.

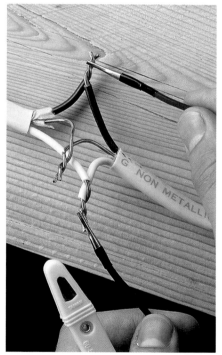

2 Test for power. Touch one probe of a circuit tester to the black hot wires, and touch other probe to the white neutral wires. The tester should not glow. If it does, the wires are still hot. Shut off power to correct circuit at the main service panel. Disconnect the spliced wires.

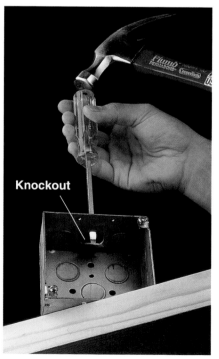

Knockout

3 Open one knockout for each cable that will enter the box, using a hammer and screwdriver. Any unopened knockouts should remain sealed.

4 Anchor the electrical box to a wooden framing member, using screws or nails.

Cable clamp

Cable sheathing

5 Thread each cable through a cable clamp. Tighten the clamp with a screwdriver. Do not overtighten. Overtightening can damage cable sheathing.

Locknut

6 Insert the cables into the electrical box, and screw a locknut onto each cable clamp.

Locknut

Lugs

7 Tighten the locknuts by pushing against the lugs with the blade of a screwdriver.

Grounding screw

8 Use wire connectors to reconnect the wires. Pigtail the copper grounding wires to the green grounding screw in the back of the box.

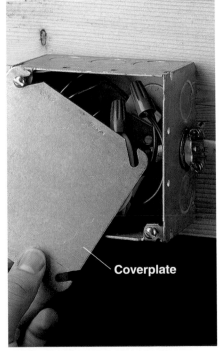

Coverplate

9 Carefully tuck the wires into the box, and attach the coverplate. Turn on the power to the circuit at the main service panel. Make sure the box remains accessible, and is not covered with finished walls or ceilings.

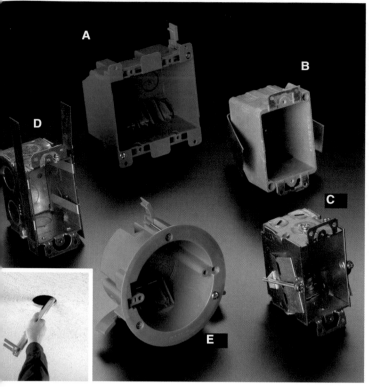

Cut-in boxes come in variety of styles. For walls, they include plastic retrofit boxes with flip-out wings (A), metal or plastic boxes with compression tabs or brackets (B), metal retrofit boxes with flip-out wings (C), and metal boxes with bendable brackets (D). For ceilings, plastic fixture boxes with flip-out wings (D) are available. For retrofitting heavy ceiling fixtures, retrofit bracing is available (inset).

Installing Cut-in Retrofit Boxes

Attaching an electrical box to a wall stud during new construction is relatively easy (pages 184 to 189). The task becomes complicated, however, when you're working in finished walls during remodeling or repair. In most cases, it's best to use an electronic stud finder, make a large cutout in the wall, and attach a new box directly to a framing member or bracing (and then replace and refinish the wall materials). But there are occasions when this isn't possible or practical and you just need to retrofit an electrical box without making a large hole in the wall. You also may find that an older switch or receptacle box is too shallow to accommodate a new dimmer or GFCI safely. These situations call for a cut-in retrofit box (sometimes called an "old work" box).

A cut-in box typically has wings, tabs, or brackets that are drawn tight against the wall surface on the wall cavity side, holding the box in place. They can be made either of metal or plastic. You can also purchase an adapter that is mounted to the front edges of a typical rectangular box, converting it to a cut-in-type box.

Everything You Need

Tools: Screwdriver, pencil, wallboard saw.

Materials: Template (if provided), plastic or metal cut-in box.

How to Install a Cut-in Box

1 Use a template to trace a cutout for the box at the intended location. If no template is provided, press the cut-in box against the wall surface and trace its front edges (but not the tabs on the top and bottom).

2 Puncture the wallboard with the tip of a wallboard saw or by drilling a small hole inside the lines, and make the cutout for the box.

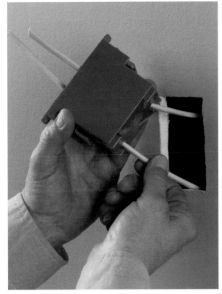

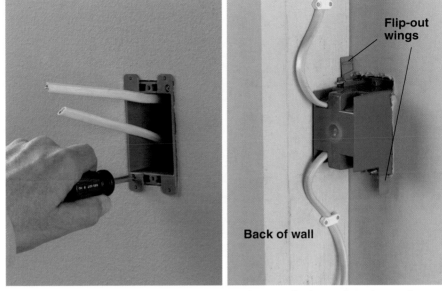

Flip-out wings

Back of wall

3 Pull NM cable through a knockout in the box (no cable clamp is required with a plastic box, just be sure not to break the pressure tab that holds the cable in place).

4 Insert the box into the cutout so the tabs are flush against the wall surface. Tighten the screws that cause the flip-out wings to pivot (right) until the box is held firmly in place. Connect the switch or receptacle that the box will house.

Variation: Metal Cut-in Boxes

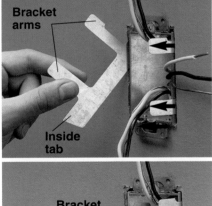

Bracket arms

Inside tab

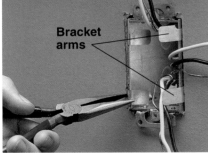

Bracket arms

1 Feed cable into the new box and secure it in the opening after clamping the cables. With this cut-in box, bracket arms are inserted at the sides of the box (top) and then bent around the front edges to secure the box in the opening (bottom).

Variation: How to Replace an Electrical Box

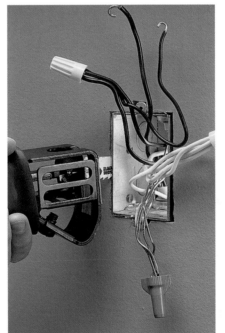

2 To install a dimmer switch or GFCI receptacle, you may have to replace an old, overcrowded box. Shut off power and remove the old switch or receptacle. Identify the location of nails holding the box to the framing member and cut the nails with a hacksaw or reciprocating saw with a metal blade inserted between the box and the stud.

3 Bind the cable ends together and attach string so they do not fall into the wall cavity when the old box is removed. Disconnect the cable clamps and slide the old box out. Install a new cut-in box.

Rotary snap switches are found in many installations completed between 1900 and 1920. Handle is twisted clockwise to turn light on and off. The switch is enclosed in a ceramic housing.

Push-button switches were widely used from 1920 until about 1940. Many switches of this type are still in operation. Reproductions of this switch type are available for restoration projects.

Toggle switches were introduced in the 1930s. This early design has a switch mechanism that is mounted in a ceramic housing sealed with a layer of insulating paper.

Common Wall-switch Problems

An average wall switch is turned on and off more than 1,000 times each year. Because switches receive constant use, wire connections can loosen and switch parts gradually wear out. If a switch no longer operates smoothly, it must be repaired or replaced.

The methods for repairing or replacing a switch vary slightly, depending on the switch type and its location along an electrical circuit. When working on a switch, use the photographs on pages 44 to 51 to identify your switch type and its wiring configuration. Individual switch styles may vary from manufacturer to manufacturer, but the basic switch types are universal.

It is possible to replace most ordinary wall switches with a specialty switch, like a timer switch or an electronic switch. When installing a specialty switch (pages 50 to 51), make sure it is compatible with the wiring configuration of the switch box.

See Inspector's Notebook:
- Common Cable Problems (pages 125 to 127).
- Checking Wire Connections (pages 128 to 129).
- Inspecting Receptacles & Switches (pages 134 to 135).

Metal arm

Screw terminals

Hot wire

Typical wall switch has a movable metal arm that opens and closes the electrical circuit. When the switch is ON, the arm completes the circuit and power flows between the screw terminals and through the black hot wire to the light fixture. When the switch is OFF, the arm lifts away to interrupt the circuit, and no power flows. Switch problems can occur if the screw terminals are not tight or if the metal arm inside the switch wears out.

Toggle switches were improved during the 1950s, and are now the most commonly used type. This switch type was the first to use a sealed plastic housing that protects the inner switch mechanism from dust and moisture.

Mercury switches became common in the early 1960s. They conduct electrical current by means of a sealed vial of mercury. Although more expensive than other types, mercury switches are durable: some are guaranteed for 50 years.

Electronic motion-sensor switch has an infrared eye that senses movement and automatically turns on lights when a person enters a room. Motion-sensor switches can provide added security against intruders.

Problem	Repair
Fuse burns out or circuit breaker trips when the switch is turned on.	1. Tighten any loose wire connections on switch (pages 56 to 57). 2. Move lamps or plug-in appliances to other circuits to prevent overloads (page 34). 3. Test switch (pages 52 to 55), and replace, if needed (pages 56 to 59). 4. Repair or replace faulty fixture (pages 78 to 97) or faulty appliance.
Light fixture or permanently installed appliance does not work.	1. Replace burned-out lightbulb. 2. Check for blown fuse or tripped circuit breaker to make sure circuit is operating (pages 28 to 29). 3. Check for loose wire connections on switch (pages 56 to 57). 4. Test switch (pages 52 to 55), and replace, if needed (pages 56 to 59). 5. Repair or replace light fixture (pages 78 to 97) or appliance.
Light fixture flickers.	1. Tighten lightbulb in the socket. 2. Check for loose wire connections on switch (pages 56 to 57). 3. Repair or replace light fixture (pages 78 to 97) or switch (pages 56 to 59).
Switch buzzes or is warm to the touch.	1. Check for loose wire connections on switch (pages 56 to 57). 2. Test switch (pages 52 to 55), and replace, if needed (pages 56 to 59). 3. Move lamps or appliances to other circuits to reduce demand (page 34).
Switch lever does not stay in position.	Replace worn-out switch (pages 56 to 59).

NOTE: Position of the screw terminals on switch may vary, depending on manufacturer

Underwriters Laboratories (UL) approved

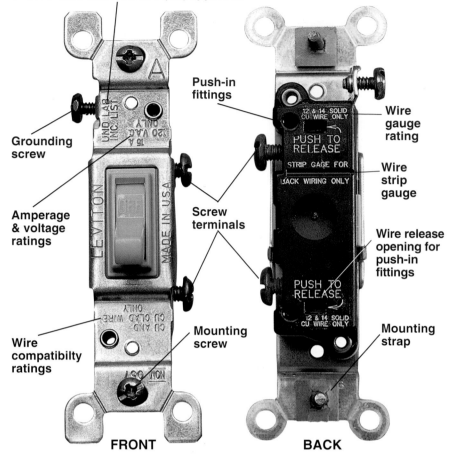

Push-in fittings

Grounding screw

Amperage & voltage ratings

Screw terminals

Wire compatibilty ratings

Wire gauge rating

Wire strip gauge

Wire release opening for push-in fittings

Mounting screw

Mounting strap

FRONT

BACK

Wall switches are available in three general types. To repair or replace a switch, it is important to identify its type.

Single-pole switches are used to control a set of lights from one location. **Three-way switches** are used to control a set of lights from two different locations and are always installed in pairs. **Four-way switches** are used in combination with a pair of three-way switches to control a set of lights from three or more locations.

Identify switch types by counting the screw terminals. Single-pole switches have two screw terminals, three-way switches have three screw terminals, and four-way switches have four.

Most switches include a grounding screw terminal, which is identified by its green color. Technically, grounded switches are required only when the switch is installed in a plastic box. However, many electricians make it a practice to always install grounded switches. When pigtailed to the grounding wires, a grounding screw provides added protection against shock.

When replacing a switch, choose a new switch that has the same number of screw terminals as the old one. The location of the screws on the switch body varies, depending on the manufacturer, but these differences will not affect the switch operation.

Whenever possible, connect switches using the screw terminals rather than push-in fittings. Some specialty switches (pages 50 to 51) have wire leads instead of screw terminals. They are connected to circuit wires with wire connectors.

A wall switch is connected to circuit wires with screw terminals or with push-in fittings on the back of the switch. A switch may have a stamped strip gauge that indicates how much insulation must be stripped from the circuit wires to make the connections.

The switch body is attached to a metal mounting strap that allows it to be mounted in an electrical box. Several rating stamps are found on the strap and on the back of the switch. The abbreviation UL or UND. LAB. INC. LIST means that the switch meets the safety standards of the Underwriters Laboratories. Switches also are stamped with maximum voltage and amperage ratings. Standard wall switches are rated 15A, 125V. Voltage ratings of 110, 120, and 125 are considered to be identical for purposes of identification.

For standard wall switch installations, choose a switch that has a wire gauge rating of #12 or #14. For wire systems with solid-core copper wiring, use only switches marked COPPER or CU. For aluminum wiring (page 124), use only switches marked CO/ALR. Switches marked AL/CU can no longer be used with aluminum wiring, according to the National Electrical Code.

Single-pole Wall Switches

A single-pole switch is the most common type of wall switch. It usually has ON-OFF markings on the switch lever and is used to control a set of lights, an appliance, or a receptacle from a single location. A single-pole switch has two screw terminals and a grounding screw. When installing a single-pole switch, check to make sure the ON marking shows when the switch lever is in the up position.

In a correctly wired single-pole switch, a hot circuit wire is attached to each screw terminal. However, the color and number of wires inside the switch box will vary, depending on the location of the switch along the electrical circuit.

If two cables enter the box, then the switch lies in the middle of the circuit. In this installation, both of the hot wires attached to the switch are black.

If only one cable enters the box, then the switch lies at the end of the circuit. In this installation (sometimes called a switch loop), one of the hot wires is black, but the other hot wire usually is white. A white hot wire sometimes is coded with black tape or paint.

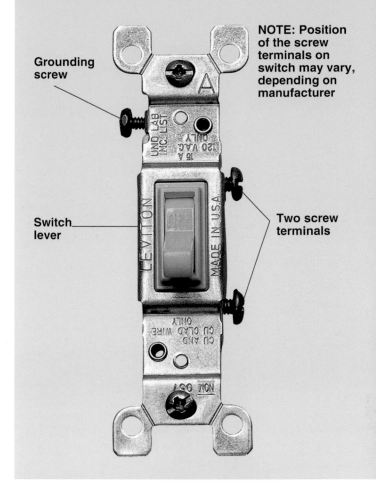

Grounding screw

Switch lever

Two screw terminals

NOTE: Position of the screw terminals on switch may vary, depending on manufacturer

Typical Single-pole Switch Installations

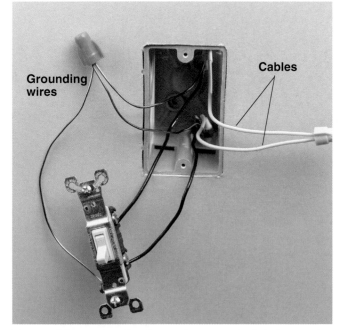

Grounding wires

Cables

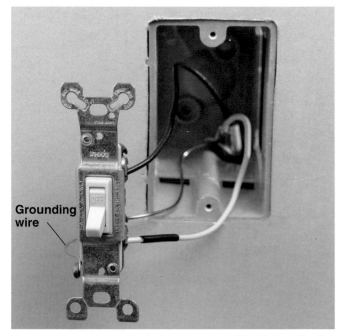

Grounding wire

Two cables enter the box when a switch is located in the middle of a circuit. Each cable has a white and a black insulated wire, plus a bare copper grounding wire. The black wires are hot and are connected to the screw terminals on the switch. The white wires are neutral and are joined together with a wire connector. Grounding wires are pigtailed to the switch.

One cable enters the box when a switch is located at the end of a circuit. The cable has a white and a black insulated wire, plus a bare copper grounding wire. In this installation, both of the insulated wires are hot. The white wire may be labeled with black tape or paint to identify it as a hot wire. The grounding wire is connected to the switch grounding screw.

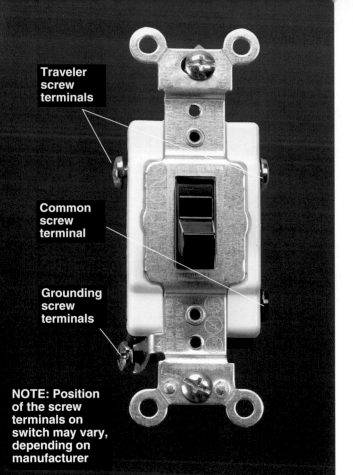

Traveler screw terminals

Common screw terminal

Grounding screw terminals

NOTE: Position of the screw terminals on switch may vary, depending on manufacturer

Three-way Wall Switches

Three-way switches have three screw terminals and do not have ON-OFF markings. Three-way switches are always installed in pairs and are used to control a set of lights from two locations.

One of the screw terminals on a three-way switch is darker than the others. This screw is the **common screw terminal.** The position of the common screw terminal on the switch body may vary, depending on the manufacturer. Before disconnecting a three-way switch, always label the wire that is connected to the common screw terminal. It must be reconnected to the common screw terminal on the new switch.

The two lighter-colored screw terminals on a three-way switch are called the **traveler screw terminals.** The traveler terminals are interchangeable, so there is no need to label the wires attached to them.

Because three-way switches are installed in pairs, it sometimes is difficult to determine which of the switches is causing a problem. The switch that receives greater use is more likely to fail, but you may need to inspect both switches to find the source of the problem.

Typical Three-way Switch Installations

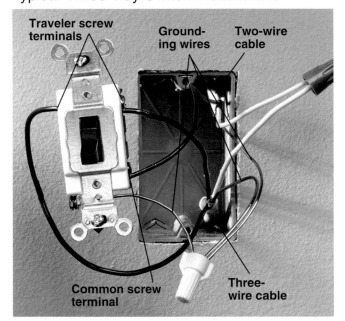

Traveler screw terminals

Grounding wires

Two-wire cable

Common screw terminal

Three-wire cable

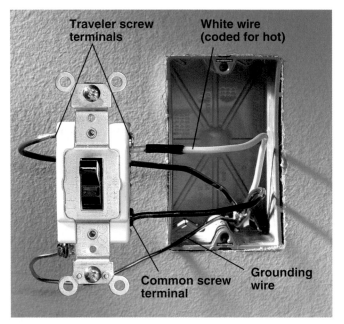

Traveler screw terminals

White wire (coded for hot)

Common screw terminal

Grounding wire

Two cables enter the box if the switch lies in the middle of a circuit. One cable has two wires, plus a bare copper grounding wire; the other cable has three wires, plus a ground. The black wire from the two-wire cable is connected to the dark, common screw terminal. The red and black wires from the three-wire cable are connected to the traveler screw terminals. The white neutral wires are joined together with a wire connector, and the grounding wires are pigtailed to the grounded metal box.

One cable enters the box if the switch lies at the end of the circuit. The cable has a black wire, red wire, and white wire, plus a bare copper grounding wire. The black wire must be connected to the common screw terminal, which is darker than the other two screw terminals. The white and red wires are connected to the two traveler screw terminals. The white wire is taped to indicate that it is hot. The bare copper grounding wire is connected to the grounded metal box.

Four-way Wall Switches

Four-way switches have four screw terminals and do not have ON-OFF markings. Four-way switches are always installed between a pair of three-way switches. This switch combination makes it possible to control a set of lights from three or more locations. Four-way switches are common in homes where large rooms contain multiple living areas, such as a kitchen opening into a dining room. Switch problems in a four-way installation can be caused by loose connections or worn parts in a four-way switch or in one of the three-way switches (facing page).

In a typical installation, there will be a pair of three-way cables that enter the box for the four-way switch. With most switches, the white and red wires from one cable should be attached to the bottom or top pair of screw terminals, and the white and red wires from the other cable should be attached to the remaining pair of screw terminals. However, not all switches are configured the same way, and wiring configurations in the box may vary, so always study the wiring diagram that comes with the switch.

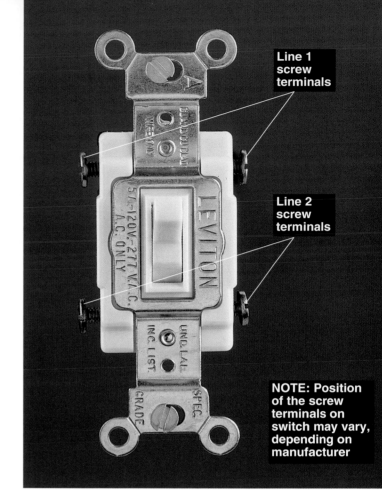

Line 1 screw terminals

Line 2 screw terminals

NOTE: Position of the screw terminals on switch may vary, depending on manufacturer

Typical Four-way Switch Installation

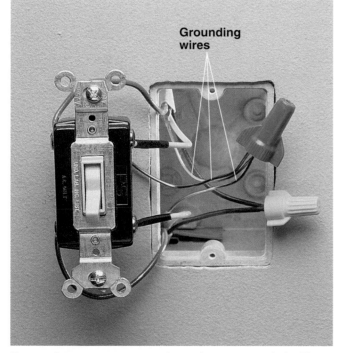

Grounding wires

Four wires are connected to a four-way switch. The red and white wires from one cable are attached to the top pair of screw terminals, while the red and white wires from the other cable are attached to the bottom screw terminals.

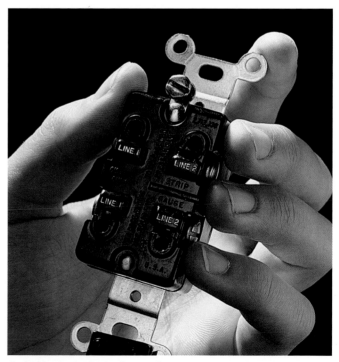

Switch variation: Some four-way switches have a wiring guide stamped on the back to help simplify installation. For the switch shown above, one pair of color-matched circuit wires will be connected to the screw terminals marked LINE 1, while the other pair of wires will be attached to the screw terminals marked LINE 2.

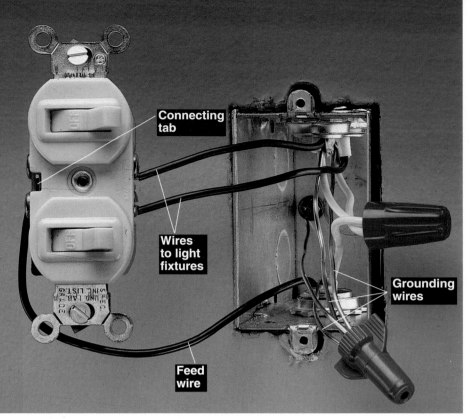

Single-circuit wiring: Three black wires are attached to the switch. The black feed wire bringing power into the box is connected to the side of the switch that has a connecting tab. The wires carrying power out to the light fixtures or appliances are connected to the side of the switch that **does not** have a connecting tab. The white neutral wires are connected together with a wire connector.

Double Switches

A double switch has two switch levers in a single housing. It is used to control two light fixtures or appliances from the same switch box.

In most installations, both halves of the switch are powered by the same circuit. In these **single-circuit** installations, three wires are connected to the double switch. One wire, called the "feed" wire, supplies power to both halves of the switch. The other wires carry power out to the individual light fixtures or appliances.

In rare installations, each half of the switch is powered by a separate circuit. In these **separate-circuit** installations, four wires are connected to the switch, and the metal connecting tab joining two of the screw terminals is removed (photo below).

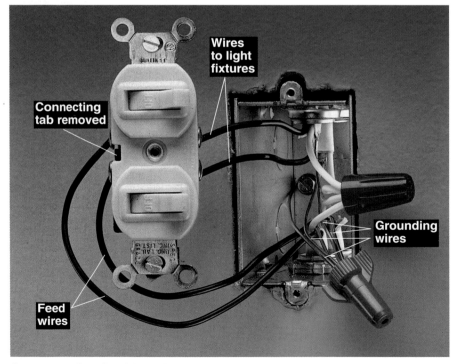

Separate-circuit wiring: Four black wires are attached to the switch. Feed wires from the power source are attached to the side of switch that has a connecting tab, and the connecting tab is removed (photo, right). Wires carrying power from the switch to light fixtures or appliances are connected to the side of the switch that **does not** have a connecting tab. White neutral wires are connected together with a wire connector.

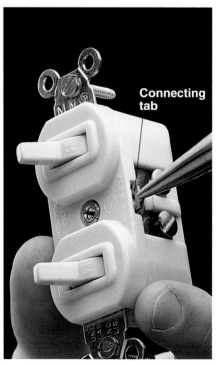

Remove the connecting tab on a double switch when wired in a separate-circuit installation. The tab can be removed with needle-nose pliers or a screwdriver.

Pilot-light Switches

A pilot-light switch has a built-in bulb that glows when power flows through the switch to a light fixture or appliance. Pilot-light switches often are installed for convenience if a light fixture or appliance cannot be seen from the switch location. Basement lights, garage lights, and attic exhaust fans frequently are controlled by pilot-light switches.

A pilot-light switch requires a neutral wire connection. A switch box that contains a single two-wire cable has only hot wires and cannot be fitted with a pilot-light switch.

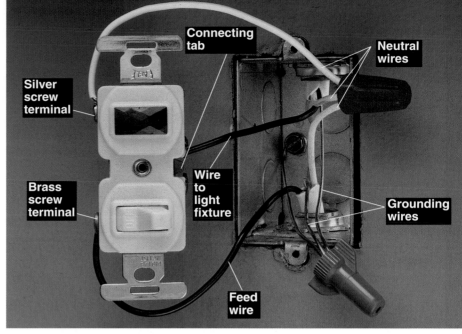

Pilot-light switch wiring: Three wires are connected to the switch. One black wire is the feed wire that brings power into the box. It is connected to the brass screw terminal on the side of the switch that **does not** have a connecting tab. The white neutral wires are pigtailed to the silver screw terminal. Black wire carrying power out to light fixture or appliance is connected to screw terminal on side of the switch that has a connecting tab.

Switch/receptacles

A switch/receptacle combines a grounded receptacle with a single-pole wall switch. In a room that does not have enough wall receptacles, electrical service can be improved by replacing a single-pole switch with a switch/receptacle.

A switch/receptacle requires a neutral wire connection. A switch box that contains a single two-wire cable has only hot wires and cannot be fitted with a switch/receptacle.

A switch/receptacle can be installed in one of two ways. In the most common installations, the receptacle is hot even when the switch is off (photo, right).

In rare installations, a switch/ receptacle is wired so the receptacle is hot only when the switch is on. In this installation, the hot wires are reversed, so that the feed wire is attached to the brass screw terminal on the side of the switch that does not have a connecting tab.

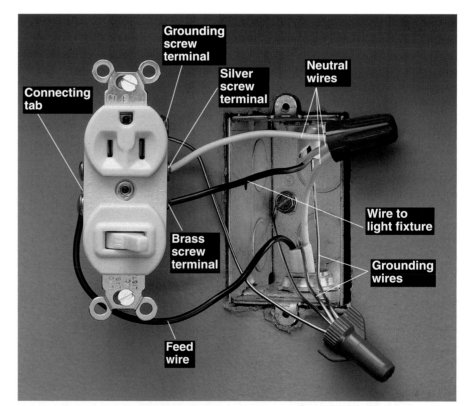

Switch/receptacle wiring: Three wires are connected to the switch/ receptacle. One of the hot wires is the feed wire that brings power into the box. It is connected to the side of the switch that has a connecting tab. The other hot wire carries power out to the light fixture or appliance. It is connected to the brass screw terminal on the side that **does not** have a connecting tab. The white neutral wire is pigtailed to the silver screw terminal. The grounding wires must be pigtailed to the green grounding screw on the switch/receptacle and to the grounded metal box.

Specialty Switches

Your house may have several types of specialty switches. **Dimmer switches** (pages 60 to 61) are used frequently to control light intensity in dining and recreation areas. **Timer switches** and **time-delay switches** (below) are used to control light fixtures and exhaust fans automatically. **Electronic switches** (facing page) provide added convenience and home security, and are easy to install. Electronic switches are durable, and they rarely need repair.

Most specialty switches have preattached wire leads instead of screw terminals and are connected to circuit wires with wire connectors.

Some motor-driven timer switches require a neutral wire connection and cannot be installed in switch boxes that have only one cable with two hot wires.

If a specialty switch is not operating correctly, you may be able to test it with a continuity tester (pages 52 to 55). Timer switches and time-delay switches can be tested for continuity, but dimmer switches cannot be tested. With electronic switches, the manual switch can be tested for continuity (page 55), but the automatic features cannot be tested.

Timer Switches

Timer switches have an electrically powered control dial that can be set to turn lights on and off automatically once each day. They are commonly used to control outdoor light fixtures.

Timer switches have three preattached wire leads. The black wire lead is connected to the hot feed wire that brings power into the box, and the red lead is connected to the wire carrying power out to the light fixture. The remaining wire lead is the neutral lead. It must be connected to any neutral circuit wires. A switch box that contains only one cable has no neutral wires, so it cannot be fitted with a timer switch.

After a power failure, the dial on a timer switch must be reset to the proper time.

Time-delay Switches

A time-delay switch has a spring-driven dial that is wound by hand. The dial can be set to turn off a light fixture after a delay ranging from 1 to 60 minutes. Time-delay switches often are used for exhaust fans, electric space heaters, bathroom vent fans, and heat lamps.

The black wire leads on the switch are connected to the hot circuit wires. If the switch box contains white neutral wires, these are connected together with a wire connector. The bare copper grounding wires are pigtailed to the grounded metal box.

A time-delay switch needs no neutral wire connection, so it can be fitted in a switch box that contains either one or two cables.

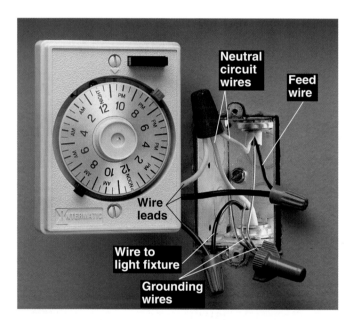

Neutral circuit wires
Feed wire
Wire leads
Wire to light fixture
Grounding wires

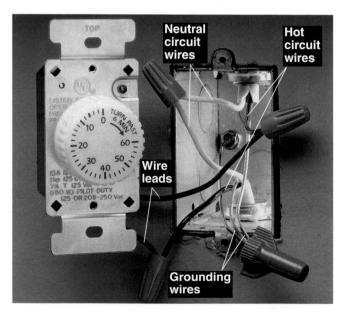

Neutral circuit wires
Hot circuit wires
Wire leads
Grounding wires

Automatic Switches

An automatic switch uses a narrow infrared beam to detect movement. When a hand passes within a few inches of the beam, an electronic signal turns the switch on or off. Some automatic switches have a manual dimming feature.

Automatic switches can be installed wherever a standard single-pole switch is used. Automatic switches are especially convenient for children and persons with disabilities.

Automatic switches require no neutral wire connections. For this reason, an automatic switch can be installed in a switch box containing either one or two cables. The wire leads on the switch are connected to hot circuit wires with wire connectors.

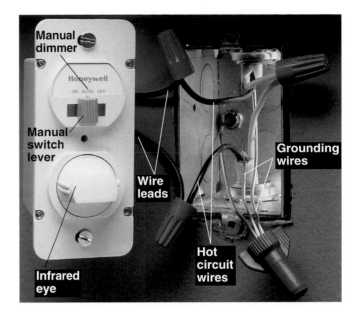

Motion-sensor Security Switches

A motion-sensor switch uses a wide-angle infrared beam to detect movement over a large area and turns on a light fixture automatically. A time-delay feature turns off lights after movement stops.

Most motion-sensor switches have an override feature that allows the switch to be operated manually. Better switches include an adjustable sensitivity control and a variable time-delay shutoff control.

Motion-sensor switches require no neutral wire connections. They can be installed in switch boxes containing either one or two cables. The wire leads on the switch are connected to hot circuit wires with wire connectors.

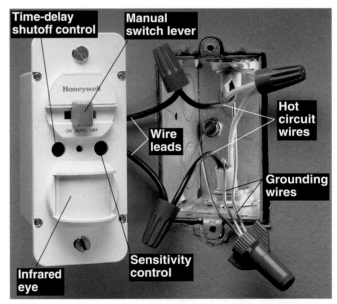

Programmable Switches

Programmable switches represent the latest in switch design. They have digital controls and can provide four on-off cycles each day.

Programmable switches frequently are used to provide security when a homeowner is absent from the house. Law enforcement experts say that programmed lighting is a proven crime deterrent. For best protection, programmable switches should be set to a random on-off pattern.

Programmable switches require no neutral wire connections. They can be installed in switch boxes containing either one or two cables. The wire leads on the switch are connected to hot circuit wires with wire connectors.

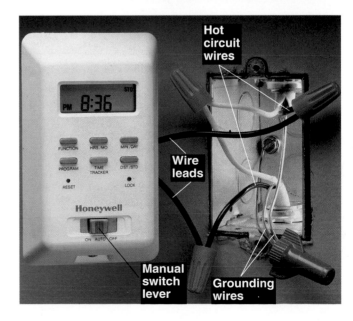

51

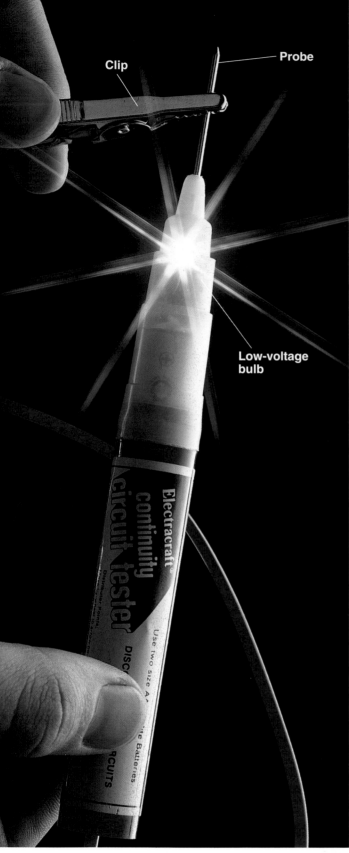

Clip — Probe

Low-voltage bulb

Continuity tester uses battery-generated current to test the metal pathways running through switches and other electrical fixtures. Always "test" the tester before use. Touch the tester clip to the metal probe. The tester should glow. If not, then the battery or lightbulb is dead and must be replaced.

Testing Switches for Continuity

A switch that does not work properly may have worn or broken internal parts. Test for internal wear with a battery-operated continuity tester. The continuity tester detects any break in the metal pathway inside the switch. Replace the switch if the continuity tester shows the switch to be faulty.

Never use a continuity tester on wires that might carry live current. Always shut off the power and disconnect the switch before testing for continuity.

Some specialty switches, like dimmers, cannot be tested for continuity. Electronic switches can be tested for manual operation using a continuity tester, but the automatic operation of these switches cannot be tested.

Everything You Need

Tools: Continuity tester.

How to Test a Single-pole Wall Switch

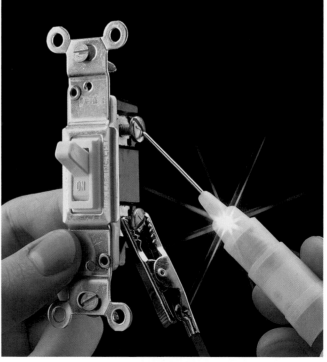

Attach clip of tester to one of the screw terminals. Touch the tester probe to the other screw terminal. Flip switch lever from ON to OFF. If switch is good, tester glows when lever is ON, but not when OFF.

How to Test a Three-way Wall Switch

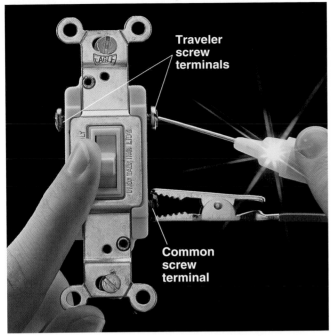

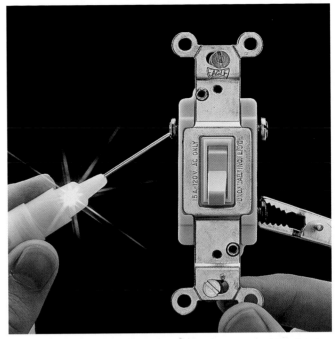

1 Attach tester clip to the dark common screw terminal. Touch the tester probe to one of the traveler screw terminals, and flip switch lever back and forth. If switch is good, the tester should glow when the lever is in one position, but not both.

2 Touch probe to the other traveler screw terminal, and flip the switch lever back and forth. If switch is good, the tester will glow only when the switch lever is in the position opposite from the positive test in step 1.

How to Test a Four-way Wall Switch

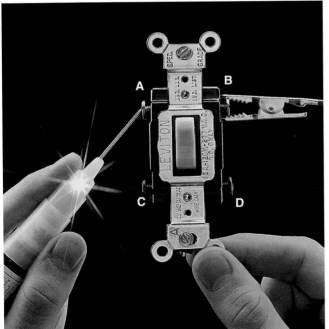

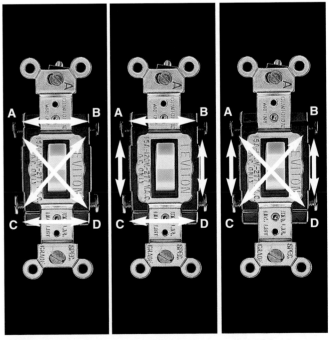

1 Test switch by touching probe and clip of continuity tester to each pair of screw terminals (A-B, C-D, A-D, B-C, A-C, B-D). The test should show continuous pathways between two different pairs of screw terminals. Flip lever to opposite position, and repeat test. Test should show continuous pathways between two different pairs of screw terminals.

2 If switch is good, test will show a total of four continuous pathways between screw terminals—two pathways for each lever position. If not, then switch is faulty and must be replaced. (The arrangement of the pathways may differ, depending on the switch manufacturer. The photo above shows the three possible pathway arrangements.)

How to Test a Pilot-light Switch

1 Test pilot light by flipping the switch lever to the ON position. Check to see if the light fixture or appliance is working. If the pilot light does not glow even though the switch operates the light fixture or appliance, then the pilot light is defective and the unit must be replaced.

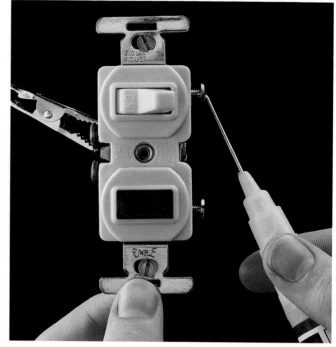

2 Test the switch by disconnecting the unit. With the switch lever in the ON position, attach the tester clip to the top screw terminal on one side of the switch. Touch tester probe to top screw terminal on opposite side of the switch. If switch is good, tester will glow when switch is ON, but not when OFF.

How to Test a Timer Switch

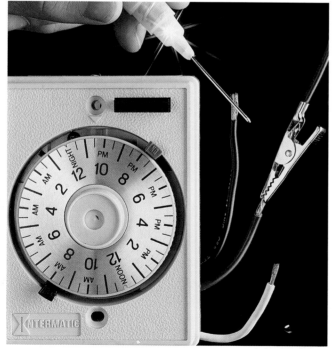

1 Attach the tester clip to the red wire lead on the timer switch, and touch the tester probe to the black hot lead. Rotate the timer dial clockwise until the ON tab passes the arrow marker. Tester should glow. If it does not, the switch is faulty and must be replaced.

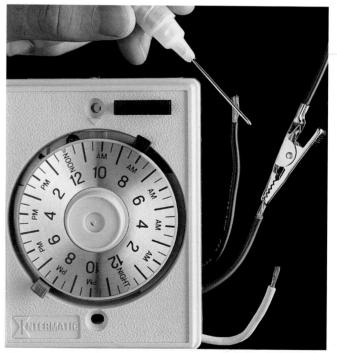

2 Rotate the dial clockwise until the OFF tab passes the arrow marker. Tester should not glow. If it does, the switch is faulty and must be replaced.

How to Test Switch/receptacle

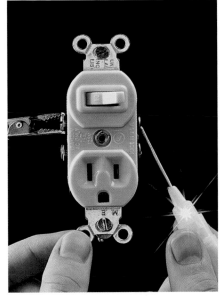

Attach tester clip to one of the top screw terminals. Touch the tester probe to the top screw terminal on the opposite side. Flip the switch lever from ON to OFF position. If the switch is working correctly, the tester will glow when the switch lever is ON, but not when OFF.

How to Test a Double Switch

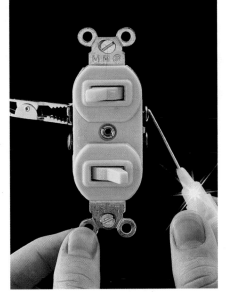

Test each half of switch by attaching the tester clip to one screw terminal and touching the probe to the opposite side. Flip switch lever from ON to OFF position. If switch is good, tester glows when the switch lever is ON, but not when OFF. Repeat test with the remaining pair of screw terminals. If either half tests faulty, replace the unit.

How to Test a Time-delay Switch

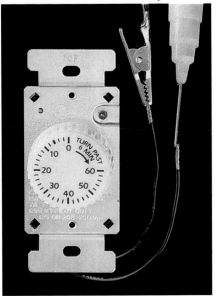

Attach tester clip to one of the wire leads, and touch the tester probe to the other lead. Set the timer for a few minutes. If switch is working correctly, the tester will glow until the time expires.

How to Test Manual Operation of Electronic Switches

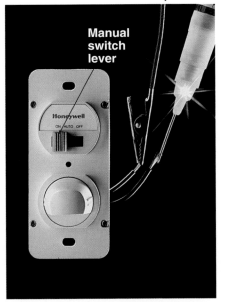

Automatic switch: Attach the tester clip to a black wire lead, and touch the tester probe to the other black lead. Flip the manual switch lever from ON to OFF position. If switch is working correctly, tester will glow when the switch lever is ON, but not when OFF.

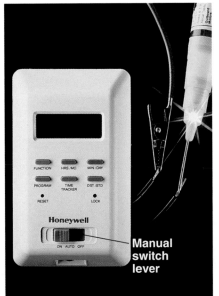

Programmable switch: Attach the tester clip to a wire lead, and touch the tester probe to the other lead. Flip the manual switch lever from ON to OFF position. If the switch is working correctly, the tester will glow when the switch lever is ON, but not when OFF.

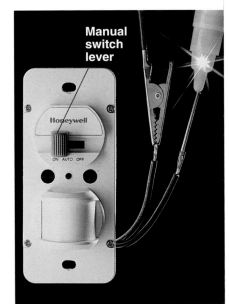

Motion-sensor switch: Attach the tester clip to a wire lead, and touch the tester probe to the other lead. Flip the manual switch lever from ON to OFF position. If the switch is working correctly, the tester will glow when the switch lever is ON, but not when OFF.

Fixing & Replacing Wall Switches

Most switch problems are caused by loose wire connections. If a fuse blows or a circuit breaker trips when a switch is turned on, a loose wire may be touching the metal box. Loose wires also can cause switches to overheat or buzz.

Switches sometimes fail because internal parts wear out. To check for wear, the switch must be removed entirely and tested for continuity (pages 52 to 55). If the continuity test shows the switch is faulty, replace it.

Everything You Need

Tools: Screwdriver, circuit tester, continuity tester, combination tool.

Materials: Fine sandpaper, antioxidant paste (for aluminum wiring), masking tape.

See Inspector's Notebook:

• Common Cable Problems (pages 125 to 127).
• Checking Wire Connections (pages 128 to 129).
• Electrical Box Inspection (pages 129 to 131).
• Inspecting Receptacles & Switches (pages 134 to 135).

How to Fix or Replace a Single-pole Wall Switch

1 Turn off the power to the switch at the main service panel, then remove the switch coverplate.

2 Remove the mounting screws holding the switch to the electrical box. Holding the mounting straps carefully, pull the switch from the box. Be careful not to touch any bare wires or screw terminals until the switch has been tested for power.

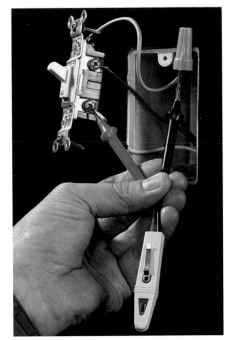

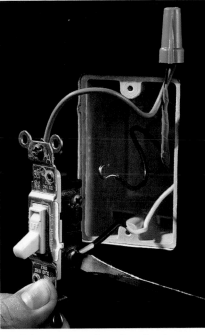

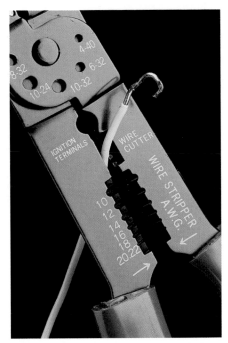

3 Test for power by touching one probe of the neon circuit tester to the grounded metal box or to the bare copper grounding wire, and touching other probe to each screw terminal. Tester should not glow. If it does, there is still power entering the box. Return to service panel, and turn off correct circuit.

4 Disconnect the circuit wires and remove the switch. Test the switch for continuity (page 52), and buy a replacement if the switch is faulty. If circuit wires are too short, lengthen them by adding pigtail wires (page 130).

5 If wires are broken or nicked, clip off damaged portion, using a combination tool. Strip wires so there is about ¾" of bare wire at the end of each wire.

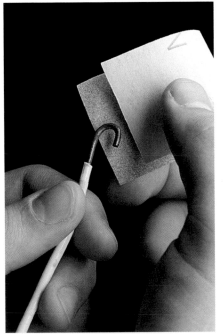

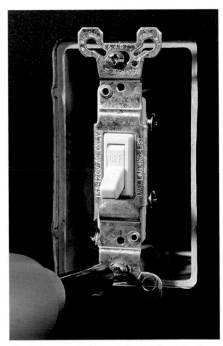

6 Clean the bare copper wires with fine sandpaper if they appear darkened or dirty. If wires are aluminum, apply an antioxidant paste before connecting the wires.

7 Connect the wires to the screw terminals on the switch. Tighten the screws firmly, but do not over-tighten. Overtightening may strip the screw threads.

8 Remount the switch, carefully tucking the wires inside the box. Reattach the switch cover-plate, and turn on the power to the switch at the main service panel.

How to Fix or Replace a Three-way Wall Switch

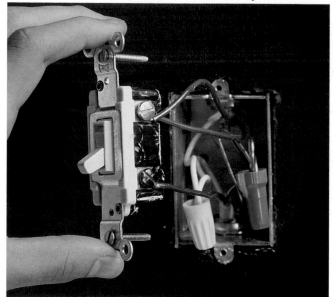

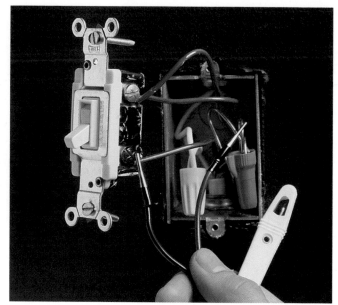

1 Turn off the power to the switch at the main service panel, then remove the switch coverplate and mounting screws. Holding the mounting strap carefully, pull the switch from the box. Be careful not to touch the bare wires or screw terminals until they have been tested for power.

2 Test for power by touching one probe of the neon circuit tester to the grounded metal box or to the bare copper grounding wire, and touching the other probe to each screw terminal. Tester should not glow. If it does, there is still power entering the box. Return to the service panel, and turn off the correct circuit.

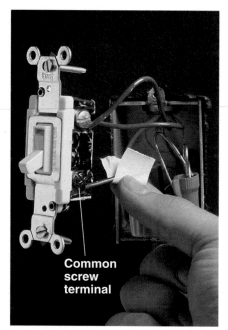

Common screw terminal

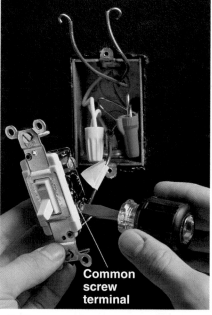

Common screw terminal

3 Locate dark common screw terminal, and use masking tape to label the "common" wire attached to it. Disconnect wires and remove switch. Test switch for continuity (page 53). If it tests faulty, buy a replacement. Inspect wires for nicks and scratches. If necessary, clip damaged wires and strip them (page 23).

4 Connect the common wire to the dark common screw terminal on the switch. On most three-way switches the common screw terminal is copper. Or it may be labeled with the word COMMON stamped on the back of the switch. If the switch has a grounding screw, connect it to the circuit grounding wires with a pigtail.

5 Connect the remaining two circuit wires to the screw terminals. These wires are interchangeable and can be connected to either screw terminal. Carefully tuck the wires into the box. Remount the switch, and attach the coverplate. Turn on the power at the main service panel.

How to Fix or Replace a Four-way Wall Switch

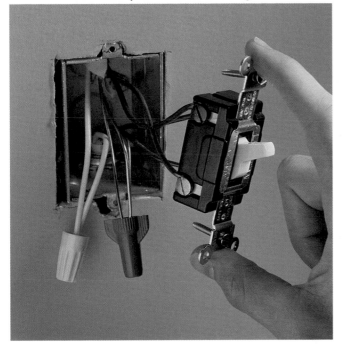

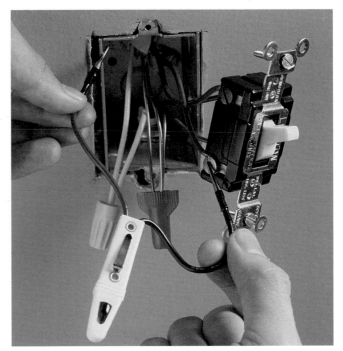

1 Turn off the power to the switch at the main service panel, then remove the switch coverplate and mounting screws. Holding the mounting strap carefully, pull the switch from the box. Be careful not to touch any bare wires or screw terminals until they have been tested for power.

2 Test for power by touching one probe of the neon circuit tester to the grounded metal box or bare copper grounding wire, and touching the other probe to each of the screw terminals. Tester should not glow. If it does, there is still power entering the box. Return to the service panel, and turn off the correct circuit.

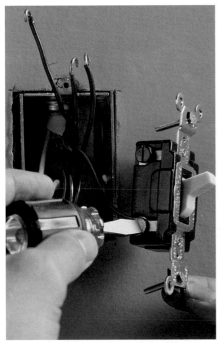

3 Disconnect the wires and inspect them for nicks and scratches. If necessary, clip damaged wires and strip them (page 23). Test the switch for continuity (page 53). Buy a replacement if the switch tests faulty.

4 Connect two wires from one incoming cable to the top set of screw terminals.

5 Attach remaining wires to the other set of screw terminals. Pigtail the grounding wires to the grounding screw. Carefully tuck the wires inside the switch box, then remount the switch and coverplate. Turn on power at main service panel.

Toggle-type dimmer resembles standard switches. Toggle dimmers are available in both single-pole and three-way designs.

Dial-type dimmer is the most common style. Rotating the dial changes the light intensity.

...e-action dimmer has an ...ted face that makes the ...sy to locate in the dark.

...omatic dimmer has an electronic sensor that adjusts the light fixture to compensate for the changing levels of natural light. An automatic dimmer also can be operated manually.

Dimmer Switches

A dimmer switch makes it possible to vary the brightness of a light fixture. Dimmers are often installed in dining rooms, recreation areas, or bedrooms.

Any standard single-pole switch can be replaced with a dimmer, as long as the switch box is of adequate size. Dimmer switches have larger bodies than standard switches. They also generate a small amount of heat that must dissipate. For these reasons, dimmers should not be installed in undersized electrical boxes or in boxes that are crowded with circuit wires. Always follow the manufacturer's specifications for installation.

In lighting configurations that use three-way switches (pages 46 to 47), replace the standard switches with special three-way dimmers. If replacing both the switches with dimmers, buy a packaged pair of three-way dimmers designed to work together.

Dimmer switches are available in several styles (photo, left). All types have wire leads instead of screw terminals, and they are connected to circuit wires using wire connectors. Some types have a green grounding lead that should be connected to the grounded metal box or to the bare copper grounding wires.

Everything You Need

Tools: Screwdriver, circuit tester, needlenose pliers.

Materials: Wire connectors, masking tape.

See Inspector's Notebook:

• Electrical Box Inspection (pages 129 to 131).

How to Install a Dimmer Switch

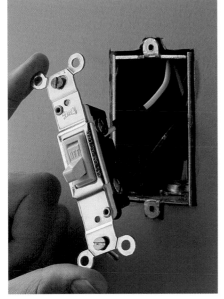

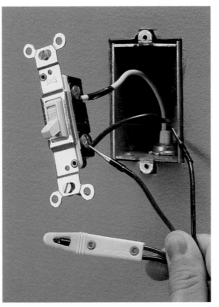

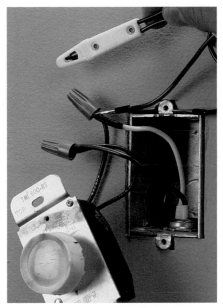

1 Turn off power to switch at the main service panel, then remove the coverplate and mounting screws. Holding the mounting straps carefully, pull switch from the box. Be careful not to touch bare wires or screw terminals until they have been tested for power.

2 Test for power by touching one probe of neon circuit tester to the grounded metal box or to the bare copper grounding wires, and touching other probe to each screw terminal. Tester should not glow. If it does, there is still power entering the box. Return to the service panel and turn off the correct circuit.

If replacing an old dimmer, test for power by touching one probe of circuit tester to the grounded metal box or bare copper grounding wires, and inserting the other probe into each wire connector. Tester should not glow. If it does, there is still power entering the box. Return to the service panel, and turn off the correct circuit.

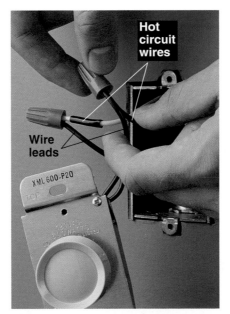

Hot circuit wires

Wire leads

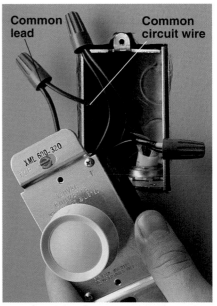

Common lead

Common circuit wire

3 Disconnect the circuit wires and remove the switch. Straighten the circuit wires, and clip the ends, leaving about ½" of the bare wire end exposed.

4 Connect the wire leads on the dimmer switch to the circuit wires, using wire connectors. The switch leads are interchangeable and can be attached to either of the two circuit wires.

Three-way dimmer has an additional wire lead. This "common" lead is connected to the common circuit wire. When replacing a standard three-way switch with a dimmer, the common circuit wire is attached to the darkest screw terminal on the old switch (page 58).

The earliest receptacles were modifications of the screw-in type light bulb. This receptacle was used in the early 1900s.

The polarized receptacle became standard in the 1920s. The different sized slots direct current flow for safety.

The ground-fault circuit-interrupter, or GFCI receptacle, is a modern safety device. When it detects slight changes in current, it instantly shuts off power

Common Receptacle Problems

Household receptacles, also called outlets, have no moving parts to wear out and usually last for many years without servicing. Most problems associated with receptacles are actually caused by faulty lamps and appliances, or their plugs and cords. However, the constant plugging in and removal of appliance cords can wear out the metal contacts inside a receptacle. Any receptacle that does not hold plugs firmly should be replaced.

A loose wire connection is another possible problem. A loose connection can spark (called arcing), trip a circuit breaker, or cause heat to build up in the receptacle box, creating a potential fire hazard.

Wires can come loose for a number of reasons. Everyday vibrations caused by walking across floors, or from nearby street traffic, may cause a connection to shake loose. In addition, because wires heat and cool with normal use, the ends of the wires will expand and contract slightly. This movement also may cause the wires to come loose from the screw terminal connections.

See Inspector's Notebook:
• Checking Wire Connections (pages 128 to 129).
• Electrical Box Inspection (pages 129 to 131).
• Inspecting Receptacles & Switches (pages 134 to 135).

Problem	Repair
Circuit breaker trips repeatedly, or fuse burns out immediately after being replaced.	1. Repair or replace worn or damaged lamp or appliance cord. 2. Move lamps or appliances to other circuits to prevent overloads (page 34). 3. Tighten any loose wire connections (pages 72 to 73). 4. Clean dirty or oxidized wire ends (page 72).
Lamp or appliance does not work.	1. Make sure lamp or appliance is plugged in. 2. Replace burned-out bulbs. 3. Repair or replace worn or damaged lamp or appliance cord. 4. Tighten any loose wire connections (pages 72 to 73). 5. Clean dirty or oxidized wire ends (page 72). 6. Repair or replace any faulty receptacle (pages 72 to 73).
Receptacle does not hold plugs firmly.	1. Repair or replace worn or damaged plugs (pages 98 to 99). 2. Replace faulty receptacle (pages 72 to 73).
Receptacle is warm to the touch, buzzes, or sparks when plugs are inserted or removed.	1. Move lamps or appliances to other circuits to prevent overloads (page 34). 2. Tighten any loose wire connections (pages 72 to 73). 3. Clean dirty or oxidized wire ends (page 72). 4. Replace faulty receptacle (pages 72 to 73).

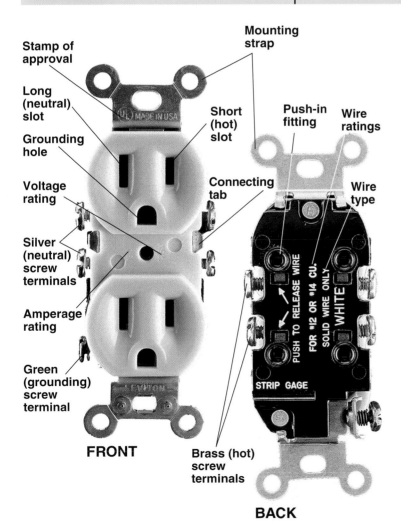

FRONT

BACK

The standard duplex receptacle has two halves for receiving plugs. Each half has a long (neutral) slot, a short (hot) slot, and a U-shaped grounding hole. The slots fit the wide prong, narrow prong, and grounding prong of a three-prong plug. This ensures that the connection between receptacle and plug will be polarized and grounded for safety (page 16).

Wires are attached to the receptacle at screw terminals or push-in fittings. A connecting tab between the screw terminals allows a variety of different wiring configurations. Receptacles also include mounting straps for attaching to electrical boxes.

Stamps of approval from testing agencies are found on the front and back of the receptacle. Look for the symbol UL or UND. LAB. INC. LIST to make sure the receptacle meets the strict standards of Underwriters Laboratories.

The receptacle is marked with ratings for maximum volts and amps. The common receptacle is marked 15A, 125V. Receptacles marked CU or COPPER are used with solid copper wire. Those marked CU-CLAD ONLY are used with copper-coated aluminum wire. Only receptacles marked CO/ALR may be used with solid aluminum wiring (page 124). Receptacles marked AL/CU no longer may be used with aluminum wire, according to code.

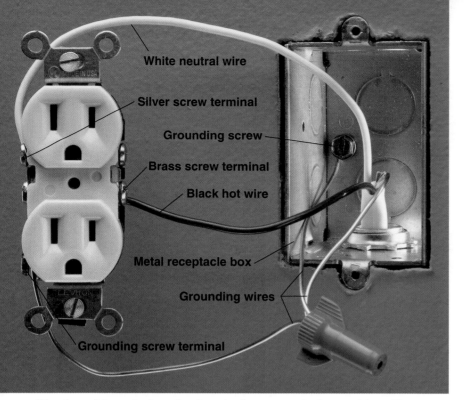

White neutral wire

Silver screw terminal

Grounding screw

Brass screw terminal

Black hot wire

Metal receptacle box

Grounding wires

Grounding screw terminal

Single cable entering the box indicates end-of-run wiring. The black hot wire is attached to a brass screw terminal, and the white neutral wire is connected to a silver screw terminal. If the box is metal, the grounding wire is pigtailed to the grounding screws of the receptacle and the box. In a plastic box, the grounding wire is attached directly to the grounding screw terminal of the receptacle.

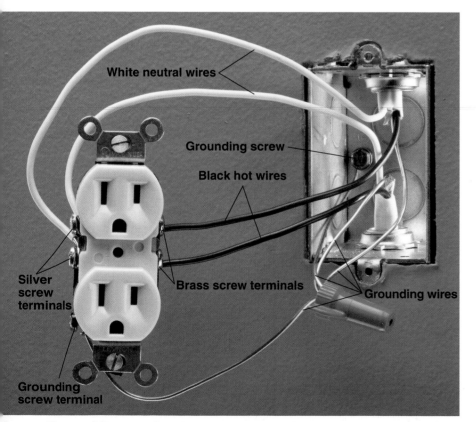

White neutral wires

Grounding screw

Black hot wires

Silver screw terminals

Brass screw terminals

Grounding wires

Grounding screw terminal

Two cables entering the box indicate middle-of-run wiring. Black hot wires are connected to brass screw terminals, and white neutral wires to silver screw terminals. The grounding wire is pigtailed to the grounding screws of the receptacle and the box.

Receptacle Wiring

A 125-volt duplex receptacle can be wired to the electrical system in a number of ways. The most common are shown on these pages.

Wiring configurations may vary slightly from these photographs, depending on the kind of receptacles used, the type of cable, or the technique of the electrician who installed the wiring. To make dependable repairs or replacements, use masking tape and label each wire according to its location on the terminals of the existing receptacle.

Receptacles are wired as either **end-of-run** or **middle-of-run.** These two basic configurations are easily identified by counting the number of cables entering the receptacle box. End-of-run wiring has only one cable, indicating that the circuit ends. Middle-of-run wiring has two cables, indicating that the circuit continues on to other receptacles, switches, or fixtures.

A **split-circuit receptacle** is shown on the next page. Each half of a split-circuit receptacle is wired to a separate circuit. This allows two appliances of high wattage to be plugged into the same receptacle without blowing a fuse or tripping a breaker. This wiring configuration is similar to a receptacle that is controlled by a wall switch. Code requires a **switch-controlled receptacle** in any room that does not have a built-in light fixture operated by a wall switch.

Split-circuit and switch-controlled receptacles are connected to two hot wires, so use caution during repairs or replacements. Make sure the connecting tab between the hot screw terminals is removed.

Two-slot receptacles are common in older homes. There is no grounding wire attached to the receptacle, but the box may be grounded with armored cable or conduit (page 20).

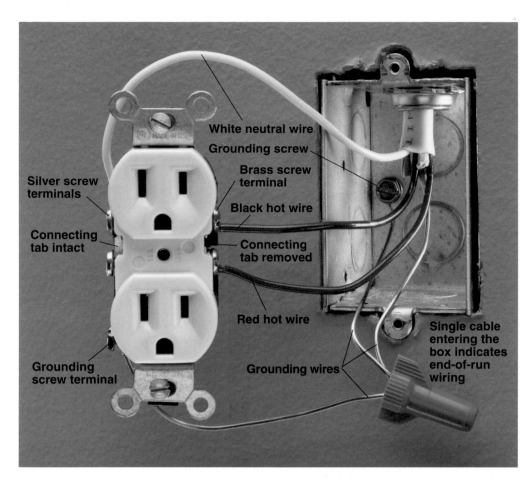

Silver screw terminals

White neutral wire

Grounding screw

Brass screw terminal

Black hot wire

Connecting tab intact

Connecting tab removed

Red hot wire

Grounding screw terminal

Grounding wires

Single cable entering the box indicates end-of-run wiring

Split-circuit receptacle is attached to a black hot wire, a red hot wire, a white neutral wire, and a bare grounding wire. The wiring is similar to a switch-controlled receptacle.

The hot wires are attached to the brass screw terminals, and the connecting tab or fin between the brass terminals is removed. The white wire is attached to a silver screw terminal, and the connecting tab on the neutral side remains intact. The grounding wire is pigtailed to the grounding screw terminal of the receptacle and to the grounding screw attached to the box.

Black hot wires

White neutral wires

Silver screw terminal

Brass screw terminal

Two cables entering the box indicates middle-of-run wiring

Two-slot receptacle is often found in older homes. The black hot wires are connected to the brass screw terminals, and the white neutral wires are pigtailed to a silver screw terminal.

Two-slot receptacles may be replaced with three-slot types, but only if a means of grounding exists at the receptacle box.

Basic Types of Receptacles

Several different types of receptacles are found in the typical home. Each has a unique arrangement of slots that accepts only a certain kind of plug, and each is designed for a specific job.

Household receptacles provide two types of voltage: normal and high voltage. Although voltage ratings have changed slightly over the years, normal receptacles should be rated for 110, 115, 120, or 125 volts. For purposes of replacement, these ratings are considered identical. High-voltage receptacles are rated at 220, 240, or 250 volts. These ratings are considered identical.

When replacing a receptacle, check the amperage rating of the circuit at the main service panel, and buy a receptacle with the correct amperage rating (page 28).

15 amps, 125 volts. Polarized two-slot receptacle is common in homes built before 1960. Slots are different sizes to accept polarized plugs.

15 amps, 125 volts. Three-slot grounded receptacle has two different size slots and a U-shaped hole for grounding. It is required in all new wiring installations.

20 amps, 125 volts. This three-slot grounded receptacle features a special T-shaped slot. It is installed for use with large appliances or portable tools that require 20 amps of current.

15 amps, 250 volts. This receptacle is used primarily for window air conditioners. It is available as a single unit or as half of a duplex receptacle with the other half wired for 125 volts.

30 amps, 125/250 volts. This receptacle is used for clothes dryers. It provides high-voltage current for heating coils and 125-volt current to run lights and timers.

50 amps, 125/250 volts. This receptacle is used for ranges. The high-voltage current powers heating coils, and the 125-volt current runs clocks and lights.

Older Receptacles

Older receptacles may look different from more modern types, but most will stay in good working order. Follow these simple guidelines for evaluating or replacing older receptacles:

• Never replace an older receptacle with one of a different voltage or higher amperage rating.
• Any two-slot, unpolarized receptacle should be replaced with a two- or three-slot polarized receptacle.
• If no means of grounding is available at the receptacle box, install a GFCI (pages 74 to 77).
• If in doubt, seek the advice of a qualified electrician.

Never alter the prongs of a plug to fit an older receptacle. Altering the prongs may remove the grounding or polarizing features of the plug.

Unpolarized receptacles have slots that are the same length. Modern plug types may not fit these receptacles. Never modify the prongs of a polarized plug to fit the slots of an unpolarized receptacle.

Surface-mounted receptacles were popular in the 1940s and 1950s for their ease of installation. Wiring often ran in the back of hollowed-out base moldings. Surface-mounted receptacles are usually ungrounded.

Ceramic duplex receptacles were manufactured in the 1930s. They are polarized but ungrounded, and they can be wired for either 125 volts or 250 volts.

Twist-lock receptacles are designed to be used with plugs that are inserted and rotated. A small tab on the end of one of the prongs prevents the plug from being pulled from the receptacle.

Ceramic duplex receptacle has a unique hourglass shape. The receptacle shown above is rated for 250 volts but only 5 amps, and would not be allowed by today's electrical codes.

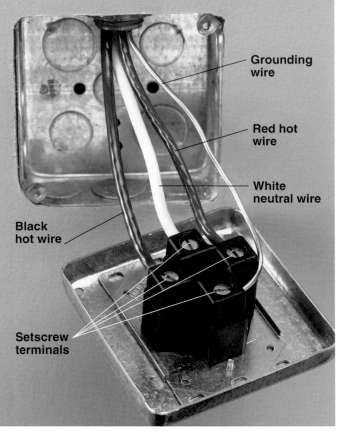

A receptacle rated for 125/250 volts has two incoming hot wires, each carrying 125 volts, a white neutral wire, and a bare copper grounding wire. Connections are made with setscrew terminals at the back of the receptacle.

High-voltage Receptacles

High-voltage receptacles provide current to large appliances like clothes dryers, ranges, water heaters, and air conditioners. The slot configuration of a high-voltage receptacle (page 66) will not accept a plug rated for 125 volts.

A high-voltage receptacle can be wired in one of two ways. In a standard high-voltage receptacle, voltage is brought to the receptacle with two hot wires, each carrying a maximum of 125 volts. No white neutral wire is necessary, but a grounding wire should be attached to the receptacle and to the metal receptacle box. Conduit can also act as a ground from the metal receptacle box back to the service panel.

A clothes dryer or range also may require normal current (a maximum of 125 volts) to run lights, timers and clocks. If so, a white neutral wire will be attached to the receptacle. The appliance itself will split the incoming current into a 125-volt circuit and a 250-volt circuit.

Repair or replace a high-voltage receptacle using the techniques shown on pages 72 to 73. It is important to identify and tag all wires on the existing receptacle so that the new receptacle will be properly wired.

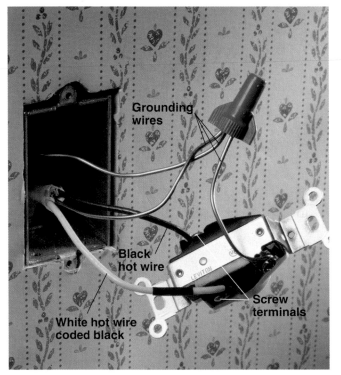

Standard receptacle rated for 250 volts has two incoming hot wires and no neutral wire. A grounding wire is pigtailed to the receptacle and to the metal receptacle box.

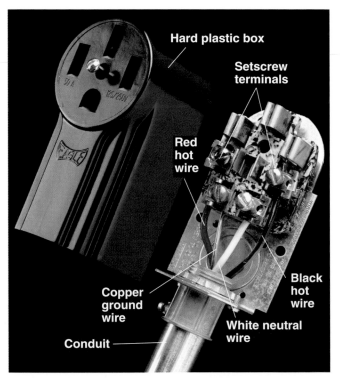

Surface-mounted receptacle rated for 250 volts has a hard plastic box that can be installed on concrete or block walls. Surface-mounted receptacles are often found in basements and utility rooms.

Childproof Receptacles & Other Accessories

Childproof your receptacles or adapt them for special uses by adding receptacle accessories. Before installing an accessory, be sure to read the manufacturer's instructions.

Homeowners with small children should add inexpensive caps or covers to guard against accidental electric shocks.

Plastic caps do not conduct electricity and are virtually impossible for small children to remove. A receptacle cover attaches directly to the receptacle and fits over plugs, preventing the cords from being removed.

Prevent accidents by installing a receptacle cover to prevent cords and plugs from being removed.

Tamper resistant outlets are another way to prevent shocks. Thermoplastic shutters seal the slots of the outlet unless the two prongs of a plug are inserted at the same time, effectively keeping foreign objects out. Use plastic caps (inset) to protect standard outlets.

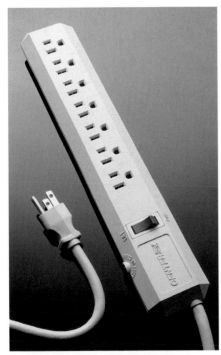

Install more than two plugs in a single duplex receptacle by using a multi-outlet power strip. A multi-outlet strip should have a built-in circuit breaker or fuse to protect against overloads.

Protect electronic equipment, such as a home computer or stereo, with a surge protector. The surge protector prevents any damage to sensitive wiring or circuitry caused by sudden drops or surges in power.

Recessed wall receptacle permits a plug-in clock to be hung flush against a wall surface.

Metal probes

Testing Receptacles for Power, Grounding & Polarity

For testing receptacles and other devices for power, grounding, and polarity, neon circuit testers are inexpensive and easy to use. But they are less sensitive than auto-ranging multimeters. In some cases, neon testers won't detect the presence of lower voltage in a circuit. This can lead you to believe that a circuit is shut off when it is not—a dangerous mistake. The small probes on a neon circuit tester also force you to get too close to live terminals and wires. For a quick check and confirmation, a neon circuit tester (or a plug-in tester) is adequate. But for the most reliable readings, buy and learn to use a multimeter.

The best multimeters are auto-ranging models with a digital readout. Unlike manual multimeters, auto-ranging models do not require you to preset the voltage range to get an accurate reading. Unlike neon testers, multimeters may be used for a host of additional diagnostic functions, such as testing fuses, measuring battery voltage, testing internal wiring in appliances, and checking light fixtures to determine if they're functional.

Everything You Need

Tools: Multimeter, neon circuit tester, plug-in tester, screwdriver.

How to Use a Plug-in Tester

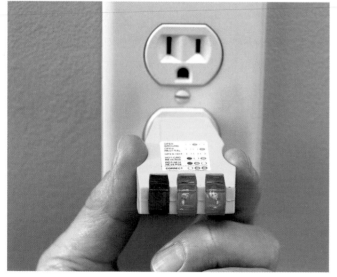

Use a plug-in tester to test a three-slot receptacle. With the power on, insert the tester into the suspect outlet. The face of the tester has three colored lights that will light up in different combinations, according to the outlet's problem. A reference chart is provided with tester, and many have a chart on the tester itself.

How to Test Quickly for Power

Use a neon circuit tester for quick testing to verify that power is not flowing to a receptacle before removing the cover plate. Insert one probe in each slot of the receptacle. If the bulb does not glow, remove the cover plate to access the receptacle and the screw terminals. Confirm that power is not flowing by testing the terminals with a multimeter.

How to Test a Receptacle for Power

1 Set the selector dial for alternating-current voltage. Plug the black probe lead into the common jack on the multimeter (labeled COM). Plug the red probe lead into the V-labeled jack.

2 Insert the test ends of the probe into the receptacle slots. It does not make a difference which probe goes into which slot as long as they're in the same receptacle. If power is present and flowing normally, you will see a voltage reading (usually between 115 and 125 volts) on the readout screen.

3 If the multimeter reads 0 or gives a very low reading (less than 1 or 2 volts), power is not present in the receptacle and it is safe to remove the cover plate and work on the fixture (although it's always a good idea to confirm your reading by touching the probes directly to the screw terminals on the receptacles).

How to Test for Hot Wires

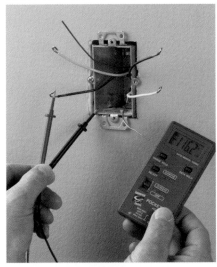

When a receptacle or switch is in the middle of a circuit, it is difficult to tell which wires are carrying current. Use a multimeter to check. With power off, remove the receptacle and separate the wires. Restore power. Touch one probe to the bare ground or the grounded metal box and touch the other probe to the end of each wire. The wire that shows current on the meter is hot.

How to Test a Two-Slot Receptacle for Grounding

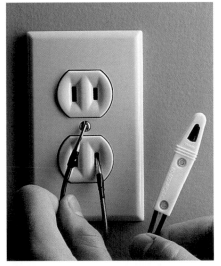

1 Confirm that the receptacle has power. Place one probe of a neon tester or multimeter in the short (hot) slot and the other on the coverplate screw (screw must be unpainted). If the tester shows current, the receptacle is grounded. If the tester doesn't show current, proceed to step 2.

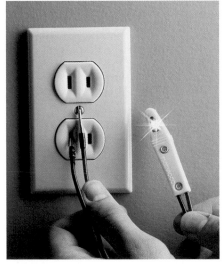

2 Place one probe in the long (neutral) slot and the other on the coverplate screw. If the tester shows current, the hot and neutral wires are reversed (page 135). If not, the box is ungrounded.

Repairing & Replacing Receptacles

Receptacles are easy to repair. After shutting off power to the receptacle circuit, remove the coverplate and inspect the receptacle for any obvious problems such as a loose or broken connection, or wire ends that are dirty or oxidized. Remember that a problem at one receptacle may affect other receptacles in the same circuit. If the cause of a faulty receptacle is not readily apparent, test other receptacles in the circuit for power (page 70).

When replacing a receptacle, check the amperage rating of the circuit at the main service panel, and buy a replacement receptacle with the correct amperage rating (page 28).

When installing a new receptacle, always test for grounding (page 71). Never install a three-slot receptacle where no grounding exists. Instead, install a two-slot polarized or GFCI receptacle.

Everything You Need

Tools: Circuit tester, screwdriver, vacuum cleaner (if needed).

Materials: Fine sandpaper, antioxidant paste, masking tape (if needed).

See Inspector's Notebook:

• Electrical Box Inspection (pages 129 to 131).
• Inspecting Receptacles & Switches (pages 134 to 135).

How to Repair a Receptacle

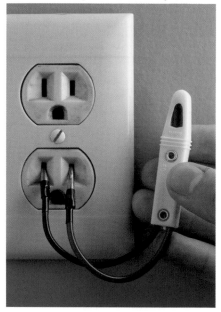

1 Turn off power at the main service panel. Test the receptacle for power with a neon circuit tester (page 70). Test both ends of a duplex receptacle. Remove the coverplate, using a screwdriver.

2 Remove the mounting screws that hold the receptacle to the box. Carefully pull the receptacle from the box. Take care not to touch any bare wires.

3 Confirm that the power to the receptacle is off (page 70), using a neon circuit tester. If wires are attached to both sets of screw terminals, test both sets. The tester should not glow. If it does, you must turn off the correct circuit at the service panel.

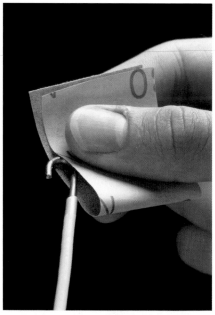

4 If the ends of the wires appear darkened or dirty, disconnect them one at a time, and clean them with fine sandpaper. If the wires are aluminum, apply an antioxidant paste before reconnecting. Antioxidant paste is available at hardware stores.

5 Tighten all connections, using a screwdriver. Take care not to overtighten and strip the screws.

6 Check the box for dirt or dust and, if necessary, clean it with a vacuum cleaner and narrow nozzle attachment.

7 Reinstall the receptacle, and turn on power at the main service panel. Test the receptacle for power with a neon circuit tester. If the receptacle does not work, check other receptacles in the circuit before making a replacement.

How to Replace a Receptacle

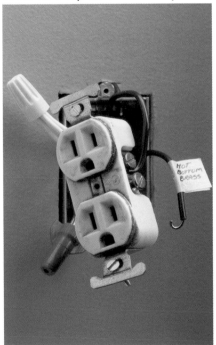

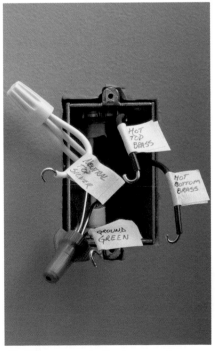

1 To replace a receptacle, repeat steps 1 to 3 on the opposite page. With the power off, label each wire for its location on the receptacle screw terminals, using masking tape and a felt-tipped pen.

2 Disconnect all wires and remove the receptacle.

3 Replace the receptacle with one rated for the correct amperage and voltage (page 28). Replace coverplate, and turn on power. Test receptacle with a neon circuit tester or multimeter (pages 70 to 71).

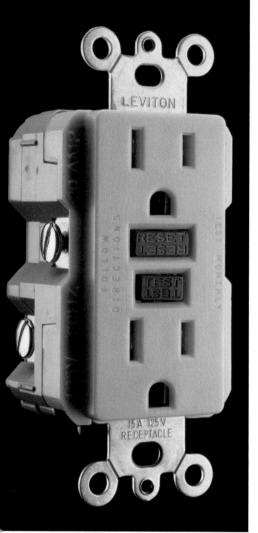

GFCI Receptacles

The ground-fault circuit-interrupter (GFCI) receptacle protects against electrical shock caused by a faulty appliance, or a worn cord or plug. It senses small changes in current flow and can shut off power in as little as 1/40 of a second.

GFCIs are now required in bathrooms, kitchens, garages, crawl spaces, unfinished basements, and outdoor receptacle locations. Consult your local codes for any requirements regarding the installation of GFCI receptacles. Most GFCIs use standard screw terminal connections, but some have wire leads and are attached with wire connectors. Because the body of a GFCI receptacle is larger than a standard receptacle, small crowded electrical boxes may need to be replaced with more spacious boxes (pages 40 to 41).

The GFCI receptacle may be wired to protect only itself (single location), or it can be wired to protect all receptacles, switches, and light fixtures from the GFCI "forward" to the end of the circuit (multiple locations).

Because the GFCI is so sensitive, it is most effective when wired to protect a single location. The more receptacles any one GFCI protects, the more susceptible it is to "phantom tripping," shutting off power because of tiny, normal fluctuations in current flow.

Everything You Need

Tools: Circuit tester, screwdriver.

Materials: Wire connectors, masking tape.

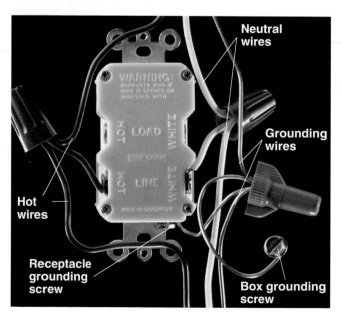

A GFCI wired for single-location protection (shown from the back) has hot and neutral wires connected only to the screw terminals marked LINE. A GFCI connected for single-location protection may be wired as either an end-of-run or middle-of-run configuration (page 64).

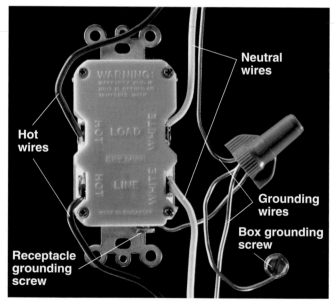

A GFCI wired for multiple-location protection (shown from the back) has one set of hot and neutral wires connected to the LINE pair of screw terminals, and the other set connected to the LOAD pair of screw terminals. A GFCI receptacle connected for multiple-location protection may be wired only as a middle-of-run configuration.

How to Install a GFCI for Single-location Protection

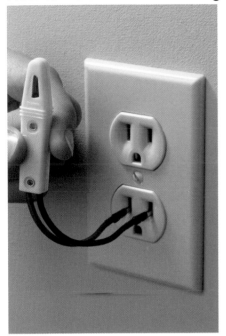

1 Shut off power to the receptacle at the main service panel. Test for power with a neon circuit tester (page 70). Be sure to check both halves of the receptacle.

2 Remove coverplate. Loosen mounting screws, and gently pull receptacle from the box. Do not touch wires. Confirm power is off with a circuit tester (page 70).

3 Disconnect all white neutral wires from the silver screw terminals of the old receptacle.

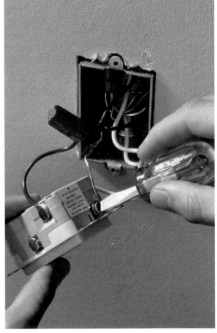

4 Pigtail all the white neutral wires together, and connect the pigtail to the terminal marked WHITE LINE on the GFCI (see photo on opposite page).

5 Disconnect all black hot wires from the brass screw terminals of the old receptacle. Pigtail these wires together, and connect them to the terminal marked HOT LINE on the GFCI.

6 If a grounding wire is available, connect it to the green grounding screw terminal of the GFCI. Mount the GFCI in the receptacle box, and reattach the coverplate. Restore power, and test the GFCI according to the manufacturer's instructions.

How to Install a GFCI for Multiple-location Protection

1 Use a map of your house circuits (pages 30 to 33) to determine a location for your GFCI. Indicate all receptacles that will be protected by the GFCI installation.

2 Turn off power to the correct circuit at the main service panel. Test all the receptacles in the circuit with a neon circuit tester to make sure the power is off. Always check both halves of each duplex receptacle.

3 Remove the coverplate from the receptacle that will be replaced with the GFCI. Loosen the mounting screws and gently pull the receptacle from its box. Take care not to touch any bare wires. Confirm the power is off with a neon circuit tester (page 70).

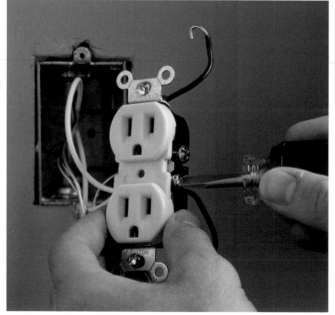

4 Disconnect all black hot wires. Carefully separate the hot wires and position them so that the bare ends do not touch anything. Restore power to the circuit at the main service panel. Determine which black wire is the "feed" wire by testing for hot wires (page 71). The feed wire brings power to the receptacle from the service panel. Use caution: This is a "live" wire test, during which the power is turned on temporarily.

5 When you have found the hot feed wire, turn off power at the main service panel. Identify the feed wire by marking it with masking tape.

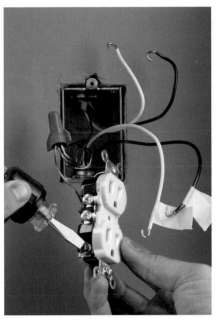

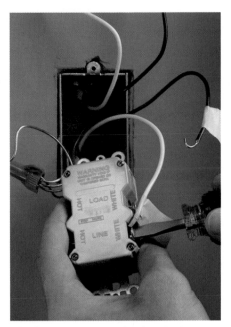

6 Disconnect the white neutral wires from the old receptacle. Identify the white feed wire and label it with masking tape. The white feed wire will be the one that shares the same cable as the black feed wire.

7 Disconnect the grounding wire from the grounding screw terminal of the old receptacle. Remove the old receptacle. Connect the grounding wire to the grounding screw terminal of the GFCI.

8 Connect the white feed wire to the terminal marked WHITE LINE on the GFCI. Connect the black feed wire to the terminal marked HOT LINE on the GFCI.

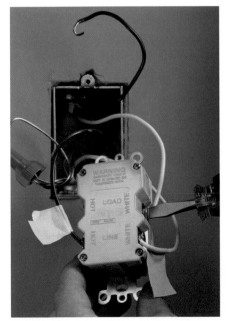

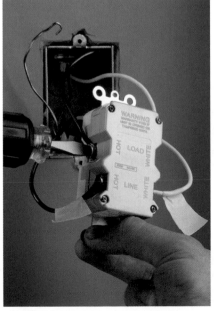

9 Connect the other white neutral wire to the terminal marked WHITE LOAD on the GFCI.

10 Connect the other black hot wire to the terminal marked HOT LOAD on the GFCI.

11 Carefully tuck all wires into the receptacle box. Mount the GFCI in the box and attach the coverplate. Turn on power to the circuit at the main service panel. Test the GFCI according to the manufacturer's instructions.

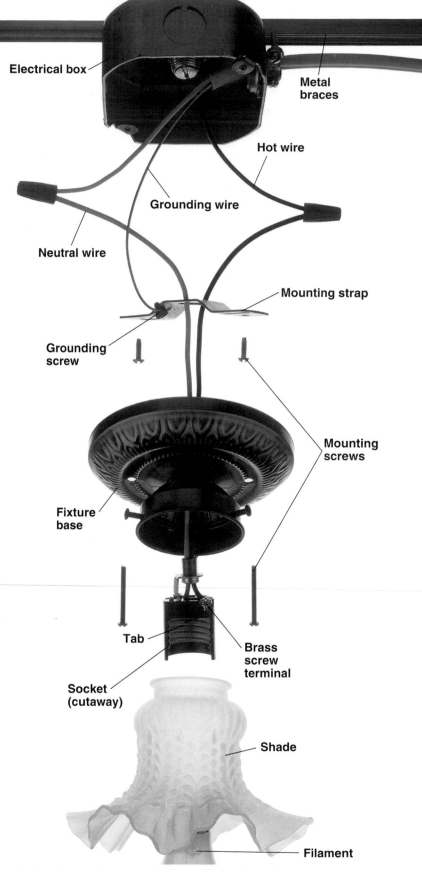

Electrical box

Metal braces

Hot wire

Grounding wire

Neutral wire

Mounting strap

Grounding screw

Mounting screws

Fixture base

Brass screw terminal

Tab

Socket (cutaway)

Shade

Filament

Repairing & Replacing Incandescent Light Fixtures

Incandescent light fixtures are attached permanently to ceilings or walls. They include wall-hung sconces, ceiling-hung globe fixtures, recessed light fixtures, and chandeliers. Most incandescent light fixtures are easy to repair, using basic tools and inexpensive parts.

If a light fixture fails, always make sure the lightbulb is screwed in tightly and is not burned out. A faulty lightbulb is the most common cause of light fixture failure. If the light fixture is controlled by a wall switch, also check the switch as a possible source of problems (pages 42 to 61).

Light fixtures can fail because the sockets or built-in switches wear out. Some fixtures have sockets and switches that can be removed for minor repairs. These parts are held to the base of the fixture with mounting screws or clips. Other fixtures have sockets and switches that are joined permanently to the base. If this type of fixture fails, purchase and install a new light fixture.

Damage to light fixtures often occurs because homeowners install lightbulbs with wattage ratings that are too high. Prevent overheating and light fixture failures by using only

In a typical incandescent light fixture, a black hot wire is connected to a brass screw terminal on the socket. Power flows to a small tab at the bottom of the metal socket and through a metal filament inside the bulb. The power heats the filament and causes it to glow. The current then flows through the threaded portion of the socket and through the white neutral wire back to the main service panel.

lightbulbs that match the wattage ratings printed on the fixtures.

Techniques for repairing fluorescent lights are different from those for incandescent lights. Refer to pages 92 to 97 to repair or replace a fluorescent light fixture.

Everything You Need

Tools: Circuit tester, screwdriver, continuity tester, combination tool.

Materials: Replacement parts, as needed.

See Inspector's Notebook:

- Common Cable Problems (pages 125 to 127)
- Checking Wire Connections (pages 128 to 129).
- Electrical Box Inspection (pages 129 to 131).

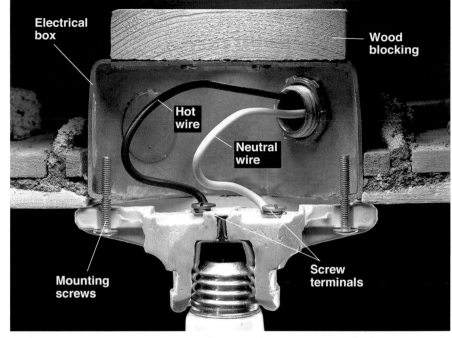

Before 1959, incandescent light fixtures (shown cut away) often were mounted directly to an electrical box or to plaster lath. Electrical codes now require that fixtures be attached to mounting straps that are anchored to the electrical boxes (page 78). If you have a light fixture attached to plaster lath, install an approved electrical box with a mounting strap to support the fixture (pages 38 to 41).

Problem	Repair
Wall- or ceiling-mounted fixture flickers or does not light.	1. Check for faulty lightbulb. 2. Check wall switch, and repair or replace, if needed (pages 42 to 61). 3. Check for loose wire connections in electrical box. 4. Test socket, and replace, if needed (pages 80 to 81). 5. Replace light fixture (page 82).
Built-in switch on fixture does not work.	1. Check for faulty lightbulb. 2. Check for loose wire connections on switch. 3. Replace switch (page 81). 4. Replace light fixture (page 82).
Chandelier flickers or does not light.	1. Check for faulty lightbulb. 2. Check wall switch, and repair or replace, if needed (pages 42 to 61). 3. Check for loose wire connections in electrical box. 4. Test sockets and fixture wires, and replace, if needed (pages 86 to 87).
Recessed fixture flickers or does not light.	1. Check for faulty lightbulb. 2. Check wall switch, and repair or replace, if needed (pages 42 to 61). 3. Check for loose wire connections in electrical box. 4. Test fixture, and replace, if needed (pages 83 to 85).

How to Remove a Light Fixture & Test a Socket

1 Turn off the power to the light fixture at the main service panel. Remove the lightbulb and any shade or globe, then remove the mounting screws holding the fixture base to the electrical box or mounting strap. Carefully pull the fixture base away from box.

2 Test for power by touching one probe of a neon circuit tester to green grounding screw, then inserting other probe into each wire connector. Tester should not glow. If it does, there is still power entering box. Return to the service panel, and turn off power to correct circuit.

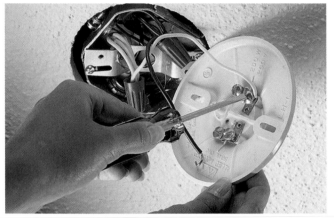

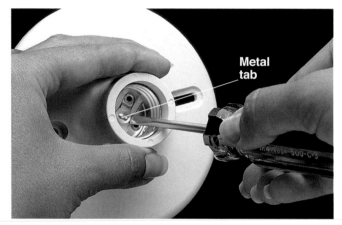

3 Disconnect the light fixture base by loosening the screw terminals. If fixture has wire leads instead of screw terminals, remove the light fixture base by unscrewing the wire connectors.

4 Adjust the metal tab at the bottom of the fixture socket by prying it up slightly with a small screwdriver. This adjustment will improve the contact between the socket and the lightbulb.

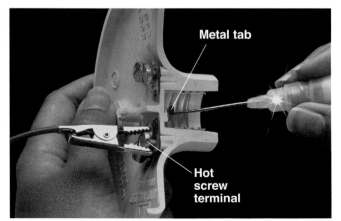

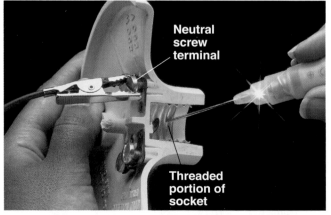

5 Test the socket (shown cutaway) by attaching the clip of a continuity tester to the hot screw terminal (or black wire lead) and touching probe of tester to metal tab in bottom of socket. Tester should glow. If not, socket is faulty and must be replaced.

6 Attach tester clip to neutral screw terminal (or white wire lead), and touch probe to threaded portion of socket. Tester should glow. If not, socket is faulty and must be replaced. If socket is permanently attached, replace the fixture (page 82).

How to Replace a Socket

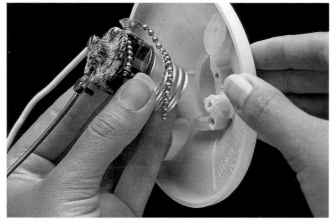 

1 Remove light fixture (steps 1 to 3, page 80). Remove the socket from the fixture. Socket may be held by a screw, clip, or retaining ring. Disconnect wires attached to the socket.

2 Purchase an identical replacement socket. Connect white wire to silver screw terminal on socket, and connect black wire to brass screw terminal. Attach socket to fixture base, and reinstall fixture.

How to Test & Replace a Built-in Light Switch

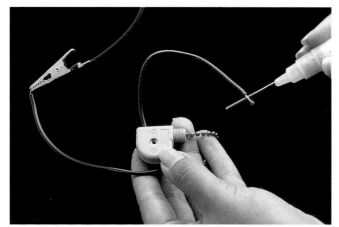 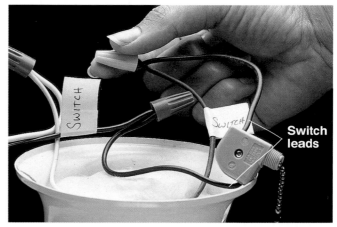

Retaining ring

1 Remove light fixture (steps 1 to 3, page 80). Unscrew the retaining ring holding the switch.

Switch leads

2 Label the wires connected to the switch leads. Disconnect the switch leads and remove switch.

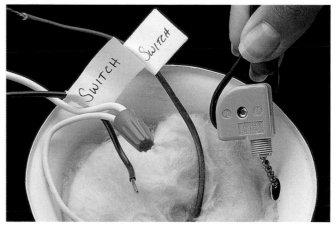

3 Test switch by attaching clip of continuity tester to one of the switch leads and holding tester probe to the other lead. Operate switch control. If switch is good, tester will glow when switch is in one position, but not both.

4 If the switch is faulty, purchase and install an exact duplicate switch. Remount the light fixture, and turn on the power at the main service panel.

How to Replace an Incandescent Light Fixture

1 Turn off the power, and remove the old light fixture, following the directions for standard light fixtures (page 80, steps 1 to 3) or chandeliers (pages 86 to 87, steps 1 to 4).

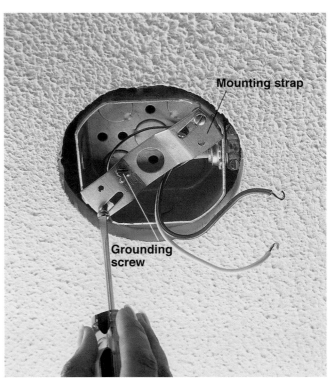

2 Attach a mounting strap to the electrical box, if box does not already have one. The mounting strap, included with the new light fixture, has a pre-installed grounding screw.

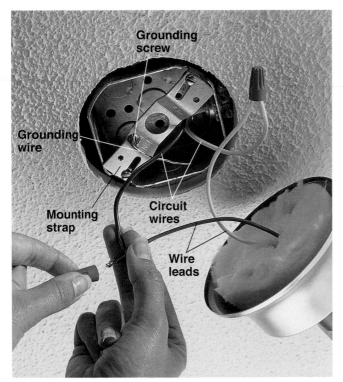

3 Connect the circuit wires to the base of the new fixture, using wire connectors. Connect the white wire lead to the white circuit wire, and the black wire lead to the black circuit wire. Pigtail the bare copper grounding wire to the grounding screw on the mounting strap.

4 Attach the light fixture base to the mounting strap, using the mounting screws. Attach the globe, and install a lightbulb with a wattage rating that is the same as or lower than the rating indicated on the fixture. Turn on the power at the main service panel.

Repairing & Replacing Recessed Light Fixtures

Most problems with recessed light fixtures occur because heat builds up inside the metal canister and melts the insulation on the socket wires. On some recessed light fixtures, sockets with damaged wires can be removed and replaced. However, most newer fixtures have sockets that cannot be removed. With this type, you will need to buy a new fixture if the socket wires are damaged.

When buying a new recessed light fixture, choose a replacement that matches the old fixture. Install the new fixture in the metal mounting frame that is already in place.

Unless the fixture is rated IC (insulated covered), make sure building insulation is at least 3" away from the canister to dissipate heat.

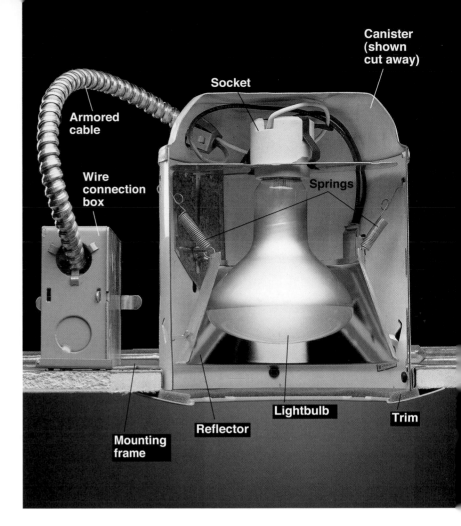

How to Remove & Test a Recessed Light Fixture

1 Turn off the power to the light fixture at the main service panel. Remove the trim, lightbulb, and reflector. The reflector is held to the canister with small springs or mounting clips.

2 Loosen the screws or clips holding the canister to the mounting frame. Carefully raise the canister and set it away from the frame opening.

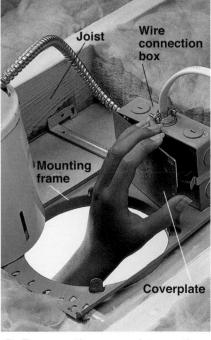

3 Remove the coverplate on the wire connection box. The box is attached to the mounting frame between the ceiling joists.

(continued next page)

How to Remove & Test a Recessed Light Fixture (continued)

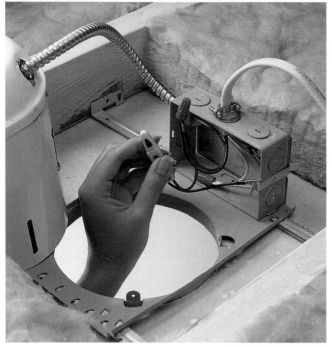

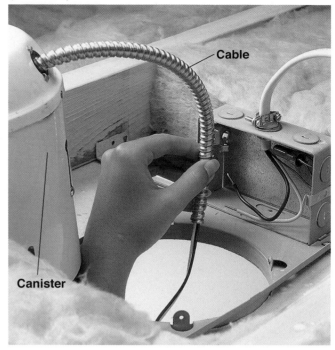

Cable

Canister

4 Test for power by touching one probe of neon circuit tester to grounded wire connection box and inserting other probe into each wire connector. Tester should not glow. If it does, there is still power entering box. Return to the service panel and turn off correct circuit.

5 Disconnect the white and black circuit wires by removing the wire connectors. Pull the armored cable from the wire connection box. Remove the canister through the frame opening.

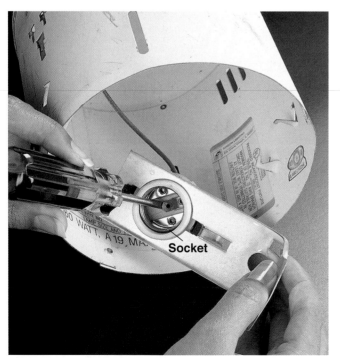

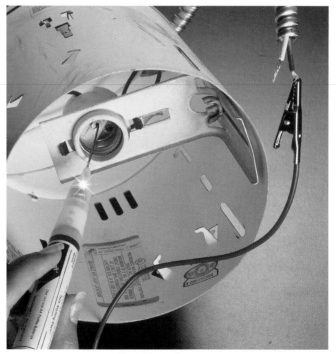

Socket

6 Adjust the metal tab at the bottom of the fixture socket by prying it up slightly with a small screwdriver. This adjustment will improve contact with the lightbulb.

7 Test the socket by attaching the clip of a continuity tester to the black fixture wire and touching tester probe to the metal tab in bottom of the socket. Attach the tester clip to white fixture wire, and touch probe to the threaded metal socket. Tester should glow for both tests. If not, then socket is faulty. Replace the socket (page 81), or install a new light fixture (next page).

How to Replace a Recessed Light Fixture

1 Remove the old light fixture (pages 83 to 84). Buy a new fixture that matches the old fixture. Although the new light fixture comes with its own mounting frame, it is easier to mount the new fixture using the frame that is already in place.

2 Set the fixture canister inside the ceiling cavity, and thread the fixture wires through the opening in the wire connection box. Push the armored cable into the wire connection box to secure it.

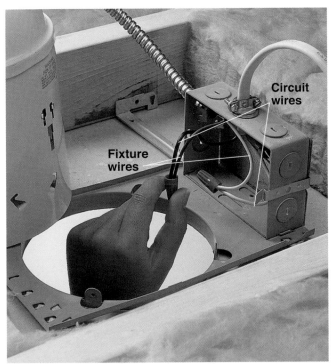

3 Connect the white fixture wire to the white circuit wire, and the black fixture wire to the black circuit wire, using wire connectors. Attach the coverplate to the wire connection box. Make sure any building insulation is at least 3" from canister and wire connection box.

4 Position the canister inside the mounting frame, and attach the mounting screws or clips. Attach the reflector and trim. Install a lightbulb with a wattage rating that is the same as or lower than rating indicated on the fixture. Turn on power at main service panel.

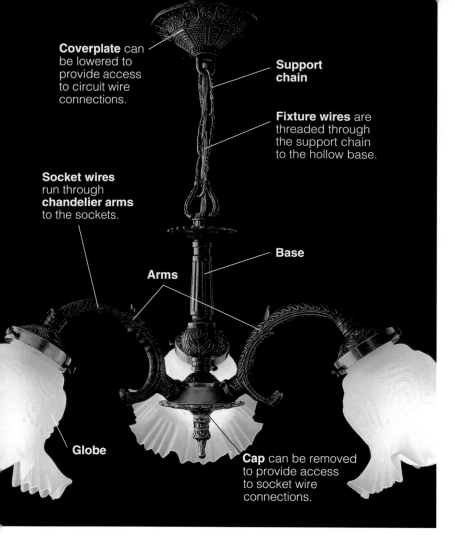

Coverplate can be lowered to provide access to circuit wire connections.

Support chain

Fixture wires are threaded through the support chain to the hollow base.

Socket wires run through **chandelier arms** to the sockets.

Base

Arms

Globe

Cap can be removed to provide access to socket wire connections.

Repairing Chandeliers

Repairing a chandelier requires special care. Because chandeliers are heavy, it is a good idea to work with a helper when removing a chandelier. Support the fixture to prevent its weight from pulling against the wires.

Chandeliers have two fixture wires that are threaded through the support chain from the electrical box to the hollow base of the chandelier. The socket wires connect to the fixture wires inside this base.

Fixture wires are identified as hot and neutral. Look closely for printed lettering or a colored stripe on one of the wires. This is the neutral wire that is connected to the white circuit wire and white socket wire. The other, unmarked, fixture wire is hot and is connected to the black wires.

If you have a new chandelier, it may have a grounding wire that runs through the support chain to the electrical box. If this wire is present, make sure it is connected to the grounding wires in the electrical box.

How to Repair a Chandelier

1 Label any lights that are not working, using masking tape. Turn off power to the fixture at the main service panel. Remove light-bulbs and all shades or globes.

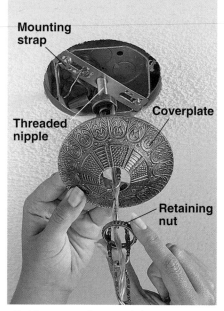

Mounting strap

Threaded nipple

Coverplate

Retaining nut

2 Unscrew the retaining nut and lower the decorative coverplate away from the electrical box. Most chandeliers are supported by a threaded nipple attached to a mounting strap.

Mounting strap

Mounting bolt

Bolt cap nut

Mounting variation: Some chandeliers are supported only by the coverplate that is bolted to the electrical box mounting strap. These types do not have a threaded nipple.

3 Test for power by touching one probe of neon circuit tester to the green grounding screw and inserting other probe into each wire connector. Tester should not glow. If it does, there is still power entering box. Return to service panel, and turn off power to correct circuit.

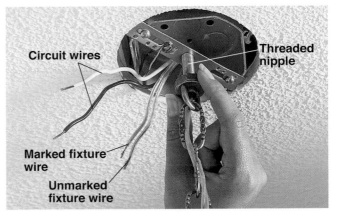

4 Disconnect fixture wires by removing the wire connectors. Marked fixture wire is neutral, and is connected to white circuit wire. Unmarked fixture wire is hot, and is connected to black circuit wire. Unscrew threaded nipple, and carefully place chandelier on a flat surface.

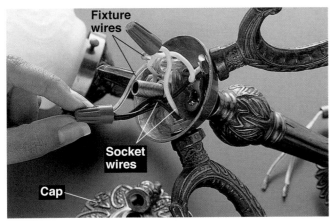

5 Remove the cap from the bottom of the chandelier, exposing the wire connections inside the hollow base. Disconnect the black socket wires from the unmarked fixture wire, and disconnect the white socket wires from the marked fixture wire.

6 Test socket by attaching clip of continuity tester to black socket wire and touching probe to tab in socket. Repeat test with threaded portion of socket and white socket wire. Tester should glow for both tests. If not, the socket is faulty and must be replaced.

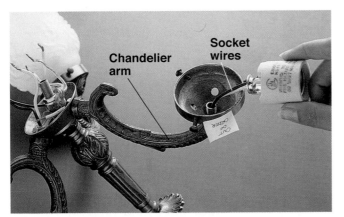

7 Remove a faulty socket by loosening any mounting screws or clips, and pulling the socket and socket wires out of the fixture arm. Purchase and install a new chandelier socket, threading the socket wires through the fixture arm.

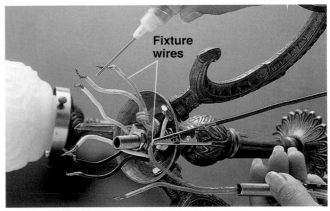

8 Test each fixture wire by attaching clip of continuity tester to one end of wire and touching probe to other end. If tester does not glow, wire is faulty and must be replaced. Install new wires, if needed, then reassemble and rehang the chandelier.

Repairing Track Lights

Like other light fixtures, track lights are connected to an electrical box in the ceiling. The circuit wires in the box provide power to the entire track, and the current runs along two metal power strips inside the track. Each fixture on the track has a contact arm with metal contacts that draw current from the strips to power the fixture.

Common fixture problems are dirty or corroded contacts or power strips, and bad sockets. Track lights are easy to work on because you can quickly remove individual fixtures to get to the source of the problem.

Everything You Need

Tools: Screwdriver, continuity tester, combination tool.

Materials: Fine sandpaper, crimp-style wire connectors.

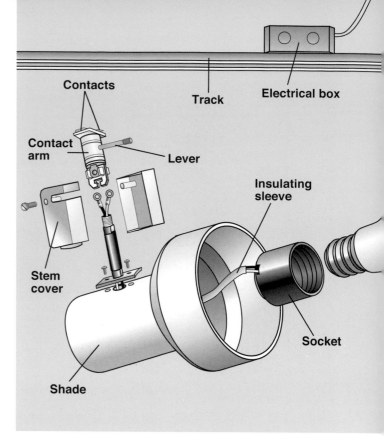

Track lights are powered by an electrical box connected to the middle of, or at the end of, a track. With multiple track sections, special connectors provide the links to power the entire system.

How to Clean Track Light Contacts

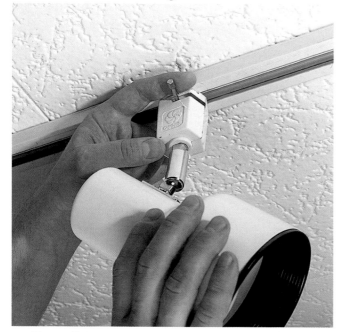

1 Turn off the power to the circuit at the main service panel. Shift the lever on the fixture stem to release the fixture from the track. Use fine sandpaper to clean the metal power strips inside the track in the general area where the fixture hangs.

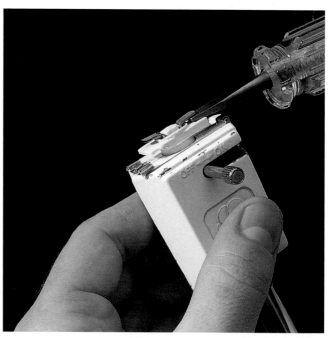

2 Sand the metal contacts on the top of the fixture's contact arm, then use a screwdriver to pry up the tabs slightly. Reattach the fixture to the track, and restore the power. If the fixture doesn't light, test the socket (next page).

How to Test & Replace a Track Light Socket

1 Turn off the power to the circuit at the main service panel. Remove the problem fixture from the track (page 88). Loosen the screws on the stem cover, and remove the cover.

2 Remove the screws securing the socket, and test the socket with a continuity tester. Attach the clip to the brass track contact, and touch the tester probe to the black wire connection on the socket. Repeat the test with the white contact and white wire connection. If the tester fails to light in either test, replace the socket.

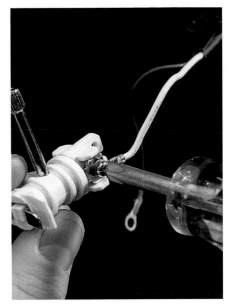

3 To remove the old socket, pull the contact arm from the stem housing, and disconnect the socket wires from the screw terminals. Pull the socket and wires from the shade. If the wires have an insulating sleeve, remove it and set it aside.

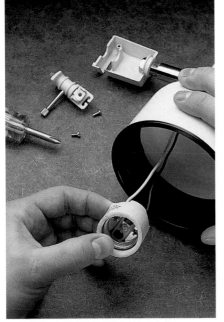

4 Buy a replacement socket with the same wattage rating as the old one. Feed the wires of the new socket into the shade and up through the stem. Attach the socket to the shade.

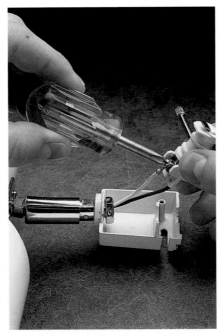

5 Use a combination tool to strip ¼" of insulation from each wire end, and attach a crimp-style wire connector to each wire. Fasten the connectors to the proper screw terminals on the contact arm.

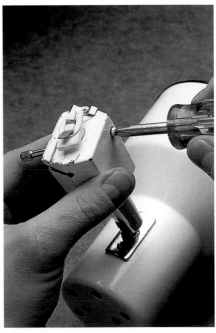

6 Reinstall the socket and contact arm, and reattach the stem cover. Remount the fixture.

Repairing Ceiling Fans

Ceiling fans contain rapidly moving parts, making them more susceptible to trouble than many other electrical fixtures. Installation is a relatively simple matter (see page 238 to 239), but repairing a ceiling fan can be very frustrating. The most common problems you'll encounter are balance and noise issues and switch failure, usually precipitated by the pull chain breaking. In most cases, both problems can be corrected without removing the fan from the ceiling. But if you have difficulty on ladders or simply don't care to work overhead, consider removing the fan when replacing the switch.

Ceiling fans are subject to a great deal of vibration and stress, so it's not uncommon for switches and motors to fail. Minimize wear and tear by making sure blades are in balance so the fan doesn't wobble.

Everything You Need
Tools: Screwdriver, combination tool.
Materials: Replacement switch.

How to Troubleshoot Blade Wobble

1 Start by checking and tightening all hardware used to attach the blades to the mounting arms and the mounting arms to the motor. Hardware tends to loosen over time and this is frequently the cause of wobble.

2 If wobble persists, try switching around two of the blades. Often, this is all it takes to get the fan back into balance. If a blade is damaged or warped, replace it.

3 If the blades are tight and you still have wobble, turn the power off at the panel, remove the fan canopy, and inspect the mounting brace and the connection between the mounting pole and the fan motor. If any connections are loose, tighten them and then replace the canopy.

How to Replace a Pull-chain Switch on a Ceiling Fan

1 Shut off power to the fan circuit at the panel, and then detach the bottom of the fan unit to expose the wires inside. Test the wires by placing one probe of a tester into the wire connecter that joins the black wires and the other to the grounding screw.

2 Locate the plastic switch unit (the part that the pull chain used to be attached to if it broke off). You'll need to replace the switch, which may be attached to the power source with wire connectors or soldered connection that require you to cut the wires. Fans have four to eight feed wires, depending on the number of speed settings. Label the wires before you remove the old switch (this is very important). Remove the old switch.

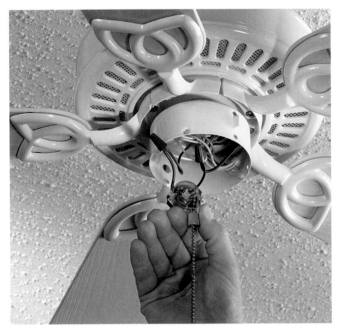

3 Using the old switch as a reference, purchase an identical new switch. Hook up the new switch using the same wiring configuration as on the old model. On newer fans, this probably require inserting the wires from the fan into the switch and crimping them (most switches come with installation instructions).

4 Secure the new switch in the housing and make sure all wires are tucked neatly inside. Restore power and test the switch before replacing the cap. (If you have improperly wired the switch, it may run only at one or two speeds, so test all settings). Reattach the base cap.

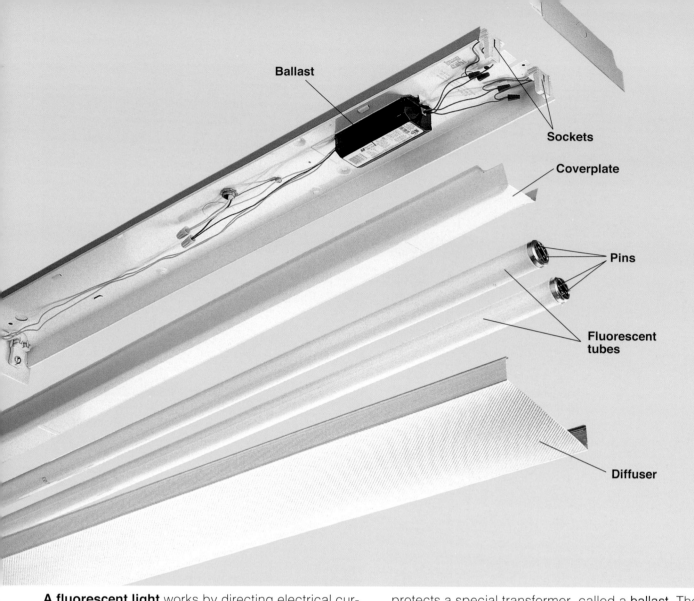

Ballast

Sockets

Coverplate

Pins

Fluorescent
tubes

Diffuser

A fluorescent light works by directing electrical current through a special gas-filled **tube** that glows when energized. A white translucent **diffuser** protects the fluorescent tube and softens the light. A **coverplate** protects a special transformer, called a **ballast**. The ballast regulates the flow of 120-volt household current to the **sockets**. The sockets transfer power to metal **pins** that extend into the tube.

Repairing & Replacing Fluorescent Lights

Fluorescent lights are relatively trouble-free and use less energy than incandescent lights. A typical fluorescent tube lasts about three years and produces two to four times as much light per watt as a standard incandescent light bulb.

The most frequent problem with a fluorescent light fixture is a worn-out tube. If a fluorescent light fixture begins to flicker, or does not light fully, remove and examine the tube. If the tube has bent or broken pins, or black discoloration near the ends, replace it. Light gray discoloration is normal in working fluorescent tubes. When replacing an old tube, read the wattage rating printed on the glass surface, and buy a new tube with a matching rating. Never dispose of old tubes by breaking them. Fluorescent tubes contain a small amount of hazardous mercury. Check with your local environmental control agency or health department for disposal guidelines.

Fluorescent light fixtures also can malfunction if the sockets are cracked or worn. Inexpensive replacement sockets are available at any hardware store and can be installed in a few minutes.

If a fixture does not work even after the tube and sockets have been serviced, the ballast probably is defective. Faulty ballasts may leak a black, oily substance and can cause a fluorescent light

Problem	Repair
Tube flickers, or lights partially.	1. Rotate tube to make sure it is seated properly in the sockets. 2. Replace tube (page 94) and the starter (where present) if tube is discolored or if pins are bent or broken. 3. Replace the ballast (page 96) if replacement cost is reasonable. Otherwise, replace the entire fixture (page 97).
Tube does not light.	1. Check wall switch, and repair or replace, if needed (pages 42 to 61). 2. Rotate the tube to make sure it is seated properly in sockets. 3. Replace tube (page 94) and the starter (where present) if tube is discolored or if pins are bent or broken. 4. Replace sockets if they are chipped or if tube does not seat properly (page 95). 5. Replace the ballast (page 96) or the entire fixture (page 97).
Noticeable black substance around ballast.	Replace ballast (page 96) if replacement cost is reasonable. Otherwise, replace the entire fixture (page 97).
Fixture hums.	Replace ballast (page 96) if replacement cost is reasonable. Otherwise, replace the entire fixture (page 97).

fixture to make a loud humming sound. Although ballasts can be replaced, always check prices before buying a new ballast. It may be cheaper to purchase and install a new fluorescent fixture rather than to replace the ballast in an old fluorescent light fixture.

Everything You Need

Tools: Screwdriver, ratchet wrench, combination tool, circuit tester.

Materials: Replacement tubes, starters, or ballast (if needed); replacement fluorescent light fixture (if needed).

See Inspector's Notebook:

• Common Cable Problems (pages 125 to 127).
• Checking Wire Connections (pages 128 to 129)
• Electrical Box Inspection (pages 129 to 131).

Older fluorescent lights may have a small cylindrical device, called a starter, located near one of the sockets. When a tube begins to flicker, replace both the tube and the starter. Turn off the power, then remove the starter by pushing it slightly and turning counterclockwise. Install a replacement that matches the old starter.

How to Replace a Fluorescent Tube

1 Turn off power to the light fixture at the main service panel. Remove the diffuser to expose the fluorescent tube.

2 Remove the fluorescent tube by rotating it ¼ turn in either direction and sliding the tube out of the sockets. Inspect the pins at the end of the tube. Tubes with bent or broken pins should be replaced.

3 Inspect the ends of the fluorescent tube for discoloration. New tube in good working order (top) shows no discoloration. Normal, working tube (middle) may have gray color. A worn-out tube (bottom) shows black discoloration.

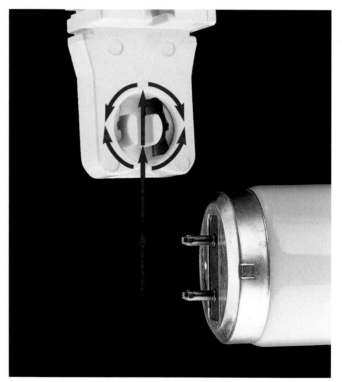

4 Install a new tube with the same wattage rating as the old tube. Insert the tube so that pins slide fully into sockets, then twist tube ¼ turn in either direction until it is locked securely. Reattach the diffuser, and turn on the power at the main service panel.

How to Replace a Socket

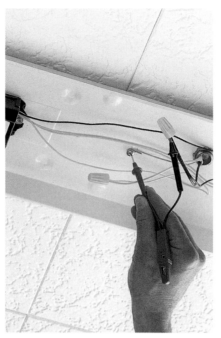

Coverplate

1 Turn off the power at the main service panel. Remove the diffuser, fluorescent tube, and the coverplate.

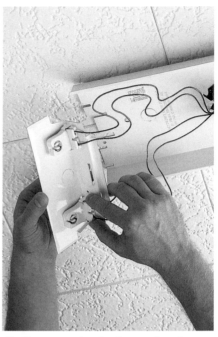

2 Test for power by touching one probe of a neon circuit tester to the grounding screw and inserting the other probe into each wire connector. Tester should not glow. If it does, power is still entering the box. Return to the service panel, and turn off correct circuit.

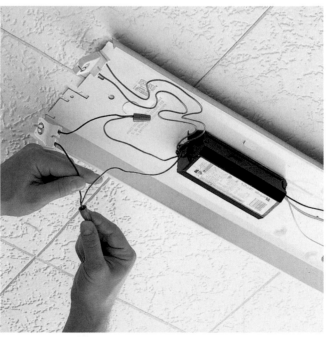

3 Remove the faulty socket from the fixture housing. Some sockets slide out, while others must be unscrewed.

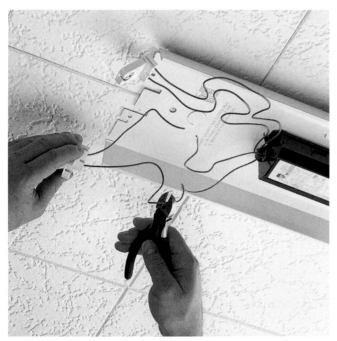

4 Disconnect wires attached to socket. For push-in fittings (above) remove the wires by inserting a small screwdriver into the release openings. Some sockets have screw terminal connections, while others have preattached wires that must be cut before the socket can be removed.

5 Purchase and install a new socket. If socket has preattached wire leads, connect the leads to the ballast wires using wire connectors. Replace coverplate, then the fluorescent tube, making sure that it seats properly. Replace the diffuser. Restore power to the fixture at the main service panel.

How to Replace a Ballast

1 Turn off the power at the main service panel, then remove the diffuser, fluorescent tube, and coverplate. Test for power, using a neon circuit tester (page 95, step 2).

2 Remove the sockets from the fixture housing by sliding them out, or by removing the mounting screws and lifting the sockets out.

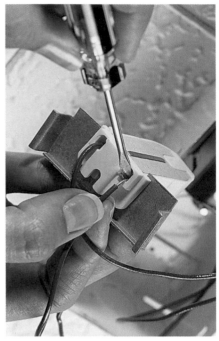

3 Disconnect the wires attached to the sockets by pushing a small screwdriver into the release openings (above), by loosening the screw terminals, or by cutting wires to within 2" of sockets.

4 Remove the old ballast, using a ratchet wrench or screwdriver. Make sure to support the ballast so it does not fall.

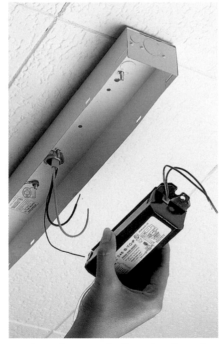

5 Install a new ballast that has the same ratings as the old ballast.

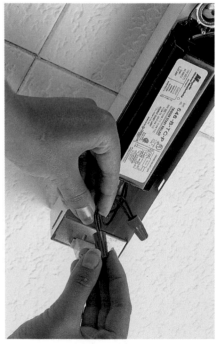

6 Attach the ballast wires to the socket wires, using wire connectors, screw terminal connections, or push-in fittings. Reinstall the coverplate, fluorescent tube, and diffuser. Turn on power to the light fixture at the main service panel.

How to Replace a Fluorescent Light Fixture

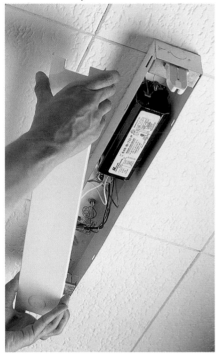

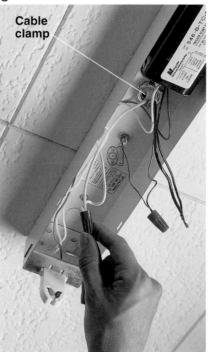

Cable clamp

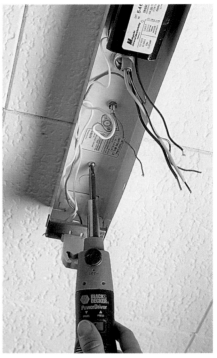

1 Turn off power to the light fixture at the main service panel. Remove the diffuser, tube, and coverplate. Test for power, using a neon circuit tester (page 95, step 2).

2 Disconnect the insulated circuit wires and the bare copper grounding wire from the light fixture. Loosen the cable clamp holding the circuit wires.

3 Unbolt the fixture from the wall or ceiling, and carefully remove it. Make sure to support the fixture so it does not fall.

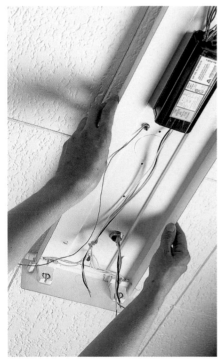

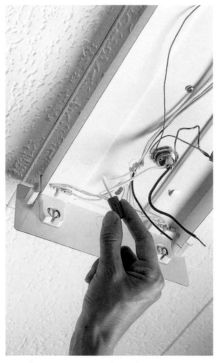

4 Position the new fixture, threading the circuit wires through the knockout opening in the back of the fixture. Bolt the fixture in place so it is firmly anchored to framing members.

5 Connect the circuit wires to the fixture wires, using wire connectors. Follow the wiring diagram included with the new fixture. Tighten the cable clamp holding the circuit wires.

6 Attach the fixture coverplate, then install the fluorescent tubes, and attach the diffuser. Turn on power to the fixture at the main service panel.

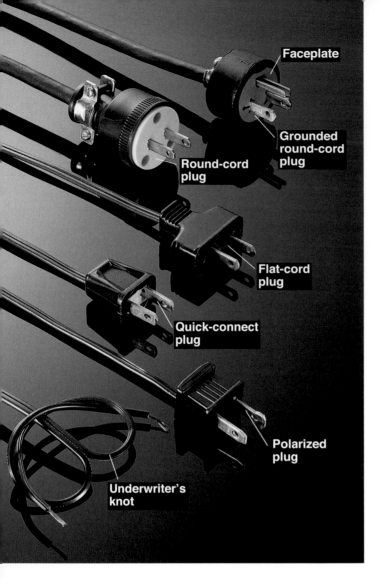

Faceplate

Grounded round-cord plug

Round-cord plug

Flat-cord plug

Quick-connect plug

Polarized plug

Underwriter's knot

Replacing a Plug

Replace an electrical plug whenever you notice bent or loose prongs, a cracked or damaged casing, or a missing insulating faceplate. A damaged plug poses a shock and fire hazard.

Replacement plugs are available in different styles to match common appliance cords. Always choose a replacement that is similar to the original plug. Flat-cord and quick-connect plugs are used with light-duty appliances, like lamps and radios. Round-cord plugs are used with larger appliances, including those that have three-prong grounding plugs.

Some tools and appliances use polarized plugs. A polarized plug has one wide prong and one narrow prong, corresponding to the hot and neutral slots found in a standard receptacle.

If there is room in the plug body, tie the individual wires in an **underwriter's knot** to secure the plug to the cord.

Everything You Need

Tools: Combination tool, needlenose pliers, screwdriver.

Materials: Replacement plug.

How to Install a Quick-connect Plug

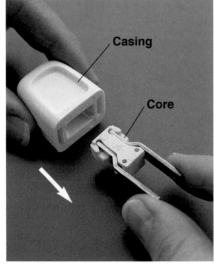

Casing

Core

1 Squeeze the prongs of the new quick-connect plug together slightly and pull the plug core from the casing. Cut the old plug from the flat-cord wire with a combination tool, leaving a clean cut end.

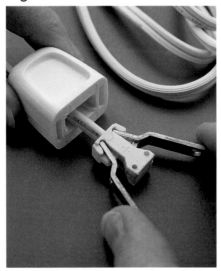

2 Feed unstripped wire through rear of plug casing. Spread prongs, then insert wire into opening in rear of core. Squeeze prongs together; spikes inside core penetrate cord. Slide casing over core until it snaps into place.

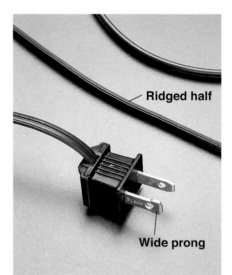

Ridged half

Wide prong

When replacing a polarized plug, make sure that the ridged half of the cord lines up with the wider (neutral) prong of the plug.

How to Replace a Round-cord Plug

1 Cut off round cord near the old plug, using a combination tool. Remove the insulating faceplate on the new plug, and feed cord through rear of plug. Strip about 3" of outer insulation from the round cord. Strip ¾" insulation from the individual wires.

Underwriter's knot

2 Tie an underwriter's knot with the black and white wires. Make sure the knot is located close to the edge of the stripped outer insulation. Pull the cord so that the knot slides into the plug body.

3 Hook end of black wire clockwise around brass screw and white wire around silver screw. On a three-prong plug, attach third wire to grounding screw. If necessary, excess grounding wire can be cut away.

4 Tighten the screws securely, making sure the copper wires do not touch each other. Replace the insulating faceplate.

How to Replace a Flat-cord Plug

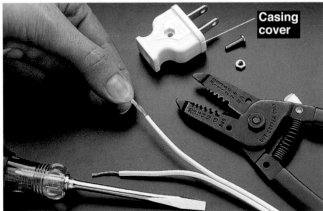

Casing cover

1 Cut old plug from cord using a combination tool. Pull apart the two halves of the flat cord so that about 2" of wire are separated. Strip ¾" insulation from each half. Remove casing cover on new plug.

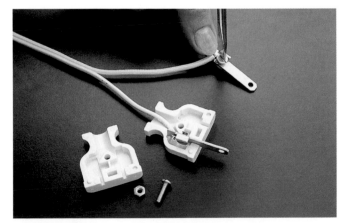

2 Hook ends of wires clockwise around the screw terminals, and tighten the screw terminals securely. Reassemble the plug casing. Some plugs may have an insulating faceplate that must be installed.

Replacing a Lamp Socket

Next to the cord plug, the most common source of trouble in a lamp is a worn lightbulb socket. When a lamp socket assembly fails, the problem is usually with the socket-switch unit, although replacement sockets may include other parts you do not need.

Lamp failure is not always caused by a bad socket. You can avoid unnecessary repairs by checking the lamp cord, plug, and lightbulb before replacing the socket.

Everything You Need:

Tools & Materials: Replacement socket, continuity tester, screwdriver.

Tip: When replacing a lamp socket, you can improve a standard ON-OFF lamp by installing a three-way socket.

Types of Sockets

Socket-mounted switch types are usually inter-changeable: choose a replacement you prefer. Clockwise from top left: twist knob, remote switch, pull chain, push lever.

How to Repair or Replace a Lamp Socket

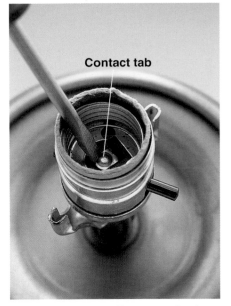

1 Unplug lamp. Remove shade, lightbulb, and harp (shade bracket). Scrape contact tab clean with a small screwdriver. Pry contact tab up slightly if flattened inside socket. Replace bulb, plug in lamp, and test. If lamp does not work, unplug, remove bulb, and continue with next step.

2 Squeeze outer shell of socket near PRESS marking, and lift it off. On older lamps, socket may be held by screws found at the base of the screw socket. Slip off cardboard insulating sleeve. If sleeve is damaged, replace entire socket.

3 Check for loose wire connections on screw terminals. Refasten any loose connections, then reassemble lamp, and test. If connections are not loose, remove the wires, lift out the socket, and continue with the next step.

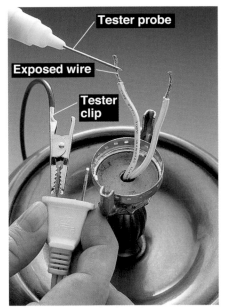

4 Test for lamp cord problems with continuity tester. Place clip of tester on one prong of plug. Touch probe to one exposed wire, then to the other wire. Repeat test with other prong of plug. If tester fails to light for either prong, then replace the cord and plug. Retest the lamp.

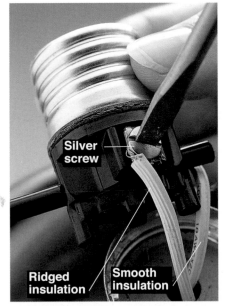

5 If cord and plug are functional, then choose a replacement socket marked with the same amp and volt ratings as the old socket. One half of flat-cord lamp wire is covered by insulation that is ridged or marked: attach this wire to the silver screw terminal. Connect other wire to brass screw.

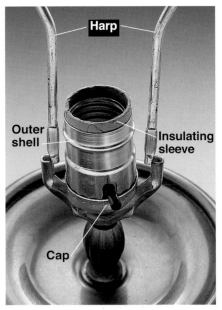

6 Slide insulating sleeve and outer shell over socket so that socket and screw terminals are fully covered and switch fits into sleeve slot. Press socket assembly down into cap until socket locks into place. Replace harp, lightbulb, and shade.

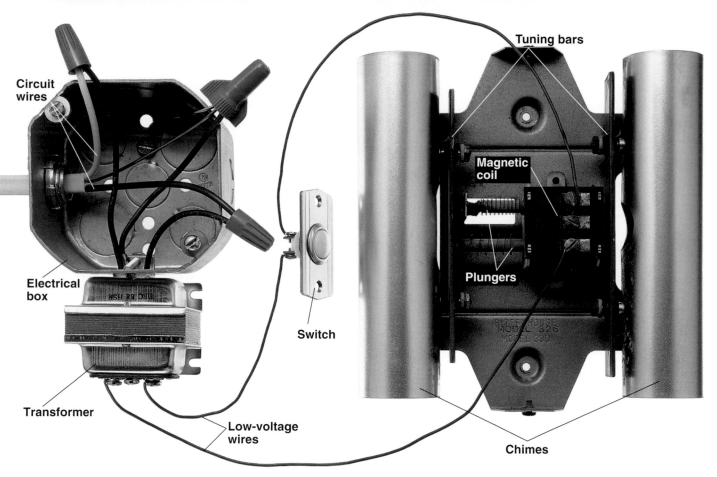

Circuit wires

Tuning bars

Magnetic coil

Plungers

Electrical box

Switch

Transformer

Low-voltage wires

Chimes

Home doorbell system is powered by a transformer that reduces 120-volt current to low-voltage current of 20 volts or less. Current flows from the transformer to one or more push-button switches. When pushed, the switch activates a magnet coil inside the chime unit, causing a plunger to strike a musical tuning bar.

Fixing & Replacing Doorbells

Most doorbell problems are caused by loose wire connections or worn-out switches. Reconnecting loose wires or replacing a switch requires only a few minutes. Doorbell problems also can occur if the chime unit becomes dirty or worn, or if the low-voltage transformer burns out. Both parts are easy to replace. Because doorbells operate at low voltage, the switches and the chime unit can be serviced without turning off power to the system. However, when replacing a transformer, always turn off the power at the main service panel.

Most houses have other low-voltage transformers in addition to the doorbell transformer. These transformers control heating and air-conditioning thermostats (page 106 to 113), or other low-voltage systems. When testing and repairing a doorbell system, it is important to identify the correct transformer. A doorbell transformer has a voltage rating of 20 volts or less. This rating is printed on the face of the transformer. A doorbell transformer often is located near the main service panel and in some homes is attached directly to the service panel. The transformer that controls a heating/

air-conditioning thermostat system is located near the furnace and has a voltage rating of 24 volts or more.

Occasionally, a doorbell problem is caused by a broken low-voltage wire somewhere in the system. You can test for wire breaks with a battery-operated multi-tester. If the test indicates a break, new low-voltage wires must be installed between the transformer and the switches, or between the switches and chime unit. Replacing low-voltage wires is not a difficult job, but it can be time-consuming. You may choose to have an electrician do this work.

Everything You Need:

Tools: Continuity tester, screwdriver, multimeter, needlenose pliers.

Materials: Cotton swab, rubbing alcohol, replacement doorbell switch (if needed), masking tape, replacement chime unit (if needed).

How to Test a Doorbell System

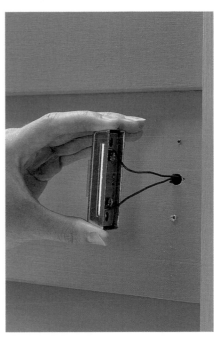

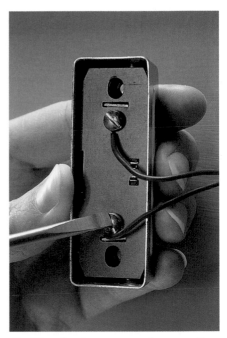

1 Remove the mounting screws holding the doorbell switch to the house.

2 Carefully pull the switch away from the wall.

3 Check wire connections on the switch. If wires are loose, reconnect them to the screw terminals. Test the doorbell by pressing the button. If the doorbell still does not work, disconnect the switch and test it with a continuity tester.

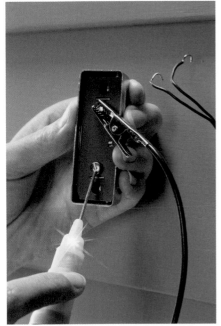

4 Test the switch by attaching the clip of a continuity tester to one screw terminal and touching the probe to the other screw terminal. Press the switch button. Tester should glow. If not, then the switch is faulty and must be replaced (page 105).

5 Twist the doorbell switch wires together temporarily to test the other parts of the doorbell system.

6 Locate the doorbell transformer, often located near the main service panel. Transformer may be attached to an electrical box, or may be attached directly to the side of the service panel.

(continued next page)

7 Identify the doorbell transformer by reading its voltage rating. Doorbell transformers have a voltage rating of 20 volts or less. Turn off power to transformer at main service panel. Remove cover on electrical box, and test wires for power (page 111, step 3). Reconnect any loose wires. Replace taped connections with wire connectors.

8 Reattach coverplate. Inspect the low-voltage wire connections, and reconnect any loose wires, using needlenose pliers. Turn on power to the transformer at the main service panel.

9 Touch the probes of the multitester to the low-voltage screw terminals on the transformer. Set the dial of the multimeter to the 50-volt (AC) range if the meter is not auto ranging. If transformer is operating properly, the meter will detect power within 2 volts of transformer's rating. If not, the transformer is faulty and must be replaced (page 111).

10 Test the chime unit. Remove the coverplate on the doorbell chime unit. Inspect the low-voltage wire connections, and reconnect any loose wires.

11 Test that the chime unit is receiving current. Touch probes of a multimeter to screw terminals marked TRANSFORMER and FRONT. If the multimeter detects power within 2 volts of the transformer rating, then the unit is receiving proper current. If it detects no power or very low power, there is a break in the low-voltage wiring, and new wires must be installed.

12 Clean the chime plungers with a cotton swab dipped in rubbing alcohol. Reassemble doorbell switches, then test the system by pushing one of the switches. If doorbell still does not work, then the chime unit is faulty and must be replaced (page 105).

How to Replace a Doorbell Switch

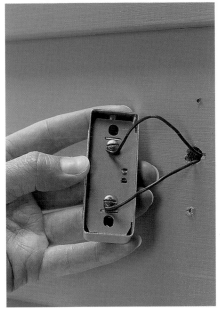

1 Remove the doorbell switch mounting screws, and carefully pull the switch away from the wall.

2 Disconnect wires from switch. Tape wires to the wall to prevent them from slipping into the wall cavity.

3 Purchase a new doorbell switch, and connect wires to screw terminals on new switch. (Wires are interchangeable and can be connected to either terminal.) Anchor the switch to the wall.

How to Replace a Doorbell Chime Unit

1 Turn off power to the doorbell at the main panel. Remove the coverplate from the old chime. Label the low-voltage wires FRONT, REAR, or TRANS to identify their screw terminal locations. Disconnect the wires. Remove the old chime unit. Tape the wires to the wall to prevent them from slipping into the wall cavity (inset).

2 Purchase a new chime unit that matches the voltage rating of the old unit. Thread the low-voltage wires through the base of the new chime unit. Attach the chime unit to the wall, using the mounting screws included with the installation kit.

3 Connect the low-voltage wires to the screw terminals on the new chime unit. Attach the coverplate and turn on the power at the main service panel.

Electronic programmable thermostats can be set to make up to four temperature changes each day. They are available in low-voltage designs (right) for central heating/cooling systems and in line-voltage designs (left) for electric baseboard heating. Most electronic programmable thermostats have an internal battery that saves the program in case of a power failure.

Fixing & Replacing Thermostats

A thermostat is a temperature-sensitive switch that automatically controls home heating and air-conditioning systems. There are two types of thermostats used to control heating and air-conditioning systems. **Low-voltage thermostats** control whole-house heating and air conditioning from one central location. **Line-voltage thermostats** are used in zone heating systems, where each room has its own heating unit and thermostat.

A low-voltage thermostat is powered by a transformer that reduces 120-volt current to about 24 volts. A low-voltage thermostat is very durable, but failures can occur if wire connections become loose or dirty, if thermostat parts become corroded, or if a transformer wears out. Some thermostat systems have two transformers. One transformer controls the heating unit, and the other controls the air-conditioning unit.

Line-voltage thermostats are powered by the same circuit as the heating unit, usually a 240-volt circuit. Always make sure to turn off the power before servicing a line-voltage thermostat.

A thermostat can be replaced in about one hour. Many homeowners choose to replace standard low-voltage or line-voltage thermostats with programmable setback thermostats. These programmable thermostats can cut energy use by up to 35%.

When buying a new thermostat, make sure the new unit is compatible with your heating/air-conditioning system. For reference, take along the brand name and model number of the old thermostat and of your heating/air-conditioning units. When buying a new low-voltage transformer, choose a replacement with voltage and amperage ratings that match the old thermostat.

Everything You Need:

Tools: Soft-bristled paint brush, multimeter, screwdriver, combination tool, continuity tester.

Materials: Masking tape, short piece of wire.

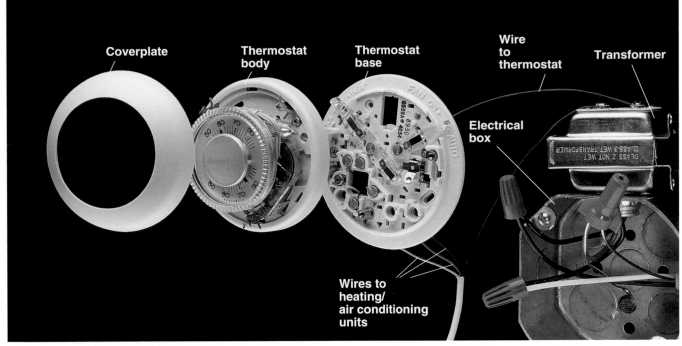

Low-voltage thermostat system has a transformer that is either connected to an electrical junction box or mounted inside a furnace access panel. Very thin wires (18 to 22 gauge) send current to the **thermostat**. The thermostat constantly monitors room temperatures, and sends electrical signals to the heating/cooling unit through additional wires. The number of wires connected to the thermostat varies from two to six, depending on the type of heating/air conditioning system. In the common four-wire system shown above, power is supplied to the thermostat through a single wire attached to screw terminal R. Wires attached to other screw terminals relay signals to the furnace heating unit, the air-conditioning unit, and the blower unit. Before removing a thermostat, make sure to label each wire to identify its screw terminal location.

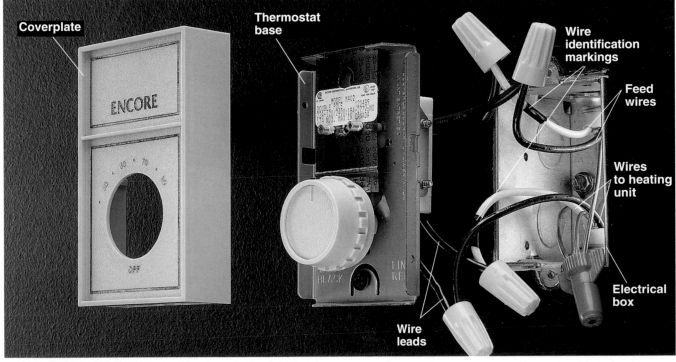

Line-voltage thermostat for 240-volt baseboard heating unit usually has four wire leads, although some models have only two leads. On a four-wire thermostat, the two red wire leads (sometimes marked LINE or L) are attached to the two hot feed wires bringing power into the box from the service panel. The black wire leads (sometimes marked LOAD) are connected to the circuit wires that carry power to the heating unit.

How to Inspect & Test a Low-voltage Thermostat System

Coverplate

Mounting screws

1 Turn off power to the heating/ air-conditioning system at the main service panel. Remove the thermostat coverplate.

2 Clean dust from the thermostat parts using a small, soft-bristled paint brush.

3 Remove the thermostat body by loosening the mounting screws with a screwdriver.

Thermostat base

4 Inspect the wire connections on the thermostat base. Reattach any loose wires. If wires are broken or corroded, they should be clipped, stripped, and reattached to the screw terminals.

5 Locate the low-voltage transformer that powers the thermostat. This transformer usually is located near the heating/air-conditioning system or inside a furnace access panel. Tighten any loose wire connections.

6 Set a multimeter to the 50-volt (AC) range. Turn on power to the heating/air-conditioning system at the main service panel.

7 Touch one probe of multimeter to each of the low-voltage screw terminals. If tester does not detect current, then the transformer is defective and must be replaced (page 111).

8 Turn on power to heating system. Set thermostat control levers to AUTO and HEAT.

9 Strip ½" from each end of a short piece of insulated wire. Touch one end of the wire to terminal marked W and the other end to terminal marked R. If heating system begins to run, then the thermostat is faulty and must be replaced (page 110).

How to Install a Programmable Low-voltage Thermostat

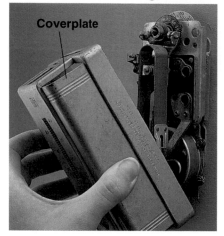

Coverplate

1 Turn off power to the heating/ air-conditioning system at the main service panel. Remove the thermostat coverplate.

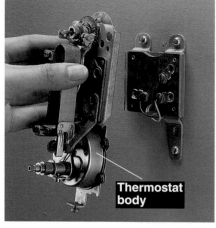

Thermostat body

2 Unscrew the thermostat mounting screws, and remove the thermostat body.

3 Label the low-voltage wires to identify their screw terminal locations, using masking tape. Disconnect all low-voltage wires.

4 Remove the thermostat base by loosening the mounting screws. Tape the wires against the wall to make sure they do not fall into the wall cavity.

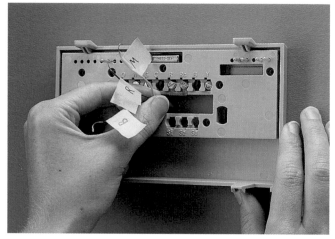

5 Thread the low-voltage wires through base of new thermostat. Mount the thermostat base on the wall, using the screws included with the thermostat.

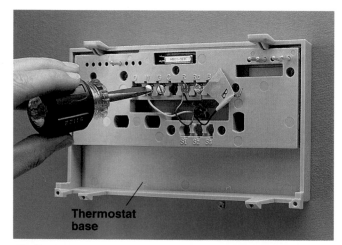

Thermostat base

6 Connect the low-voltage wires to the screw terminals on the thermostat base. Use the manufacturer's connection chart as a guide.

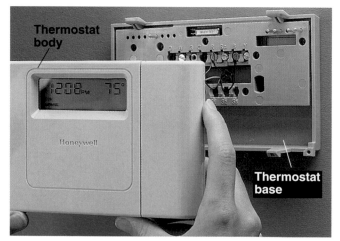

Thermostat body

Thermostat base

7 Install batteries in thermostat body, then attach the body to thermostat base. Turn on power, and program the thermostat as desired.

How to Replace a Low-voltage Transformer

1 Turn off power to the heating/air-conditioning system at the main service panel. Remove the coverplate on the transformer electrical box.

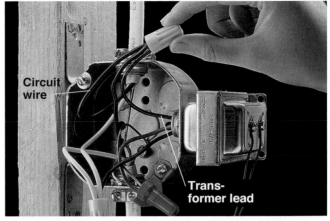

2 Carefully remove the wire connector joining the black circuit wire to the transformer lead. Be careful not to touch bare wires.

3 Test for power by touching one probe of neon circuit tester to grounded metal box and other probe to exposed wires. Remove wire connector from white wires and repeat test. Tester should not glow for either test. If it does, power is still entering box. Return to service panel, and turn off correct circuit.

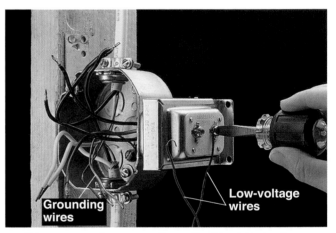

4 Disconnect the grounding wires inside the box, then disconnect low-voltage wires attached to the screw terminals on the transformer. Unscrew the transformer mounting bracket inside the box, and remove transformer. Purchase a new transformer with the same voltage rating as the old transformer.

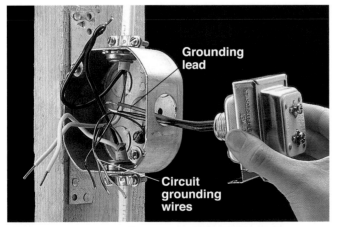

5 Attach new transformer to electrical box. Reconnect circuit wires to transformer leads. Connect circuit grounding wires to transformer grounding lead.

6 Connect the low-voltage wires to the transformer, and reattach the electrical box coverplate. Turn on the power at the main service panel.

How to Test & Replace a Line-voltage Thermostat

1 Turn off power to the heating unit at the main service panel. Remove the thermostat coverplate.

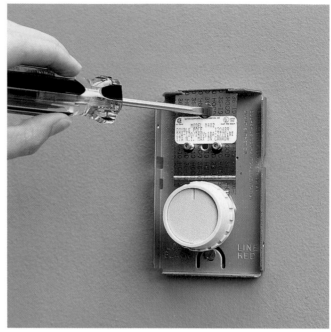

2 Loosen the thermostat mounting screws, and carefully pull the thermostat from the electrical box.

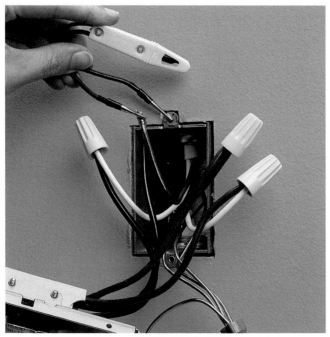

3 Unscrew one wire connector. Test for power by touching one probe of neon circuit tester to grounded metal box and touching other probe to exposed wires. Tester should not glow. Repeat test with other wire connections. Tester should not glow. If it does, then power is still entering box. Return to service panel, and turn off correct circuit.

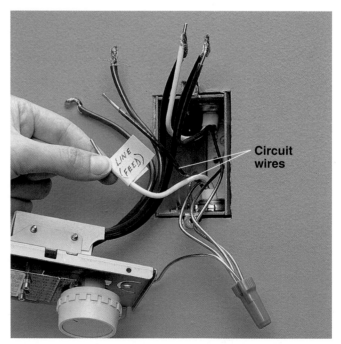

Circuit wires

4 Identify the two circuit wires that are attached to the thermostat leads marked LINE. The circuit wires attached to the LINE leads bring power into the box and are known as feed wires. Label the feed wires with masking tape, then disconnect all wires.

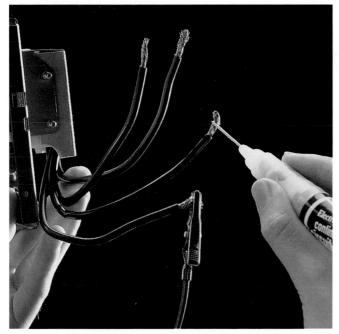

5 Test thermostat by attaching the clip of a continuity tester to one of the two leads marked LINE then touching probe to wire lead marked LOAD on same side of thermostat. Turn temperature dial from HIGH to LOW. Tester should glow in both positions. Repeat test with other pair of wire leads. If tester does not glow for both positions, thermostat is faulty and must be replaced.

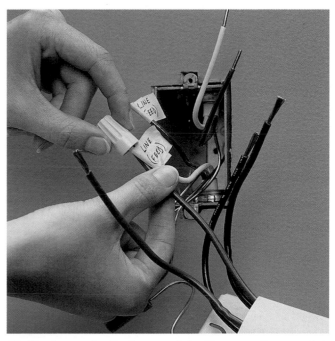

6 Replace a faulty thermostat with a new thermostat that has the same voltage and amperage ratings as the old one. Connect the new thermostat by attaching the circuit feed wires to the wire leads marked LINE, using wire connectors.

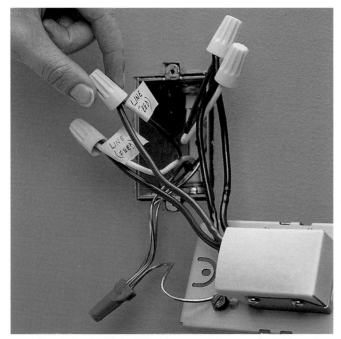

7 Connect the remaining circuit wires to the thermostat leads marked LOAD, using wire connectors. Connect the grounding wires together with a wire connector.

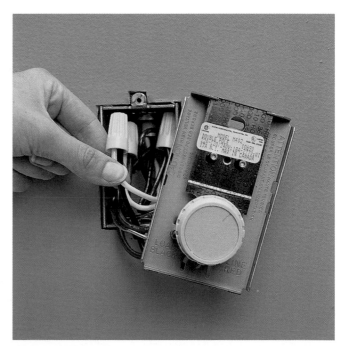

8 Carefully fold the wires inside the electrical box, then attach the thermostat mounting screws and the coverplate. Turn on the power at the main service panel. If new thermostat is programmable (page 106), set the program as desired.

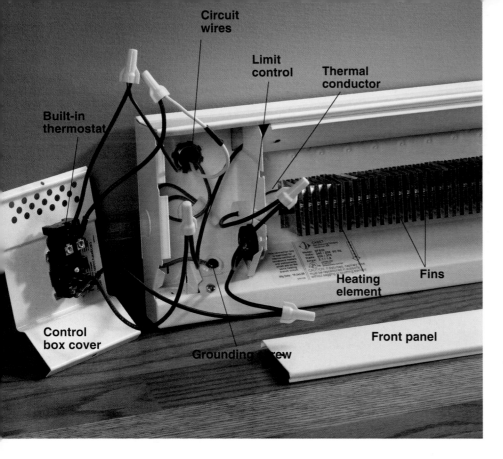

Built-in thermostat

Circuit wires

Limit control

Thermal conductor

Fins

Heating element

Control box cover

Grounding screw

Front panel

Repairing Electric Baseboard Heaters

Baseboard heaters are simple electrical units consisting of a heating **element** with attached metal **fins** for transferring heat, and a **limit control**—a switch that prevents the element from overheating. To control the temperature, some models have a built-in thermostat; others are controlled by a **line voltage**, or *zone* thermostat (page 106)—a wall-mounted thermostat that is wired directly to the heater.

Most heaters are wired to a 240-volt circuit, which means both the black and white circuit wires are hot and carry voltage. Others use 120 volts and are wired to a circuit or plugged into a standard receptacle. The tests for all three types are nearly the same.

If the heater is wired to a household circuit, shut off the power at the main service panel, and test for power before proceeding (left).

NOTE: Wiring for heaters and thermostats varies. For the best—and safest—results, check the manufacturer's wiring instructions, and label all wires before disconnecting.

How to Test for Power Before Making Repairs

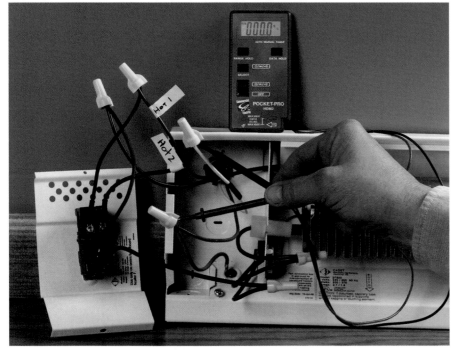

Turn off the power to the heater at the main service panel. Remove the heater's control box cover, and label the black hot circuit wire. Insert one probe of a neon circuit tester or multimeter into the wire connector at the end of the circuit wire, and touch the other probe to the grounding screw on the heater casing. Then, label the other circuit wire (with a 240-volt heater, this wire will also carry voltage). Insert the tester probe into its wire connector, and touch the other probe to the grounding screw. Finally, insert one probe into each of the wire connectors you've just tested. If the tester shows current for any of the tests, the power is still on. Return to the service panel, and turn off the correct circuit.

Everything You Need

Tools: Screwdriver, multimeter, vacuum or brush, needlenose pliers.

Materials: (As needed) replacement parts, masking tape, pen.

How to Test & Service Electric Baseboard Heater

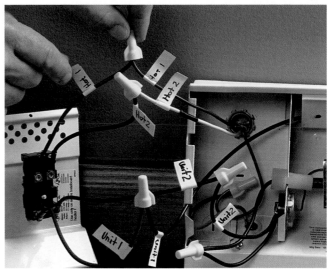

1 Begin by testing the limit control. Shut off the power at the main service panel, and confirm it is off by testing the unit (page 114). Pull a limit control lead from its terminal. Set multimeter to test continuity. Touch one probe to each limit control terminal. If the tester shows continuity, it means the limit control is working correctly, and you should move on to testing the thermostat (step 2). If the tester does not show continuity, remove the limit control and thermal conductor from the unit, and replace it with a duplicate part from the manufacturer.

2 To test the thermostat, start by labeling each thermostat lead and wire connected to it, giving both wires the same name. Designate circuit wires and their respective leads as HOT, and heater wires and their respective leads as UNIT.

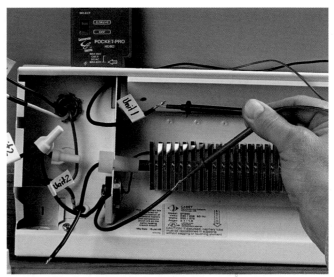

3 Disconnect wires, and remove thermostat. Turn thermostat dial to highest (hottest) setting. Set multimeter to test continuity. Touch one probe to a HOT wire lead and the other to each UNIT wire. The tester should indicate continuity in one of the connections. Repeat test for the other HOT wire lead and each UNIT wire. If there is continuity for both HOT wires, move on to step 4. If the thermostat fails either test, replace with duplicate part from manufacturer.

4 Test the heating element. Find the heating element wire that connects to a thermostat lead. (This wire may come from the far end of the element.) Unscrew wire connector, and separate wires. Set a multimeter to test continuity. Touch one probe to the free heating element wire and the other to the wire running from limit control to the other end of the element. Multitester should indicate continuity, meaning element is sound and the problem may lie in the circuit. If not, the element is bad, and the entire unit should be replaced.

Repairing Wall-mounted Electric Heaters

Wall-mounted electric heaters are installed between studs in an interior wall, typically in small areas, such as entryways or bathroom additions, where no other heat source is available. They work on the same principles as electric baseboard heaters (pages 114 to 115), generating heat by running electrical current through a heating element.

Wall-mounted heaters often contain a fan to help distribute heat to the room. If the heater won't turn on or shut off when the room temperature changes or when you turn the control knob, minor repairs may solve the problem.

The heater may have one or two limit controls near the heating element. They are designed to shut off the heater if it overheats. If there is a slight burning smell and the heater doesn't shut itself off, one or both limit controls may be faulty.

If the heater doesn't respond when adjusting the control knob, the thermostat may be faulty. Starting at OFF, turn the thermostat knob, and listen for a click. If the unit doesn't click, test the thermostat for continuity, using a multi-tester. Replace the thermostat if it is faulty.

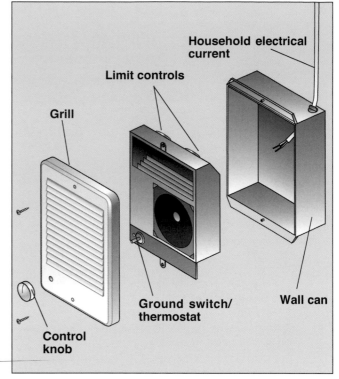

Inspect a wall-mounted heater before the start of the heating season. Dirt and dust can build up around the heating element, resulting in a burning smell when the heater is back in service. A careful cleaning with a soft-bristled brush is important for safe, reliable use.

How to Remove the Heater and Check for Power

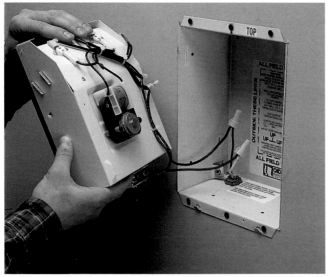

1 To remove and test the heater, shut off the power to the heater at the main service panel. Remove the control knob. Loosen the mounting screws on the grill, and slide the heater out of the wall can. Lift the top out first, disengaging the tabs at the base.

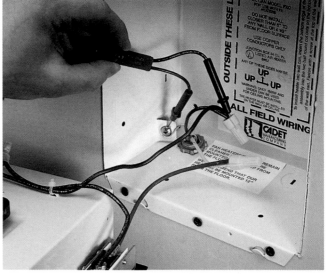

2 Insert one end of a neon circuit tester into the wire connector holding the black circuit wire, and touch the other probe to the grounding screw. Repeat, touching the probes to the white circuit connector and grounding screw. Finally, insert one probe into each of the wire connectors. The tester should not glow for any of these tests. If it does, shut off the correct circuit breaker on the main service panel. Repeat the tests until the tester does not glow.

116

How to Test & Replace a Limit Control

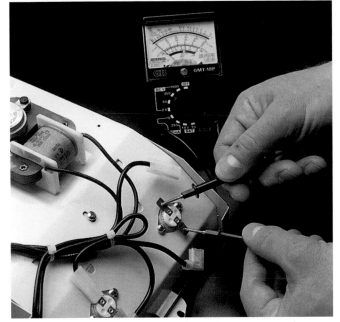

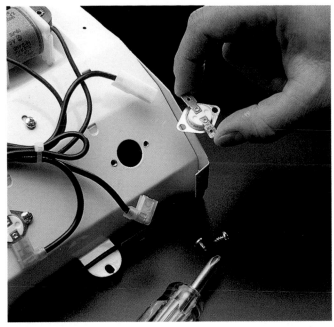

1 Shut off the power to the heater at the main service panel, and check for power (page 116). Use needlenose pliers to remove a single limit control lead from its terminal on the back of the heater, and test for continuity with a multimeter. Touch one probe of the multimeter to each limit control terminal. Repeat the test for the other limit control.

2 If the tester doesn't indicate continuity, remove the limit control and thermal conductor assembly from the heater. When purchasing a replacement, bring the old limit control with you for identification. Install the new limit control, and reassemble the heater.

How to Test & Replace a Thermostat

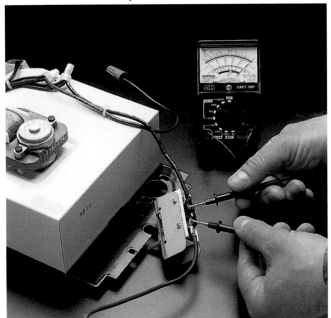

1 Shut off the power to the heater at the main service panel, and check for power (page 116). Disconnect one lead from the back of the control switch/thermostat unit by prying it loose with a needlenose pliers or unscrewing it. With the multimeter set to test for continuity, place one probe on each terminal.

2 If the multimeter doesn't indicate continuity, remove the other lead, and unscrew the control switch/thermostat unit from the base of the heater. Install an identical replacement unit.

Repairing & Replacing Phone Jacks

Although the telephone company owns the wires that bring telephone service to the house, repair and new installation can take place in any part of the telephone system that extends past the company's demarcation jack. The demarcation jack is usually located in a basement or utility area, although it may also be mounted on a baseboard in a home's living quarters.

Because the voltage running through telephone wires is very low, there is little danger of shock when working on the wiring. Still, it is best not to work in wet conditions when repairing any wiring. Also, do not work on a phone system if you wear a cardiac pacemaker, because the mild electrical currents in phone lines can interfere with the device.

Common telephone repairs include replacing a loose or broken modular connection (page 119), installing a modular jack in place of an outdated jack (page 120), and installing a junction box (page 121) that allows additional phone jacks to be run anywhere in the house.

A phone can be plugged directly into the demarcation jack to find out if a problem lies in the house wiring or in the phone company's wires and equipment. If there is no dial tone at the demarcation jack, the problem lies outside the home and should be fixed by the phone company. If there is a dial tone, however, this means that any problem lies inside the house.

NOTE: As the needs for Internet service and network data links in the home become increasingly important, larger and stronger telecommunication cables are needed in place of standard two-way telephone lines. Pages 310 to 329 contain information on telecommunication cable and home network systems available for home installation that allow faster and more reliable pathways for data and telephone transference.

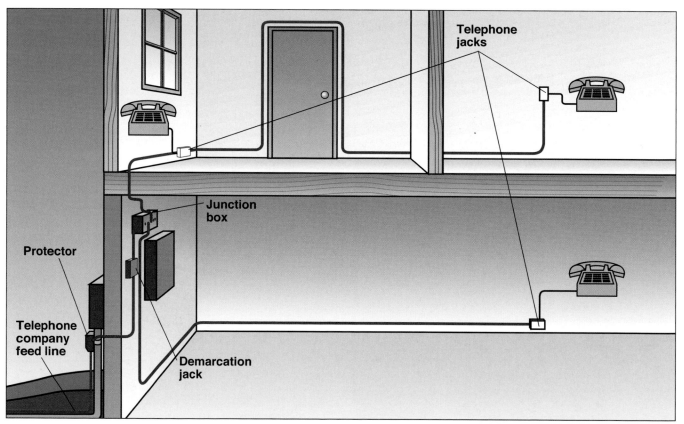

Two methods are used to wire phone systems. Relatively new systems are wired using the **home run** method (shown above), in which a wire distribution hub, or junction box, feeds individual lines to various phone jacks in the house. A junction box allows new jacks to easily be added by running new wires from the box to the new location. If one line becomes damaged, the other jacks will still operate. Older systems use a **continuous loop** method. With this method, various jacks are installed along a single loop of wire running throughout the house. A continuous loop is easier to install but less reliable since a single problem in the wire can render all the jacks inoperable.

Troubleshooting Phone Problems

Problems	Possible causes	Solutions
Dead air; no sound on line.	Wires may be crossed.	Make sure bare copper wires inside jack aren't touching.
Static on line.	Wires may be wet. Wire connections may be loose.	Check for moisture in phone jacks. Check all connections.
Buzzing on line.	Wires may be touching metal. Wires may be connected to wrong terminals.	Check all wires and connections. Check color coding of connections.

Wire Assignments

Most phone cords have four wires: red, green, yellow, and black. But there are two other possible color schemes. Use the following as a guide to connecting the wires:

The red terminal will accept:
- a red wire
- a blue wire
- a blue wire w/white stripe

The green terminal will accept:
- a green wire
- a white wire w/blue stripe

The yellow terminal will accept:
- a yellow wire
- an orange wire
- an orange wire w/white stripe

The black terminal will accept:
- a black wire
- a white wire w/orange stripe

If there are extra wires in the cord (usually these will be green and white), they can be tucked into the jack and left unconnected. The phone company will use these wires to connect additional phone lines if you should ever need them.

How to Replace a Modular Connector

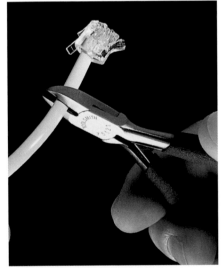  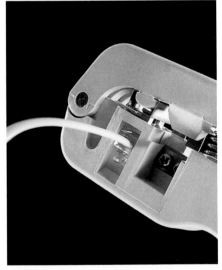

1 Remove the telephone cord from the wall jack and telephone. Use wire cutters to snip off the cord just below the connector to be replaced. Make sure to trim the cord at a straight angle.

2 Insert the cord into the stripper section of the tool. Squeeze the handle just enough to sever the outer insulation. Tug on the cord to pull the wires free of the insulation. Make sure not to cut the inner insulation on the individual wires.

3 Insert the individual wires into a plastic connector in the opposite sequence from that at the other end of the cord. Make sure the wires are flush with the top of connector and touching the metal contacts. Use a crimper tool to secure the connector to the wires.

How to Install a Modular Jack

1 Disconnect the phone cord from the jack. Unscrew the phone jack from the wall or baseboard with a screwdriver. Gently pull the jack away from the wall.

2 Disconnect the individual wires from the terminals on the jack. Clip off the bare copper ends of the wire, using a wire cutter.

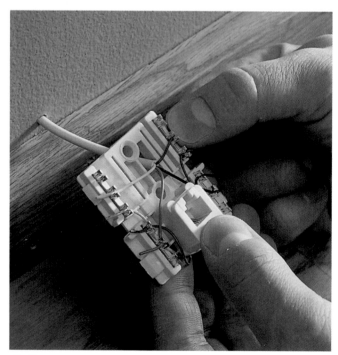

3 Remove casing from the connection block on the new modular jack, and feed phone cables through the back of the base piece. Force each colored wire into one of the metal slots on the terminal block that has a wire of the same or acceptable color (page 119). About ½" of wire should extend through the slot.

4 Screw the connection block to the wall with the screw included with the jack, and snap coverplate in place. Attach a phone to the new jack, and test it to make sure it works.

How to Install a Telephone Junction Box

1 Select a location that allows the cable for the junction box to reach the demarcation jack. Snap off the cover of the junction box. Attach the box to a wall, baseboard, or framing member, using the mounting screws that are included with it. Run phone cable to the demarcation jack. Secure to wall or framing members with staples every 24".

2 Trim all but 5" of cable, and strip off 3" of outer insulation, using a crimper. Strip 1" of inner insulation from each of the four individual wires, using a utility knife. Loop the bare copper wires clockwise around demarcation jack screw terminals, matching the colors. Tighten screws. NOTE: Some junction boxes have attached cords with modular connections that plug directly into demarcation jacks.

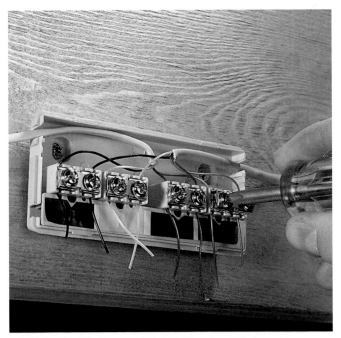

3 Loosen one terminal screw on each of the four color-coded sections of the junction box. Insert each wire into a slot in the corresponding section. About ½" of wire should extend through the slot.

4 For each phone extension line, attach the cable to the junction box following the same procedure used for the cable running to the demarcation jack. Screw the terminals down tight, then bend the wires upright so they don't touch each other. Snap the cover back on the junction box.

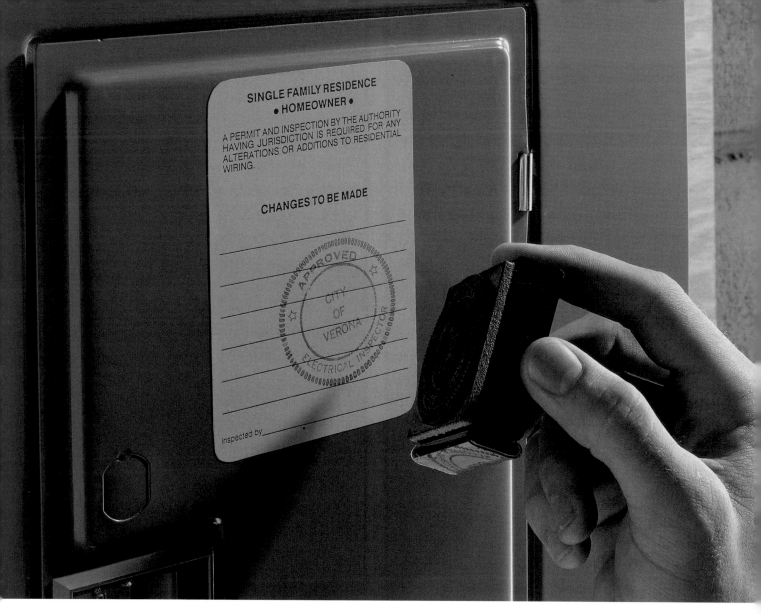

Inspector's Notebook

An electrical inspector visiting your home might identify a number of situations that are not "up to code." These situations may not be immediate problems. In fact, it is possible that the wiring in your home has remained trouble-free for many years.

Nevertheless, any wiring or device that is not up to code carries the potential for problems, often at risk to your home and your family. In addition, you may have trouble selling your home if it is not wired according to accepted methods.

Most local electrical codes are based on the National Electrical Code (NEC), a book updated and published every three years by the National Fire Protection Agency. This code book contains rules and regulations for the proper installation of electrical wiring and devices. Most public libraries carry reference copies of the NEC.

All electrical inspectors are required to be well versed in the NEC. Their job is to know the NEC regulations and to make sure these rules are followed in order to prevent fires and ensure safety. If you have questions regarding your home wiring system, your local inspector will be happy to answer them.

While a book like *The Complete Guide to Home Wiring* cannot possibly identify all potential wiring problems in your house, we have created the "Inspector's Notebook" to help you identify some of the most common wiring defects and show you how to correct them. When working on home wiring repair or replacement projects, refer to this section to help identify any conditions that may be hazardous.

Service Panel Inspection

Problem: Rust stains are found inside the main service panel. This problem occurs because water seeps into the service head outside the house and drips down into the service panel.

Solution: Have an electrician examine the service head and the main service panel. If the panel or service wires have been damaged, new electrical service must be installed.

Problem: This problem is actually a very old and very dangerous solution. A penny or a knockout behind a fuse effectively bypasses the fuse, preventing an overloaded circuit from blowing the fuse. This is very dangerous and can lead to overheated wiring.

Solution: Remove the penny and replace the fuse. Have a licensed electrician examine the panel and circuit wiring. If the fuse has been bypassed for years, wiring may be dangerously compromised, and the circuit may need to be replaced.

Service Panel Inspection (continued)

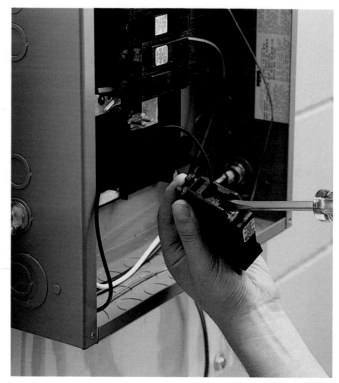

Problem: Two wires connected to one single-pole breaker is a sign of an overcrowded panel and also a dangerous code violation unless the breaker is approved for such a connection.

Solution: If there is room in the panel, install a separate breaker for the extra wire. If the panel is overcrowded have an electrician upgrade the panel or install a subpanel.

Recognizing Aluminum Wire

Inexpensive aluminum wire was used in place of copper in many wiring systems installed during the late 1960s and early 1970s, when copper prices were high. Aluminum wire is identified by its silver color and by the AL stamp on the cable sheathing. A variation, copper-clad aluminum wire, has a thin coating of copper bonded to a solid aluminum core.

By the early 1970s, all-aluminum wire was found to pose a safety hazard if connected to a switch or receptacle with brass or copper screw terminals. Because aluminum expands and contracts at a different rate than copper or brass, the wire connections could become loose. In some instances, fires resulted.

Existing aluminum wiring in homes is considered safe if proper installation methods have been followed, and if the wires are connected to special switches and receptacles designed to be used with aluminum wire. **If you have aluminum wire** in your home, have a qualified electrical inspector review the system. Copper-coated aluminum wire is not a hazard.

For a short while, switches and receptacles with an Underwriters Laboratories (UL) wire compatibility rating of AL-CU were used with both aluminum and copper wiring. However, these devices proved to be hazardous when connected to aluminum wire. AL-CU devices should not be used with aluminum wiring.

In 1971, switches and receptacles designed for use with aluminum wiring were introduced. They are marked CO/ALR. This mark is now the only approved rating for aluminum wires. If your home has aluminum wires connected to a switch or receptacle without a CO/ALR rating stamp, replace the device with a switch or receptacle rated CO/ALR.

A switch or receptacle that has no wire compatibility rating printed on the mounting strap or casing should not be used with aluminum wires. These devices are designed for use with copper wires only.

124

Inspecting the Grounding Jumper Wire

Problem: Grounding system jumper wire is missing or is disconnected. In most homes the grounding jumper wire attaches to water pipes on either side of the water meter. Because the ground pathway is broken, this is a dangerous situation that should be fixed immediately.

Solution: Attach a jumper wire to the water pipes on either side of the water meter, using pipe clamps. Use #6-gauge or #4-gauge bare copper wire for the jumper wire.

Common Cable Problems

Problem: Cable running across joists or studs is attached to the edge of framing members. Electrical codes forbid this type of installation in exposed areas, like unfinished basements or walk-up attics.

Solution: Protect cable by drilling holes in framing members at least 2" from exposed edges, and threading the cable through the holes.

(continued next page)

Common Cable Problems (continued)

Problem: Cable running along joists or studs hangs loosely. Loose cables can be pulled accidentally, causing damage to wires.

Solution: Anchor the cable to the side of the framing members at least 1¼" from the edge, using plastic staples. NM (nonmetallic) cable should be stapled every 4½ feet and within 12" of each electrical box.

Problem: Cable threaded through studs or joists lies close to the edge of the framing members. NM (non-metallic) cable (shown cutaway) can be damaged easily if nails or screws are driven into the framing members during remodeling projects.

Solution: Install metal nail guards to protect cable from damage. Nail guards are available at hardware stores and home centers.

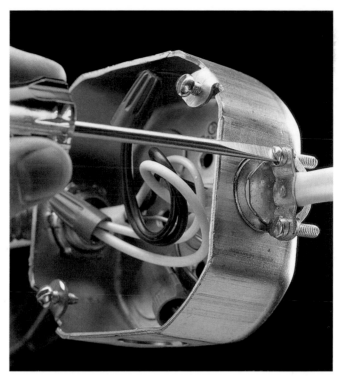

Problem: Unclamped cable enters a metal electrical box. Edges of the knockout can rub against the cable sheathing and damage the wires. (NOTE: With plastic boxes, clamps are not required if cables are anchored to framing members within 12" of box.)

Solution: Anchor the cable to the electrical box with a cable clamp (page 39). Several types of cable clamps are available at hardware stores and home centers.

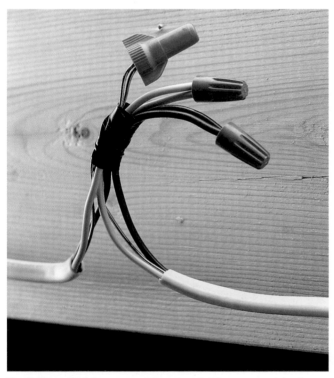

Problem: Cables are spliced outside an electrical box. Exposed splices can spark and create a risk of shock or fire.

Solution: Bring installation "up to code" by enclosing the splice inside a metal or plastic electrical box (pages 38 to 39). Make sure the box is large enough for the number of wires it contains (page 36).

Checking Wire Connections

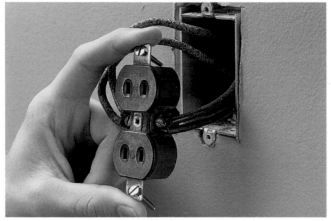

Problem: Two or more wires are attached to a single screw terminal. This type of connection is seen in older wiring but is now prohibited by the National Electrical Code.

Pigtail

Solution: Disconnect the wires from the screw terminal, then join them to a short length of wire (called a pigtail), using a wire connector (page 25). Connect the other end of the pigtail to the screw terminal.

Exposed wire

Problem: Bare wire extends past a screw terminal. Exposed wire can cause a short circuit if it touches the metal box or another circuit wire.

Solution: Clip the wire, and reconnect it to the screw terminal. In a proper connection, the bare wire wraps completely around the screw terminal, and the plastic insulation just touches the screw head (page 24).

Problem: Wires are connected with electrical tape. Electrical tape was used frequently in older installations, but it can deteriorate over time, leaving bare wires exposed inside the electrical box.

Solution: Replace electrical tape with wire connectors (page 25). You may need to clip away a small portion of the wire so the bare end will be covered completely by the connector.

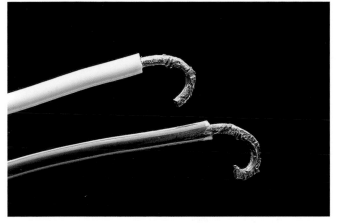

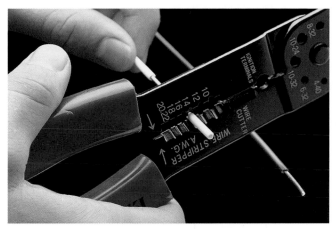

Problem: Nicks and scratches in bare wires interfere with the flow of current. This can cause the wires to overheat.

Solution: Clip away damaged portion of wire, then restrip about ¾" of insulation and reconnect the wire to the screw terminal (page 24).

Electrical Box Inspection

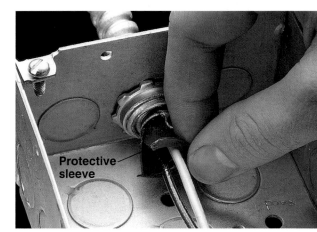

Problem: No protective sleeve on armored cable. Sharp edges of the cable can damage the wire insulation, creating a shock hazard and fire risk.

Solution: Protect the wire insulation by installing plastic or fiber sleeves around the wires. Sleeves are available at hardware stores. Wires that are damaged must be replaced.

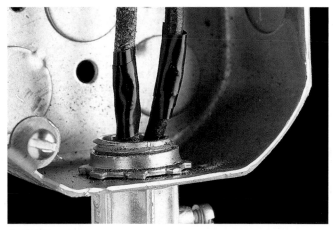

Problem: Insulation on wires is cracked or damaged. If damaged insulation exposes bare wire, a short circuit can occur, posing a shock hazard and fire risk.

Solution: Wrap damaged insulation temporarily with plastic electrical tape. Damaged circuit wires should be replaced by an electrician.

(continued next page)

Electrical Box Inspection (continued)

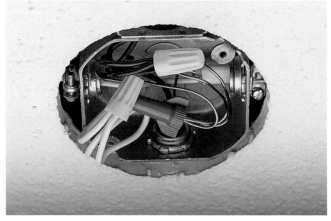

Problem: Open electrical boxes create a fire hazard if a short circuit causes sparks (arcing) inside the box.

Solution: Cover the open box with a solid metal cover-plate, available at any hardware store. Electrical boxes must remain accessible and cannot be sealed inside ceilings or walls.

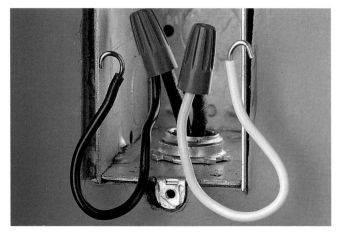

Problem: Short wires are difficult to handle. The National Electrical Code (NEC) requires that each wire in an electrical box have at least 6" of workable length.

Solution: Lengthen circuit wires by connecting them to short pigtail wires, using wire connectors (page 25). Pigtails can be cut from scrap wire, but should be the same gauge and color as the circuit wires.

Problem: Recessed electrical box is hazardous, especially if the wall or ceiling surface is made from a flammable material, like wood paneling. The National Electrical Code prohibits this type of installation.

Solution: Add an extension ring to bring the face of the electrical box flush with the surface. Extension rings come in several sizes, and are available at hardware stores.

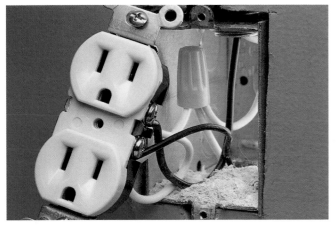

Problem: Dust and dirt in electrical box can cause hazardous high-resistance short circuits (pages 136 to 139). When making routine electrical repairs, always check the electrical boxes for dust and dirt buildup.

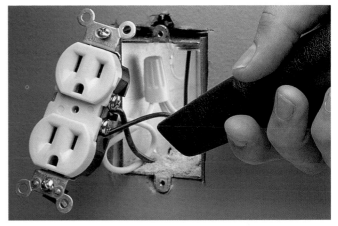

Solution: Vacuum electrical box clean, using a narrow nozzle attachment. Make sure power to box is turned off at main service panel before vacuuming.

Problem: Crowded electrical box (shown cutaway) makes electrical repairs difficult. This type of installation is prohibited because wires can be damaged easily when a receptacle or switch is installed.

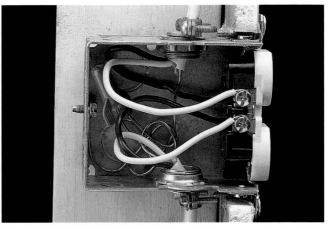

Solution: Replace the electrical box with a deeper electrical box (pages 36 to 39).

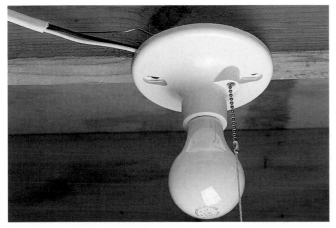

Problem: Light fixture is installed without an electrical box. This installation exposes the wiring connections, and provides no support for the light fixture.

Solution: Install an approved electrical box (pages 36 to 39) to enclose the wire connections and support the light fixture.

Common Electrical Cord Problems

Problem: Lamp or appliance cord runs underneath a rug. Foot traffic can wear off insulation, creating a short circuit that can cause fire or shock.

Solution: Reposition the lamp or appliance so that cord is visible. Replace worn cords.

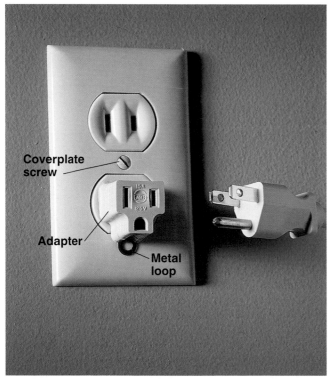

Coverplate screw

Adapter

Metal loop

Problem: Three-prong appliance plugs do not fit two slot receptacle. Do not use three-prong adapters unless the metal loop on the adapter is tightly connected to the coverplate screw on receptacle (page 17).

GFCI receptacle

Solution: Install a three-prong grounded receptacle if a means of grounding exists at the box (pages 70 to 71). Install a GFCI (ground-fault circuit-interrupter) receptacle (pages 74 to 77) in kitchens and bathrooms, or if the electrical box is not grounded.

Problem: Lamp or appliance plug is cracked, or electrical cord is frayed near plug. Worn cords and plugs create a fire and shock hazard.

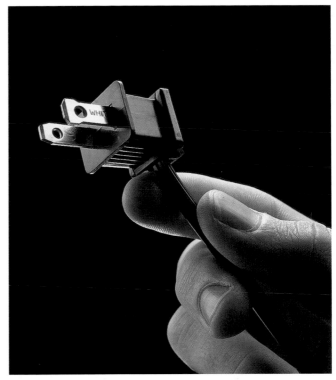

Solution: Cut away damaged portion of wire and install a new plug (pages 98 to 99). Replacement plugs are available at appliance stores and home centers.

Problem: Extension cord is too small for the power load drawn by a tool or appliance. Undersized extension cords can overheat, melting the insulation and leaving bare wires exposed.

Solution: Use an extension cord with wattage and amperage ratings that meet or exceed the rating of the tool or appliance. Extension cords are for temporary use only. Never use an extension cord for a permanent installation.

Inspecting Receptacles & Switches

Problem: Octopus receptacle attachments used permanently can overload a circuit and cause overheating of the receptacle.

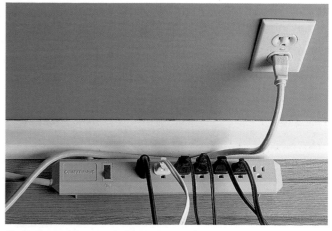

Solution: Use a multi-receptacle power strip with built-in overload protection. This is for temporary use only. If the need for extra receptacles is frequent, upgrade the wiring system.

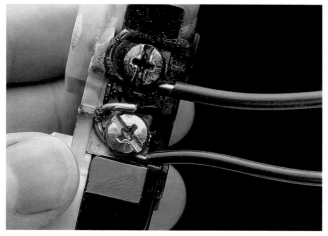

Problem: Scorch marks near screw terminals indicate that electrical arcing has occurred. Arcing usually is caused by loose wire connections.

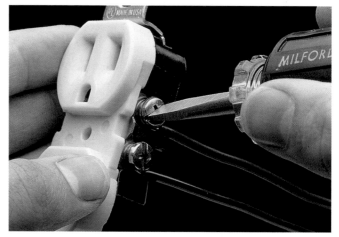

Solution: Clean wires with fine sandpaper, and replace the receptacle if it is badly damaged. Make sure wires are connected securely to screw terminals.

Problem: Two-slot receptacle in outdoor installation is hazardous because it has no grounding slot. In case of a short circuit, a person plugging in a cord becomes a conductor for current to follow to ground.

Solution: Install a GFCI (ground-fault circuit-interrupter) receptacle. Electrical codes now require that GFCIs be used for all outdoor receptacles, as well as for basement, kitchen, and bathroom receptacles.

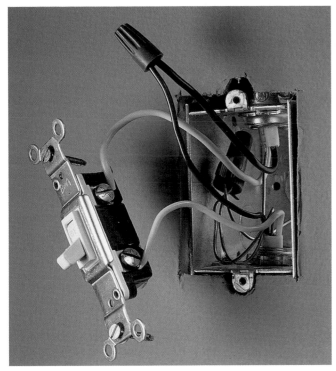

Problem: White neutral wires are connected to switch. Although switch appears to work correctly in this installation, it is dangerous because light fixture carries voltage when the switch is off.

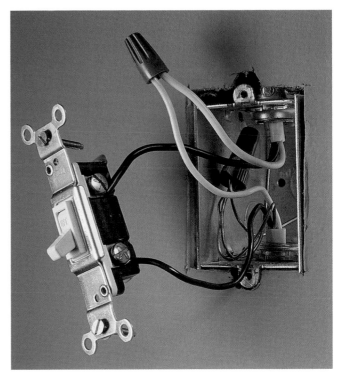

Solution: Connect the black hot wires to the switch, and join the white wires together with a wire connector.

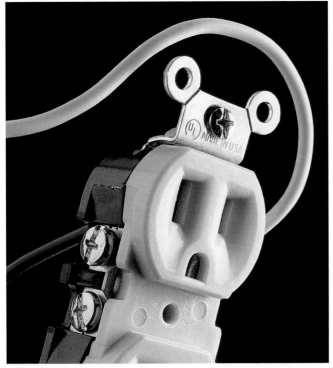

Problem: White neutral wires are connected to the brass screw terminals on the receptacle, and black hot wires are attached to silver screw terminals. This installation is hazardous because live voltage flows into the long neutral slot on the receptacle.

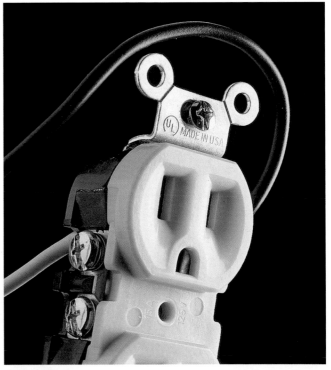

Solution: Reverse the wire connections so that the black hot wires are attached to brass screw terminals and white neutral wires are attached to silver screw terminals. Live voltage now flows into the short slot on the receptacle.

Evaluating Old Wiring

If the wiring in your home is more than 30 years old, it may have a number of age-related problems. Many problems associated with older wiring can be found by inspecting electrical boxes for dirty wire connections (page 72), signs of arcing (page 134), cracked or damaged wire insulation (page 129), or dirt buildup (page 131).

However, it is difficult to identify problems with wiring that is hidden inside the walls. If old wires are dusty and have damaged insulation, they can "leak" electrical current. The amount of current that leaks through dust usually is very small, too small to trip a breaker or blow a fuse. Nevertheless, by allowing current to leave its normal path, these leaks consume power in much the same way that a dripping faucet wastes water.

This kind of electrical leak is called a high-resistance short circuit. A high-resistance short circuit can produce heat and should be considered a fire hazard.

It is possible to check for high-resistance short circuits by using your electric meter to test the wires of each circuit. The goal of the test is to determine if electricity is being consumed even if none of the lights and appliances are drawing power. To do this, you must turn on all wall switches to activate the hot circuit wires, then stop power consumption by removing lightbulbs and fluorescent tubes, and disconnecting all lamps and appliances.

Then examine the electric meter, usually located on the outside of the house near the service head (page 12). If the flat, circular rotor inside the meter is turning, it means that a high-resistance short circuit is causing an electrical leak somewhere in the wiring. High-resistance short circuits consume very small amounts of power, so you should watch the rotor for a full minute to detect any movement.

If the test shows there is a high-resistance short circuit in your wiring, contact a licensed electrician to have it repaired.

Everything You Need

Tools: Screwdriver.

Materials: Wire connectors, masking tape, pen.

How to Evaluate Old Wiring for High-resistance Short Circuits

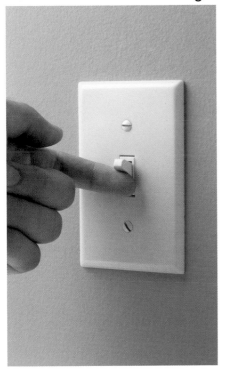

1 Switch on all light fixtures. Remember to turn on closet lights, basement lights, and exterior lights.

2 Stop all power consumption by removing all lightbulbs and fluorescent tubes. Turn off all thermostats.

3 Disconnect all plug-in lamps and appliances from the receptacles.

4 Shut off power to all permanently wired appliances by turning off the correct breakers or removing the correct fuses at the service panel. Permanently wired appliances include attic fans, water heaters, garage door openers, and ceiling fans.

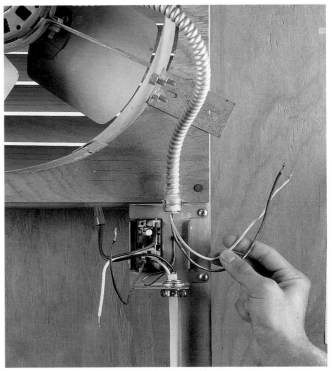

5 With the power turned off, disconnect circuit wires from each permanently wired appliance. Cap the wire ends with wire connectors. Next, turn on power and make sure all appliance wall switches are turned on.

(continued next page)

6 Watch the circular rotor located inside the electric meter for at least one minute. If the rotor does not move, then your wiring is in good condition. If the rotor moves, it means there is a high-resistance short circuit somewhere in the wiring system: proceed to step 7.

7 Turn off power to all circuits at the main service panel by switching off circuit breakers or removing fuses. Do not turn off main shutoff. Watch the rotor inside the meter. If rotor moves, then the high-resistance short circuit is located in the main service panel or service wiring. In this case, consult a licensed electrician. If rotor does not move, proceed to step 8.

8 Turn on individual circuits, one at a time, by switching on the circuit breaker or inserting the fuse. Watch for rotor movement in the electric meter. If rotor does not move, wiring is in good condition. Turn off power to the circuit, then proceed to the next circuit.

9 If the rotor is moving, then use masking tape to mark the faulty circuit. Turn off power to the circuit, then proceed to the next circuit.

10 If circuit contains three-way or four-way switches, flip the lever on each switch individually, and watch for rotor movement after each flip of a switch.

11 For each faulty circuit, identify the appliances, lights, switches, receptacles, and electrical junction boxes powered by the circuit. Use a map of your home wiring system as a guide (pages 30 to 33).

12 Recheck all lights and appliances along each faulty circuit to make sure they are not consuming power. If they are, disconnect them and repeat test.

13 Inspect the electrical boxes along each faulty circuit for dirty wire connections (page 72), damaged wire insulation (page 129), dirt buildup (page 131), or signs of arcing (page 134).

14 If no problems are found in electrical boxes, then the high-resistance short circuit is in wiring contained inside the walls. In this case, consult a licensed electrician.

1. Examine your main service (page 142). The amp rating of the electrical service and the size of the circuit breaker panel will help you determine if a service upgrade is needed.

2. Learn about codes (pages 143 to 147). The National Electrical Code (NEC), and local electrical codes and building codes, provide guidelines for determining how much power and how many circuits your home needs. Your local electrical inspector can tell you which regulations apply to your job.

Planning a Wiring Project

Careful planning of a wiring project ensures you will have plenty of power for present and future needs. Whether you are adding circuits in a room addition, wiring a remodeled kitchen, or adding an outdoor circuit, consider all possible ways the space might be used, and plan for enough electrical service to meet peak needs.

For example, when wiring a room addition, remember that the way a room is used can change. In a room used as a spare bedroom, a single 15-amp circuit provides plenty of power, but if you ever choose to convert the same room to a family recreation space, it will need at least two 20-amp circuits.

When wiring a remodeled kitchen, it is a good idea to install circuits for an electric oven and countertop range, even if you do not have these electric appliances. Installing these circuits now makes it easy to convert from gas to electric appliances at a later date.

A large wiring project adds a considerable load to your main electrical service. In about 25% of all homes, some type of service upgrade is needed before new wiring can be installed. For example, many homeowners will need to replace an older 60-amp electrical service with a new service rated for 100 amps or more. This is a job for a licensed electrician but is well worth the investment. In other cases, the existing main service provides adequate power, but the main circuit breaker panel is too full to hold any new circuit breakers. In this case it is necessary to install a circuit breaker subpanel to provide room for hooking up added circuits. Installing a subpanel is a job most homeowners can do themselves (pages 218 to 221).

This chapter gives an easy five-step method for determining your electrical needs and planning new circuits.

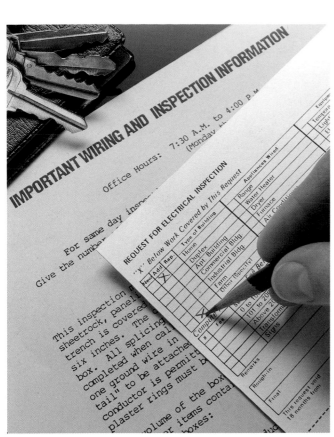

3. Prepare for inspections (pages 148 to 149). Remember that your work must be reviewed by your local electrical inspector. When planning your wiring project, always follow the inspector's guidelines for quality workmanship.

4. Evaluate electrical loads (pages 150 to 153). New circuits put an added load on your electrical service. Make sure that total load of the existing wiring and the planned new circuits does not exceed the main service capacity.

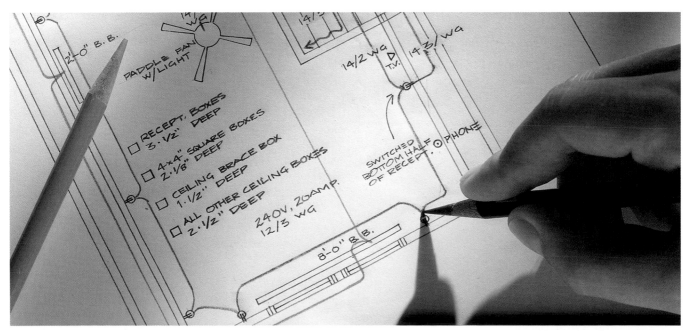

5. Draw a wiring diagram and get a permit (pages 154 to 155). Your inspector needs to see an accurate wiring diagram and materials list before he will issue a work permit for your project. This wiring plan also helps you organize your work.

1: Examine Your Main Service

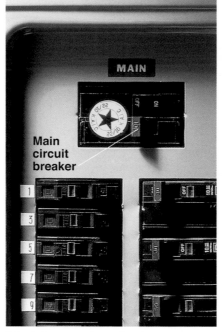

The first step in planning a new wiring project is to look in your main circuit breaker panel and find the size of the service by reading the amperage rating on the main circuit breaker. As you plan new circuits and evaluate electrical loads, knowing the size of the main service helps you determine if you need a service upgrade.

Also look for open circuit breaker slots in the panel. The number of open slots will determine if you need to add a circuit breaker subpanel.

Find the service size by opening the main service panel and reading the amp rating printed on the main circuit breaker. In most cases, 100-amp service provides enough power to handle the added loads of projects like the ones shown in this book. A service rated for 60 amps or less may need to be upgraded.

Older service panels use fuses instead of circuit breakers. Have an electrician replace this type of panel with a circuit breaker panel that provides enough power and enough open breaker slots for the new circuits you are planning.

Look for open circuit breaker slots in the main circuit breaker panel or in a circuit breaker subpanel, if your home already has one. You will need one open slot for each 120-volt circuit you plan to install and two slots for each 240-volt circuit. If your main circuit breaker panel has no open breaker slots, install a subpanel (pages 218 to 221) to provide room for connecting new circuits.

2: Learn about Codes

To ensure public safety, your community requires that you get a permit to install new wiring and have the completed work reviewed by an appointed inspector. Electrical inspectors use the National Electrical Code (NEC) as the primary authority for evaluating wiring, but they also follow the local Building Code and Electrical Code standards.

As you begin planning new circuits, call or visit your local electrical inspector and discuss the project with him. The inspector can tell you which of the national and local code requirements apply to your job, and may give you a packet of information summarizing these regulations. Later, when you apply to the inspector for a work permit, he will expect you to understand the local guidelines as well as a few basic National Electrical Code requirements.

The National Electrical Code is a set of standards that provides minimum safety requirements for wiring installations. It is revised every three years. The national code requirements for the projects shown in this book are thoroughly explained on the following pages. For more information, you can find copies of the current NEC, as well as a number of excellent handbooks based on the NEC, at libraries and bookstores.

In addition to being the final authority of code requirements, inspectors are electrical professionals with years of experience. Although they have busy schedules, most inspectors are happy to answer questions and help you design well-planned circuits.

Basic Electrical Code Requirements

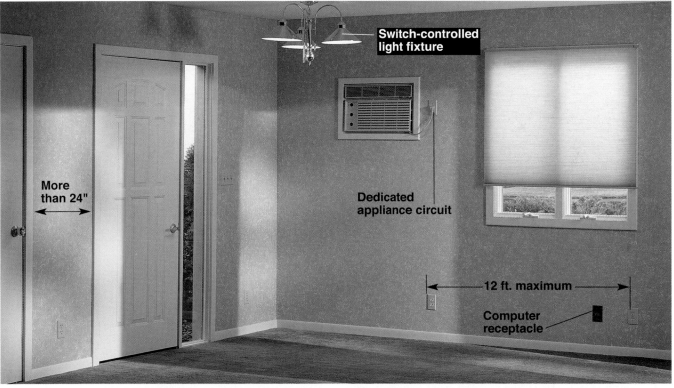

Electrical Code requirements for living areas: Living areas need at least one 15-amp or 20-amp basic lighting/receptacle circuit for each 600 square feet of living space and should have a "dedicated" circuit for each type of permanent appliance, like an air conditioner, computer, or a group of baseboard heaters. Receptacles on basic lighting/receptacle circuits should be spaced no more than 12 feet apart. Many electricians and electrical inspectors recommend even closer spacing. Any wall more than 24" wide also needs a receptacle. Every room should have a wall switch at the point of entry to control either a ceiling light or plug-in lamp. Kitchens and bathrooms must have a ceiling-mounted light fixture.

(continued next page)

Basic Electrical Code Requirements (continued)

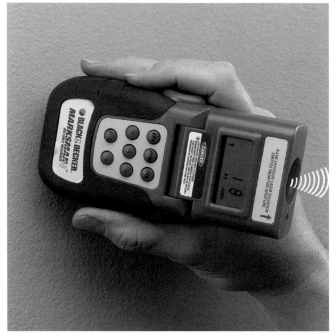

Measure the living areas of your home, excluding closets and unfinished spaces. A sonic measuring tool gives room dimensions quickly and contains a built-in calculator for figuring floor area. You will need a minimum of one basic lighting/receptacle circuit for every 600 sq. ft. of living space. The total square footage also helps you determine heating and cooling needs for new room additions (page 147).

Stairways with six steps or more must have lighting that illuminates each step. The light fixture must be controlled by three-way switches at the top and bottom landings.

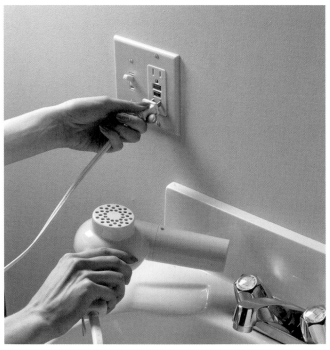

Kitchen and bathroom receptacles must be protected by a ground-fault circuit-interrupter (GFCI). Also, all outdoor receptacles and general-use receptacles in an unfinished basement or crawl space must be protected by a GFCI.

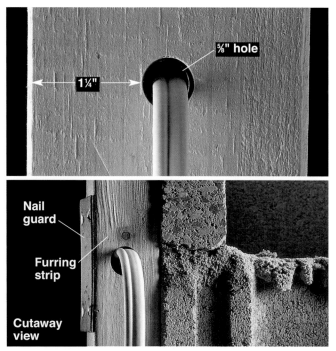

Cables must be protected against damage by nails and screws by at least 1¼" of wood (top). When cables pass through 2 × 2 furring strips (bottom), protect the cables with metal nail guards.

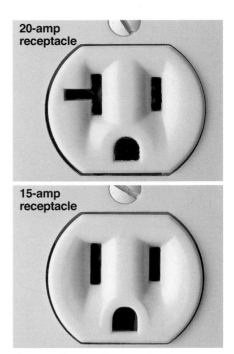

20-amp receptacle

15-amp receptacle

Closets and other storage spaces need at least one light fixture that is controlled by a wall switch near the entrance. Prevent fire hazards by positioning the light fixtures so the outer globes are at least 12" away from all shelf areas.

Hallways more than 10 feet long need at least one receptacle. All hallways should have a switch-controlled light fixture.

Amp ratings of receptacles must match the size of the circuit. A common mistake is to use 20-amp receptacles (top) on 15-amp circuits—a potential cause of dangerous circuit overloads.

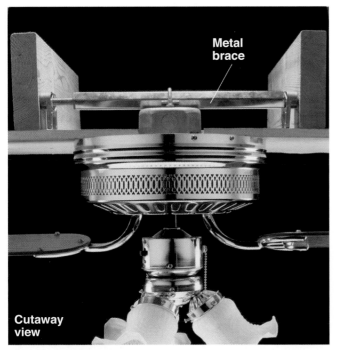

Metal brace

Cutaway view

A metal brace attached to framing members is required for ceiling fans and large light fixtures that are too heavy to be supported by an electrical box.

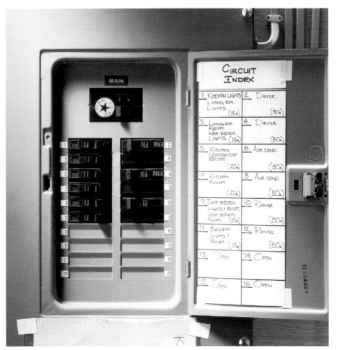

Label new circuits on an index attached to the circuit breaker panel. List the rooms and appliances controlled by each circuit. Make sure the area around the panel is clean, well lighted, and accessible.

Common Electrical Code Requirements

By Material

Service Panel (pages 26 to 33)
- Maintain a minimum 30" × 36" of clearance in front of the service panel.
- Ground all 120-volt and 240-volt circuits.
- Match the amperage rating of the circuit when replacing fuses.
- Locate service panels and subpanels a maximum of 79" above floor level.
- Use handle-tie breakers for 240-volt loads (line to line).
- Close all unused service panel openings.
- Label each fuse and breaker clearly on the panel.

Electrical Boxes (pages 36 to 41)
- Use boxes that are large enough to accommodate the number of wires entering the box.
- Locate all receptacle boxes 12" above the finished floor (standard).
- Locate all switch boxes 48" above the finished floor (standard).
  For special circumstances, inspectors will allow switch and location measurements to be altered, such as a switch at 36" above the floor in a child's bedroom or receptacles at 24" above the floor to make them more accessible for someone in a wheelchair.
- Install all boxes and conduit fittings so they remain accessible.
- Leave no gaps greater than ⅛" between wallboard and front of electrical boxes.
- Place receptacle boxes flush with combustible surfaces.
- Leave a minimum of 8" of usable cable or wire extending past the front of the electrical box.

Wires & Cables (pages 20 to 25)
- Use wires that are large enough for the amperage rating of the circuit (see Wire Size Chart, page 21).
- Drill holes at least 2" back from the exposed edge of joists to run cables through. Do not attach cables to the bottom edge of joists.
- Do not run cables diagonally between framing members.
- Run cable between receptacles 20" above the floor.
- Use nail plates to protect cable that is run through holes drilled or cut into studs less than 1¼" from front edge of stud.
- Do not crimp cables sharply.
- Contain spliced wires or connections entirely in a plastic or metal electrical box.
- Use wire connectors to join wires.
- Use staples to fasten cables within 8" of an electrical box and every 48" along its run.
- Leave a minimum ¼" (maximum 1") of sheathing where cables enter an electrical box.
- Clamp cables and wires to electrical boxes with approved NM clamp. No clamp is necessary for one-gang plastic boxes if cables are stapled within 8".

- Label all cables and wires at each electrical box to show which circuits they serve for the rough-in inspection.
- Connect only a single wire to a single screw terminal. Use pigtails to join more than one wire to a screw terminal.

Switches (pages 42 to 61)
- Use a switch-controlled receptacle in rooms without a built-in light fixture operated by a wall switch.
- Use three-way switches at the top and bottom on stairways with six steps or more.
- Use switches with grounding screw with plastic electrical boxes.
- Locate all wall switches within easy reach of the room entrance.

Receptacles (pages 62 to 77)
- Match the amp rating of a receptacle with the size of the circuit.
- Include receptacles on all walls 24" wide or greater.
- Include receptacles so a 6-ft. cord can be plugged in from any point along a wall or every 12-ft. along a wall.
- Include receptacles in any hallway that is 10-ft. long or more.
- Use three-prong, grounded receptacles for all 15- or 20-amp, 120-volt branch circuits.
- Include a switch-controlled receptacle in rooms without a built-in light fixture operated by a wall switch.
- Install GFCI-protected receptacles in bathrooms, kitchens, garages, crawl spaces, unfinished basements, and outdoor receptacle locations.
- Install an isolated-ground circuit to protect sensitive equipment, like a computer, against tiny power fluctuations. Computers should also be protected by a standard surge protector.

Light Fixtures (pages 78 to 101)
- Use mounting straps that are anchored to the electrical boxes to mount ceiling fixtures.
- Keep recessed light fixtures 3" from insulation and ½" from combustibles.
- Include at least one switch-operated lighting fixture in every room.

Grounding (pages 16 to 17)
- Ground all receptacles by connecting receptacle grounding screws to the circuit grounding wires.
- Use switches with grounding screws whenever possible. Always ground switches installed in plastic electrical boxes and all switches in kitchens, bathrooms, and basements.

By Room

Kitchens/Dining Rooms
- Install a dedicated 40- or 50-amp, 120/240-volt circuit for a range (or two circuits for separate oven and countertop units).
- Install two 20-amp small appliance circuits.
- Install dedicated 15-amp, 120-volt circuits for dishwashers and food disposals (required by many local codes).
- Use GFCI receptacles for all accessible countertop receptacles; receptacles behind fixed appliances do not need to be GFCIs.
- Position receptacles for appliances that will be installed within cabinets, such as microwaves or food disposals, according to the manufacturer's instructions.
- Include receptacles on all counters wider than 12".
- Space receptacles a maximum of 48" apart above countertops and closer together in areas where many appliances will be used.
- Locate receptacles 18" above the countertop. If the backsplash is more than the standard 4" or the bottom of the cabinet is less than 18" from the countertop, center the box in the space between the countertop and the bottom of the wall cabinet.
- Mount one receptacle within 12" of the countertop on islands and peninsulas that are 12" × 24" or greater.
- Locate at least one receptacle at table height in the dining areas for convenience in operating a small appliance.
- Do not put lights on small appliance circuits.
- Install additional lighting in work areas at a sink or range for convenience and safety.

Bathrooms
- Install a separate 20-amp circuit.
- Ground switches in bathrooms.
- Use GFCI-protected receptacles.
- Install at least one ceiling-mounted light fixture.
- Place blower heaters in bathrooms well away from the sink and tub.

Utility/Laundry Rooms
- Install a separate 20-amp circuit for a washing machine.
- Install a minimum feed 30-amp #10 THHN wire for the dryer, powered by a separate 120/240-volt major appliance circuit.
- Install metal conduit for cable runs in unfinished rooms.
- Use GFCI-protected receptacles, *except* for fixed appliances, such as freezers or dryers.

Living Room/Entertainment Rooms/Bedrooms
- Install a minimum of two 20-amp circuits in living rooms.
- Install a minimum of one 15- or 20-amp basic lighting/receptacle circuit for each 600 square feet of living space.
- Install a dedicated circuit for each permanent appliance, like an air conditioner, computer, or group of electric baseboard heaters.
- Do not use standard electrical boxes to support ceiling fans.
- Include receptacles on any wall that is 24" wide or more.
- Space receptacles on basic lighting/receptacle circuits a maximum of 12 feet apart. For convenience you can space them as close as 6 feet.
- Position permanent light fixtures in the center of the room's ceiling.
- Install permanently wired smoke alarms in room additions that include sleeping areas.

Outdoors
- Check for underground utilities before digging.
- Use UF cable for outdoor wiring needs.
- Run cable in rigid metal or schedule 40 PVC plastic (see page 205), as required by local code.
- Bury cables 12" if the circuit is no larger than 20 amps. Bury the cable at least 18" deep if the circuit is larger than 20 amps.
- Use weatherproof electrical boxes with watertight covers.
- Use GFCI-protected receptacles.
- Install receptacles a minimum of 12" above ground level.
- Anchor freestanding receptacles not attached to a structure by embedding the rigid metal conduit or schedule 40 PVC plastic conduit in a concrete footing, so that it is at least 12", but no more than 18", above ground level.
- Plan on installing a 20-amp, 120-volt circuit if the circuit contains more than one light fixture rated for 300 watts or more than four receptacles.

Stairs/Hallways
- Use three-way switches at the top and bottom on stairways with six steps or more.
- Include receptacles in any hallway that is 10 ft. long or more.
- Position stairway lights so each step is illuminated.

3: Prepare for Inspections

Electrical inspectors who issue the work permit for your wiring project will also visit your home to review the work. Make sure to allow time for these inspections as you plan the project. For most projects, inspectors make two visits.

The first inspection, called the **rough-in,** is done after the cables are run between the boxes, but before the insulation, wallboard, switches, and fixtures are installed. The second inspection, called the **final,** is done after the walls and ceilings are finished and all electrical connections are made.

When preparing for the rough-in inspection, make sure the area is neat. Sweep up sawdust and clean up any pieces of scrap wire or cable insulation. Before inspecting the boxes and cables, inspectors will check to make sure all plumbing and other mechanical work is completed. Some electrical inspectors will ask to see your building and plumbing permits.

At the final inspection, inspectors check random boxes to make sure the wire connections are correct. If they see good workmanship at the selected boxes, the inspection will be over quickly. However, if they spot a problem, inspectors may choose to inspect every connection.

Inspectors have busy schedules, so it is a good idea to arrange for an inspection several days or weeks in advance. In addition to basic compliance with code, inspectors expect your work to meet their own standards for quality. When you apply for a work permit, make sure you understand what the inspectors will look for during inspections.

You cannot put new circuits into use legally until an inspector approves them at the final inspection. Because inspectors are responsible for the safety of all wiring installations, their approval means that your work meets professional standards. If you have planned carefully and done your work well, electrical inspections are routine visits that give you confidence in your own skills.

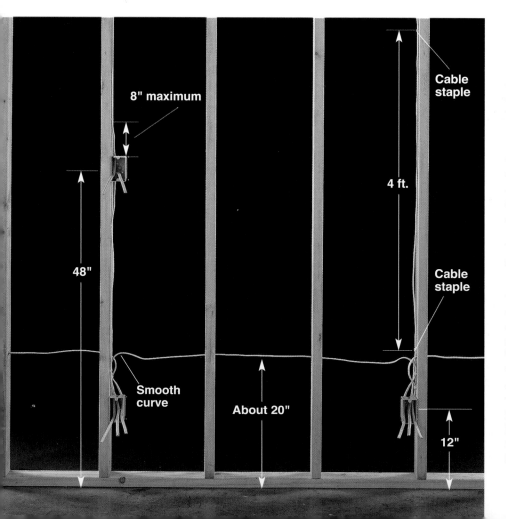

8" maximum

48"

Smooth curve

About 20"

Cable staple

4 ft.

Cable staple

12"

Inspectors measure to see that electrical boxes are mounted at consistent heights. Measured from the center of the boxes, receptacles in living areas typically are located 12" above the finished floor, and switches at 48". For special circumstances, inspectors allow you to alter these measurements. For example, you can install switches at 36" above the floor in a child's bedroom, or set receptacles at 24" to make them more convenient for someone in a wheelchair.

Inspectors will check cables to see that they are anchored by cable staples driven within 8" of each box and every 4 feet thereafter when they run along studs. When bending cables, form the wire in a smooth curve. Do not crimp cables sharply or install them diagonally between framing members. Some inspectors specify that cables running between receptacle boxes should be about 20" above the floor.

What Inspectors Look For

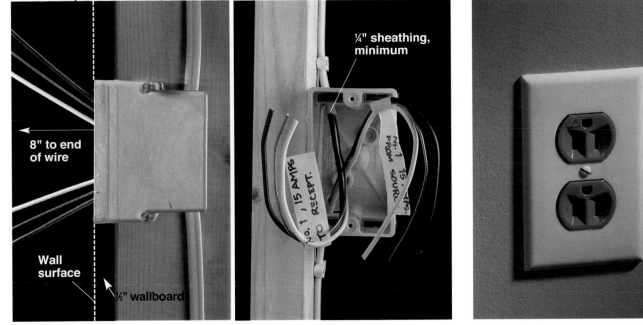

¼" sheathing, minimum

8" to end of wire

Wall surface

½" wallboard

Electrical box faces should extend past the front of framing members so the boxes will be flush with finished walls (left). Inspectors will check to see that all boxes are large enough for the wires they contain. Cables should be cut and stripped back so that 8" of usable length extends past the front of the box, and so that at least ¼" of sheathing reaches into the box (right). Label all cables to show which circuits they serve: inspectors recognize this as a mark of careful work. The labels also simplify the final hookups after the wallboard is installed.

Install an isolated-ground circuit and receptacle if recommended by your inspector. An isolated-ground circuit protects sensitive electronic equipment against tiny current fluctuations and interference. Electronics also should be protected by either a plug-in surge protector or a whole-house surge arrestor.

Heating & Air Conditioning Chart (compiled from manufacturers' literature)

Room addition living area	Recommended total heating rating	Recommended circuit size	Recommended air-conditioner rating	Recommended circuit size
100 sq. feet	900 watts	15-amp (240 volts)	5,000 BTU	15-amp (120 volts)
150 sq. feet	1350 watts		6,000 BTU	
200 sq. feet	1800 watts		7,000 BTU	
300 sq. feet	2700 watts		9,000 BTU	
400 sq. feet	3600 watts	20-amp (240 volts)	10,500 BTU	
500 sq. feet	4500 watts	30-amp (240 volts)	11,500 BTU	20-amp (120 volts)
800 sq. feet	7200 watts	two 20-amp	17,000 BTU	15-amp (240 volts)
1,000 sq. feet	9000 watts	two 30-amp	21,000 BTU	20-amp (240 volts)

Electric heating and air-conditioning for a new room addition will be checked by an inspector. Determine your heating and air-conditioning needs by finding the total area of the living space. Choose electric heating units with a combined wattage rating close to the chart recommendation above. Choose an air conditioner with a BTU rating close to the chart recom-mendation for your room size. NOTE: These recom-mendations are for homes in moderately cool climates, sometimes referred to as "Zone 4" regions. Cities in Zone 4 include Denver, Chicago, and Boston. In more severe climates, check with your electrical inspector or energy agency to learn how to find heating and air-conditioning needs.

4: Evaluate Electrical Loads

Before drawing a plan and applying for a work permit, make sure your home's electrical service provides enough power to handle the added load of the new circuits. In a safe wiring system, the current drawn by fixtures and appliances never exceeds the main service capacity.

To evaluate electrical loads, use the work sheet on page 153 or whatever evaluation method is recommended by your electrical inspector. Include the load for all existing wiring as well as that for proposed new wiring when making your evaluation.

Most of the light fixtures and plug-in appliances in your home are evaluated as part of general allowances for basic lighting/receptacle circuits (page 143) and small-appliance circuits. However, appliances that are permanently installed require their own "dedicated" circuits. The electrical loads for these appliances are added in separately when evaluating wiring.

If your evaluation shows that the load exceeds the main service capacity, you must have an electrician upgrade the main service before you can install new wiring. An electrical service upgrade is a worthwhile investment that improves the value of your home and provides plenty of power for present and future wiring projects.

Tips for Evaluating Appliance Loads

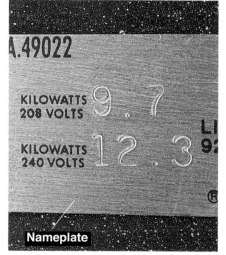

Add 1500 watts for each small appliance circuit required by the local electrical code. In most communities, three such circuits are required—two in the kitchen and one for the laundry—for a total of 4500 watts. No further calculations are needed for appliances that plug into small-appliance or basic lighting/receptacle circuits.

Find wattage ratings for permanent appliances by reading the manufacturer's nameplate. If the nameplate gives the rating in kilowatts, find the watts by multiplying kilowatts times 1000. If an appliance lists only amps, find watts by multiplying the amps times the voltage—either 120 or 240 volts.

Electric water heaters are permanent appliances that require their own dedicated 30-amp, 240-volt circuits. Most water heaters are rated between 3500 and 4500 watts. If the nameplate lists several wattage ratings, use the one labeled "total connected wattage" when figuring electrical loads.

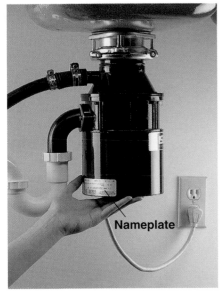

Food disposers are considered permanent appliances and require their own dedicated 15-amp, 120-volt circuits. Most disposers are rated between 500 and 900 watts.

Dishwashers installed permanently under a countertop need dedicated 15-amp, 120-volt circuits. Dishwasher ratings are usually between 1000 and 1500 watts. Portable dishwashers are regarded as part of small appliance circuits and are not added in when figuring loads.

Electric ranges can be rated for as little as 3000 watts or as much as 12,000 watts. They require dedicated 120/240-volt circuits. Find the exact wattage rating by reading the nameplate, found inside the oven door or on the back of the unit.

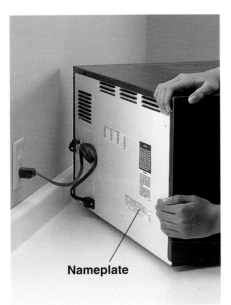

Microwave ovens are regarded by many local codes as permanent appliances. If your inspector asks you to install a separate 20-amp, 120-volt circuit for the microwave oven, add in its wattage rating when calculating loads. The nameplate is found on the back of the cabinet or inside the front door. Most microwave ovens are rated between 500 and 800 watts.

Freezers are permanent appliances that require dedicated 15-amp, 120-volt circuits. Freezer ratings are usually between 240 and 480 watts. But combination refrigerator-freezers rated for 1000 watts or less are plugged into small appliance circuits and do not need their own dedicated circuits. The nameplate for a freezer is found inside the door or on the back of the unit, just below the door seal.

Electric clothes dryers are permanent appliances that need dedicated 30-amp, 120/240-volt circuits. The wattage rating, usually between 4500 and 5500 watts, is printed on the nameplate inside the dryer door. Washing machines, and gas-heat clothes dryers with electric tumbler motors, do not need dedicated circuits. They plug into the 20-amp small-appliance circuit in the laundry room.

(continued next page)

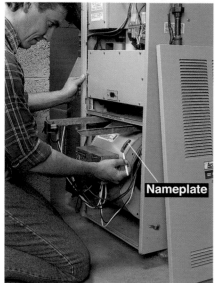

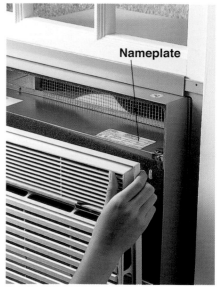

Forced-air furnaces have electric fans and are considered permanent appliances. They require dedicated 15-amp, 120-volt circuits. Include the fan wattage rating, printed on a nameplate inside the control panel, when figuring wattage loads for heating.

A central air conditioner requires a dedicated 240-volt circuit. Its wattage rating, usually between 2300 and 5500 watts, is printed on a metal plate near the electrical hookup panel. If the air conditioner relies on a furnace fan for circulation, add the fan wattage rating to the air-conditioner rating.

Window air conditioners, both 120-volt and 240-volt types, are permanent appliances that require dedicated 15-amp or 20-amp circuits. The wattage rating, which can range from 500 to 2000 watts, is found on the nameplate located inside the front grill. Make sure to include all window air conditioners in your evaluation.

Electric room heaters that are permanently installed require a dedicated circuit, and must be figured into the load calculations. Use the maximum wattage rating printed inside the cover. In general, 240-volt baseboard-type heaters are rated for 180 to 250 watts for each linear foot.

Air-conditioning and heating appliances are not used at the same time, so figure in only the larger of these two numbers when evaluating your home's electrical load.

Outdoor receptacles and fixtures are not included in basic lighting calculations. When evaluating electrical loads, add in the nameplate wattage rating for each outdoor light fixture, and add in 180 watts for each outdoor receptacle. Receptacles and light fixtures in garages also are considered to be outdoor fixtures when evaluating loads.

How to Evaluate Electrical Loads (photocopy this work sheet as a guide; blue sample calculations will not reproduce)

1. Find the basic lighting/receptacle load by multiplying the square footage of all living areas (including any room additions) times 3 watts.	Existing space: _____1100_____ square ft. New additions: _____400_____ square ft. _____1500_____ total square ft. × 3 watts =	4500 watts
2. Add 1500 watts for each kitchen small-appliance circuit and for the laundry circuit.	_____3_____ circuits × 1500 watts =	4500 watts
3. Add ratings for permanent electrical appliances, including: range, food disposer, dishwasher, freezer, water heater, and clothes dryer.	RANGE 12.3 K.W. = 12,300 watts	12,300 watts
	DRYER 5000	5,000 watts
	DISHWASHER 1200	1,200 watts
	FREEZER 550	550 watts
	FOOD DISPOSER 800	800 watts
Find total wattages for the furnace and heating units, and for air conditioners. Add in only the larger of these numbers.	Furnace heat: _1,200_ watts Space heaters: _5,450_ watts Total heating = _6,650_ watts Central air conditioner: _3,500_ watts Window air conditioners: _1,100_ watts Total cooling = _4,600_ watts	6,650 watts
4. For outdoor fixtures (including those in garages) find the nameplate wattage ratings.	Total fixture watts =	650 watts
Multiply the number of outdoor receptacles (including those in garages) times 180 watts.	_____3_____ receptacles × 180 watts =	540 watts
5. Total the wattages to find the gross load.		36,690 watts
6. Figure the first 10,000 watts of the gross load at 100%.	100% × 10,000 = 10,000	10,000 watts
7. Subtract 10,000 watts from the gross load, then figure the remaining load at 40%.	_36,690_ watts - 10,000 = _26,690_ watts _26,690_ watts × .40 =	10,676 watts
8. Add steps 6 and 7 to estimate the true electrical load.		20,676 watts
9. Convert the estimated true electrical load to amps by dividing by 230.	_20,676_ watts ÷ 230 =	89.9 amps
10. Compare the load with the amp rating of your home's electrical service, printed on the main circuit breaker (page 142). If the load is less than main circuit breaker rating, the system is safe. If the load exceeds the main circuit breaker rating, your service should be upgraded.	OK ☒ Upgrade ☐	

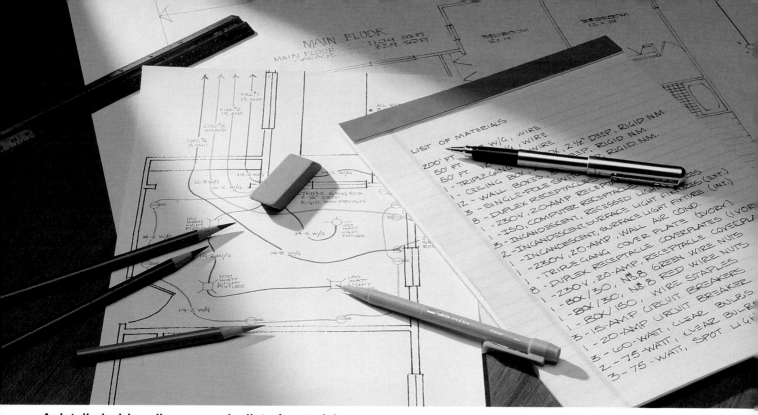

A detailed wiring diagram and a list of materials is required before electrical inspectors will issue a work permit. If blueprints exist for the space you are remodeling, start your electrical diagram by tracing the wall outlines from the blueprint. Use standard electrical symbols (next page) to clearly show all the receptacles, switches, light fixtures, and permanent appliances. Make a copy of the symbol key, and attach it to the wiring diagram for the inspectors' convenience. Show each cable run, and label its wire size and circuit amperage.

Planning a Wiring Project

5: Draw a Wiring Diagram & Get a Permit

Drawing a wiring diagram is the last step in planning a circuit installation. A detailed wiring diagram helps you get a work permit, makes it easy to create a list of materials, and serves as a guide for laying out circuits and installing cables and fixtures. Use the circuit maps on pages 165 to 179 as a guide for planning wiring configurations and cable runs. Bring the diagram and materials list when you visit electrical inspectors to apply for a work permit.

Never install new wiring without following your community's permit and inspection procedure. A work permit is not expensive, and it ensures that your work will be reviewed by a qualified inspector to guarantee its safety. If you install new wiring without the proper permit, an accident or fire traced to faulty wiring could cause your insurance company to discontinue your policy and can hurt the resale value of your home.

When electrical inspectors look over your wiring diagram, they will ask questions to see if you have a basic understanding of the electrical code and fundamental wiring skills. Some inspectors ask these questions informally, while others give a short written test. Inspectors may allow you to do some, but not all, of the work. For example, they may ask that all final circuit connections at the circuit breaker panel be made by a licensed electrician, while allowing you to do all other work.

A few communities allow you to install wiring only when supervised by an electrician. This means you can still install your own wiring but must hire an electrician to apply for the work permit and to check your work before inspectors review it. The electrician is held responsible for the quality of the job.

Remember that it is the inspectors' responsibility to help you do a safe and professional job. Feel free to call them with questions about wiring techniques or materials.

154

How to Draw a Wiring Plan

1 Draw a scaled diagram of the space you will be wiring, showing walls, doors, windows, plumbing pipes and fixtures, and heating and cooling ducts. Find the floor space by multiplying room length by width, and indicate this on the diagram. Do not include closets or storage areas when figuring space.

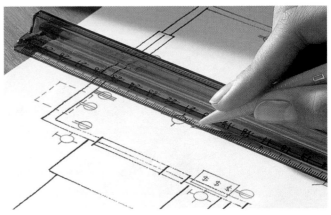

2 Mark the location of all switches, receptacles, light fixtures, and permanent appliances, using the electrical symbols shown below. Where you locate these devices along the cable run determines how they are wired. Use the circuit maps on pages 165 to 179 as a guide for drawing wiring diagrams.

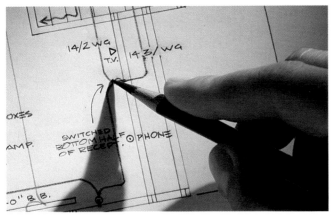

3 Draw in cable runs between devices. Indicate cable size and type, and the amperage of the circuits. Use a different-colored pencil for each circuit.

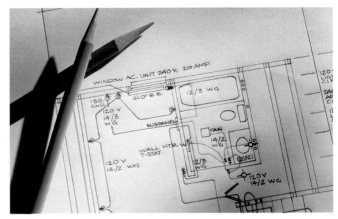

4 Identify the wattages for light fixtures and permanent appliances, and the type and size of each electrical box. On another sheet of paper, make a detailed list of all materials you will use.

Electrical Symbol Key (copy this key and attach it to your wiring plan)

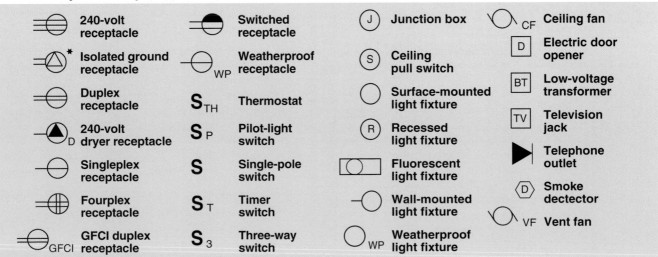

Symbol	Description	Symbol	Description	Symbol	Description	Symbol	Description
	240-volt receptacle		Switched receptacle	J	Junction box	CF	Ceiling fan
	Isolated ground receptacle	WP	Weatherproof receptacle	S	Ceiling pull switch	D	Electric door opener
	Duplex receptacle	S_{TH}	Thermostat		Surface-mounted light fixture	BT	Low-voltage transformer
D	240-volt dryer receptacle	S_P	Pilot-light switch	R	Recessed light fixture	TV	Television jack
	Singleplex receptacle	S	Single-pole switch		Fluorescent light fixture		Telephone outlet
	Fourplex receptacle	S_T	Timer switch		Wall-mounted light fixture	D	Smoke dectector
GFCI	GFCI duplex receptacle	S_3	Three-way switch	WP	Weatherproof light fixture	VF	Vent fan

Case Study: Wiring a Room Addition
Construction View

The photo below shows the circuits you would likely want to install in a large room addition. This example shows the framing and wiring of an un- finished attic converted to an office or entertain- ment room with a bathroom. This room includes a subpanel and five new circuits plus telephone

14/2 cable

Vent fan

Circuit breaker subpanel

Vanity light fixture

GFCI recept.

12/2 cable

12/2 cable

Timer & light fixture switch

14/3 cable

Blower heater

10/3 cable

Individual Circuits

■ #1: Bathroom circuit. This 15-amp, 120-volt circuit supplies power to bathroom fix- tures and to fixtures in the adjacent closet. All general-use recepta- cles in a bathroom must be protected by a GFCI.

■ #2: Computer circuit. A 15-amp, 120- volt dedicated circuit with an extra isolated grounding wire that protects computer equipment.

Circuit breaker sub- panel receives power through a 10-gauge, three-wire feeder cable connected to a 30-amp, 240-volt circuit breaker at the main circuit breaker panel. Larger room additions may require a 40-amp or a 50-amp "feeder" circuit breaker.

■ #3: Air-conditioner circuit. A 20-amp, 240-volt dedicated cir- cuit. In cooler climates, or in a smaller room, you may need an air conditioner and circuit rated for only 120 volts.

and cable-TV lines.

A wiring project of this sort is a potentially complicated undertaking that can be made simpler by breaking the project into convenient steps, and finishing one step before moving on to the next.

14/3 cable

14/3 cable

Phone cable

Coaxial cable

These cables continue through the foreground wall to complete the circuits. This wall has been removed for clarity.

12/2 cable

14/2 cable

■ **#4: Basic lighting/ receptacle circuit.** This 15-amp, 120-volt circuit supplies power to most of the fixtures in the bedroom and study areas.

■ **#5: Heater circuit.** This 20-amp, 240-volt circuit supplies power to the bathroom blower-heater and to the baseboard heaters. Depending on the size of your room and the wattage rating of the baseboard heaters, you may need a 30-amp, 240-volt heating circuit.

Telephone outlet is wired with 22-gauge four-wire phone cable. If your home phone system has two or more separate lines, you may need to run a cable with eight wires, commonly called "four-pair" cable.

Cable television jack is wired with coaxial cable running from an existing television junction in the utility area.

Diagram View

The diagram below shows the layout of the five circuits and the locations of their receptacles, switches, fixtures, and devices, as shown in the photo on the previous pages. The circuits and receptacles are based on the needs of a 400-sq. ft. space. An inspector will want to see a dia-

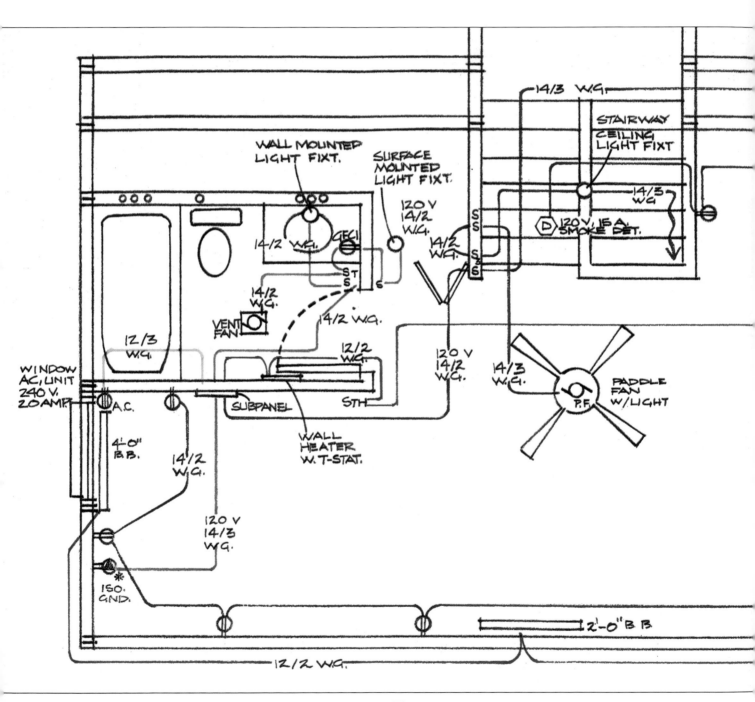

■ **Circuit #1:** A 15-amp, 120-volt circuit serving the bathroom and closet area. Includes: 14/2 NM cable, double-gang box, timer switch, single-pole switch, 4" × 4" box with single-gang adapter plate, GFCI receptacle, 2 plastic light fixture boxes, vanity light fixture, closet light fixture, 15-amp single-pole circuit breaker.

■ **Circuit #2:** A 15-amp, 120-volt computer circuit. Includes: 14/3 NM cable, single-gang box, 15-amp isolated-ground receptacle, 15-amp single-pole circuit breaker.

gram like this one before issuing a permit. After you've received approval for your addition, the wiring diagram will serve as your guide as you complete your project.

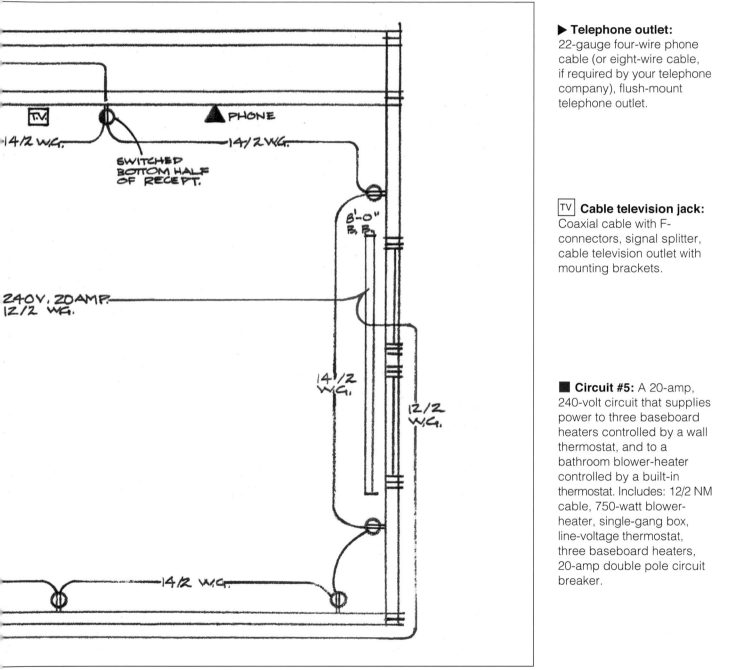

▶ **Telephone outlet:** 22-gauge four-wire phone cable (or eight-wire cable, if required by your telephone company), flush-mount telephone outlet.

TV **Cable television jack:** Coaxial cable with F-connectors, signal splitter, cable television outlet with mounting brackets.

■ **Circuit #5:** A 20-amp, 240-volt circuit that supplies power to three baseboard heaters controlled by a wall thermostat, and to a bathroom blower-heater controlled by a built-in thermostat. Includes: 12/2 NM cable, 750-watt blower-heater, single-gang box, line-voltage thermostat, three baseboard heaters, 20-amp double pole circuit breaker.

Circuit #3: A 20-amp, 240-volt air-conditioner circuit. Includes: 12/2 NM cable; single-gang box; 20-amp, 240-volt receptacle (duplex or singleplex style); 20-amp double-pole circuit.

■ **Circuit #4:** A 15-amp, 120-volt basic lighting/receptacle circuit serving most of the fixtures in the bedroom and study areas. Includes: 14/2 and 14/3 NM cable, 2 double-gang boxes, fan speed-control switch, dimmer switch, single-pole switch, 2 three-way switches, 2 plastic light fixture boxes, light fixture for stairway, smoke detector, metal light fixture box with brace bar, ceiling fan with light fixture, 10 single-gang boxes, 4" × 4" box with single-gang adapter plate, 10 duplex receptacles (15-amp), 15-amp single-pole circuit breaker.

14/2 cable

12/3 cable

12/2 cable

6/3 cable

14/2 cable

Individual Circuits

■ **#1 & #2: Small-appliance circuits.** Two 20-amp, 120-volt circuits supply power to countertop and eating areas for small appliances. All general-use receptacles must be on these circuits. One 12/3 cable, fed by a 20-amp double-pole breaker, wires both circuits. These circuits share one electrical box with the disposer circuit (#5), and another with the basic lighting circuit (#7).

■ **#3: Range circuit.** A 50-amp, 120/240-volt dedicated circuit supplies power to the range/oven appliance. It is wired with 6/3 cable.

□ **#4: Microwave circuit.** A dedicated 20-amp, 120-volt circuit supplies power to the microwave. It is wired with 12/2 cable. Microwaves that use less than 300 watts can be installed on a 15-amp circuit or plugged into the small-appliance circuits.

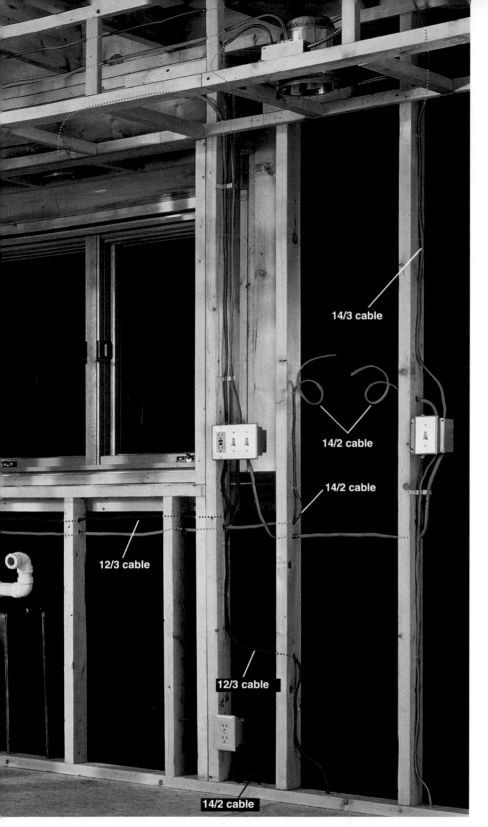

14/3 cable

14/2 cable

14/2 cable

12/3 cable

12/3 cable

14/2 cable

Case Study: Wiring a Remodeled Kitchen
Construction View

The photo at left shows the circuits you would probably want to install in a total kitchen remodel. Kitchens require a wide range of electrical services, from simple 15-amp lighting circuits to 120/240, 60 amp appliance circuits. This kitchen example has seven circuits, including separate dedicated circuits for a dishwasher and food disposer. Some codes allow the disposer and dishwasher to share a single circuit.

All rough carpentry and plumbing should be in place before beginning any electrical work. As always, divide a project of this scale into manageable steps, and finish one step before moving on.

■ **#5: Food disposer circuit.** A dedicated 15-amp, 120-volt circuit supplies power to the disposer. It is wired with 14/2 cable. Some local codes allow the disposer to be on the same circuit as the dishwasher.

■ **#6: Dishwasher circuit.** A dedicated 15-amp, 120-volt circuit supplies power to the dishwasher. It is wired with 14/2 cable. Some local codes allow the dishwasher to be on the same circuit as the disposer.

■ **#7: Basic lighting circuit.** A 15-amp, 120-volt circuit powers the ceiling fixture, recessed fixtures, and under-cabinet task lights. 14/2 and 14/3 cables connect the fixtures and switches in the circuit. Each task light has a self-contained switch.

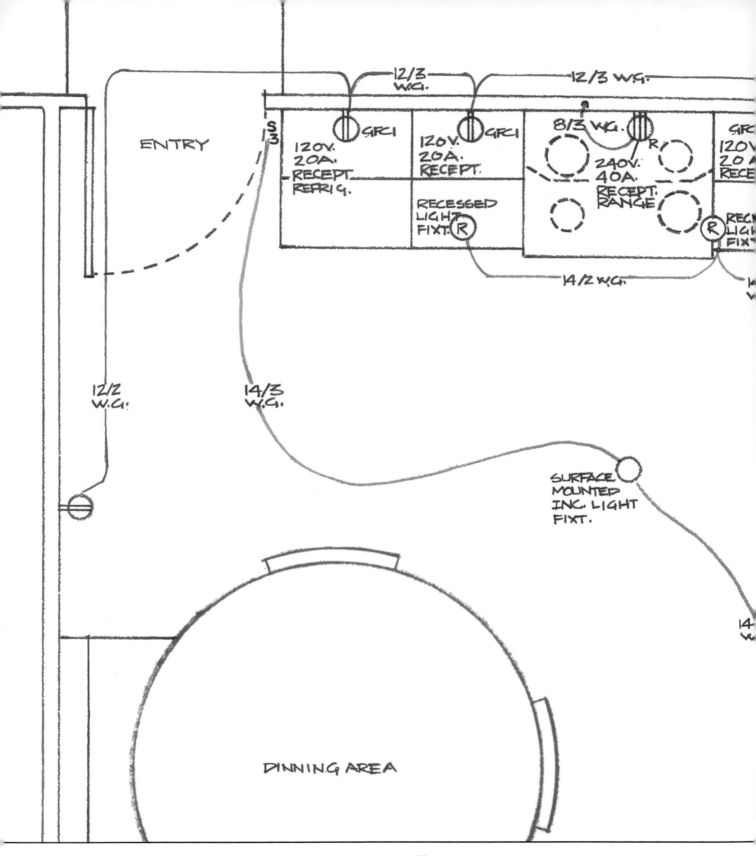

ENTRY

12/3
W.G.

12/3 W.G.

S3

GFCI

120V.
20A.
RECEPT.
REFRIG.

120V.
20A.
RECEPT.

GFCI

8/3 W.G.

R

240V.
40A.
RECEPT.
RANGE

GFCI

120V
20A
RECE

R

REC
LIGH
FIX

RECESSED
LIGHT
FIXT. R

14/2 W.G.

12/2
W.G.

14/3
W.G.

SURFACE
MOUNTED
INC. LIGHT
FIXT.

14
W

DINNING AREA

Circuits #1 & #2: Two 20-amp, 120-volt small-appliance circuits wired with one cable. All general-use receptacles must be on these circuits, and they must be GFCI units. Includes: 7 GFCI receptacles rated for 20 amps, 5 electrical boxes that are 4" × 4", and 12/3 cable. One GFCI shares a double-gang box with circuit #5, and another GFCI shares a triple-gang box with circuit #7.

Circuit #3: A 50-amp, 120/240-volt dedicated circuit for the range. Includes: a 4" × 4" box; a 120/240-volt, 50-amp range receptacle; and 6/3 NM cable.

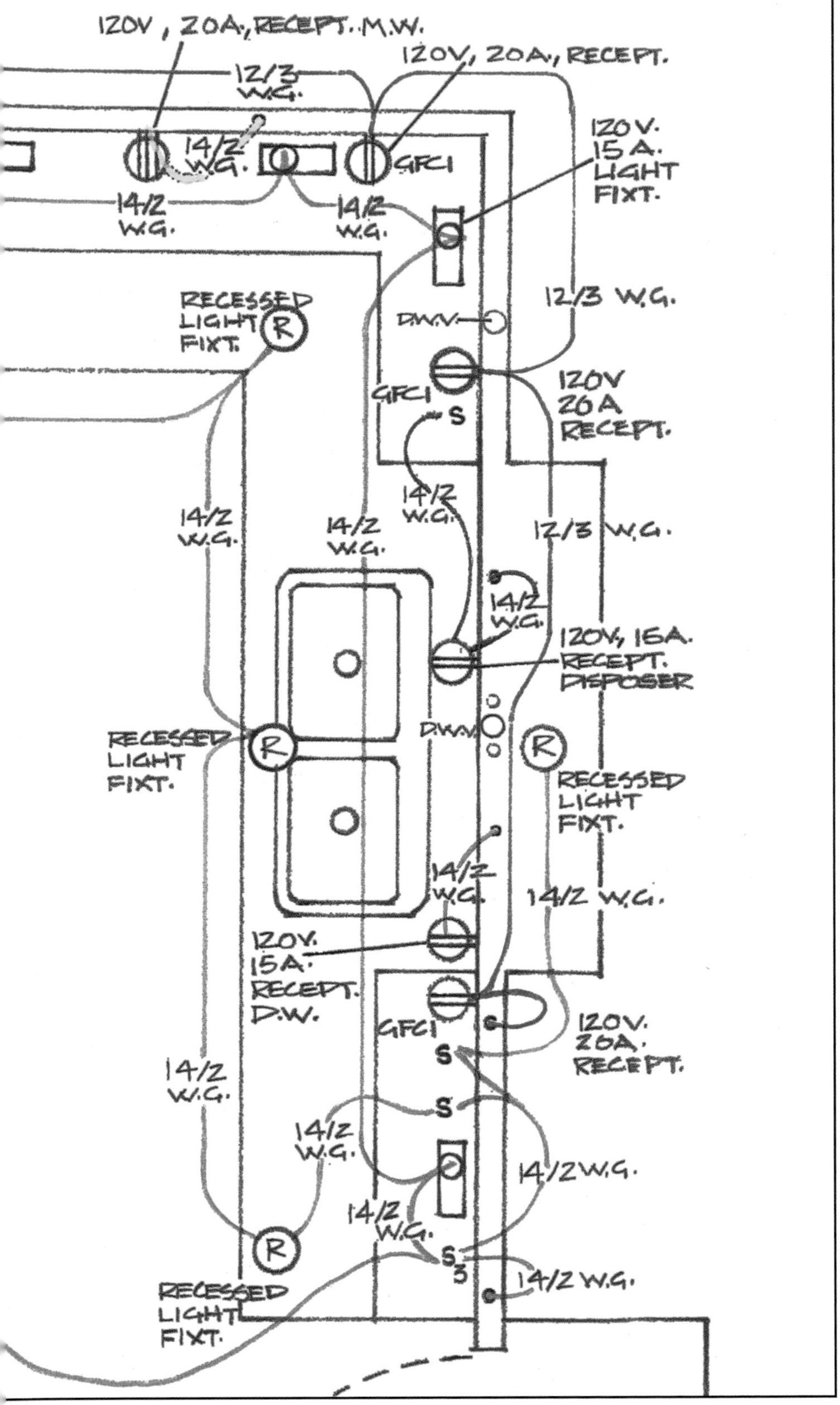
120V, 20A, RECEPT. M.W.
120V, 20A, RECEPT.
12/3 W.G.
14/2 W.G.
GFCI
120V. 15A. LIGHT FIXT.
14/2 W.G.
14/2 W.G.
RECESSED LIGHT FIXT.
D.W.V.
12/3 W.G.
GFCI
S
120V 20A RECEPT.
14/2 W.G.
14/2 W.G.
14/2 W.G.
12/3 W.G.
14/2 W.G.
120V, 15A. RECEPT. DISPOSER
RECESSED LIGHT FIXT.
D.W.V.
R
RECESSED LIGHT FIXT.
14/2 W.G.
14/2 W.G.
120V. 15A. RECEPT. D.W.
GFCI
S
120V. 20A. RECEPT.
14/2 W.G.
S
14/2 W.G.
14/2W.G.
14/2 W.G.
R
RECESSED LIGHT FIXT.
14/2 W.G.

Diagram View

The diagram at left shows the layout of the seven circuits and the locations of their receptacles, switches, fixtures, and devices, as shown in the photo on the previous pages. The circuits and receptacles are based on the needs of a 175-sq. ft. space kitchen. An inspector will want to see a diagram like this one before issuing a permit. After you've received approval for your addition, the wiring diagram will serve as your guide as you complete your project.

Circuit #7: A 15-amp, 120-volt basic lighting circuit serving all of the lighting needs in the kitchen. Includes: 2 single-pole switches, 2 three-way switches, single-gang box, 4" × 4" box, triple-gang box (shared with one of the GFCI receptacles from the small-appliance circuits), plastic light fixture box with brace, ceiling light fixture, 4 fluorescent under-cabinet light fixtures, 6 recessed light fixtures, 14/2 and 14/3 cables.

Circuit #6: A 15-amp, 120-volt dedicated circuit for the dishwasher. Includes: a 15-amp duplex receptacle, one single-gang box, and 14/2 cable.

Circuit #4: A 20-amp, 120-volt dedicated circuit for the microwave. Includes: a 20-amp duplex receptacle, a single-gang box, and 12/2 NM cable.

Circuit #5: A 15-amp, 120-volt dedicated circuit for the food disposer. Includes: a 15-amp duplex receptacle, a single-pole switch (installed in a double-gang box with a GFCI receptacle from the small-appliance circuits), one single-gang box, and 14/2 cable.

Circuit Maps for 31 Common Wiring Layouts

The arrangement of switches and appliances along an electrical circuit differs for every project. This means that the configuration of wires inside an electrical box can vary greatly, even when fixtures are identical.

The circuit maps on the following pages show the most common wiring variations for typical electrical devices. Most new wiring you install will match one or more of the examples shown. By finding the examples that match your situation, you can use these maps to plan circuit layouts.

The 120-volt circuits shown on the following pages are wired for 15 amps, using 14-gauge wire and receptacles rated at 15 amps. If you

are installing a 20-amp circuit, substitute 12-gauge cables and use receptacles rated for 20 amps.

In configurations where a white wire serves as a hot wire instead of a neutral, both ends of the wire are coded with black tape to identify it as hot. In addition, each of the circuit maps shows a box grounding screw. This grounding screw is required in all metal boxes, but plastic electrical boxes do not need to be grounded.

NOTE: For clarity, all grounding conductors in the circuit maps are colored green. In practice, the grounding wires inside sheathed cables usually are bare copper.

1. 120-volt Duplex Receptacles Wired in Sequence

Use this layout to link any number of duplex receptacles in a basic lighting/receptacle circuit. The last receptacle in the cable run is connected like the receptacle shown at the right side of the circuit map below. All other receptacles are wired like the receptacle shown on the left side. Requires two-wire cables.

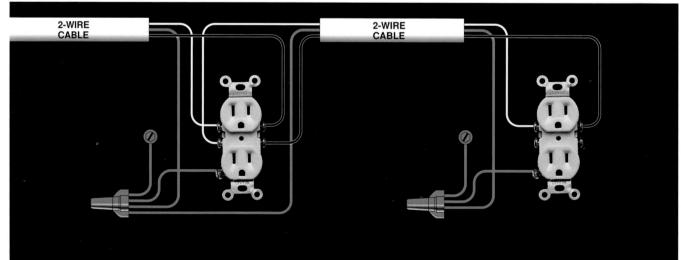

164

2. GFCI Receptacles (Single-location Protection)

Use this layout when receptacles are within 6 feet of a water source, like those in kitchens and bathrooms. To prevent nuisance tripping caused by normal power surges, GFCIs should be connected only at the LINE screw terminal, so they protect a single location, not the fixtures on the LOAD side of the circuit. Requires two-wire cables. Where a GFCI must protect other fixtures, use circuit map 3.

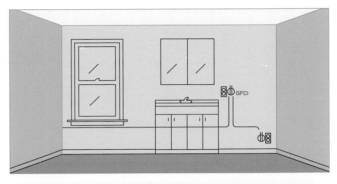

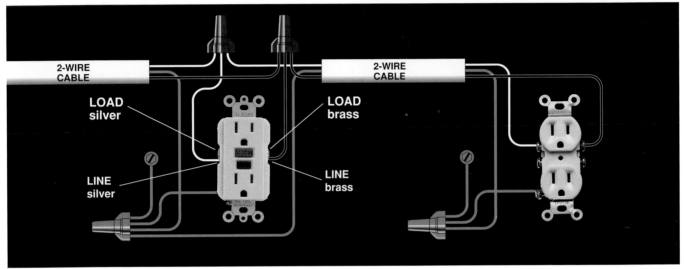

3. GFCI Receptacle, Switch & Light Fixture (Wired for Multiple-location Protection)

In some locations, such as an outdoor circuit, it is a good idea to connect a GFCI receptacle so it also provides shock protection to the wires and fixtures that continue to the end of the circuit. Wires from the power source are connected to the LINE screw terminals; outgoing wires are connected to LOAD screws. Requires two-wire cables.

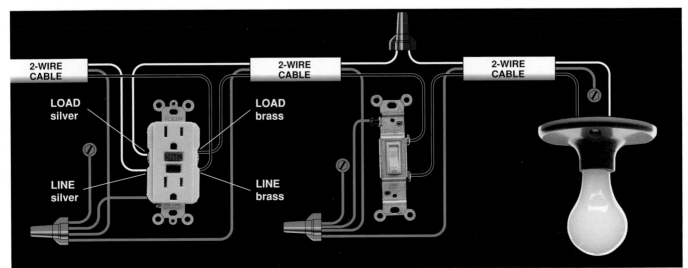

4. Single-pole Switch & Light Fixture (Light Fixture at End of Cable Run)

Use this layout for light fixtures in basic lighting/ receptacle circuits throughout the home. It is often used as an extension to a series of receptacles (circuit map 1). Requires two-wire cables.

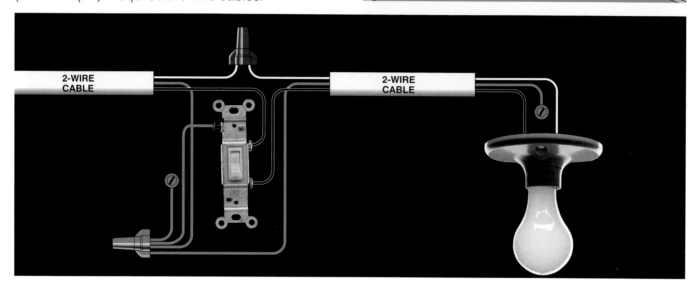

5. Single-pole Switch & Light Fixture (Switch at End of Cable Run)

Use this layout, sometimes called a **switch loop**, where it is more practical to locate a switch at the end of the cable run. In the last length of cable, both insulated wires are hot; the white wire is tagged with black tape at both ends to indicate it is hot. Requires two-wire cables.

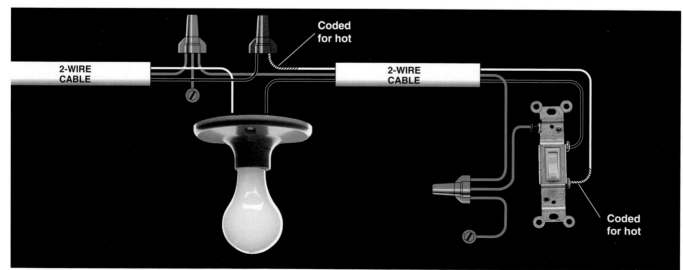

6. Single-pole Switch & Two Light Fixtures (Switch Between Light Fixtures, Light at Start of Cable Run)

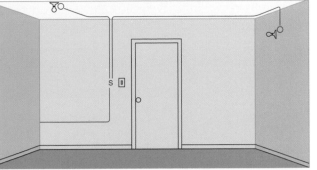

Use this layout when you need to control two fixtures from one single-pole switch and the switch is between the two lights in the cable run. Power feeds to one of the lights. Requires two-wire and three-wire cables.

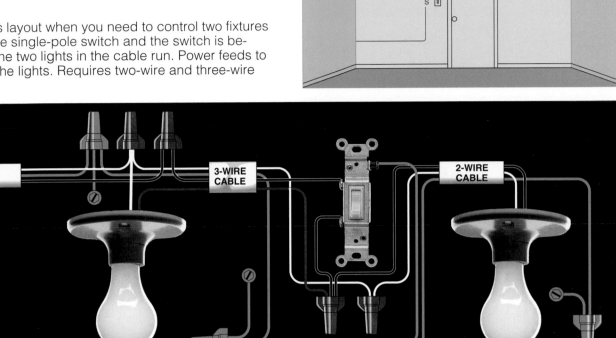

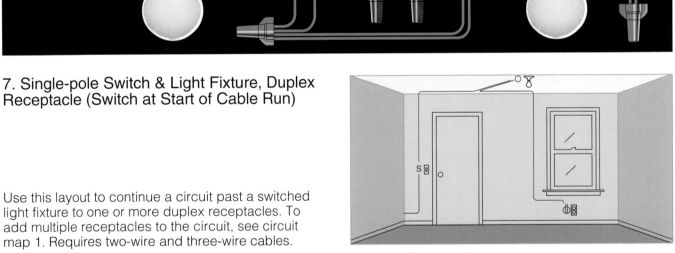

7. Single-pole Switch & Light Fixture, Duplex Receptacle (Switch at Start of Cable Run)

Use this layout to continue a circuit past a switched light fixture to one or more duplex receptacles. To add multiple receptacles to the circuit, see circuit map 1. Requires two-wire and three-wire cables.

8. Switch-controlled Split Receptacle, Duplex Receptacle (Switch at Start of Cable Run)

This layout lets you use a wall switch to control a lamp plugged into a wall receptacle. This configuration is required by code for any room that does not have a switch-controlled ceiling fixture. Only the bottom half of the first receptacle is controlled by the wall switch; the top half of the receptacle and all additional receptacles on the circuit are always hot. Requires two-wire and three-wire cables.

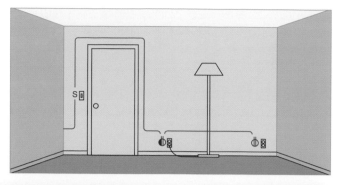

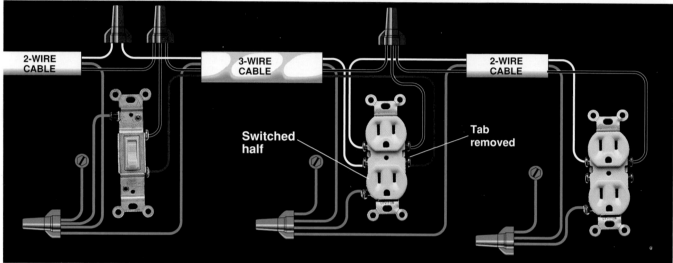

2-WIRE CABLE

3-WIRE CABLE

2-WIRE CABLE

Switched half

Tab removed

9. Switch-controlled Split Receptacle (Switch at End of Cable Run)

Use this switch loop layout to control a split receptacle (see circuit map 7) from an end-of-run circuit location. The bottom half of the receptacle is controlled by the wall switch, while the top half is always hot. White circuit wire attached to the switch is tagged with black tape to indicate it is hot. Requires two-wire cable.

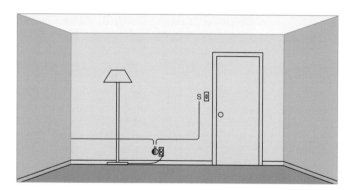

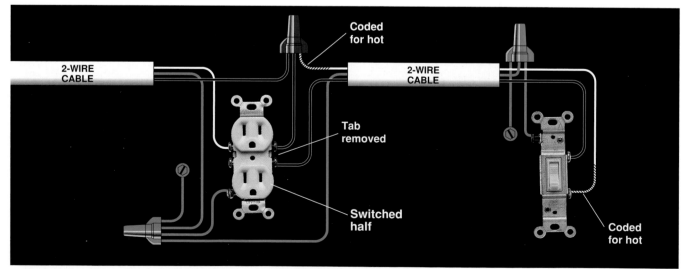

Coded for hot

2-WIRE CABLE

2-WIRE CABLE

Tab removed

Switched half

Coded for hot

10. Switch-controlled Split Receptacle, Duplex Receptacle (Split Receptacle at Start of Run)

Use this variation of circuit map 7 where it is more practical to locate a switch-controlled receptacle at the start of a cable run. Only the bottom half of the first receptacle is controlled by the wall switch; the top half of the receptacle, and all other receptacles on the circuit, are always hot. Requires two-wire cables.

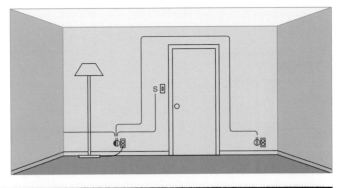

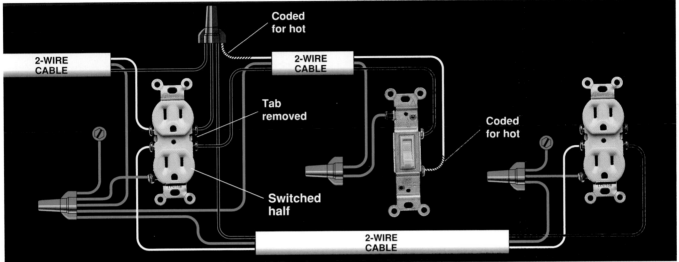

11. Double Receptacle Circuit with Shared Neutral Wire (Receptacles Alternate Circuits)

This layout features two 120-volt circuits wired with one three-wire cable connected to a double-pole circuit breaker. The black hot wire powers one circuit; the red wire powers the other. The white wire is a shared neutral that serves both circuits. When wired with 12/2 and 12/3 cable, and receptacles rated for 20 amps, this layout can be used for the two small-appliance circuits required in a kitchen.

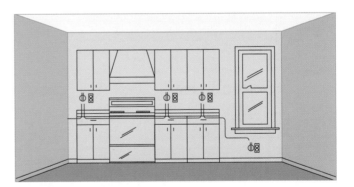

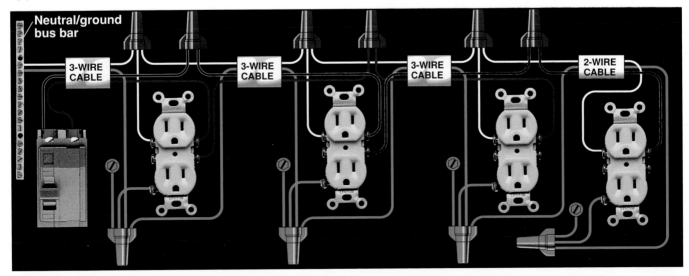

12. Double Receptacle Small Appliance Circuit with GFCIs & Shared Neutral Wire

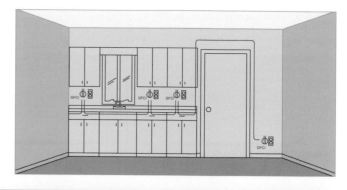

Use this layout variation of circuit map 10 to wire a double receptacle circuit when code requires that some of the receptacles by GFCIs. The GFCIs should be wired for single-location protection (see circuit map 2). Requires three-wire and two-wire cables.

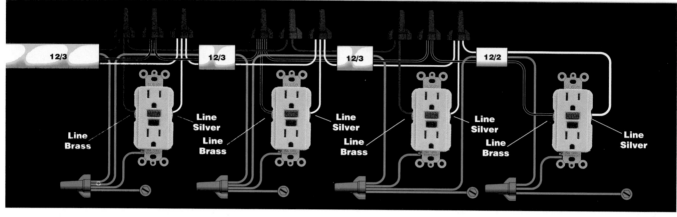

13. Double Receptacle Small Appliance Circuit with GFCIs & Separate Neutral Wires

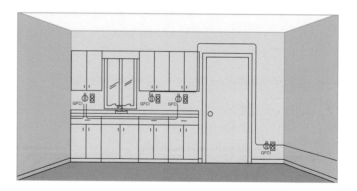

If the room layout or local codes do not allow for a shared neutral wire, use this layout instead. The GFCIs should be wired for single-location protection (see circuit map 2). Requires two-wire cable.

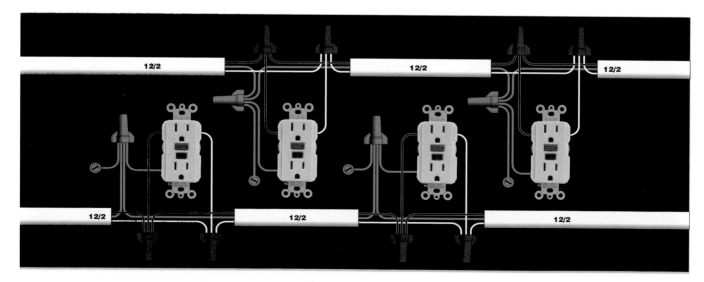

14. 120/240-volt Range Receptacle

This layout is for a 50- or 60-amp, 120/240-volt dedicated appliance circuit wired with 6/3 cable, as required by code for a large kitchen range. The black and red circuit wires, connected to a double-pole circuit breaker in the circuit breaker panel, each bring 120 volts of power to the setscrew terminals on the receptacle. The white circuit wire attached to the neutral bus bar in the circuit breaker panel is connected to the neutral setscrew terminal on the receptacle.

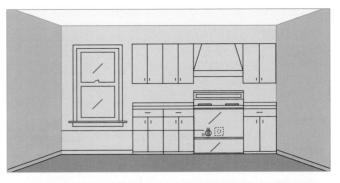

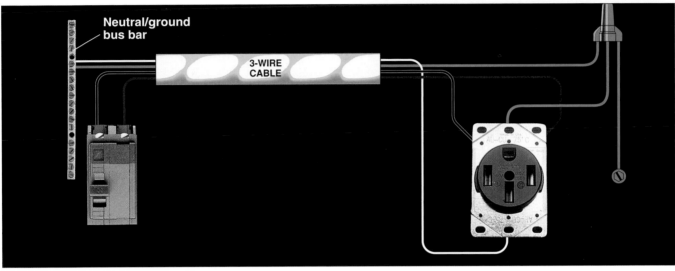

15. 240-volt Baseboard Heaters, Thermostat

This layout is typical for a series of 240-volt baseboard heaters controlled by wall thermostat. Except for the last heater in the circuit, all heaters are wired as shown below. The last heater is connected to only one cable. The size of the circuit and cables are determined by finding the total wattage of all heaters (page 149). Requires two-wire cable.

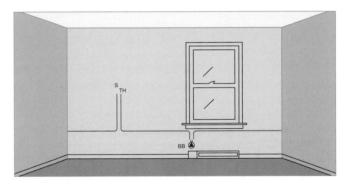

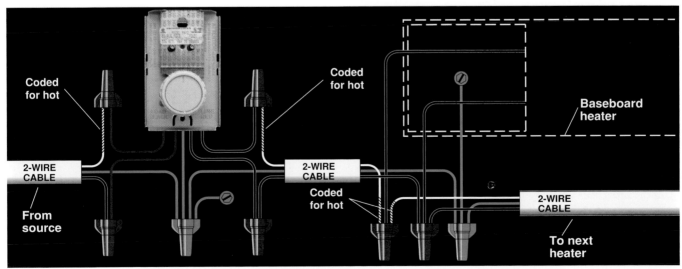

16. Dedicated 120-volt Computer Circuit, Isolated-ground Receptacle

This 15-amp isolated-ground circuit provides extra protection against surges and interference that can harm electronics. It uses 14/3 cable with the red wire serving as an extra grounding conductor. The red wire is tagged with green tape for identification. It is connected to the grounding screw on an "isolated-ground" receptacle and runs back to the grounding bus bar in the circuit breaker panel without touching any other house wiring.

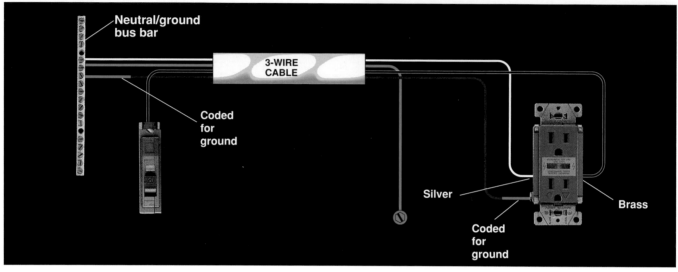

17. 240-volt Appliance Receptacle

This layout represents a 20-amp, 240-volt dedicated appliance circuit wired with 12/2 cable, as required by code for a large window air conditioner. Receptacles are available in both singleplex (shown) and duplex styles. The black and white circuit wires connected to a double-pole breaker each bring 120 volts of power to the receptacle. The white wire is tagged with black tape to indicate it is hot.

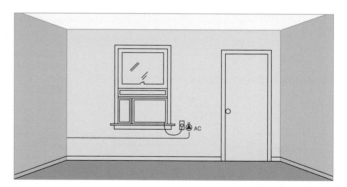

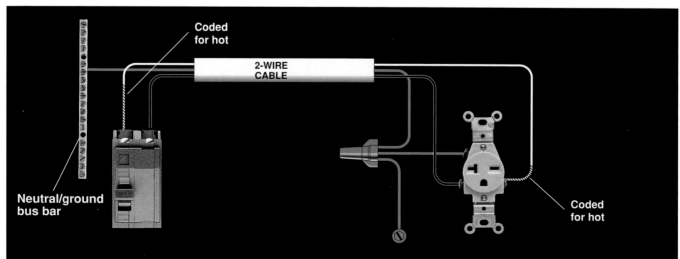

18. Ganged Single-pole Switches Controlling Separate Light Fixtures

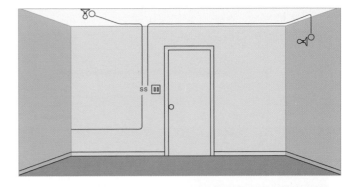

This layout lets you place two switches controlled by the same 120-volt circuit in one double-gang electrical box. A single feed cable provides power to both switches. A similar layout with two feed cables can be used to place switches from different circuits in the same box. Requires two-wire cable.

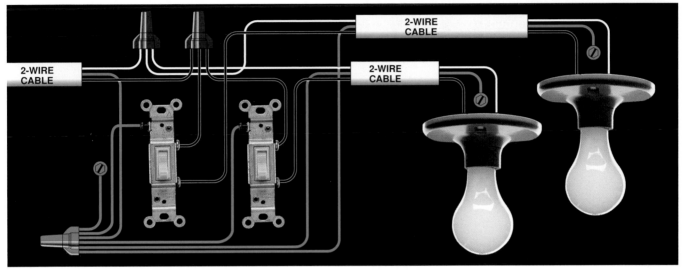

19. Ganged Switches Controlling a Light Fixture and a Vent Fan

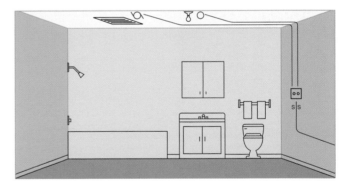

This layout lets you place two switches controlled by the same 120-volt circuit in one double-gang electrical box. A single feed cable provides power to both switches. A standard switch controls the light fixture and time-delay switch controls the vent fan.

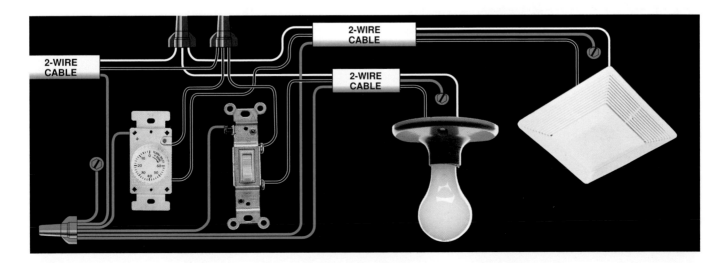

20. Three-way Switches & Light Fixture (Fixture Between Switches)

This layout for three-way switches lets you control a light fixture from two locations. Each switch has one COMMON screw terminal and two TRAVELER screws. Circuit wires attached to the TRAVELER screws run between the two switches, and hot wires attached to the COMMON screws bring current from the power source and carry it to the light fixture. Requires two-wire and three-wire cables.

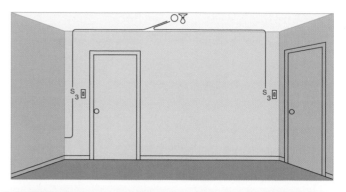

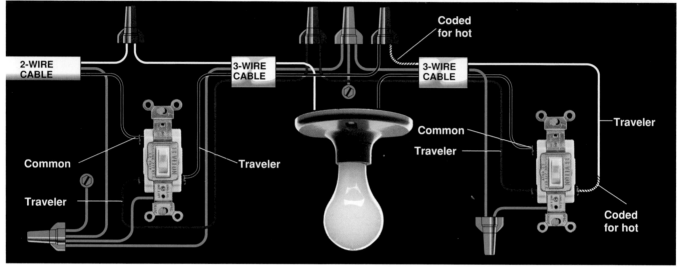

21. Three-way Switches & Light Fixture (Fixture at Start of Cable Run)

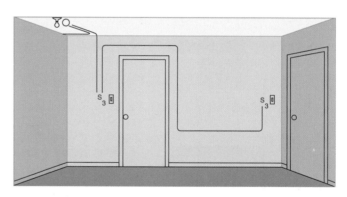

Use this layout variation of circuit map 19 where it is more convenient to locate the fixture ahead of the three-way switches in the cable run. Requires two-wire and three-wire cables.

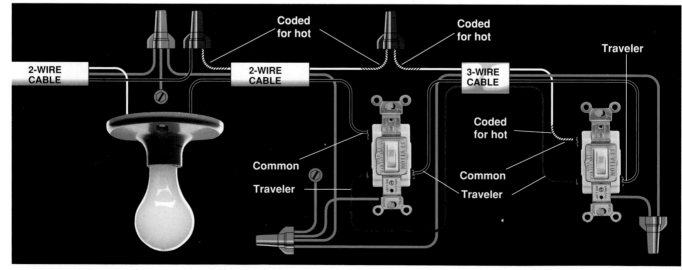

22. Three-way Switches & Light Fixture
(Fixture at End of Cable Run)

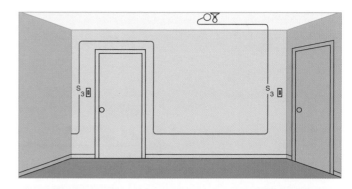

This variation of the three-way switch layout (circuit map 19) is used where it is more practical to locate the fixture at the end of the cable run. Requires two-wire and three-wire cables.

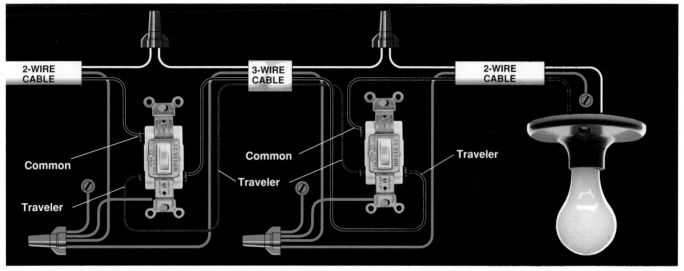

23. Three-way Switches & Light Fixture
with Duplex Receptacle

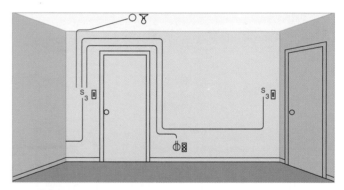

Use this layout to add a receptacle to a three-way switch configuration (circuit map 19). Requires two-wire and three-wire cables.

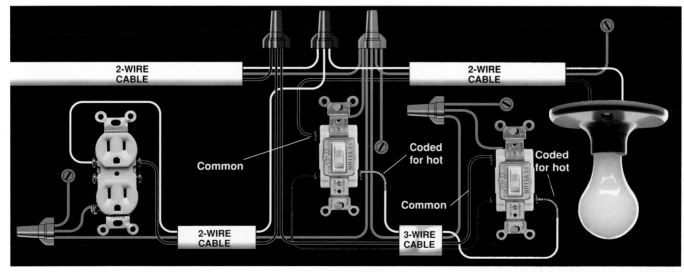

24. Three-way Switches & Multiple Light Fixtures (Fixtures Between Switches)

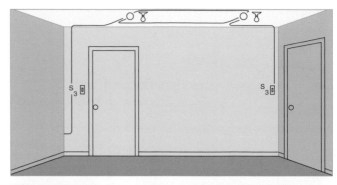

This is a variation of circuit map 20. Use it to place multiple light fixtures between two three-way switches, where power comes in at one of the switches. Requires two- and three-wire cable.

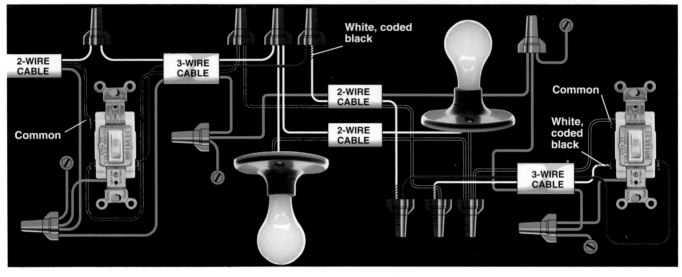

25. Three-way Switches & Multiple Light Fixtures (Fixtures at Beginning of Run)

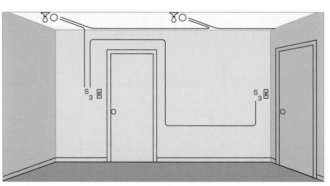

This is a variation of circuit map 21. Use it to place multiple light fixtures at the beginning of a run controlled by two three-way switches. Power comes in at the first fixture. Requires two- and three-wire cable.

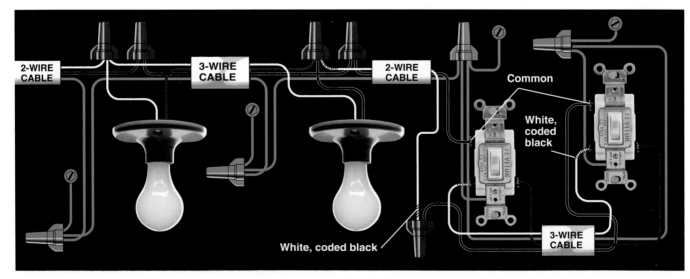

26. Four-way Switch & Light Fixture (Fixture at Start of Cable Run)

This layout lets you control a light fixture from three locations. The end switches are three way and the middle is four way. A pair of three-wire cables enter the box of the four-way switch. The white and red wires from one cable attach to the top pair of screw terminals (line 1) and the white and red wires from the other cable attaches to the bottom screw terminals (line 2). Requires two three-way switches and one four-way switch and two-wire and three-wire cables.

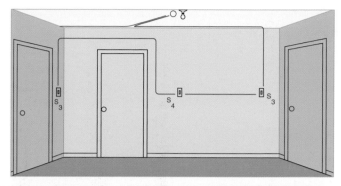

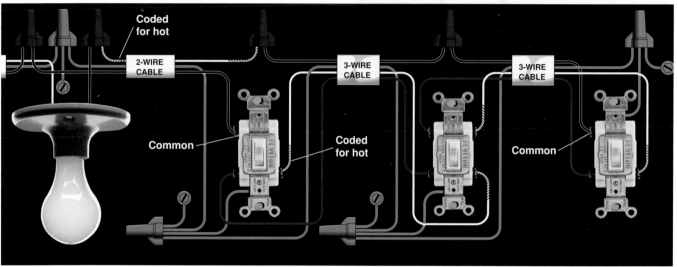

27. Four-way Switch & Light Fixture (Fixture at End of Cable Run)

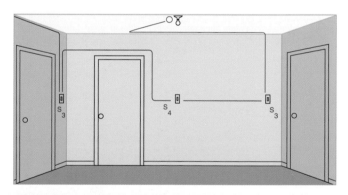

Use this layout variation of circuit map 26 where it is more practical to locate the fixture at the end of the cable run. Requires two three-way switches and one four-way switch and two-wire and three-wire cables.

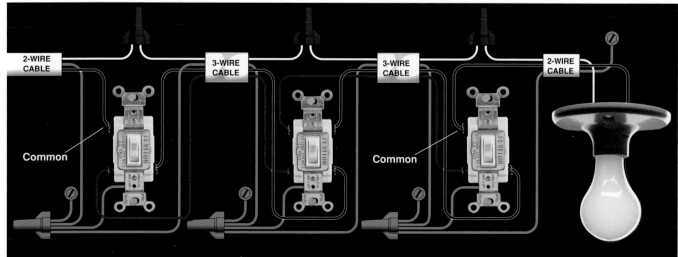

28. Multiple Four-way Switches Controlling a Light Fixture

This alternate variation of the four-way switch layout (circuit map 27) is used where three or more switches will control a single fixture. The outer switches are three way and the middle are four way. Requires two three-way switches and two four-way switches and two-wire and three-wire cables.

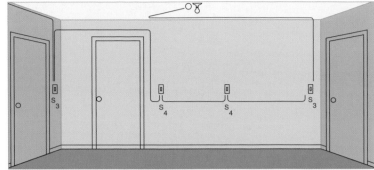

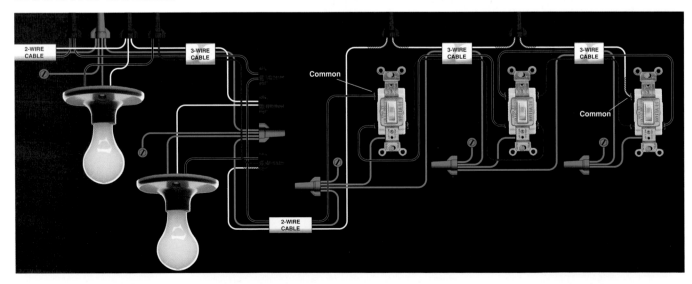

29. Four-way Switches & Multiple Light Fixtures

This variation of the four-way switch layout (circuit map 26) is used where two or more fixtures will be controlled from multiple locations in a room. Outer switches are three way and the middle switch is a four way. Requires two three-way switches and one four-way switch and two-wire and three-wire cables.

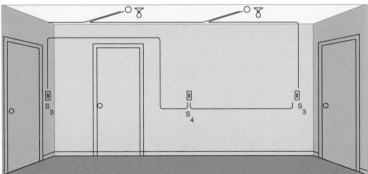

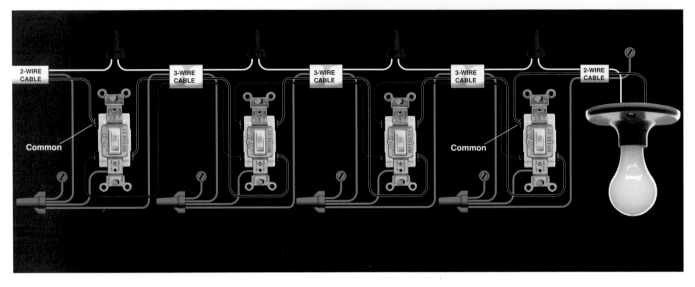

30. Ceiling Fan/Light Fixture Controlled by Ganged Switches (Fan at End of Cable Run)

This layout is for a combination ceiling fan/light fixture, controlled by a speed-control switch and dimmer in a double-gang switch box. Requires two-wire and three-wire cables.

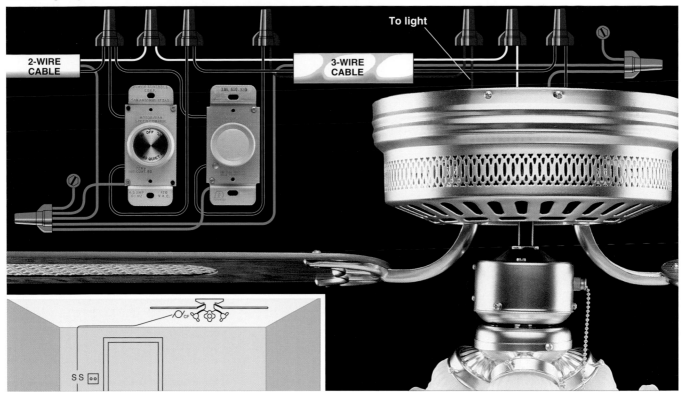

31. Ceiling Fan/Light Fixture Controlled by Ganged Switches (Switches at End of Cable Run)

Use this "switch loop" layout variation when it is more practical to install the ganged speed control and dimmer switches for the ceiling fan at the end of the cable run. Requires two-wire and three-wire cables.

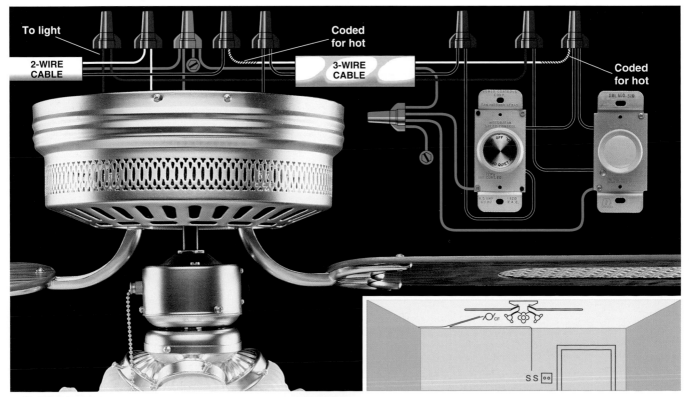

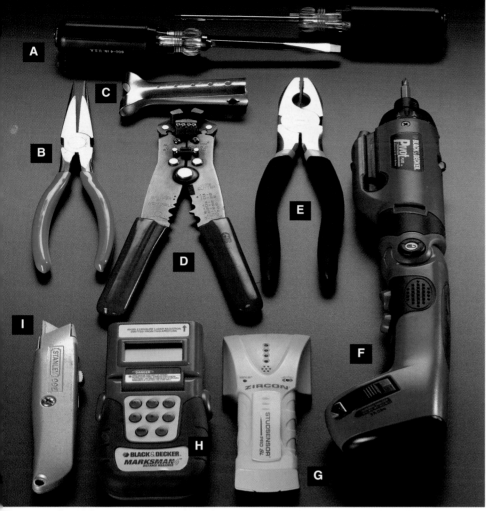

Screwdrivers with insulated handles (A) are used to make wire connections. Needlenose pliers (B) are used to hold and shape wires. A cable ripper (C) removes sheathing from NM cables. A combination tool (D) cuts cable and strips insulation from wires. Linesman's pliers (E) are used to cut wires. An electric screwdriver (F) is handy for mounting fixtures and coverplates. A sonic measuring tool (H) helps compute room areas when calculating electrical loads. A stud finder (G) helps locate framing members in finished walls; better models also locate wires and plumbing behind walls. A utility knife (I) trims excess cable sheathing.

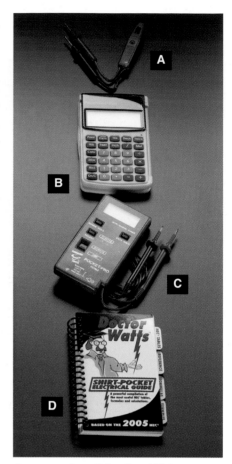

A neon circuit tester (A) is convenient for quickly checking wires for power. A calculator (B) is used to evaluate electrical loads. A multimeter (C) takes precise measurements of the amount of current on a line. A pocket wiring reference book (D) provides quick answers to electrical code questions.

Tools, Materials & Techniques for Projects

To complete the wiring projects shown in this book, you need a few specialty electrical tools (above), as well as a collection of basic hand tools. As with any tool purchase, invest in good-quality products when you buy tools for electrical work. Keep your tools clean, and sharpen or replace any cutting tools that have dull edges.

The materials used for electrical wiring have changed dramatically in the last 20 years, making it much easier for homeowners to do their own electrical work. The following pages show how to work with the following components for your projects:

- Electrical Boxes: Projects (pages 182 to 189).
- Wires & Cables: Projects (pages 190 to 203).
- Conduit (pages 204 to 207).
- Circuit Breaker Panels (pages 212 to 213).
- Circuit Breakers (pages 214 to 217).
- Subpanels (pages 212 to 213, 218 to 221).

Plastic electrical boxes for indoor installations are ideal for do-it-yourself electrical work. They have preattached mounting nails for easy installation and are much less expensive than metal boxes.

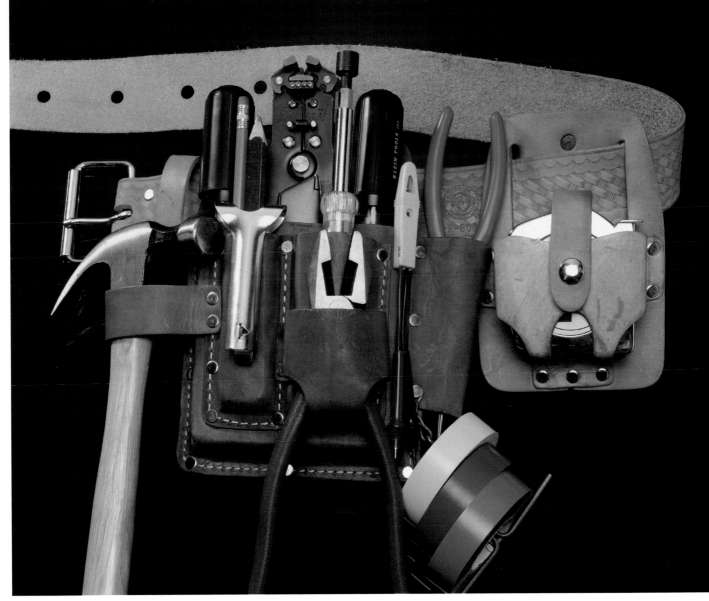

Use a tool belt to keep frequently used tools within easy reach. Electrical tapes in a variety of colors are used for marking wires and for attaching cables to a fish tape.

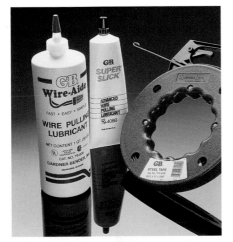

A fish tape is useful for installing cables in finished wall cavities and for pulling wires through conduit. Products designed for lubrication reduce friction and make it easier to pull cables and wires.

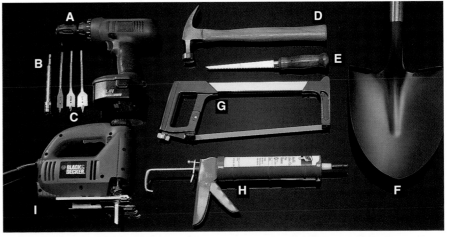

These basic tools are used for advanced wiring projects: drill (A), drill bit extension (B), and spade bits (C) for boring holes in framing members; hammer (D) for attaching electrical boxes; wallboard saw (E) for making cutouts in indoor walls; shovel (F) to dig trenches for outdoor wiring; hacksaw (G) for cutting conduit; caulk gun (H) for sealing gaps in exterior walls; jig saw (I) for making wall cutouts.

3½"-deep plastic boxes with preattached mounting nails are used for any indoor wiring project that will be protected by finished walls, such as a room addition or a rewired kitchen. Common styles include single-gang (A), double-gang (B), and triple-gang (C). Double-gang and triple-gang boxes require internal cable clamps.

Metal boxes should be used for exposed indoor wiring, such as conduit installations in an unfinished basement. Metal boxes, available in the same variety of sizes and shapes as plastic boxes, also can be used for wiring that will be covered by finished walls. Metal boxes are good electrical conductors, so they must be pigtailed to the circuit grounding wires to reduce the chance of shock caused by a short circuit.

Plastic retrofit boxes are used when a new switch or receptacle must fit inside a finished wall. Use internal cable clamps with these boxes.

Electrical Boxes

Use the chart below to select the proper type of box for your wiring project. For most indoor wiring done with NM cable, use plastic electrical boxes. Plastic boxes are inexpensive, lightweight, and easy to install.

Metal boxes also can be used for indoor NM cable installations and are still favored by some electricians, especially for supporting heavy ceiling light fixtures.

If you have a choice of box depths, always choose the deepest size available. Wire connections are easier to make if boxes are roomy. Check with your local inspector if you have questions regarding the proper box size to use.

Box type	Typical uses
Plastic	• Protected indoor wiring, used with NM cable. • Not suited for heavy light fixtures and fans.
Metal	• Exposed indoor wiring, used with metal conduit. • Protected indoor wiring, used with NM cable.
Cast aluminum	• Outdoor wiring, used with metal conduit.
PVC plastic	• Outdoor wiring, used with PVC conduit. • Exposed indoor wiring, used with PVC conduit.

Tips for Using Electrical Boxes

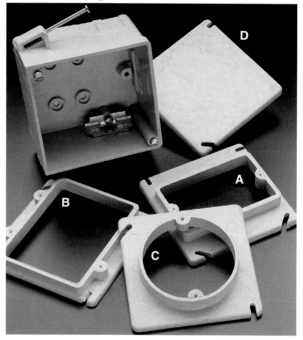

A square plastic box, 4" × 4" × 3" deep, provides extra space for making wire connections. It has preattached nails for easy mounting. A variety of adapter plates are available for 4" × 4" boxes, including single-gang (A), double-gang (B), light fixture (C), and junction box coverplate (D). Adapter plates come in several thicknesses to match different wall constructions.

Plastic retrofit light fixture box lets you install a new fixture in an existing wall or ceiling.

Plastic light fixture boxes with brace bars let you position a fixture between framing members.

Metal light fixture boxes with heavy-duty brace bars are recommended when installing heavy light fixtures or hanging a ceiling fan.

B

A

Cast aluminum boxes are required for outdoor electrical fixtures connected with metal conduit. Cast aluminum boxes have sealed seams and threaded openings to keep moisture out. A variety of weatherproof coverplates are available, including duplex receptacle plates (A), GFCI receptacle plates (B), and switch plates.

PVC plastic boxes are used with PVC conduit in outdoor wiring and exposed indoor wiring. Many local codes now allow the use of PVC plastic boxes. PVC coverplates are available to fit switches, standard duplex receptacles, and GFCI receptacles.

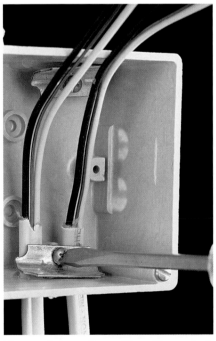

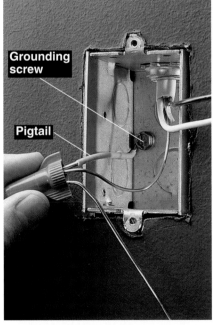

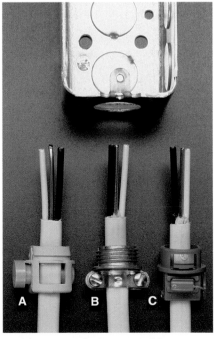

Boxes larger than 2" × 4", and all retrofit boxes, must have internal cable clamps. After installing cables in the box, tighten the cable clamps over the cables so they are gripped firmly, but not so tightly that the cable sheathing is crushed.

Metal boxes must be grounded to the circuit grounding system. Connect the circuit grounding wires to the box with a green insulated pigtail wire and wire connector (as shown) or with a grounding clip (page 204).

Cables entering a metal box must be clamped. A variety of clamps are available, including plastic clamps (A, C) and threaded metal clamps (B).

Nonmetallic boxes for home use include: Single-gang, double-gang, triple gang, and quad boxes (A); thermoset and fiberglass boxes for heavier duty (B); round fixture box (C) for ceiling installation (nail-in and with integral metal bracket).

Working With Nonmetallic Boxes

Nonmetallic electrical boxes have taken over much of the do-it-yourself market. Most are sold prefitted with installation hardware—from metal wings to 10d common nails attached at the perfect angle for a nail-in box. The bulk of the nonmetallic boxes sold today are inexpensive blue PVC. You can also purchase heavier-duty fiberglass or thermoset plastic models that provide a nonmetallic option for installing heavier fixtures such as ceiling fans and chandeliers.

In addition to cost and availability, nonmetallic boxes hold a big advantage over metal boxes in that their resistance to conducting electricity will prevent a sparking short circuit if a hot wire contacts the box. Nonmetallic boxes generally are not approved for exposed areas where they may be susceptible to damage. Their lack of rigidity also allows them to compress or distort, which can reduce the interior capacity beyond code minimums or make outlets difficult to attach.

Low cost is the primary reason that the blue PVC nail-in box is so popular. Not only are they inexpensive (about a quarter apiece when purchased in quantity), they also feature built-in cable clamps so you may not need to buy extra hardware to install them. The standard PVC nail-in box is prefitted with a pair of 10d common nails for attaching to exposed wall studs.

Tips for Working With Nonmetallic Boxes

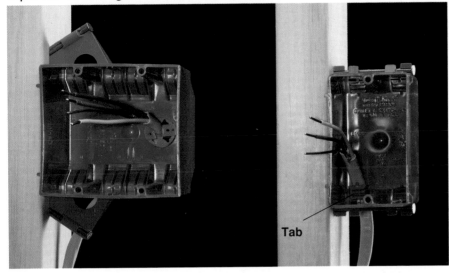

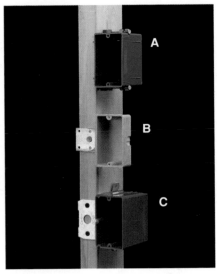

Tab

Do not break off the tabs that cover cable entry holes in plastic boxes. These are not knockouts as you would find in metal boxes. In single-gang boxes (right), the pressure from the tab is sufficient to secure the cable as long as it enters with sheathing intact and is stapled no more than 8" from the box. On larger boxes (left), you will find traditional knockouts intended to be used with plastic cable clamps that resemble metal cable clamps. Use these for heavier gauge cable and cable with more than three wires.

Nail-on boxes (A) are prefitted with 10d nails that are attached perpendicular to the face of single-gang boxes and at inward angle for better gripping power on larger boxes. Side-mount boxes (B) feature a nailing plate that is attached to the front of the stud to automatically create the correct setback; adjustable side-mount boxes (C) are installed the same way but can be moved on the bracket.

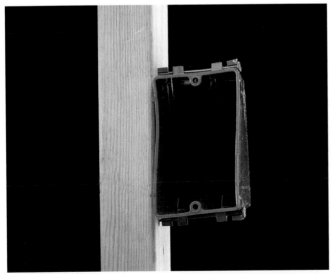

Ribs

Distortion can occur in nonmetallic boxes when nails or other fasteners are overdriven or installed at improper angles, or when the semiflexible boxes are compressed into improperly sized or shaped openings. This can reduce the box capacity and prevent outlets and faceplates from fitting.

Integral ribs cast into many nonmetallic boxes are used to register the box against the wall studs so the front edges of the box will be flush with the wall surface after drywall is installed. Most are set for ½" drywall, but if your wall will be a different thickness you may be able to find a box with corresponding ribs. Otherwise, use a piece of the wallcovering material as a reference.

Installing Electrical Boxes

Install electrical boxes for receptacles, switches, and fixtures only after your wiring project plan has been approved by your inspector. Use your wiring plan as a guide, and follow electrical code height and spacing guidelines when laying out box positions.

Always use the deepest electrical boxes that are practical for your installation. Using deep boxes ensures that you will meet code regulations regarding box volume and makes it easier to make the wire connections.

Some electrical fixtures, like recessed light fixtures, electric heaters, and exhaust fans, have built-in wire connection boxes. Install the frames for these fixtures at the same time you are installing the other electrical boxes.

Electrical boxes in adjacent rooms should be positioned close together when they share a common wall and are controlled by the same circuit. This simplifies the cable installations and also reduces the amount of cable needed.

Fixtures That Do Not Need Electrical Boxes

Wire connection box

Recessed fixtures that fit inside wall cavities have built-in wire connection boxes and require no additional electrical boxes. Common recessed fixtures include electric blower-heaters (left), bathroom vent fans (right), and recessed light fixtures (page 228). Install the frames for these fixtures at the same time you are installing the other electrical boxes along the circuit. Surface-mounted fixtures, like electric baseboard heaters (pages 254 to 255) and under-cabinet fluorescent lights (pages 232 to 233), also have built-in wire connection boxes. These fixtures are not installed until it is time to make the final hookups.

How to Install Electrical Boxes for Receptacles

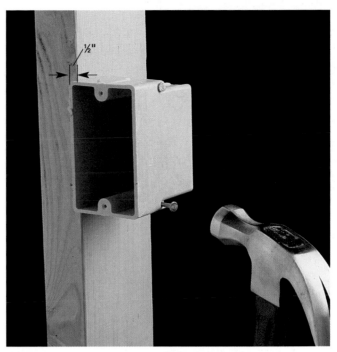

1 Mark the location of each box on studs. Standard receptacle boxes should be centered 12" above floor level. GFCI receptacle boxes in a bathroom should be mounted so they will be about 10" above the finished countertop.

2 Position each box against a stud so the front face will be flush with the finished wall. For example, if you will be installing ½" wallboard, position the box so it extends ½" past the face of the stud. Anchor the box by driving the mounting nails into the stud.

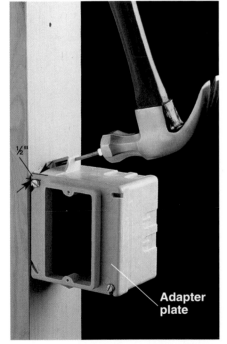

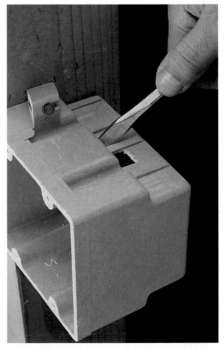

Adapter plate

3 If installing 4" × 4" boxes, attach the adapter plates before positioning the boxes. Use adapter plates that match the thickness of the finished wall. Anchor the box by driving the mounting nails into the stud.

4 Open one knockout for each cable that will enter the box, using a hammer and screwdriver.

5 Break off any sharp edges that might damage vinyl cable sheathing by rotating a screwdriver in the knockout.

How to Install Boxes for Light Fixtures

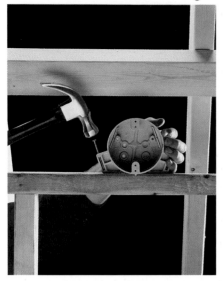

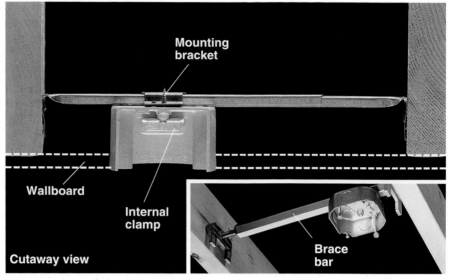

Position the light fixture box for a vanity light above the frame opening for a mirror or medicine cabinet. Place the box for a ceiling light fixture in the center of the room. Position each box against a framing member so the front face will be flush with the finished wall or ceiling, then anchor the box by driving the mounting nails into the framing.

To position a light fixture between joists, attach an electrical box to an adjustable brace bar. Nail the ends of the brace bar to joists so the face of the box will be flush with the finished ceiling surface. Slide the box along the brace bar to the desired position, then tighten the mounting screws. Use internal cable clamps when using a box with a brace bar. NOTE: For ceiling fans and heavy fixtures, use a metal box and a heavy-duty brace bar rated for heavy loads (inset photo).

How to Install Boxes for Switches

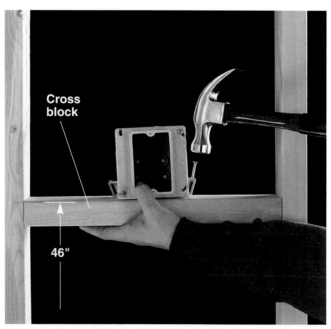

Install switch boxes at accessible locations, usually on the latch side of a door, with the center of the box 48" from the floor. In a bathroom or kitchen with partially tiled walls, switches are installed at 54" to 60" to keep them above the tile. The box for a thermostat is mounted at 48" to 60". Position each box against the side of a stud so the front face will be flush with the finished wall, and drive the mounting nails into the stud.

To install a switch box between studs, first install a cross block between studs, with the top edge 46" above the floor. Position the box on the cross block so the front face will be flush with the finished wall, and drive the mounting nails into the cross block.

How to Install Boxes for a Kitchen

Heights of electrical boxes in a kitchen vary depending on use. In the kitchen shown here, boxes above the countertop are 45" above the floor, in the center of 18" backsplashes that extend from the countertop to the cabinets. All boxes for wall switches also are installed at this height. The center of the box for the microwave receptacle is 72" off the floor. The centers of the boxes for the range and food disposer receptacles are 12" off the floor, but the center of the box for the dishwasher receptacle is 6" off the floor.

How to Install Electrical Boxes to Match Finished Wall Depth

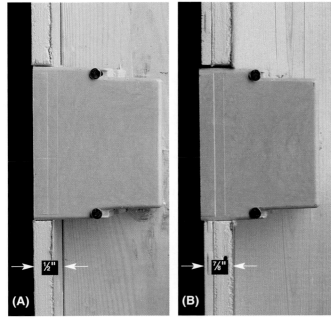

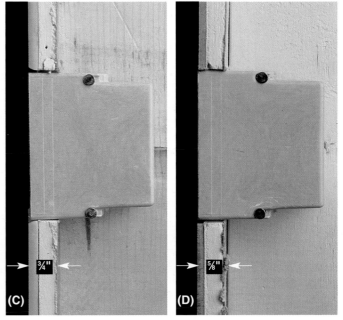

Consider the thickness of finished walls when mounting electrical boxes against framing members. Code requires that the front face of boxes be flush with the finished wall surface, so how you install boxes will vary depending on the type of wall finish that will be used. For example, if the walls will be finished with ½" wallboard (A), attach the boxes so the front faces extend ½" past the front of the framing members. With ceramic tile and wall board (B), extend the boxes ⅞" past the framing members. With ¼" Corian® over wallboard (C), boxes should extend ¾"; and with wallboard and laminate (D), boxes extend ⅝".

NM (nonmetallic) sheathed cable

should be used for most indoor wiring projects in dry locations. NM cable is available in a wide range of wire sizes, and in either "2-wire with ground" or "3-wire with ground" types. NM cable is sold in boxed rolls that contain from 25 to 250 ft. of cable.

Coaxial cable

Coaxial cable is used to connect cable television jacks (page 202). Coaxial cable is available in lengths up to 25 ft. with preattached fittings called F-connectors (A). Or you can buy bulk coaxial cable (B) in any length and attach your own F-connectors.

Large-appliance cable

Large-appliance cable, also called service entrance round (SER) cable, is used for kitchen ranges (page 223) and other 50-amp or 60-amp appliances that require 8-gauge or larger wire. Large-appliance cable is similar to NM cable, but each individual conducting wire is made from fine-stranded copper wires so the cable is easier to bend. Large-appliance cable is available in both 2-wire and 3-wire types.

THHN/THWN wire

THHN/THWN wire is a versatile product that can be used in all conduit applications (pages 204 to 207). Each conducting wire, purchased individually, is covered with a color-coded thermoplastic insulating jacket similar to the insulation on the wires inside NM cable. Make sure the wire you buy has the THHN/THWN rating. Other wire types have a similar appearance but are less resistant to heat and moisture than THHN/THWN wire.

UF (underground feeder) cable

is used for wiring in damp or wet locations, such as in an outdoor circuit (pages 268 to 288). It has a white or gray solid-core vinyl sheathing that protects the conducting wires and ground wire inside. Most codes allow UF cable to be buried directly in the ground. It also can be used indoors wherever NM cable is allowed.

Telephone cable

Telephone cable is used to connect telephone outlets (page 202). Your phone company may recommend four-wire cable (shown below) or eight-wire cable, sometimes called **four-pair.** Telephone outlet connections are identical for both types of cable, but eight-wire cable has extra wires that are left unattached. These extra wires allow for future expansion of the system.

Wire & Cables

Many types of wire and cable are available at home centers, but only a few are used in most home wiring projects. Check your local electrical code to learn which type of wire to use, and choose wire large enough for the circuit "ampacity" (next page). Cables are identified by the wire gauge and number of insulated circuit wires they contain. In addition, all cables have a grounding wire. For example, a cable labeled "12/2 W G" contains two insulated 12-gauge wires, plus a grounding wire.

Use NM cable for new wiring installed inside walls. NM cable is easy to install when walls and ceilings are unfinished; these techniques are shown throughout the book. However, some jobs require that you run cable through finished walls, such as when you make the feeder cable connection linking a new circuit to the circuit-breaker panel. Running cable in finished walls requires extra planning and often is easier if you work with a helper. Sometimes cables can be run through a finished wall by using the gaps around a chimney or plumbing soil stack. Other techniques for running NM cable inside finished walls are shown on pages 192 to 201.

Tips for Working With Wire

Wire gauge		Ampacity	Maximum wattage load
	14-gauge	15 amps	1440 watts (120 volts)
	12-gauge	20 amps	1920 watts (120 volts) 3840 watts (240 volts)
	10-gauge	30 amps	2880 watts (120 volts) 5760 watts (240 volts)
	8-gauge	40 amps	7680 watts (240 volts)
	6-gauge	50 amps	9600 watts (240 volts)

Wire "ampacity" is a measurement of how much current a wire can carry safely. Ampacity varies according to the size of the wires, as shown above. When installing a new circuit, choose wire with an ampacity rating matching the circuit size. For dedicated appliance circuits, check the wattage rating of the appliance and make sure it does not exceed the maximum wattage load of the circuit.

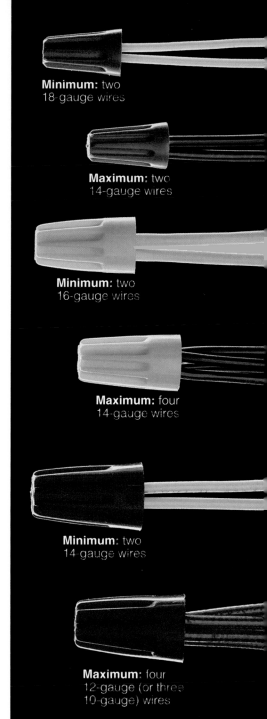

Minimum: two 18-gauge wires

Maximum: two 14-gauge wires

Minimum: two 16-gauge wires

Maximum: four 14-gauge wires

Minimum: two 14-gauge wires

Maximum: four 12-gauge (or three 10-gauge) wires

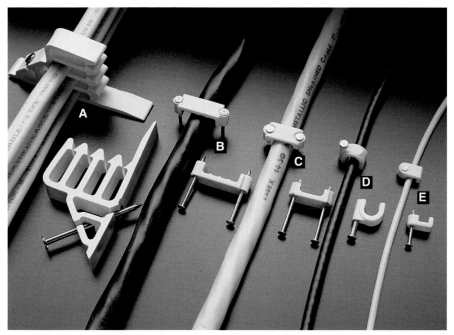

Use plastic cable staples to anchor cables to the sides of framing members. Choose staples sized to match the cables they anchor: Stack-It® staples (A) for attaching up to four 2-wire cables to the side of a framing member; ¾" staples (B) for 12/2, 12/3, and all 10-gauge cables; ½" staples (C) for 14/2, 14/3, or 12/2 cables; coaxial staples (D) for anchoring television cables; bell wire staples (E) for attaching telephone cables. Cables should be anchored within 8" of each electrical box, and every 4 feet thereafter.

Use wire connectors rated for the wires you are connecting. Wire connectors are color-coded by size, but the coding scheme varies according to manufacturer. The wire connectors shown above come from one major manufacturer. To ensure safe connections, each connector is rated for both minimum and maximum wire capacity. These connectors can be used to connect both conducting wires and grounding wires. Green wire connectors are used only for grounding wires.

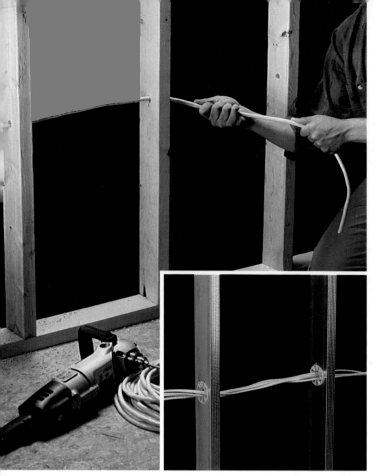

Installing NM Cable

NM cable is used for all indoor wiring projects except those requiring conduit (see pages 204 to 207). Cut and install the cable after all electrical boxes have been mounted. Refer to your wiring plan to make sure each length of cable is correct for the circuit size and configuration.

Cable runs are difficult to measure exactly, so leave plenty of extra wire when cutting each length. Cable splices inside walls are not allowed by code. When inserting cables into a circuit breaker panel, make sure the power is shut off (page 214).

After all cables are installed, call your electrical inspector to arrange for the rough-in inspection. Do not install wallboard or attach light fixtures and other devices until this inspection is done.

Pulling cables through studs is easier if you drill smooth, straight holes at the same height. Prevent kinks by straightening the cable before pulling it through the studs. Use plastic grommets to protect cables on steel studs (inset).

Everything You Need

Tools: Drill, bits, tape measure, cable ripper, combination tool, screwdrivers, needlenose pliers, hammer, fish tape.

Materials: NM cable, cable clamps, cable staples, masking tape, grounding pigtails, wire connectors, cable-pulling lubricant.

Framing member	Maximum hole size	Maximum notch size
2 × 4 loadbearing stud	1⁷⁄₁₆" diameter	⅞" deep
2 × 4 non-loadbearing stud	2½" diameter	1⁷⁄₁₆" deep
2 × 6 loadbearing stud	2¼" diameter	1⅜" deep
2 × 6 non-loadbearing stud	3⁵⁄₁₆" diameter	2³⁄₁₆" deep
2 × 6 joists	1½" diameter	⅞" deep
2 × 8 joists	2⅜" diameter	1¼" deep
2 × 10 joists	3¹⁄₁₆" diameter	1½" deep
2 × 12 joists	3¾" diameter	1⅞" deep

This framing member chart shows the maximum sizes for holes and notches that can be cut into studs and joists when running cables. When boring holes, there must be at least 1¼" of wood between the edge of a stud and the hole, and at least 2" between the edge of a joist and the hole. Joists can be notched only in the end ⅓ of the overall span; never in the middle ⅓ of the joist.

How to Install NM Cable

1 Drill ⅝" holes in framing members for the cable runs. This is done easily with a right-angle drill, available at rental centers. Holes should be set back at least 1¼" from the front face of the framing members.

2 Where cables will turn corners (step 6, page 194), drill intersecting holes in adjoining faces of studs. Measure and cut all cables, allowing 2 ft. extra at ends entering breaker panel and 1 foot for ends entering electrical box.

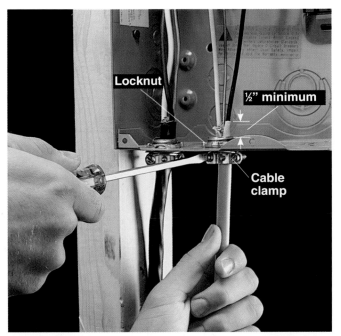

Locknut

½" minimum

Cable clamp

3 **Shut off power to circuit breaker panel**. Use a cable stripper to strip cable, leaving at least ¼" of sheathing to enter the circuit breaker panel. Clip away the excess sheathing.

4 Open a knockout in the circuit breaker panel, using a hammer and screwdriver. Insert a cable clamp into the knockout, and secure it with a locknut. Insert the cable though the clamp so that at least ½" of sheathing extends inside the circuit breaker panel. Tighten the mounting screws on the clamp so the cable is gripped securely, but not so tightly that the sheathing is crushed.

(continued next page)

How to Install NM Cable (continued)

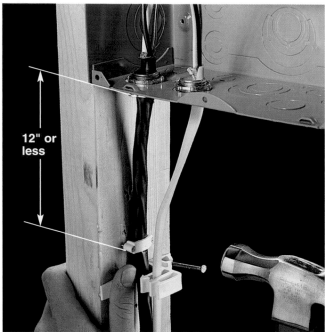

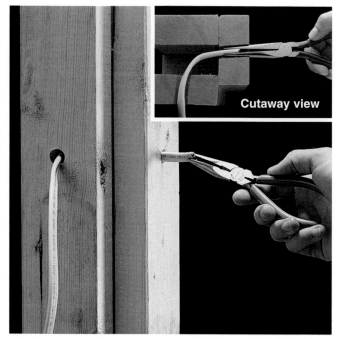

Cutaway view

5 Anchor the cable to the center of a framing member within 12" of the circuit breaker panel, using a cable staple. Stack-It® staples work well where two or more cables must be anchored to the same side of a stud. Run the cable to the first electrical box. Where the cable runs along the sides of framing members, anchor it with cable staples no more than 4 ft. apart.

6 At corners, form a slight L-shaped bend in the end of the cable and insert it into one hole. Retrieve cable through the other hole, using needlenose pliers (inset).

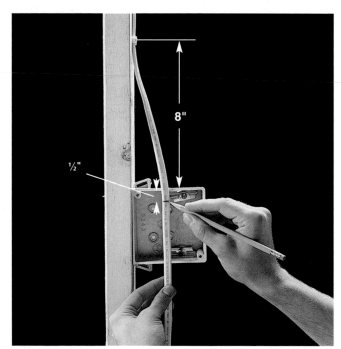

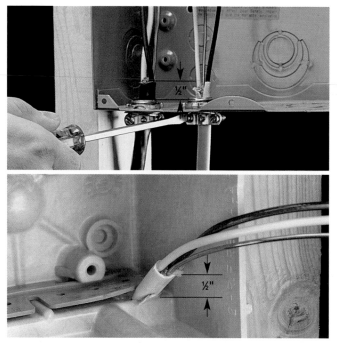

7 Staple the cable to a framing member 8" from the box. Hold the cable taut against the front of the box, and mark a point on the sheathing ½" past the box edge. Remove sheathing from the marked line to the end, using a cable ripper, and clip away excess sheathing with a combination tool. Insert the cable through the knockout in the box.

Variation: Different types of boxes have different clamping devices. Make sure cable sheathing extends ½" past the edge of the clamp to ensure that the cable is secure and that the wire won't be damaged by the edges of the clamp.

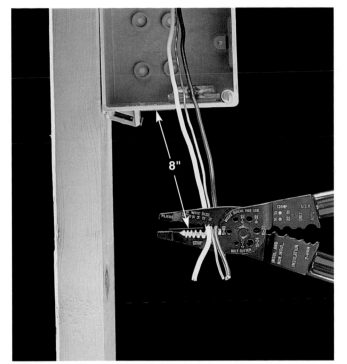

8 As each cable is installed in a box, clip back each wire so that 8" of workable wire extends past the front edge of the box.

9 Strip ¾" of insulation from each circuit wire in the box, using a combination tool. Take care not to nick the copper.

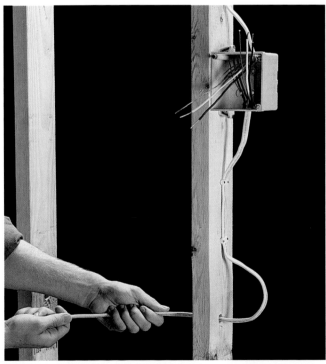

10 Continue the circuit by running cable between each pair of electrical boxes, leaving an extra 1 ft. of cable at each end.

11 At metal boxes and recessed fixtures, open knockouts, and attach cables with cable clamps. From inside fixture, strip away all but ¼" of sheathing. Clip back wires so there is 8" of workable length, then strip ¾" of insulation from each wire.

(continued next page)

How to Install NM Cable (continued)

12 For a surface-mounted fixture like a baseboard heater or fluorescent light fixture, staple the cable to a stud near the fixture location, leaving plenty of excess cable. Mark the floor so the cable will be easy to find after the walls are finished.

13 At each recessed fixture and metal electrical box, connect one end of a grounding pigtail to the metal frame, using a grounding clip attached to the frame (shown above) or a green grounding screw (page 204).

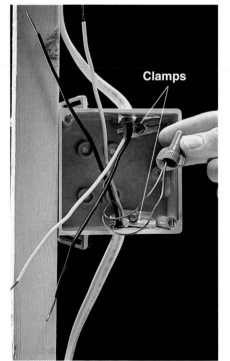

14 At each electrical box and recessed fixture, join grounding wires together with a wire connector. If box has internal clamps, tighten the clamps over the cables.

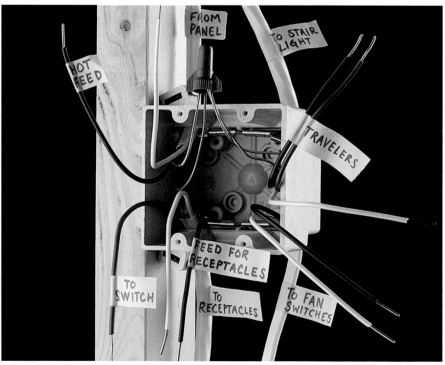

15 Label the cables entering each box to indicate their destinations. In boxes with complex wiring configurations, also tag the individual wires to make final hookups easier. After all cables are installed, your rough-in work is ready to be reviewed by the electrical inspector.

How to Run NM Cable Inside a Finished Wall

1 From the unfinished space below the finished wall, look for a reference point, like a soil stack, plumbing pipes, or electrical cables, that indicates the location of the wall above. Choose a location for the new cable that does not interfere with existing utilities. Drill a 1" hole up into the stud cavity.

2 From the unfinished space above the finished wall, find the top of the stud cavity by measuring from the same fixed reference point used in step 1. Drill a 1" hole down through the top plate and into the stud cavity, using a drill bit extender.

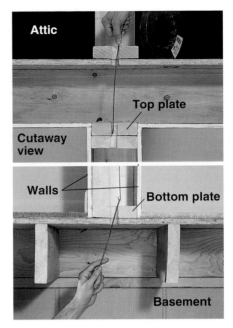

3 Extend a fish tape down through the top plate, twisting the tape until it reaches the bottom of the stud cavity. From the unfinished space below the wall, use a piece of stiff wire with a hook on one end to retrieve the fish tape through the drilled hole in the bottom plate.

4 Trim back 2" of sheathing from the end of the NM cable, then insert the wires through the loop at the tip of the fish tape.

5 Bend the wires against the cable, then use electrical tape to bind them tightly. Apply cable-pulling lubricant to the taped end of the fish tape.

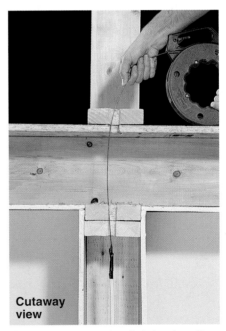

6 From above the finished wall, pull steadily on the fish tape to draw the cable up through the stud cavity. This job will be easier if you have a helper feed the cable from below as you pull.

Tips for Running Cable Inside Finished Walls

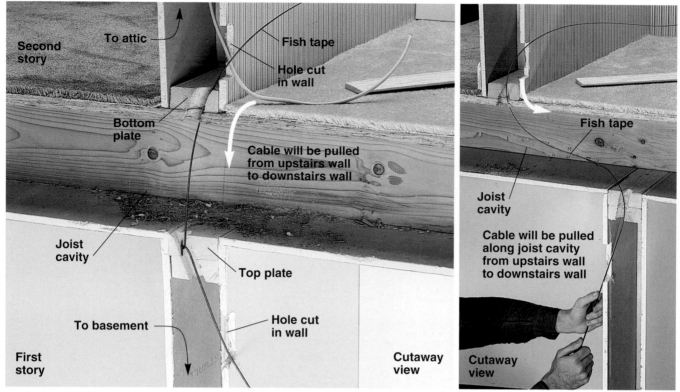

Second story

To attic

Fish tape

Hole cut in wall

Bottom plate

Cable will be pulled from upstairs wall to downstairs wall

Joist cavity

Top plate

To basement

Hole cut in wall

First story

Cutaway view

Fish tape

Joist cavity

Cable will be pulled along joist cavity from upstairs wall to downstairs wall

Cutaway view

If there is no access space above and below a wall (page 197), cut openings in the finished walls to run a cable. This often occurs in two-story homes when a cable is extended from an upstairs wall to a downstairs wall. Cut small openings in the wall near the top and bottom plates, then drill an angled 1" hole through each plate. Extend a fish tape into the joist cavity between the walls and use it to pull the cable from one wall to the next. If the walls line up one over the other (left), you can retrieve the fish tape using a piece of stiff wire. If walls do not line up (right), use a second fish tape. After running the cable, repair the holes in the walls with patching plaster, or wallboard scraps and taping compound.

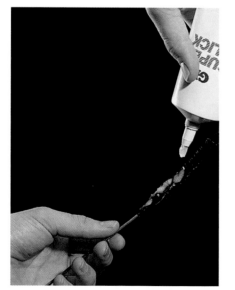

Apply cable-pulling lubricant to the taped end of the fish tape when a cable must be pulled through a sharp bend. Don't use oil or petroleum jelly, as they can damage cable sheathing.

Cutaway view

If you don't have a fish tape, use a length of sturdy string and a lead weight or heavy washer. Drop the line into the stud cavity from above, then use a piece of stiff wire to hook the line from below.

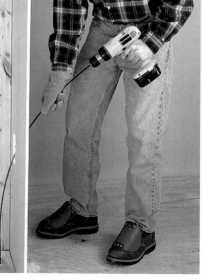

Use a flexible drill bit also called a *bell-hanger's bit* to bore holes through framing in finished walls.

How to Install NM Cable in Finished Ceilings

If you don't have access to a ceiling from above, you can run cable for a new ceiling fixture from an existing receptacle in the room up the wall and into the ceiling without disturbing much of the ceiling. To begin, run cable from the receptacle to the stud channel that aligns with the ceiling joists on which you want to install a fixture. Be sure to plan a location for the new switch. Remove short strips of drywall from the wall and ceiling. Make a notch in the center of the top plates, and protect the notch with metal nail stops. Use a fish tape to pull the new cable up through the wall cavity and the notch in top plates. Next, use the fish tape to pull the cable through the ceiling to the fixture hole. After having your work inspected, replace the drywall and install the fixture and switch.

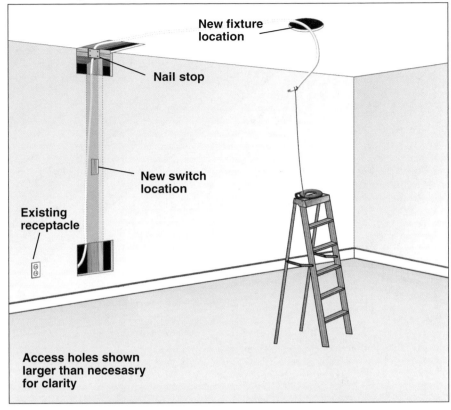

New fixture location

Nail stop

New switch location

Existing receptacle

Access holes shown larger than necesasry for clarity

1 Plan a route for running cable between electrical boxes (see illustration above). Remove drywall on the wall and ceiling surface. Where cable must cross framing members, cut a small access opening in the wall and ceiling surface; then cut a notch into the framing with a wood chisel.

2 Fish a cable from the exisiting receptacle locationup to the notch at the top of the wall. Protect the notch with a metal nail stop. Fish the cable through the ceiling to the location of the new ceiling fixture.

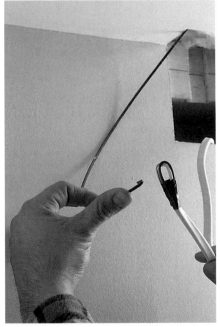

3 Fish the cable through the ceiling to the location of the new ceiling fixture.

How to Add a Receptacle in a Finished Wall

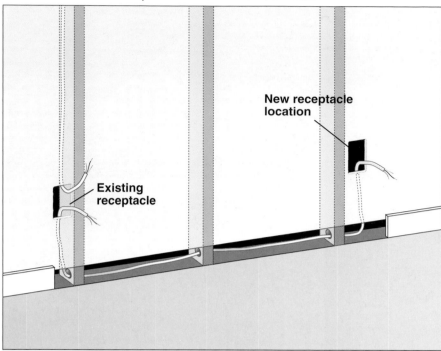

New receptacle location

Existing receptacle

Adding a new receptacle or switch to a finished wall is not nearly as difficult as it might seem, if you can remove the baseboard. If you use cut-in boxes (pages 40 to 41), this method requires no drywall refinishing. The new receptacle will draw power from an existing receptacle on the same wall. Remove the baseboard and the drywall behind it and fish cable to the new outlet location.

1 Position the new cut-in box on the wall, and trace around it. Consider the location of hidden utilities within the wall before you cut.

2 Remove baseboard between new and existing receptacle. Cut away the drywall about 1" below the baseboard with a jig saw, wallboard saw, or utility knife.

3 Drill a ⅝" hole in the center of each stud along the opening between the two receptacles. A drill bit extender or a flexible drill bit will allow you a better angle and make drilling the holes easier.

4 Run the branch cable through the holes from the new location to the existing receptacle. Staple the cable to the stud below the box. Install a metal nail plate on the front edge of each stud that the cable routes through.

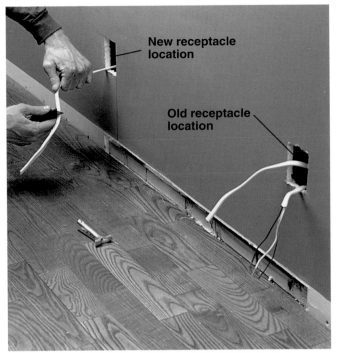

New receptacle location

Old receptacle location

5 Turn off the power at the main panel. Remove the old receptacle and its box, and pull the new branch cable up through the hole. Remove sheathing and insulation from both ends of the new cable.

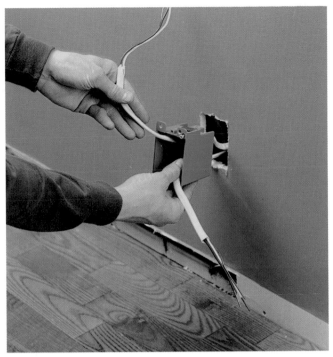

6 Thread the new and old cables into a cut-in box large enough to contain the added wires and clamp the cables. Fit the box into the old hole and attach it (page 40 to 41).

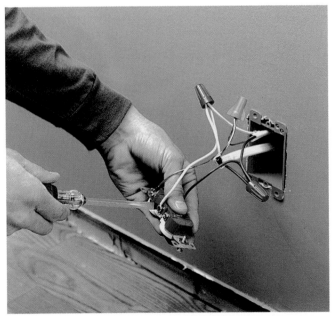

7 Reconnect the old receptacle by connecting its neutral, hot, and grounding screws to the new branch cable and the old cable from the panel with pigtails.

8 Pull the cable through another cut-in box for the new receptacle. Secure the cable and install the box. Connect the new receptacle to the new branch cable. Insert the receptacle into the box and attach the receptacle and coverplate with screws. Patch the opening with ½"-thick wood strips or drywall. Reattach the baseboard to the studs.

Coaxial cable for television jack

F-connector

Installing Telephone & Cable Television Wiring

Telephone outlets and television jacks are easy to install while you are wiring new electrical circuits. Install the accessory cables while framing members are exposed, then make the final connections after the walls are finished.

Telephone lines use four- or eight-wire cable, often called **bell wire**, while television lines use a shielded coaxial cable with threaded end fittings called F-connectors. To splice into an existing cable television line, use a fitting called a signal splitter. Signal splitters are available with two, three, or four outlet nipples.

How to Install Coaxial Cable for a Television Jack

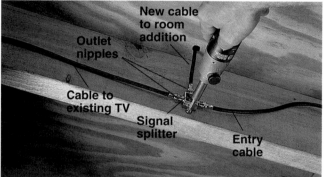

New cable to room addition

Outlet nipples

Cable to existing TV

Signal splitter

Entry cable

1 Install a signal splitter where the entry cable connects to indoor TV cables, usually in the basement or another utility area. Attach one end of new coaxial cable to an outlet nipple on the splitter. Anchor splitter to a framing member with wallboard screws.

2 Run the coaxial cable to the location of the new television jack. Keep coaxial cable at least 6" away from electrical wiring to avoid electrical interference. Mark the floor so the cable can be found easily after the walls are finished.

How to Connect a Television Jack

Mounting bracket

1 After walls are finished, make a cutout opening 1½" wide and 3¾" high at the television jack location. Pull cable through the opening, and install two television jack mounting brackets in the cutout.

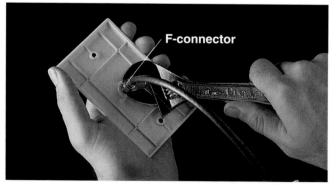

F-connector

2 Use a wrench to attach the cable F-connector to the back of the television jack. Attach the jack to the wall by screwing it onto the mounting brackets.

How to Install Cable for a Telephone Outlet

1 Locate a telephone junction in your basement or other utility area. Remove the junction cover. Use cable staples to anchor one end of the cable to a framing member near the junction, leaving 6" to 8" of excess cable.

2 Run the cable from the junction to the telephone outlet location. Keep the cable at least 6" away from circuit wiring to avoid electrical interference. Mark the floor so the cable can be located easily after the walls are finished.

How to Connect a Telephone Outlet

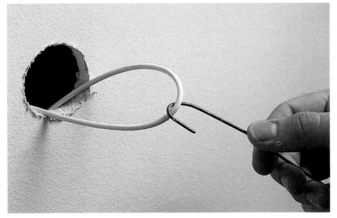

1 After walls are finished, cut a hole in the wallboard at phone outlet location, using a wallboard saw. Retrieve the cable, using a piece of stiff wire.

2 At each cable end, remove about 2" of outer sheathing. Remove about ¾" of insulation from each wire, using a combination tool.

3 Connect wires to similarly colored wire leads in phone outlet. If there are extra wires, tape them to back of the outlet, out of the way. Put the telephone outlet over the wall cutout, and attach it to the wallboard.

4 At the telephone junction, connect the cable wires to the color-coded screw terminals. If there are extra wires, wrap them with tape and tuck them inside the junction. Reattach the junction cover.

Sweep forms a gradual 90º bend for ease in wire pulling.

Elbow fitting is used in tight corners or for long conduit runs that have many bends. The elbow's cover can be removed to pull long lengths of wire.

Compression fittings are used most frequently in outdoor intermediate metallic conduit installations where a rain-tight connection is needed.

Screw-in connectors or set-screw connectors are used to connect flexible metal conduit.

Single-hole & double-hole pipe straps hold conduit in place against masonry walls or wooden framing members. Conduit should be supported within 3 feet of each electrical box and fitting, and every 10 ft. thereafter.

Nail straps are driven into wooden framing members to anchor conduit.

Flexible metal conduit, available in ½" and ¾" sizes, is used in exposed locations where rigid conduit is difficult to install. Because it bends easily, flexible metal conduit often is used to connect permanently wired appliances, like a water heater.

Conduit

Electrical wiring that runs in exposed locations must be protected by rigid tubing, called **conduit**. For example, conduit is used for wiring that runs across masonry walls in a basement laundry and for exposed outdoor wiring. THHN/THWN wire (page 190) normally is installed inside conduit, although UF or NM cable can also be installed in conduit.

There are several types of conduit available, so check with your electrical inspector to find out which type meets code requirements in your area. Conduit installed outdoors must be rated for exterior use. Metal conduit should be used only with metal boxes, never with plastic boxes.

At one time, conduit could only be fitted by using elaborate bending techniques and special tools. Now, however, a variety of shaped fittings are available to let a homeowner join conduit easily.

Electrical Grounding in Metal Conduit

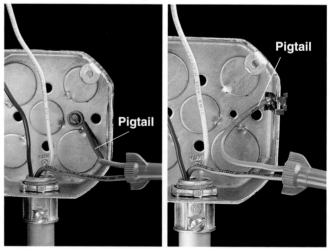

Pigtail

Pigtail

Install a green insulated grounding wire for any circuit that runs through metal conduit. Although code allows the metal conduit to serve as the grounding conductor, most electricians install a green insulated wire as a more dependable means of grounding the system. The grounding wires must be connected to metal boxes with a pigtail and grounding screw (left) or grounding clip (right).

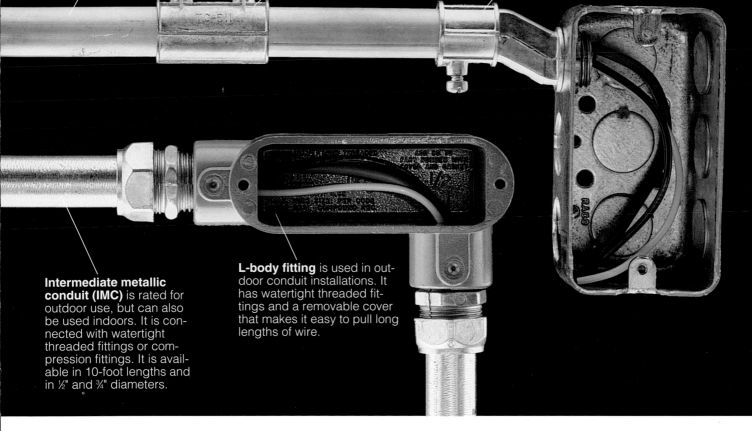

EMT conduit is available in 10-foot lengths and in ½" and ¾" diameters. EMT is used primarily for exposed indoor installations.

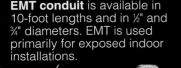

Setscrew coupling connects lengths of indoor metal conduit.

Offset fitting connects an indoor metal electrical box to a conduit anchored flush against a wall.

Intermediate metallic conduit (IMC) is rated for outdoor use, but can also be used indoors. It is connected with watertight threaded fittings or compression fittings. It is available in 10-foot lengths and in ½" and ¾" diameters.

L-body fitting is used in outdoor conduit installations. It has watertight threaded fittings and a removable cover that makes it easy to pull long lengths of wire.

Wire Capacities of Conduit

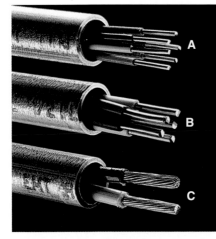

Conduit ½" in diameter can hold up to six 14-gauge or 12-gauge THHN/THWN wires (A), five 10-gauge wires (B), or two 8-gauge wires (C). Use ¾" conduit if the number of wires exceeds this capacity.

Three Metal Conduit Variations

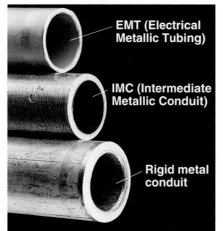

EMT (Electrical Metallic Tubing)

IMC (Intermediate Metallic Conduit)

Rigid metal conduit

EMT is lightweight and easy to install but should not be used where it can be damaged. IMC has thicker, galvanized walls and is a good choice for exposed outdoor use. Rigid metal conduit provides the greatest protection for wires, but it is more expensive and requires threaded fittings.

Plastic Conduit Variation

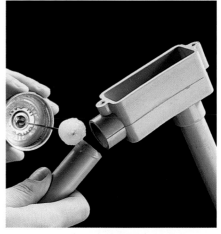

Plastic PVC conduit is allowed by many local codes. It is assembled with solvent glue and PVC fittings that resemble those for metal conduit. PVC conduit should be attached only to PVC boxes, never to metal boxes. When wiring with PVC conduit, always run a green grounding wire.

How to Install Metal Conduit & THHN/THWN Wire on Masonry Walls

1 Measure from floor to position electrical boxes on wall, and mark location for mounting screws. Boxes for receptacles in an unfinished basement or other damp area are mounted at least 2 ft. from the floor. Laundry receptacles usually are mounted at 48".

2 Drill pilot holes with a masonry bit, then mount the boxes against masonry walls with masonry anchors. Or use masonry anchors and pan-head screws.

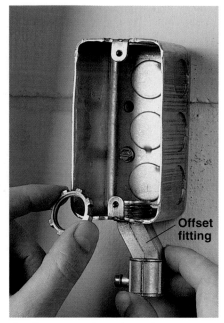

3 Open one knockout for each length of conduit that will be attached to the box. Attach an offset fitting to each knockout, using a locknut.

Offset fitting

4 Measure the first length of conduit and cut it with a hacksaw. Remove any rough inside edges with a pipe reamer or a round file. Attach the conduit to the offset fitting on the box, and tighten the setscrew.

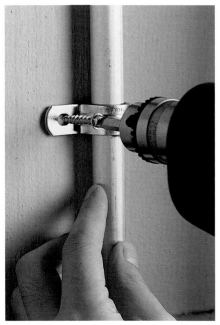

5 Anchor the conduit against the wall with pipe straps and masonry anchors. Conduit should be anchored within 3 ft. of each box and fitting, and every 10 ft. thereafter.

6 Make conduit bends by attaching a sweep fitting, using a setscrew fitting or compression fitting. Continue conduit run by attaching additional lengths, using setscrew or compression fittings.

7 Use an elbow fitting in conduit runs that have many bends, or runs that require very long wires. The cover on the elbow fitting can be removed to make it easier to extend a fish tape and pull wires.

8 At the service breaker panel, turn the power off, then remove the cover and test for power (page 214). Open a knockout in the panel, then attach a setscrew fitting, and install the last length of conduit.

9 Unwind the fish tape and extend it through the conduit from the circuit breaker panel outward. Remove the cover on an elbow fitting when extending the fish tape around tight corners.

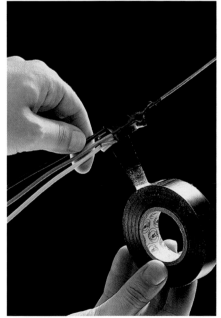

10 Trim back 2" of outer insulation from the end of the wires, then insert the wires through the loop at the tip of the fish tape.

11 Retrieve the wires through the conduit by pulling on the fish tape with steady pressure. **NOTE: Use extreme care** when using a metal fish tape inside a circuit breaker panel, even when the power is turned off.

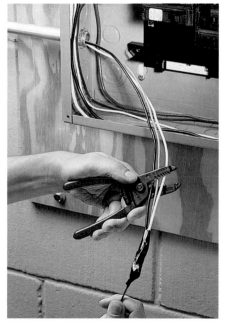

12 Clip off the taped ends of the wires. Leave at least 2 ft. of wire at the service panel and 8" at each electrical box.

Wiring a Laundry with Conduit

A typical home laundry has three electrical circuits. A 20-amp, 120-volt small-appliance circuit wired with 12-gauge THHN/THWN wire supplies power for the washing machine receptacle and all other general-use receptacles in the laundry area. A basic lighting circuit, often extended from another part of the house, powers the laundry light fixture. Finally, a 240-volt, 30-amp circuit wired with 10-gauge THHN/THWN wire provides power for the dryer.

Follow the directions on pages 206 to 207 when installing the conduit. For convenience, you can use the same conduit to hold the wires for both the 120-volt circuit and the 240-volt dryer circuit.

Everything You Need

Tools: Hacksaw, drill and ⅛" masonry bit, screwdriver, fish tape, combination tool.

Materials: Conduit, setscrew fittings, masonry anchors, THHN/THWN wire, electrical tape, wire connectors, receptacles (GFCI, 120-volt, 120/240-volt), circuit breakers (30-amp double-pole, 20-amp single-pole).

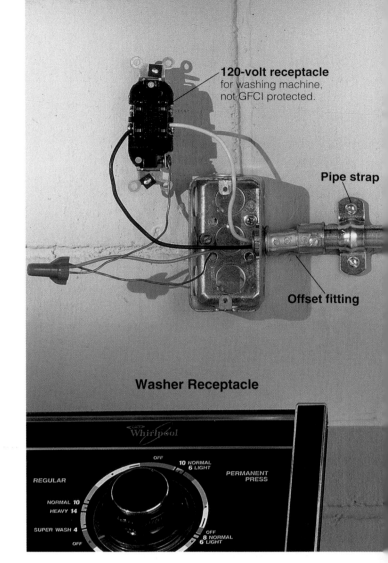

120-volt receptacle for washing machine, not GFCI protected.

Pipe strap

Offset fitting

Washer Receptacle

How to Connect a 30-amp Dryer Circuit (conduit installation)

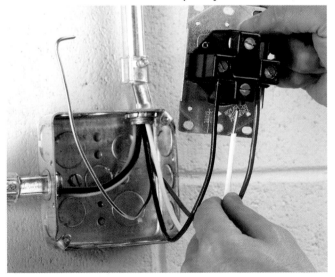

1 Connect the white circuit wire to the neutral setscrew terminal on the receptacle. Connect the black and red wires to the remaining setscrew terminals, and connect the grounding wire to the receptacle grounding screw. Attach the coverplate.

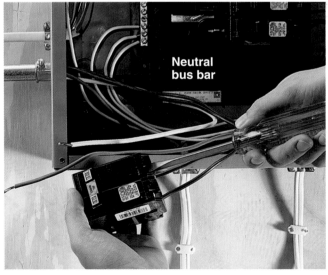

Neutral bus bar

2 With the main breaker shut off, connect the red and black circuit wires to the setscrew terminals on the 30-amp double-pole breaker. Connect the white wire to the neutral bus bar. Attach the grounding wire to the grounding bus bar. Attach the breaker panel cover, and turn the breakers on.

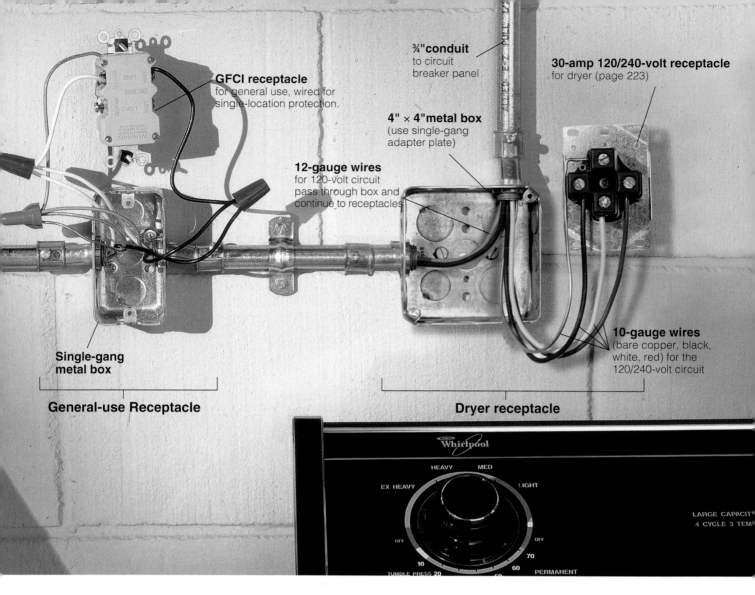

GFCI receptacle for general use, wired for single-location protection.

¾"conduit to circuit breaker panel

30-amp 120/240-volt receptacle for dryer (page 223)

4" × 4" metal box (use single-gang adapter plate)

12-gauge wires for 120-volt circuit pass through box and continue to receptacles

10-gauge wires (bare copper, black, white, red) for the 120/240-volt circuit

Single-gang metal box

General-use Receptacle

Dryer receptacle

Wiring a Water Heater with Flexible Conduit

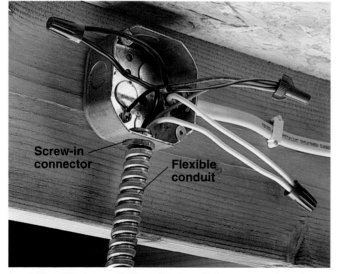

Screw-in connector

Flexible conduit

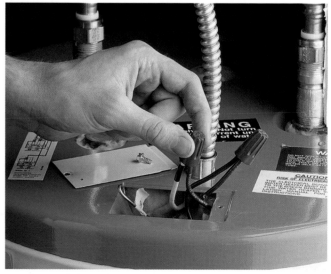

Install a 30-amp, 240-volt circuit for most electric water heaters. A water heater circuit is wired in much the same way as an air conditioner circuit (circuit map 17, page 172). Install a junction box near the water heater, then use 10/2 NM cable to bring power from the service panel to the junction box (left). Use flexible metal conduit and 10-gauge THHN/THWN wires to bring power from the junction box to the water heater wire connection box (right). Connect black and red water heater leads to the white and black circuit wires. Connect the grounding wire to the water heater grounding screw.

209

Raceway wiring can make a quick job of adding an outlet or light fixture. It is especially useful in situations where it is not possible to run cable within walls, such as in basements and garages.

Parts of a raceway system

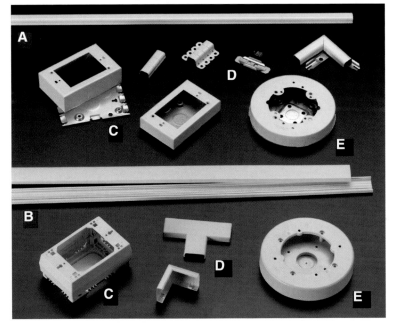

Raceway systems employ two-part tracks that are mounted directly to the wall surface to house cable. Lighter-duty plastic raceways (A), used frequently in office buildings, are made of snap-together plastic components. For home wiring, look for a heavier metal-component system (B). Both systems include box extenders for tying in to a receptacle (C), elbows, T-connectors, and couplings (D), and boxes for fixtures (E).

Raceway Wiring

Raceways are essentially decorative conduit. Often called surface-mounted wiring, a raceway is a track of flattened metal or plastic tubing that attaches to a wall and houses cable for a circuit. The systems include matching elbows, T-connectors, and various other fittings and boxes that are also surface-mounted. The main advantage to a raceway system is that, with one, you can add a new fixture onto a circuit without cutting into your walls.

Although they are extremely convenient and can even contribute to a room's decor when used thoughtfully, raceway systems do have some limitations. They are not allowed for some specific applications (such as damp areas like bathrooms) in many areas, so check with the local building authorities before beginning a project. And, the boxes that house the switches and receptacles tend to be very shallow and more difficult to work with than ordinary boxes.

In some cases, you may choose to run an entirely new circuit with raceway components (at least starting at the point where the feeder wire reaches the room from the service panel). But more often, a raceway circuit ties into an existing receptacle or switch. If you are tying into a standard switch box for power, make sure the load wire for the new raceway circuit is connected to the hot wire in the switch box before it is connected to the switch (otherwise, the raceway circuit will be off whenever the switch is off).

Everything You Need

Tools: Hacksaw, circuit tester, drill/driver, flathead screwdriver, combination tool.

Materials: Cable, raceway channels and fittings, wall anchors.

How to Install a Switch and Ceiling Light Using a Raceway System

1 Turn power off at the main panel. Remove the faceplate covering the receptacle where you'll tie into a power source. Unscrew the switch or receptacle from the existing electrical box. Check for power with a tester. Disconnect the receptacle from the wires.

2 Pull the cable through the box extension mounting plate and connect it to the existing box with screws. Remove a knockout from the box extension. Fit it over the plate and attach it with screws.

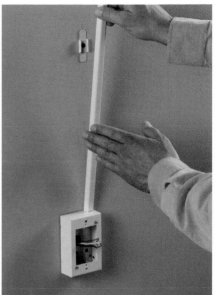

3 Connect the first section of raceway track to the knockout hole in the box extension and mount the raceway to the wall using straps or clips supplied with the product. Use a hacksaw to cut track to length and secure straps with wall anchors if a stud is not available.

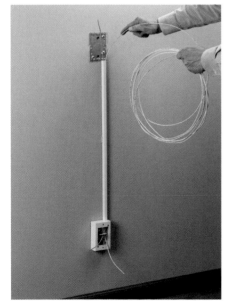

4 At the switch location, attach a switch box to the end of the track and the wall. Fish THHN wire (black, white, and green) back through the track and into the source receptacle box. Run at least 12" of extra THHN into the switch box and the source box.

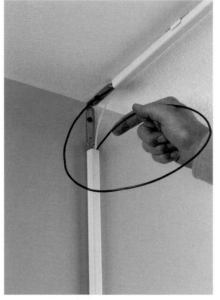

5 Install the remaining track to connect to the fixture. When turns are required, use elbows to position tracks, but don't attach the elbows. After all track is attached, continue feeding THHN from the receptacle at the beginning of the run. At the turns, feed all THHN into the next section of track, and then secure the elbow.

6 Continue until the THHN spans from the receptacle to the fixture. If you are installing a ceiling fixture, make sure the box is attached solidly to a framing member in the ceiling. Make final electrical connections.

Circuit Breaker Panels

The circuit breaker panel is the electrical distribution center for your home. It divides the current into branch circuits that are carried throughout the house. Each branch circuit is controlled by a circuit breaker that protects the wires from dangerous current overloads. When installing new circuits, the last step is to connect the wires to new circuit breakers at the panel. Working inside a circuit breaker panel is not dangerous if you follow basic safety procedures. Always shut off the main circuit breaker and test for power before touching any parts inside the panel, and **never touch the service wire lugs.** If unsure of your own skills, hire an electrician to make the final circuit connections. (If you have an older electrical service with fuses instead of circuit breakers, always have an electrician make these final hookups.)

If the main circuit breaker panel does not have enough open slots to hold new circuit breakers, install a subpanel (pages 218 to 221). This job is well within the skill level of an experienced do-it-yourselfer, although you can also hire an electrician to install the subpanel.

Main circuit breaker panel distributes the power entering the home into branch circuits. (Note: Some circuit breakers have been removed for clarity.)

Neutral service wire carries current back to the power source after it has passed through the home.

Two hot service wires provide 120 volts of power to the main circuit breaker. These wires are always HOT.

Main circuit breaker protects the hot service wires from overloads and transfers power to two hot bus bars. To work inside the service panel safely, the main circuit breaker must be shut off.

Double-pole breaker wired for a 120/240 circuit transfers power from the two hot bus bars to red and black hot wires in a 3-wire cable. This wiring is also used for double 120-volt circuits that share a common neutral wire.

Neutral bus bar has setscrew terminals for linking all neutral circuit wires to the neutral service wire.

Slimline circuit breakers require half as much space as standard single-pole breakers. Slimlines can be used in a crowded panel to make room for added circuits or a subpanel feeder breaker.

Service wire lugs: DO NOT TOUCH.

Grounding bus bar has terminals for linking circuit grounding wires to the main grounding conductor. In a main panel, the grounding bar is bonded to the neutral bus bar.

120-volt branch circuits

Subpanel feeder breaker is a double-pole circuit breaker, usually 30 to 50 amps in size. It is wired in the same way as a 120/240-volt circuit.

Two hot bus bars run through the center of the service panel, supplying power to the individual circuit breakers. Each carries 120 volts of power.

Grounding conductor connects the service panel equipment to metal grounding rods driven into the earth.

120/240-volt branch circuit

Before installing any new wiring, evaluate your electrical service to make sure it provides enough current to support both the existing wiring and any new circuits (pages 150 to 153). If your service does not provide enough power, have an electrician upgrade it to a higher amp rating. During the upgrade, the electrician will install a new circuit breaker panel with enough extra breaker slots for the new circuits you want to install.

Safety Warning:

Never touch any parts inside a circuit breaker panel until you have checked for power (page 214). Circuit breaker panels differ in appearance, depending on the manufacturer. Never begin work in a circuit breaker panel until you understand its layout and can identify the parts.

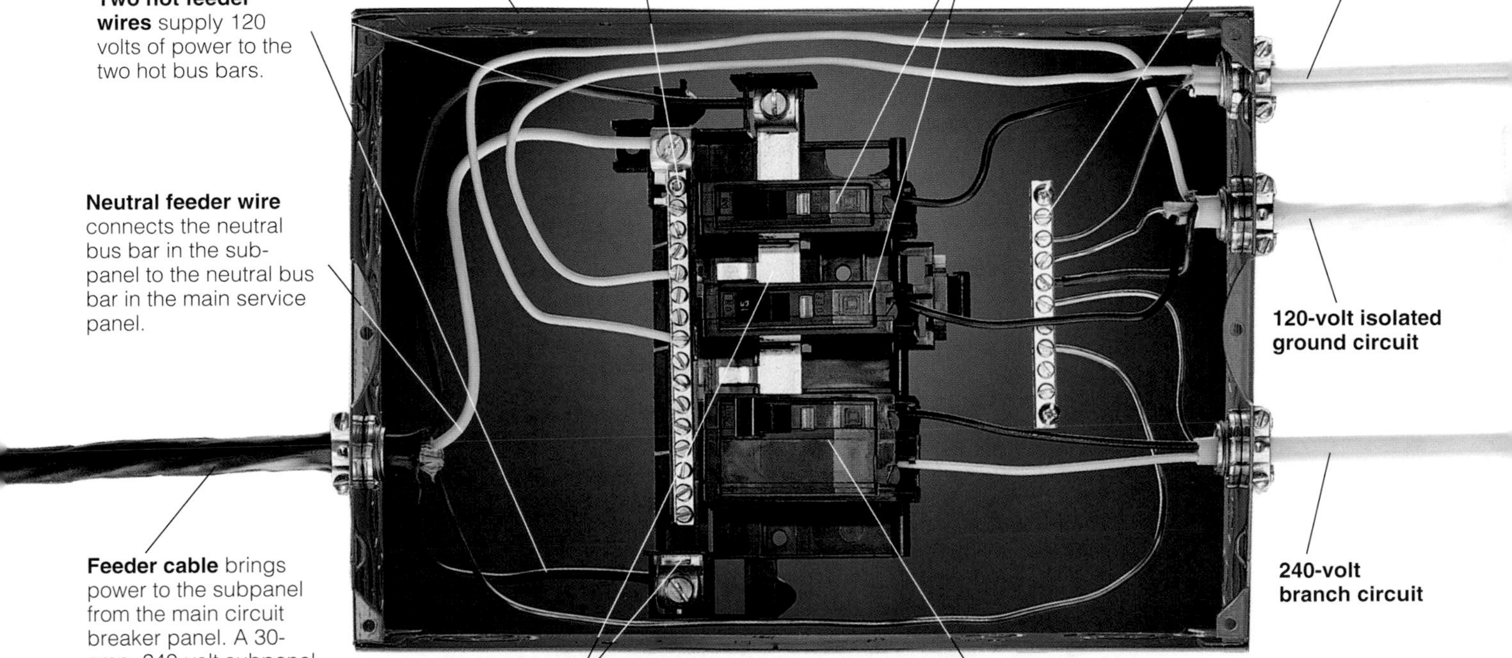

Circuit breaker subpanel can be installed when the main circuit breaker panel does not have enough space to hold circuit breakers for new circuits you want to install. (Some circuit breakers have been removed for clarity.)

Grounding bus bar has setscrew terminals for connecting circuit grounding wires. In a circuit breaker subpanel, the grounding bus bar is not bonded to the neutral bus bar.

Neutral bus bar has setscrew terminals for linking neutral circuit wires to the neutral feed wire leading back to the main circuit breaker panel.

Single-pole circuit breaker transfers 120 volts of power from one hot bus bar to the black hot wire in a 2-wire cable.

120-volt branch circuit

Two hot feeder wires supply 120 volts of power to the two hot bus bars.

Neutral feeder wire connects the neutral bus bar in the subpanel to the neutral bus bar in the main service panel.

120-volt isolated ground circuit

Feeder cable brings power to the subpanel from the main circuit breaker panel. A 30-amp, 240-volt subpanel requires a 10/3 feeder cable controlled by a 30-amp double-pole circuit breaker.

240-volt branch circuit

Two hot bus bars pass through the center of the service panel, supplying power to the individual circuit breakers. Each carries 120 volts of power.

Double-pole breaker wired for 240 volts transfers power from both hot bus bars to white and black hot wires in a 2-wire cable. A 240-volt circuit has no neutral wire connection; the white wire is tagged with black tape to identify it as a hot wire.

Test for current before touching any parts inside a circuit breaker panel. With main breaker turned off but all other breakers turned on, touch one probe of a neon tester to the neutral bus bar, and touch other probe to each setscrew on one of the double-pole breakers (not the main breaker). If tester does not light for either setscrew, it is safe to work in the panel.

Connecting Circuit Breakers

The last step in a wiring project is connecting circuits at the breaker panel. After this is done, the work is ready for the final inspection.

Circuits are connected at the main breaker panel, if it has enough open slots, or at a circuit breaker subpanel (pages 218 to 221). When working at a subpanel, make sure the feeder breaker at the main panel has been turned off, and test for power (photo, left) before touching any parts in the subpanel.

Make sure the circuit breaker amperage does not exceed the "ampacity" of the circuit wires you are connecting to it (page 191). Also be aware that circuit breaker styles and installation techniques vary according to manufacturer. Use breakers designed for your type of panel.

Everything You Need

Tools: Screwdriver, hammer, pencil, combination tool, cable ripper, circuit tester, pliers.

Materials: Cable clamps, single- and double-pole circuit breakers.

How to Connect Circuit Breakers

1 Shut off the main circuit breaker in the main circuit breaker panel (if you are working in a subpanel, shut off the feeder breaker in the main panel). Remove the panel coverplate, taking care not to touch the parts inside the panel. Test for power (photo, top).

2 Open a knockout in the side of the circuit breaker panel, using a screwdriver and hammer. Attach a cable clamp to the knockout.

3 Hold cable across the front of the panel near the knockout, and mark sheathing about ½" inside the edge of the panel. Strip the cable from marked line to end, using a cable ripper. (There should be 18" to 24" of excess cable.) Insert the cable through the clamp and into the service panel, then tighten the clamp.

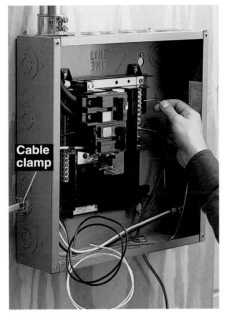

4 Bend the bare copper grounding wire around the inside edge of the panel to an open setscrew terminal on the grounding bus bar. Insert the wire into the opening on the bus bar, and tighten the setscrew. Fold excess wire around the inside edge of the panel.

5 For 120-volt circuits, bend the white circuit wire around the outside of the panel to an open setscrew terminal on the neutral bus bar. Clip away excess wire, then strip ½" of insulation from the wire, using a combination tool. Insert the wire into the terminal opening, and tighten the setscrew.

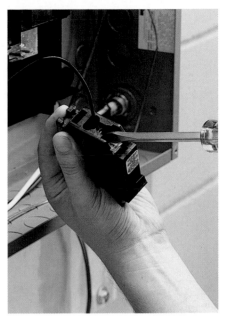

6 Strip ½" of insulation from the end of the black circuit wire. Insert the wire into the setscrew terminal on a new single-pole circuit breaker, and tighten the setscrew.

7 Slide one end of the circuit breaker onto the guide hook, then press it firmly against the bus bar until it snaps into place. (Breaker installation may vary, depending on the manufacturer.) Fold excess black wire around the inside edge of the panel.

8 **120/240-volt circuits (top):** Connect red and black wires to double-pole breaker. Connect white wire to neutral bus bar and grounding wire to grounding bus bar.
240-volt circuits (bottom): Attach white and black wires to double-pole breaker, tagging white wire with black tape. There is no neutral bus bar connection on this circuit.

9 Remove the appropriate breaker knockout on the panel cover-plate to make room for the new circuit breaker. A single-pole breaker requires one knockout, while a double-pole breaker requires two knockouts. Reattach the cover-plate, and label the new circuit on the panel index.

Connecting an AFCI or GFCI Breaker on an Existing Circuit

AFCI breakers (right) are similar in appearance to GFCI breakers (left), but they function differently. AFCI breakers trip when they sense an arc fault between the hot and neutral wires. GFCI breakers trip when they sense circuit overloads, short circuits, or a fault between the hot wire and the ground.

Everything You Need

Tools: Insulated screwdriver, circuit tester, combination tool.

Materials: AFCI or GFCI breaker.

Arc-Fault Circuit-Interrupter Breakers

Installing an arc-fault circuit interrupter (AFCI) breaker is an easy way to protect a circuit against a line-to-neutral electrical arc fault that, if uninterrupted, could cause a fire. AFCIs prevent electrical fires by sensing arcing and instantly disconnecting the damaged circuit before the arc builds enough heat to catch surrounding materials on fire.

The National Electric Code (NEC) requires that an arc-fault circuit-interrupter (AFCI) breaker be installed on all branch circuits that supply outlets or fixtures in bedrooms in newly constructed homes. They're a prudent precaution in any home, especially if it has older wiring. AFCI breakers will not interfere with the operation of GFCI receptacles, so it is safe to install an AFCI breaker on a circuit that contains GFCI receptacles.

Ground-Fault Circuit-Interrupter Breakers

A GFCI breaker is an important safety device that disconnects a circuit in the event of an overload, short circuit, or line-to-ground fault.

On new construction, GFCI protection is required on outlets located within a 6 ft. radius of laundry, utility, and kitchen or bathroom sinks and in garages and unfinished basements. In general it is a good practice to protect all receptacle and fixture locations that could encounter damp or wet circumstances. Typically, a GFCI receptacle is installed at each location, but in some cases—outdoor circuits or older homes with boxes too shallow for GFCI receptacles, for instance—it is advisable to protect the entire circuit with a GFCI breaker.

How to Install an AFCI or GFCI Breaker

1 Locate the breaker for the circuit you'd like to protect. Then, turn off the main circuit breaker. Remove the cover from the panel, and test to ensure that power is off (page 214). Remove the breaker you want to replace from the panel. Remove the black wire from the LOAD terminal of the breaker.

2 Find the white wire on the circuit you want to protect, and remove it from the neutral bus bar.

3 Flip the handle of the new AFCI or GFCI breaker to OFF. Loosen both of the breaker's terminal screws. Connect the white circuit wire to the breaker terminal labeled PANEL NEUTRAL. Connect the black circuit wire to the breaker terminal labeled LOAD POWER.

4 Connect the new breaker's coiled white wire to the neutral bus bar on the service panel.

5 Make sure all the connections are tight. Snap the new breaker into the bus bar.

6 Turn the main breaker to the ON position. Make sure all the fixtures and appliances on the AFCI or GFCI breaker circuit are off or unplugged. Turn the AFCI or GFCI breaker handle to the ON position. Press the test button to verify operation. If the breaker is wired correctly, the breaker will trip open. If the breaker does not trip, double-check all connections or consult a qualified electrician. Replace the panel cover.

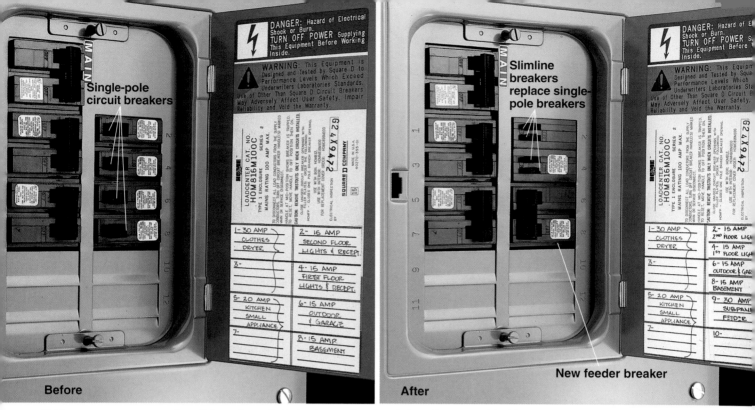

Before

After

Single-pole circuit breakers

Slimline breakers replace single-pole breakers

New feeder breaker

If there are no open circuit breaker slots in the main circuit breaker panel (left), you can make room for a sub-panel feeder breaker by replacing some of the single-pole breakers with slimline breakers (right). Slimline breakers take up half the space of standard breakers, allowing you to fit two circuits into one single slot on the service panel. In the service panel shown above, four single-pole 120-volt breakers were replaced with slimline breakers to provide the double opening needed for a 30-amp, 240-volt subpanel feeder breaker. Use slimline breakers with the same amp rating as the standard single-pole breakers you are removing, and make sure they are approved for use in your panel.

Installing a Subpanel

Install a circuit breaker subpanel if the main circuit breaker panel does not have enough open breaker slots for the new circuits you are planning. The subpanel serves as a second distribution center for connecting circuits. It receives power from a double-pole "feeder" circuit breaker you install in the main circuit breaker panel.

If the main service panel is so full that there is no room for the double-pole subpanel feeder breaker, you can reconnect some of the existing 120-volt circuits to special slimline breakers (photos, above).

Plan your subpanel installation carefully, making sure your electrical service supplies enough power to support the extra load of the new sub-panel circuits. Assuming your main service is adequate, consider installing an oversized subpanel feeder breaker in the main panel to provide enough extra amps to meet the needs of future wiring projects.

Also consider the physical size of the subpanel, and choose one that has enough extra slots to hold

circuits you may want to install later. The smallest panels have room for up to 6 single-pole breakers (or 3 double-pole breakers), while the largest models can hold up to 20 single-pole breakers.

Subpanels often are mounted near the main circuit breaker panel. Or, for convenience, they can be installed close to the areas they serve, such as in a new room addition or a garage. In a finished room, a subpanel can be painted or covered with a removable painting, bulletin board, or decorative cabinet to make it more attractive. If it is covered, make sure the subpanel is easily accessible and clearly identified.

Everything You Need

Tools: Hammer, screwdriver, circuit tester, cable ripper, combination tool.

Materials: Screws, cable clamps, 3-wire NM cable, cable staples, double-pole circuit breaker, circuit breaker subpanel, slimline circuit breakers.

How to Plan a Subpanel Installation (photocopy this work sheet as a guide; blue sample numbers will not reproduce)

1. Find the gross electrical load for only those areas that will be served by the subpanel. Refer to "Evaluate Electrical Loads" (steps 1 to 5, page 153). EXAMPLE: In the 400-sq. ft. attic room addition shown on pages 156 to 159, the gross load required for the basic lighting/receptacle circuits and electric heating is 5000 watts.	Gross electrical load:	_5000_ watts
2. Multiply the gross electrical load times 1.25. This safety adjustment is required by the National Electrical Code. EXAMPLE: In the attic room addition (gross load 5000 watts), the adjusted load equals 6250 watts.	_5,000_ watts × 1.25 =	_6,250_ watts
3. Convert the load into amps by dividing by 230. This gives the required amperage needed to power the subpanel. EXAMPLE: The attic room addition described above requires about 27 amps of power (6250 ÷ 230).	_6,250_ watts ÷ 230 =	_27.2_ amps
4. For the subpanel feeder breaker, choose a double-pole circuit breaker with an amp rating equal to or greater than the required subpanel amperage. EXAMPLE: In a room addition that requires 27 amps, choose a 30-amp double-pole feeder breaker.	☒ 30-amp breaker ☐ 40-amp breaker ☐ 50-amp breaker	
5. For the feeder cable bringing power from the main circuit breaker panel to the subpanel, choose 3-wire NM cable with an ampacity equal to the rating of the subpanel feeder breaker (page 191). EXAMPLE: For a 40-amp subpanel feeder breaker, choose 8/3 cable for the feeder.	☒ 10/3 cable ☐ 8/3 cable ☐ 6/3 cable	

How to Install a Subpanel

1 Mount the subpanel at shoulder height, following manufacturer's recommendations. The subpanel can be mounted to the sides of studs or to plywood attached between two studs. Panel shown here extends ½" past the face of studs so it will be flush with the finished wall surface.

2 Open a knockout in the subpanel, using a screwdriver and hammer. Run the feeder cable from the main circuit breaker panel to the subpanel, leaving about 2 ft. of excess cable at each end. See pages 197 to 201 if you need to run the cable through finished walls.

3 Attach a cable clamp to the knockout in the subpanel. Insert the cable into the subpanel, then anchor it to framing members within 8" of each panel, and every 4 ft. thereafter.

(continued next page)

How to Install a Subpanel (continued)

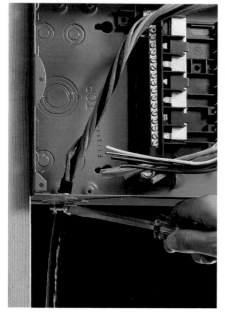

4 Strip away outer sheathing from the feeder cable, using a cable ripper. Leave at least ¼" of sheathing extending into the subpanel. Tighten the cable clamp screws so cable is held securely, but not so tightly that the wire sheathing is crushed.

5 Strip ½" of insulation from the white neutral feeder wire, and attach it to the main lug on the subpanel neutral bus bar. Connect the grounding wire to a setscrew terminal on the grounding bus bar. Fold excess wire around the inside edge of the subpanel.

6 Strip away ½" of insulation from the red and black feeder wires. Attach one wire to the main lug on each of the hot bus bars. Fold excess wire around the inside edge of the subpanel.

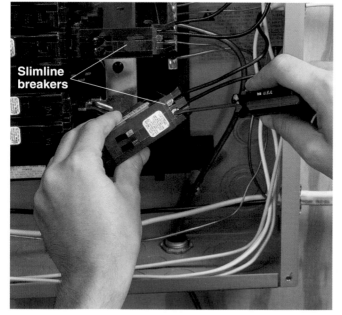

7 At the main circuit breaker panel, shut off the main circuit breaker, then remove the coverplate and test for power (page 214). If necessary, make room for the double-pole feeder breaker by removing single-pole breakers and reconnecting the wires to slimline circuit breakers. Open a knockout for the feeder cable, using a hammer and screwdriver.

8 Strip away the outer sheathing from the feeder cable so that at least ¼" of sheathing will reach into the main service panel. Attach a cable clamp to the cable, then insert the cable into the knockout, and anchor it by threading a locknut onto the clamp. Tighten the locknut by driving a screwdriver against the lugs. Tighten the clamp screws so cable is held securely, but not so tightly that the cable sheathing is crushed.

9 Bend the bare copper wire from the feeder cable around the inside edge of the main circuit breaker panel, and connect it to one of the setscrew terminals on the grounding bus bar.

10 Strip away ½" of insulation from the white feeder wire. Attach the wire to one of the setscrew terminals on the neutral bus bar. Fold excess wire around the inside edge of the service panel.

11 Strip ½" of insulation from the red and black feeder wires. Attach one wire to each of the setscrew terminals on the double-pole feeder breaker.

12 Hook the end of the feeder circuit breaker over the guide hooks on the panel, then push the other end forward until the breaker snaps onto the hot bus bars (follow manufacturer's directions). Fold excess wire around the inside edge of the circuit breaker panel.

13 If necessary, open two knockouts where the double-pole feeder breaker will fit, then reattach the coverplate. Label the feeder breaker on the circuit index. Turn main breaker on, but leave feeder breaker off until all subpanel circuits have been connected and inspected.

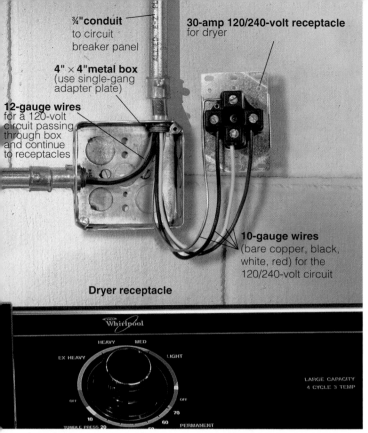

¾"conduit
to circuit
breaker panel

4" × 4" metal box
(use single-gang
adapter plate)

12-gauge wires
for a 120-volt
circuit passing
through box
and continue
to receptacles

30-amp 120/240-volt receptacle
for dryer

10-gauge wires
(bare copper, black,
white, red) for the
120/240-volt circuit

Dryer receptacle

A **240-volt installation** is no more complicated than wiring a single-pole breaker and outlet. The main difference is that the dryer circuit's double-pole breaker is designed to contact both 120-volt bus bars in the service panel. Together, these two 120-volt circuits serve the dryer's heating elements with 240 volts of power. The timer, switches, and other dryer electronics utilize the circuit's 120-volt power.

Installing a 120/240-Volt Dryer Receptacle

Many dryers require both 120- and 240-volt power. If you are installing this type of electric dryer, you will need to install a 30-amp, 120/240-volt receptacle that feeds from a dedicated 30-amp double-pole breaker in your service panel. Verify your dryer's electric requirements before wiring a new receptacle.

Begin the installation by identifying a location for the dryer receptacle. Run 10/3 NM cable from the service panel to the new receptacle. If you are mounting the dryer receptacle box on an unfinished masonry wall, run the cable in conduit and secure the box and conduit with masonry screws. If you are mounting the receptacle box in finished drywall, cut a hole, fish the cable through, and mount the receptacle in the wall opening.

Everything You Need

Tools: Combination tool, drill, circuit tester, hammer, screwdriver.

Materials: 30-amp double-pole breaker, 30-amp 120/240-volt dryer receptacle, 10/3 NM cable or 10-gauge THHN/THWN, receptacle box, conduit (for masonry walls).

How to Install a 120/240-Volt Dryer Receptacle

1 Connect the white neutral wire to the silver neutral screw terminal. Connect each of the black and red wires to either of the brass screw terminals (the terminals are interchangeable). Connect the bare copper ground wire to the receptacle grounding screw. Attach the coverplate.

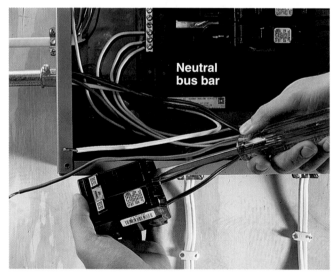

Neutral bus bar

2 With the service panel main breaker shut off, connect the dryer cable to a dedicated 30-amp double-pole breaker. Connect the ground wire to the panel grounding bar. Connect the white neutral wire to the neutral bar. Connect the red and black wires to the two brass screw terminals on the breaker. Snap the breaker into the bus bar. Attach the panel cover. Turn the breakers on and test the circuit.

Installing a 120/240-Volt Kitchen Range Receptacle

Many electric ranges require both 120- and 240-volt power. If you are installing this type of electric range, you will need to install a 50- or 60-amp 120/240-volt receptacle that feeds from a dedicated 50- or 60-amp breaker in the service panel. Breaker amperage depends on the amount of power the range draws. Verify requirements before wiring a receptacle.

A range receptacle and breaker installation is no more complicated than wiring a single-pole breaker and outlet. The main difference is that the range circuit's double-pole breaker is designed to contact both 120-volt bus bars in the service panel. Together these two 120-volt circuits serve the range's heating elements with 240 volts of power. The timer, switches, and other range electronics utilize the circuit's 120-volt power.

Modern range receptacles accept a four-prong plug configuration. The cable required is four-conductor service entrance round (SER) cable, containing three insulated wires and one ground. The two hot wires might be black and red (shown below) or black and black with a red stripe. The neutral wire is generally white or gray. The grounding wire is green or bare. The size used for a kitchen range is usually 6/3 grounded SER copper cable. The receptacle itself is generally surface mounted for easier installation (shown below), though flush-mount units are also available.

Everything You Need

Tools: Combination tool, circuit tester, drill, hammer, screwdriver, drywall saw, fish tape.

Materials: Surface-mount range receptacle, 6/3 grounded SER cable, 50- or 60-amp double-pole circuit breaker.

How to Install a Kitchen Range Receptacle

1 Identify a location for the surface-mount range receptacle. Cut a small hole in the wall. Fish the SER cable from the service panel into the wall opening. Thread the cable into a surface-mount receptacle and clamp it. Strip insulation from the individual wires.

2 Wire the receptacle. Connect the bare copper ground wire to the receptacle grounding screw. Connect the white neutral wire to the silver neutral screw terminal. Connect each of the hot (black and red) wires to either of the brass screw terminals (the terminals are interchangeable). Mount the housing on the wall and attach the coverplate.

3 Wire the SER cable to a 50- or 60-amp breaker. With the main breaker off, remove the panel cover. Remove a knockout from the panel and feed the cable into the panel. Connect the ground to the grounding bar. Connect the neutral wire from the cable to the neutral bar. Connect the red and black wires to the two brass screw terminals on the breaker. Snap it into the bus bar. Attach the panel cover. Turn the breakers on and test the circuit.

Installing an Isolated-ground Receptacle

An isolated-ground circuit is simply a receptacle wired so that it does not share a common grounding path with the rest of the electrical system. The wire connected to the grounding screw on the isolated-ground receptacle leads directly back to the grounding bar at the panel. The receptacle (typically orange in color) is isolated such that it does not ground through the box itself, so it is imperative that the isolated grounding wire be properly connected.

An isolated-ground circuit provides protection beyond standard surge suppression for computer equipment, and it also significantly reduces the potential for electromagnetic "noise" from the common grounding path. This noise may interfere with the proper function of sensitive audio and video equipment by causing an audible hum or poor picture quality. If you have a high-end home theater, isolated-ground receptacles are a good idea to ensure maximum picture and sound quality.

Typically, to install an isolated-ground receptacle, a new circuit is run from a 15-amp breaker (see circuit map 16, page 172). To create an isolated grounding path, the circuit is wired with three-wire cable. The bare grounding wire terminates at the box's grounding screw, and the red wire (coded green at its end) provides the dedicated path back to the panel's grounding or neutral bar.

Everything You Need

Tools: Hammer, screwdriver, fish tape, circuit tester, stud finder, combination tool.

Materials: 14/3 NM cable, isolated-ground receptacle, single-pole breaker.

How to Replace an Existing Receptacle with an Isolated-Ground Receptacle

Isolated-ground receptacles provide extra protection for computers and isolate audio-video equipment from interference-causing electrical noise.

1 Turn off the power to the old receptacle at the service panel. Remove the cover and test that power is off. If the receptacle is at the end of a run, disconnect it and trace the cable back to the next box in the circuit. Disconnect the cable between the old receptacle and the upstream device and remove the cable. If the box is in the middle of the run (as shown), disconnect the receptacle, and join the circuit wires so they pass uninterrupted through the box. Push the connectors to the back of the box. (You may need to install a deeper box; pages 40 to 41.)

2 Run 14/3 NM cable for the new circuit from the service panel to the receptacle box. Leave 10" of cable at the receptacle end. Clamp the cable in the box. Strip sheathing and insulation from the cable. Ground the bare copper wire to the grounding screw on the box.

3 Code the red wire with green tape and connect it to the grounding screw on the isolated-ground receptacle. Connect the white wire to the silver neutral terminal on the receptacle, and connect the black wire to the brass hot terminal. Push the wires into the box and attach the receptacle to the box. Install the coverplate.

4 At the service panel, switch off the main breaker. Remove the cover. Test that the power is off by touching one probe of a tester to the neutral bar and the other probe to each breaker's setscrew. Remove a knockout from the side of the panel and thread the end of the 14/3 NM into the panel. Secure it with a clamp.

Isolated ground wire

5 Connect the white wire from the cable to the neutral bar. Connect the bare copper wire to the grounding bar. Connect the red wire (coded green on the end) to the grounding bar or neutral bar (shown), whichever is the shortest path. Connect the black wire to a new 15-amp breaker (GFCI breaker shown; pages 214 to 215). Snap the breaker into an open space on the panel. Restore power and test the circuit. Replace the panel cover.

Replacing a basic ceiling-mounted fixture with a chandelier is usually only a matter of installing an adequately braced box.

Installing Ceiling-mounted Light Fixtures

Installing a chandelier or ceiling mounted globe is simple in new construction and not much more difficult in a retrofit or replacement installation.

With hanging fixtures, the main consideration is making sure the box is adequately braced to support the fixture's weight. This is particularly critical if you plan to replace a globe-style fixture with a chandelier. If you have access to the ceiling from above, you can install a new chandelier-approved box and brace it with 2 × 4 blocking. If the ceiling is enclosed, use an adjustable remodeling brace, as shown on 227.

Everything You Need

Tools: Circuit tester, cable ripper, combination tool, pliers, fish tape.

Materials: Hanging fixture, specified electrical box and bracing.

How to Install a Ceiling-mounted Fixture

1 If you are replacing an old fixture with a chandelier, begin by removing the existing fixture. Shut off the power at the service panel. Detach the old fixture from its box. Test to make sure the power is off. Disconnect the old fixture base by unscrewing the wire connectors.

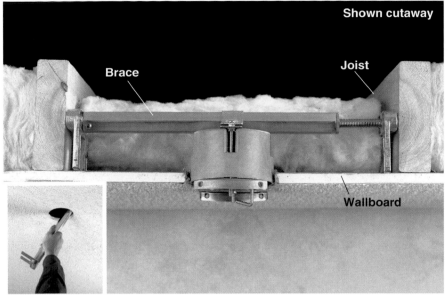

Brace

Joist

Wallboard

Shown cutaway

2 If the new fixture is much heavier than the original fixture, it will require additional bracing in the ceiling to support the electrical box and the fixture. The manufacturer's instructions should specify the size and type of box. If the ceiling is finished and there is no access from above, you can remove the old box and use an adjustable remodeling brace appropriate for your fixture (shown). The brace fits into a small hole in the ceiling (inset). Once the bracing is in place, install a new electrical box specified for the new fixture.

3 Adjust the length of the fixture's hanging support before wiring or attaching the base. Most chandeliers have chains with removable links. Some pendant fixtures use a plastic tube to make the pendant hang straight down. Test the fixture's height before making the chain length permanent. Cut the power cord a foot longer than the chain so you will have enough wire to make connections.

4 Attach the cross brace to the electrical box with screws. Thread the fixture mounting ring onto the threaded tube in the center of the cross brace. Close the top link of the hanging chain around the mounting ring.

5 Weave the cord from the fixture through the chain and push it through the threaded tube and into the box. Separate the two wires and strip ¾" of insulation from the ends. Connect the white circuit wire to the neutral cord wire. (The neutral cord wire will have ridges along its length or a colored stripe.) Connect the black circuit wire to the hot cord wire. Attach the ground circuit wire to the grounding wire from the fixture.

227

Recessed light cans come in a wide range of sizes and styles. Generally, fixtures can be purchased for new construction (A) or for retrofit installation (B) in a variety of sizes. Trim pieces are available for various can sizes in different colors and lens shapes (C). Fixtures are also available for recessed cabinet lights (D)

Installing Recessed Light Fixtures

Recessed lights are versatile fixtures, suited for a variety of situations. Fixtures rated for outdoor use can also be installed in roof soffits and overhangs for accent and security lighting. Recessed fixtures can also be installed over showers or tubs. Be sure to use fixture cans and trims rated for bathroom use.

There are recessed lighting cans in all shapes and sizes for almost every type of ceiling or cabinet. Cans are sold for unfinished ceilings (new construction) or for finished ceilings (retrofit installation). Cans are also rated as insulation compatible or for uninsulated ceilings. Be sure to use the correct one for your ceiling to prevent creating a fire hazard.

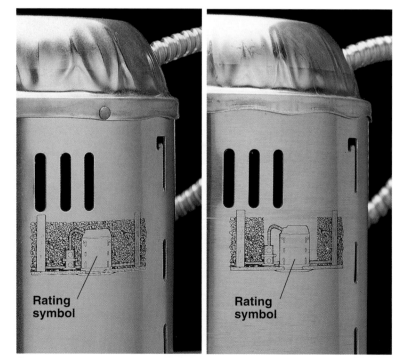

Choose the proper type of recessed light fixture for your project. There are two types of fixtures: those rated for installation within insulation (left), and those which must be kept at least 3" from insulation (right). Self-contained thermal switches shut off power if the unit gets too hot for its rating. A recessed light fixture must be installed at least ½" from combustible materials.

Everything You Need

Tools: Circuit tester, cable ripper, combination tool, pliers, fish tape, drywall saw.

Materials: Recessed-lighting can for new construction or remodeling and trim, NM cable.

How to Connect a Recessed Fixture Can in an Unfinished Ceiling

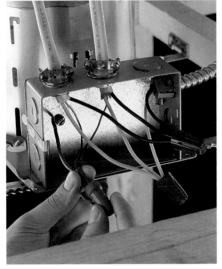

1 Extend the mounting bars on the recessed fixture to reach the framing members. Adjust the position of the light unit on the mounting bars to locate it properly. Align the bottom edges of the mounting bars with the bottom face of the framing members. Nail or screw the mounting bars to the framing members.

2 Remove the wire connection box cover and open one knockout for each cable entering the box. Install a cable clamp for each open knockout, and tighten locknut, using a screwdriver to drive the lugs. Run a 14/2 NM cable from the switch location to the fixture.

3 Make connections before installing wallboard. Connect white cable wires to white fixture lead. Connect black wires to black lead from fixture. Attach a grounding pigtail to the grounding screw on the fixture, then connect all grounding wires. Tuck wires into the junction box, and replace the cover.

How to Connect a Recessed Light Fixture in a Finished Ceiling

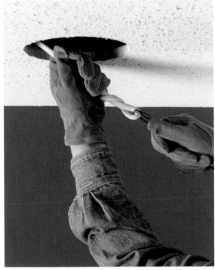

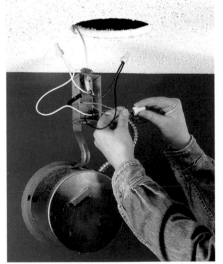

1 Make the hole for the can. Most fixtures will include a template for sizing the hole. Fish 14/2 cable from the switch location to the hole. Pull about 16" of cable out of the hole for making the connection.

2 Remove a knockout from the electrical box attached to the can. Thread the cable into the box; secure it with a cable clamp. Remove sheathing ansulation. Connect the black fixture wire to the black circuit wire, the white fixture wire to the white circuit wire, and then connect the ground wire to the grounding screw or grounding wire attached to the box.

3 Retrofit cans secure themselves in the hole with spring-loaded clips. Install the can in the ceiling by depressing the mounting clips so the can will fit into the hole. Insert the can so that its edge is tight to the ceiling. Push the mounting clips back out so they grip the drywall and hold the fixture in place. Install the trim piece.

229

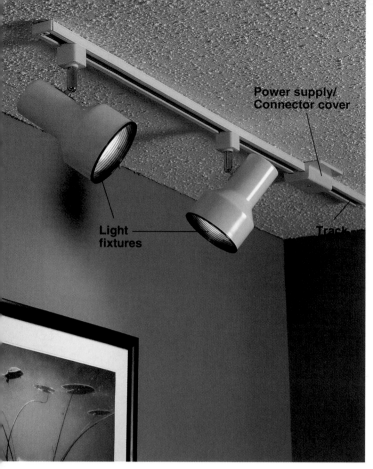

Power supply/
Connector cover

Light
fixtures

Track

Installing Track Lighting

Track lighting allows you to create custom indoor lighting at a small cost. Use it to highlight a wall, illuminate a sculpture, or brighten a dark corner; the possibilities and effects are limitless. Fixtures come in a variety of styles, which allows you to mix and match components to suit your needs.

Installing track lighting in new construction is straightforward. Run cable for the circuit and install a ceiling box before drywall is installed. It's also a good idea to map out the track locations and install blocking as necessary. It's also possible to install track on a finished ceiling. The easiest way to install it is to replace an existing ceiling fixture.

Since track lighting manufacturers and models vary, it is important to always follow product instructions.

Track light systems are easy to install. Most include spot lights for task and accent lighting.

Everything You Need

Tools: Circuit tester, drill, screwdrivers, straight-edge.

Materials: Toggle bolts, screws, track-lighting kit and additional fixtures or connectors as needed.

How to Install Track Lighting

In addition to traditional spot-light fixtures, most track systems also accept a variety of pendant-style fixtures.

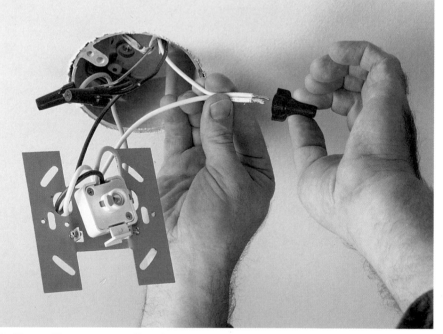

1 Turn off power to ceiling box outlet. Remove existing fixture and disconnect wires if you are replacing an existing fixture. Attach green grounding fixture wire to bare copper grounding wire, and pigtail to electrical box, if required. Attach the white circuit wire to white fixture wire. Then attach black circuit wire to black fixture wire. Carefully tuck wires into the box.

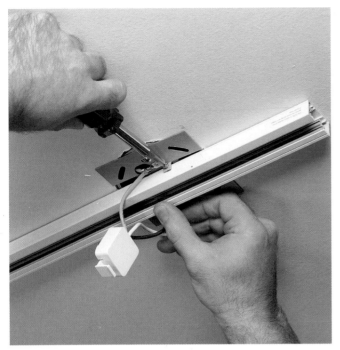

2 Mark the track location line from the power source to the end of the track. If possible, position tracks underneath ceiling joists for sturdy installation. Attach the mounting plate to ceiling box. Snap the first track onto the mounting plate and position track. Fasten track loosely with screws (or toggle bolts, if fastening to ceiling drywall).

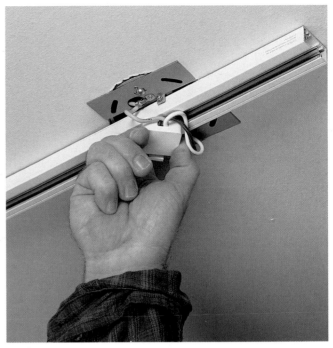

3 Insert the connector into the track, and twist into position (connector installation may vary according to manufacturer). Attach power supply/connector cover. Continue inserting connectors and attaching connector covers to each track section, using the L-connector for corners and the T-connector to join three tracks.

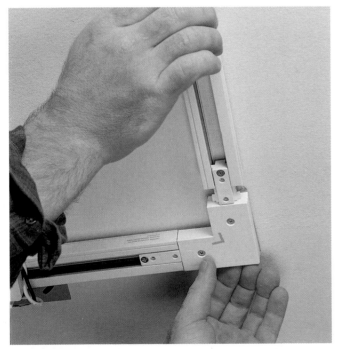

4 Hold each track section in place and mark screw or toggle bolt hole locations on the ceiling. Remove track and drill holes. Install bolts in track and hang all units, waiting to tighten until all tracks are hung. After all tracks are installed, tighten screws or bolts until tracks are flush with ceiling. Close open ends with dead-end pieces.

5 Insert lighting fixtures into the track, and twist-lock into place. Install appropriate bulbs, and turn on power to ceiling box. Turn on power to the fixture at the wall switch, and adjust beams for the desired effect.

Installing Under-cabinet Lighting

Under-cabinet lights come in numerous styles, including mini-track lights, strip lights, halogen puck lights, flexible rope lights and fluorescent task lights.

In a remodel, run cable and install boxes for under-cabinet fixtures and a switch before drywall or cabinets are installed. It's also not difficult to add under-cabinet fixtures in a finished wall by tying in to an existing kitchen circuit. Kitchen circuits often support several devices; be sure the circuit's capacity is sufficient for the additional load.

Tools and Materials

Tools: Utility knife, drywall saw, hammer, screwdriver, drill and hole saw, jig saw, combination tool, circuit tester.

Materials: Under-cabinet lighting kit, NM cable, plastic switch box, switch.

How to Install Hardwired Under-cabinet Lighting in a Finished Wall

1 Shut off the power to the receptacle you plan to draw power from. Disconnect the receptacle from its wiring. Locate and mark the studs in the installation area. Mark and cut a channel to route the cable, using a utility knife. In order to ease repair of the drywall when finished, cut a 6"-wide channel in the center of the installation area.

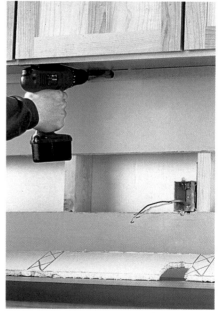

2 Drill holes through the cabinet edging and/or wall surface directly beneath the cabinets where the cable will enter each light fixture. Drill ⅝" holes through the studs to run the cable.

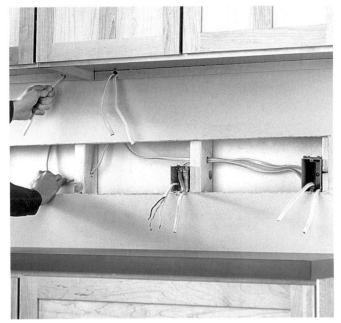

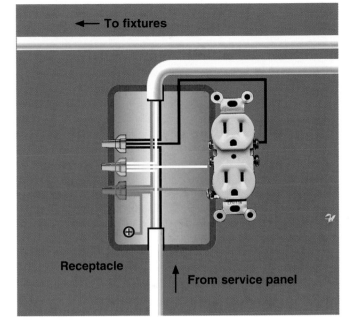

To fixtures ←

Receptacle

From service panel ↑

3 Install a switch box. Route a length of 12/2 cable from the switch location to the power-source receptacle. Route another cable from the switch to the first fixture hole. If you are installing more than one set of lights, route cables from the first fixture location to the second, and so on.

4 Clamp the cable into the receptacle box. Using wire connectors, pigtail the white wires to the silver terminal on the receptacle and the black wires to the brass terminal. Pigtail the grounding wires to the grounding screw in the electrical box. Tuck wiring into the electrical box and reattach the receptacle.

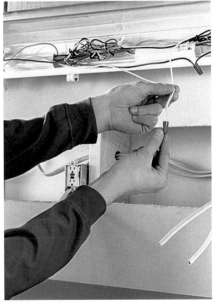

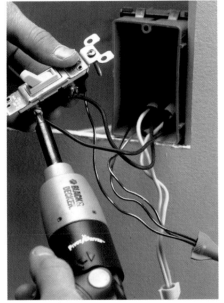

5 Remove the access cover, lens, and bulb from the light fixture. Open the knockouts for running cables into the fixture. Insert the cables into the knockouts and secure the clamps. Strip sheathing from the cables. Attach the light fixture to the bottom of the cabinet with screws.

6 Use wire connectors to join the black, white, and ground leads from the light fixture to each of the corresponding cable wires from the wall, including any cable leading to additional fixtures. Reattach the bulb, lens, and access cover to the fixture. Repeat this process for any additional fixtures.

7 Strip sheathing from each cable at the switch and clamp the cables into the switch box. Join the white wires together with wire connectors. Connect each black wire to a screw terminal on the switch. Pigtail the ground wires to the grounding screw on the switch. Install the switch and coverplate; restore power. Patch the drywall.

Low-voltage cable lights are low profile and easy to install, but they provide a surprising amount of light.

Installing Low-voltage Cable Lighting

This unique fixture system is a mainstay of retail and commercial lighting and is now becoming common in homes. Low-voltage cable systems use two parallel cables to suspend and provide electricity to fixtures mounted anywhere on the cables. A 12-volt transformer feeds low-voltage power to the cables.

The system's ease of installation, flexibility, and the wide variety of individual lights available make it perfect for all kinds of spaces. Low-voltage cable light systems are ideal for retrofits and for situations where surface-mounted track is undesirable or impossible to install.

Everything You Need

Tools: Combination tool, screwdriver, drill, fish tape.

Materials: Low-voltage cable light kit, electrical boxes, NM cable, switch.

How to Install Low-voltage Cable Lighting

1 Screw the cable hooks into the walls, spacing the hooks 6 to 10" apart. (Make sure the hooks hit wall framing or use wall anchors.) Cut the cable to the length of the span plus about 12" extra for connecting the cable to the hooks and turnbuckles. Make loops at the ends of both cables with the provided fasteners, and attach the cables. Adjust the turnbuckles until the cables are taut.

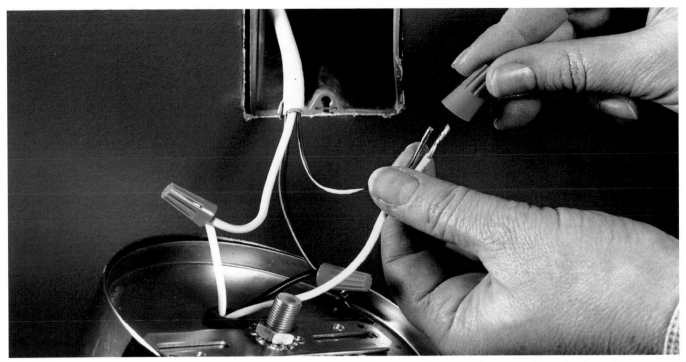

2 Turn off the power at the service panel. Remove the old fixture if you are replacing an existing fixture. If you are not replacing an old fixture, install a new electrical box for the power supply and route NM cable to it from a nearby receptacle. Thread the new cable into the box and secure it with a cable clamp. Remove sheathing and strip insulation from the ends of the wires. Install the mounting strap for the transformer onto the fixture box

with screws. Remove the cover from the transformer, and connect the black transformer wire to the black circuit wire. Connect the white transformer wire to the white circuit wire, and connect the ground transformer wire to the grounding wire. Attach the transformer to the wall, and replace the cover.

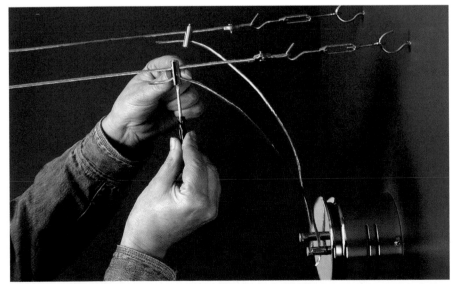

3 Connect the two low-voltage leads from the transformer to the parallel cables. The low-voltage leads carry the 12-volt current from the transformer to the parallel cables that supply the fixtures and can be connected at any point on the cable and can be cut to any length. Connect the leads to the cables using the screw-down connectors provided. (It doesn't matter which lead is connected to which cable.) Make sure the screw is tight enough that it pierces the insulation. Once the leads are attached, it's safe to restore the power. The 12-volt current is safe, and it's easier to adjust the lights when they're on.

4 Attach the fixtures with the connectors supplied by the manufacturers (fixtures connect in a variety of ways), and adjust the beams as necessary. Individual fixtures can be purchased at lighting stores, and you can generally mix and match manufacturers. Make sure you don't add more fixtures than the transformer can support.

Installing Vanity Lights

Many bathrooms have a single fixture positioned above the vanity, but a light source in this position casts shadows on the face and makes grooming more difficult. Light fixtures on either side of the mirror is a better arrangement.

For a remodel, mark the mirror location, run cable, and position boxes before drywall installation. You can also retrofit by installing new boxes and drawing power from the existing fixture.

The light sources should be at eye level; 66" is typical. The size of your mirror and its location on the wall may affect how far apart you can place the sconces, but 36" to 40" apart is a good guideline.

Vanity lights on the sides of the mirror provide the best light.

Everything You Need

Tools: Drywall saw, drill, combination tool, circuit tester, screwdrivers, hammer.

Materials: Electrical boxes and braces, wall sconces, NM cable, wire connectors.

How to Install Vanity Lights in a Finished Bathroom

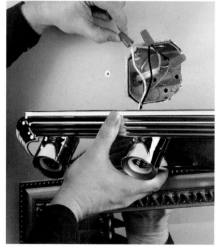

1 Turn off the power at the service panel. Remove the old fixture from the wall, and test to make sure that the power is off. Undo the connectors, and remove the old fixture. Then, remove a strip of drywall from around the old fixture to the first studs beyond the approximate location of the new sconces. Make the opening large enough that you have room to route cable from the existing fixture to the boxes for the sconces.

2 Mark the location for the sconces, and install new boxes. Install the boxes about 66" above the floor and 18 to 20" from the centerline of the mirror (the mounting base of some sconces is above or below the bulb, so adjust the height of the bracing accordingly). If the correct location is on or next to a stud, you can attach the box directly to the stud, otherwise you'll need to install blocking or use boxes with adjustable braces (shown).

3 Open the side knockouts on the electrical box above the vanity. Then, drill ⅝" holes in the centers of any studs between the old fixture and the new ones. Run two 14/2 NM cables from the new boxes for the sconces to the box above the vanity. Protect the cable with metal protector plates, and secure the new branch cables at both ends with cable clamps, leaving 11" of extra cable for making the connection to the old box and new sconces. Remove sheathing and strip insulation from the ends of the wires.

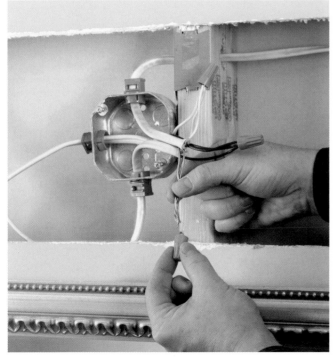

4 Connect the white wires from the new cables to the white wire from the old cable, and connect the black wires from the new cables to the black wire from the old cable. Connect the ground wires. Replace the drywall, leaving openings for the sconces and the old box. Cover the old box with a flat cover, or reconnect and reinstall the original above-mirror fixture after installing the new fixtures.

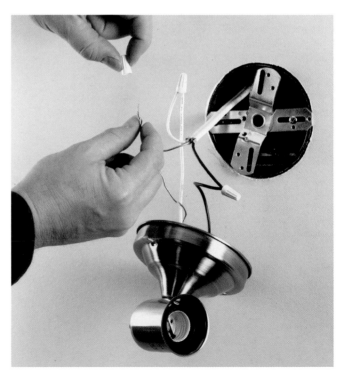

5 Install the fixture mounting braces on the boxes. Attach the fixtures by connecting the black circuit wire to the black fixture wire, and connecting the white circuit wire to the white fixture wire. Connect the ground wires. Position the fixture over the box, and attach with the mounting screws. Restore power and test the circuit.

237

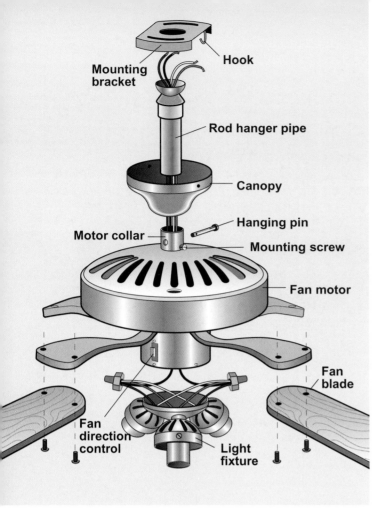

Mounting bracket

Hook

Rod hanger pipe

Canopy

Hanging pin

Motor collar

Mounting screw

Fan motor

Fan blade

Fan direction control

Light fixture

Installing Ceiling Fans

Ceiling fans are installed and wired like ceiling fixtures. They always require heavy-duty bracing and electrical boxes rated for ceiling fans.

Most standard ceiling fans work with a wall switch functioning as master power for the unit. Pull chains attached to the unit control the fan and lights. In these installations, it's fairly simple to replace an existing ceiling fixture with a fan and light.

If you will be installing a new circuit for the fan, use 3-wire cable so both the light and the motor can be controlled by wall switches (circuit maps 30 and 31, page 179).

Installation varies from fan to fan, so be sure to follow the manufacturer's instructions.

Tools and Materials

Tools: Screwdriver, combination tool, pliers or adjustable wrench, circuit tester, hammer.

Materials: Ceiling fan-light kit, 2 × 4 lumber or adjustable ceiling fan cross brace, 1½" and 3" wallboard screws.

How to Install a Ceiling Fan & Light

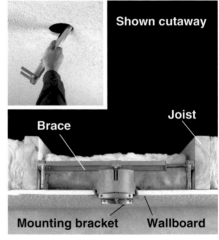

Shown cutaway

Brace

Joist

Mounting bracket

Wallboard

1 Shut off the power to the circuit at the service panel. Unscrew the existing fixture and carefully pull it away from the ceiling. Test for power by inserting the probes of a tester into the wire connectors on the black and white wires. Disconnect and remove the old fixture.

2 Determine whether the existing electrical box will support for the fan. From above, check to see that it is a metal, not plastic, box and that it has a heavy-duty cross brace rated for ceiling fans. If the box is not adequately braced, attach a 2 × 4 between the joists with 3" screws. Attach a metal electrical box to the brace from below with at least three 1½" drywall screws. Attach the fan mounting bracket to the box.

Variation: If the joists are inaccessible from above, remove the old box and install an adjustable ceiling fan brace through the rough opening in the ceiling (page 188). Insert the fan brace through the hole, adjust until it fits tightly between the joists, then attach the box with the included hardware. Make sure the lip of the box is flush with the ceiling wallboard before attaching the mounting bracket.

Rod hanger pipe   Canopy

3 Run the wires from the top of the fan motor through the canopy and then through the rod hanger pipe. Slide the rod hanger pipe through the canopy and attach the pipe to the motor collar using the included hanging pin. Tighten the mounting screws firmly.

Hanging pin

4 Hang the motor assembly by the hook on the mounting bracket. Connect the wires according to manufacturer's directions, using wire connectors to join the fixture wires to the circuit wires in the box. Gather the wires together and tuck them inside the fan canopy. Lift the canopy and attach it to the mounting bracket.

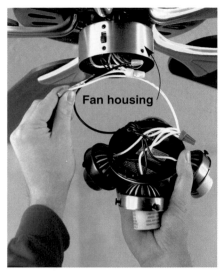

Fan housing

5 Attach the fan blades with the included hardware. Connect the wiring for the fan's light fixture according to the manufacturer's directions. Tuck all wires into the switch housing and attach the fixture. Install light bulbs. Restore power and test the fan.

Wires to fan motor and light

Remote-control receiver

Wires to circuit

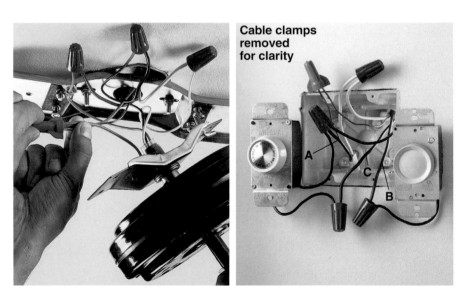

Cable clamps removed for clarity

A   C   B

Remote Control Variation: To install a remote control, fit the receiver inside the fan canopy. Follow the manufacturer's wiring diagram to wire the unit. The receiver has a set of three wires that connects to the corresponding wires from the fan motor and lights, and another set that connects to the two circuit wires from the electrical box.

Switch-controlled Fan Variation: Fans motors can also be controlled by a wall switch. This installation requires 3-wire cable from the ganged light switch and fan switch. To wire the fan (left), connect black circuit wire to black wire lead from fan, using a wire connector. Connect red circuit wire from dimmer to blue wire lead from light fixture, white circuit wire to white lead, and grounding wires to green lead. Complete assembly of fan and light fixture, following manufacturer's directions. (See also circuit maps 30 and 31, page 179.) To wire the switches (right), connect the black feed wire (A) to one of the black wire leads on each switch, using a wire connector. Connect the red circuit wire (B) running to the fan light fixture to the remaining wire lead on the dimmer switch. Connect the black circuit wire (C) running to the fan motor to the remaining wire lead on the speed-control switch. Use wire connectors to join the white wires and the grounding wires.

How to Wire a Food Disposer

1 Run a 12/2 NM cable from the service panel to the garbage disposal receptacle location under the sink. Clamp and run another 12/2 NM cable from the receptacle box to the location for the new switch (skip this step if you choose an air-activated switch). Install a switch box at the switch location, and secure the cable in the switch box. Connect a GFCI receptacle and switch.

2 Install an appliance cord on the disposer unit. Remove the coverplate from the bottom of the disposer. Connect the neutral wire from the cord to the neutral lead on the disposer. Connect the hot wire to the hot lead. Attach the grounding wire to the grounding screw. Replace the cover plate. Install the disposer on the sink and make the plumbing connections. At the service panel, with the main breaker off, install a new 15-amp breaker and connect the cable to new GFCI to the breaker. Restore power and test the disposer and GFCI.

Wiring Food Disposers

Installing a food disposer is useful kitchen upgrade and a relatively easy project. New installations will require a 120-volt single-pole switch that will control power to the disposal unit. This switch may be installed in the cabinet beneath the sink or in the wall above the cabinets. Air-activated sink-top switches are another option (see next page).

A food disposer must be plugged into a dedicated GFCI (ground-fault circuit-interrupter) receptacle or hardwired directly from the switch to the disposer unit. Many people prefer to plug the disposer into a receptacle, so that in case of malfunction, the disposer is easy to remove and replace. One of the most common installations is to install a GFCI outlet under the sink and a separate wall switch above a sink.

Code generally requires that a food disposer be installed on its own dedicated 15-amp circuit. Codes in some areas allow the disposal and dishwasher to share one circuit. Check with your inspector before beginning a disposer installation.

Everything You Need

Tools: Screwdriver, combination tool, fish tape, circuit tester.

Materials: Food disposer, electrical boxes, GFCI receptacle, switch, 12/2 NM cable, 15-amp breaker, appliance cord.

Installing an Air-activated Switch

An air-activated switch controls a food disposer from the sink with a puff of air rather than electrical current. The switch mounts easily in the standard holes found in most sinks. A power module that plugs into disposer outlet receives the puff of air from the switch and activates the disposer.

Because the switch does not require a hard-wired switch, it's ideal for a remodel or island installation. The switch offers increased safety, because there is no electricity near wet hands and fingers as they activate the switch.

Everything You Need

Tools: Drill, pliers.

Materials: Air-activated switch.

To turn the disposer on, press the switch down. This sends a puff of air down a thin plastic tube to a control unit that activates the disposer. To turn the disposer off, press the switch down again.

How To Install an Air-activated Switch to Control a Food Disposer

1 Mount the button in a standard sink accessory hole, or in the countertop by drilling a 1⅜" diameter hole. Place the supplied rubber gasket between the button and the top of the sink counter. Tighten the plastic nut under the counter to ensure a watertight seal.

2 Mount the switch's power module on a cabinet wall within three feet of the outlet and disposer using screws. Attach the air tube to the button and the power module.

3 Plug the power module cord into a dedicated GFCI receptacle. Plug the disposer into the power module. Press and release the button to test operation (disposer should turn on and off).

Installing a Vent Hood

A vent hood eliminates heat, moisture, and cooking vapors from your kitchen. It has an electric fan unit with one or more filters and a system of metal ducts to vent air to the outdoors. A ducted vent hood is more efficient than a ductless model, which filters and recirculates air without removing it.

Metal ducts for a vent hood can be round or rectangular. Elbows and transition fittings are available for both types of ducts. These fittings let you vent around corners, or join duct components that differ in shape or size.

Tools and Materials

Tools: Tape measure, screwdrivers, hammer, drill, reciprocating saw, combination tool, metal snips, masonry drill and masonry chisel (for brick or stucco exterior), circuit tester.

Materials: Duct sections, duct elbow, duct cap, vent hood, ¾", 1½", 2½" sheetmetal screws, 1¼" wallboard screws, silicone caulk, metallic duct tape, wire connectors, eye protection, pencil, 2" masonry nails (for brick or stucco exterior).

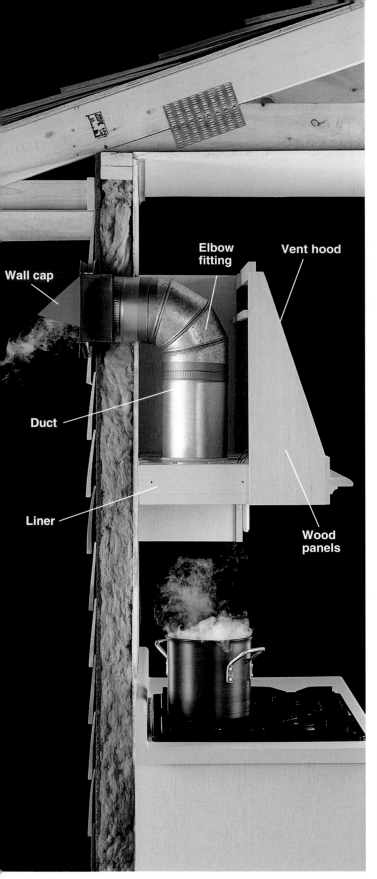

A wall-mounted vent hood (shown cutaway) is installed between wall cabinets. The fan unit is fastened to a metal liner that is anchored to cabinets. Duct and elbow fitting exhaust cooking vapors to the outdoors through a wall cap. The vent fan and duct are covered by wood or laminate panels that match the cabinet finish.

How to Install a Wall-mounted Vent Hood

1 Attach ¾" × 4" × 12" wooden cleats to sides of the cabinets with 1¼" wallboard screws. Follow manufacturer's directions for proper distance from cooking surface.

Liner

2 Position the hood liner between the cleats and attach with ¾" sheetmetal screws.

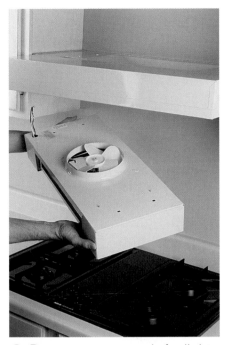

3 Remove cover panels for light, fan, and electrical compartments on fan unit, as directed by manufacturer. Position fan unit inside liner and fasten by attaching nuts to mounting bolts inside light compartments.

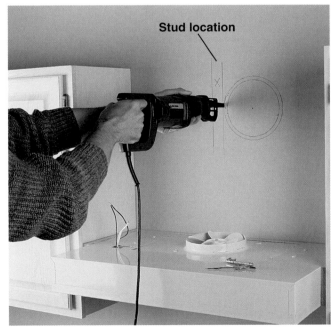

Stud location

4 Locate studs in wall where duct will pass, using a stud finder. Mark hole location. Hole should be ½" larger than diameter of duct. Complete cutout with a reciprocating saw or jig saw. Remove any wall insulation. Drill a pilot hole through outside wall.

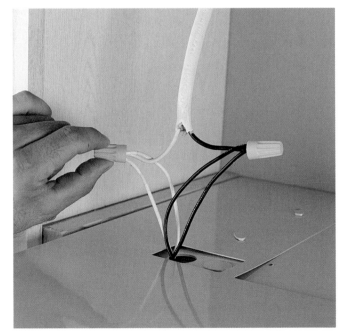

5 Run a cable (follow manufacturer's guidelines for wire gauge) from a dedicated breaker at the service panel or from a nearby receptacle. Connect the black wires from the fan and light to the black circuit wire. Connect all the white wires. Gently push the wires into the electrical box. Replace the cover panels on the light and fan compartments.

(continued next page)

6 Make duct cutout on exterior wall. On masonry, drill a series of holes around outline of cutout. Remove waste with a masonry chisel and ball-peen hammer. On wood siding, make cutout with a reciprocating saw.

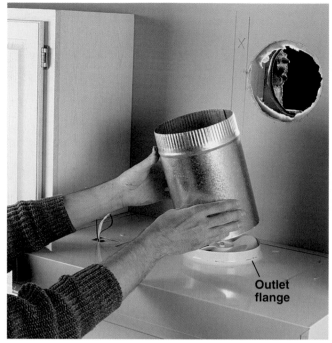

Outlet flange

7 Attach first duct section by sliding the smooth end over the outlet flange on the vent hood. Cut duct sections to length with metal snips.

8 Drill three or four pilot holes around joint through both layers of metal, using a ⅛" twist bit. Attach duct with ¾" sheetmetal screws. Seal joint with duct tape.

9 Join additional duct sections by sliding smooth end over corrugated end of preceding section. Use an adjustable elbow to change directions in duct run. Secure all joints with sheetmetal screws and duct tape.

10 Install duct cap on exterior wall. Apply a thick bead of silicone caulk to cap flange. Slide cap over end of duct.

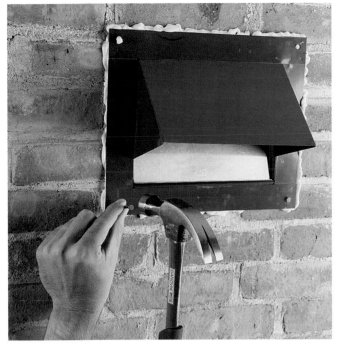

11 Attach cap to wall with 2" masonry nails, or 1½" sheetmetal screws (on wood siding). Wipe away excess caulk.

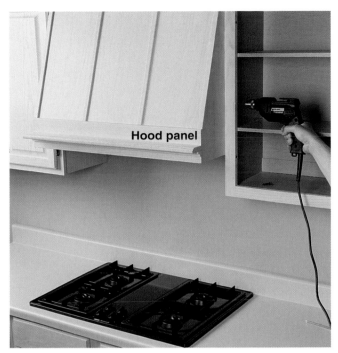

12 Slide the decorative hood panel into place between the wall cabinets. Drill pilot holes through the cabinet face frame with a counterbore bit. Attach the hood panel to the cabinets with 2½" sheetmetal screws.

Vent Hood Variations

Downdraft cooktop has a built-in blower unit that vents through the back of the bottom of a base cabinet. A downdraft cooktop is a good choice for a kitchen island or peninsula.

Cabinet-mounted vent hood is attached to the bottom of a short, 12"- to 18"-tall wall cabinet. Metal ducts run inside this wall cabinet.

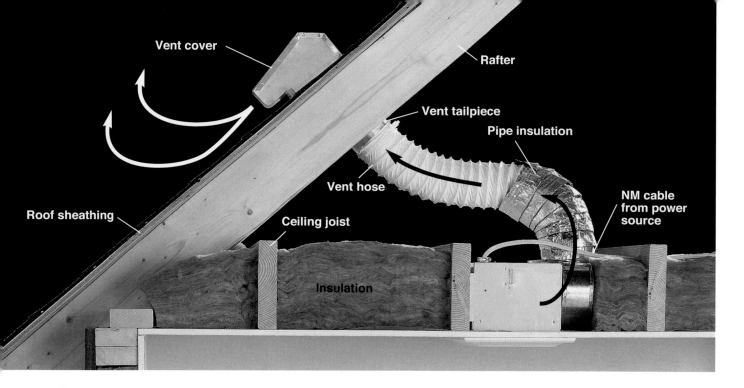

Vent cover · Rafter · Vent tailpiece · Pipe insulation · Vent hose · NM cable from power source · Roof sheathing · Ceiling joist · Insulation

Installing a Bathroom Vent Fan

Most building codes require a vent fan in any bathroom without natural ventilation. Even if you're not remodeling, retrofitting a fan is a good idea. Fans come as separate fan units, fan-light combinations, and fan-heat lamp combinations. Stand-alone fans and fans with a light fixture usually can be wired into a main bathroom electrical circuit, but units with built-in heat lamps require a separate circuit.

Most vent fans are installed in the center of the bathroom ceiling or over the toilet area. Do not install a fan over the tub or shower area unless the unit is GFCI-protected and rated for use in wet areas.

If the fan you choose doesn't come with a mounting kit, purchase one separately. A mounting kit should include a vent duct, a vent tailpiece, and an exterior vent cover.

Venting instructions vary among manufacturers, but the most common options are attic vented. Attic venting routes fan ductwork into the attic and out through the roof. Always insulate ducting in this application to keep condensation from forming and running down into the motor. And carefully install flashing around the outside vent cover to prevent roof leaks.

To prevent moisture damage, always terminate the vent outside your home—never into your attic or basement.

Consider installing a time-delay switch (page 50) to control the fan. This way, the fan will run long enough to exhaust moist air completely and then shut off automatically.

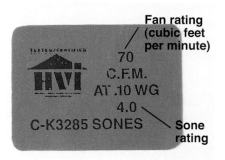

Fan rating (cubic feet per minute) · 70 C.F.M. AT .10 WG · 4.0 · C-K3285 SONES · Sone rating · TESTED/CERTIFIED · HVI

Check the information label attached to each vent fan unit. Choose a unit with a fan rating at least 5 CFM higher than the square footage of your bathroom. The *sone rating* refers to the relative quietness of the unit, rated on a scale of 1 to 7. (Quieter vent fans have lower sone ratings.)

Everything You Need

Tools: Drill, jig saw, combination tool, screwdrivers, caulk gun, reciprocating saw, pry bar.

Materials: Drywall screws, double-gang retrofit electrical box, NM cable, cable clamp, hose clamps, pipe insulation, roofing cement, self-sealing roofing nails, shingles, vent fan unit, wire connectors, switches.

How to Install a Bathroom Vent Fan

1 Position the vent fan unit against a ceiling joist. Outline the vent fan onto the ceiling surface. Remove the unit; then drill pilot holes at the corners of the outline and cut out the area with a jig saw or drywall saw.

2 Remove the grille from the fan unit, then position the unit against the joist, with the edge recessed ¼" from the finished surface of the ceiling (so the grille can be flush-mounted). Attach the unit to the joist, using drywall screws.

VARIATION: For vent fans with heaters or light fixtures, some manufacturers recommend using 2× lumber to build dams between the ceiling joists to keep the insulation at least 6" away from the fan unit.

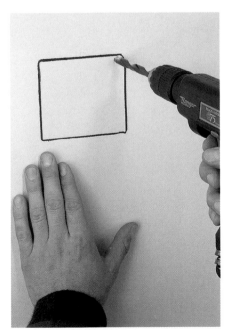

3 Shut of power to the bathroom at the main panel. Mark and cut an opening for the switch box on the wall next to the latch side of the bathroom door. Run a 3-wire NM cable from the switch cutout to the fan unit. Run a 2-wire NM cable from a nearby power source to the switch cutout.

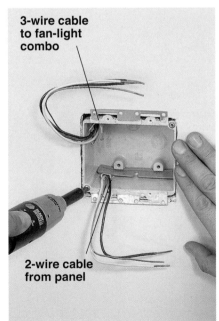

3-wire cable to fan-light combo

2-wire cable from panel

4 Feed the cables into a double-gang retrofit switch box. Clamp the cables in place. Tighten the mounting screws until the box is secure in the cutout.

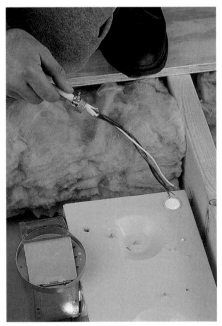

5 Strip sheathing from the end of the cable at the vent unit and clamp the cable in the fan unit.

(continued next page)

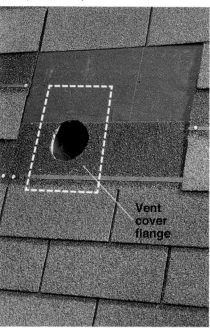

6 Mark the exit location in the roof for the vent hose, next to a rafter. Drill a pilot hole, then saw through the sheathing and roofing material with a reciprocating saw to make the cutout for the vent tailpiece.

7 Remove a section of shingles from around the cutout, leaving the roofing paper intact. Remove enough shingles to create an exposed area that is at least the size of the vent cover flange.

8 Attach a hose clamp to the rafter next to the roof cutout, about 1" below the roof sheathing (top). Insert the vent tailpiece into the cutout and through the hose clamp, then tighten the clamp screw (bottom).

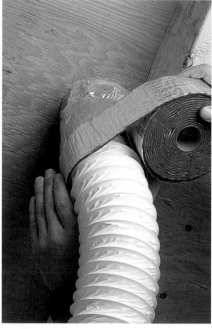

9 Slide one end of the vent hose over the tailpiece, and slide the other end over the outlet on the fan unit. Slip hose clamps or straps around each end of the vent hose, and tighten the clamps.

10 Wrap the vent hose with pipe insulation. Insulation prevents moist air inside the hose from condensing and dripping down into the fan motor.

11 Apply roofing cement to the bottom of the vent cover flange, then slide the vent cover over the tailpiece. Nail the vent cover flange in place with self-sealing roofing nails, then patch in shingles around the cover.

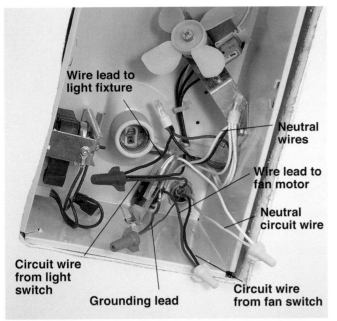

Wire lead to
light fixture

Neutral
wires

Wire lead to
fan motor

Neutral
circuit wire

Circuit wire
from light
switch

Grounding lead

Circuit wire
from fan switch

12 Make the wire connections at the fan unit. Connect the black circuit wire from the fan switch to the wire lead for the fan motor. Connect the red circuit wire from the light switch to the wire lead for the light fixture in the unit. Connect the white neutral circuit wire to the neutral wire lead and the circuit grounding wire to the grounding lead on the fan unit. Attach the coverplate.

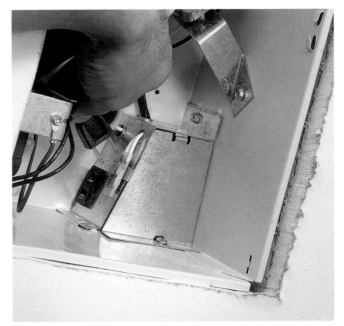

13 Connect the fan motor plug to the built-in receptacle on the wire connection box, and attach the fan grille to the frame, using the mounting clips included with the fan kit. NOTE: If you removed the wall and ceiling surfaces for the installation, install new surfaces before completing this step.

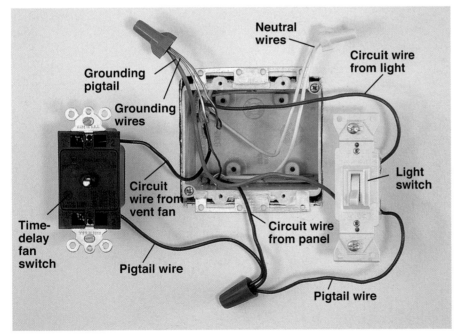

Neutral
wires

Grounding
pigtail

Grounding
wires

Circuit wire
from light

Circuit
wire from
vent fan

Circuit wire
from panel

Time-
delay
fan
switch

Light
switch

Pigtail wire

Pigtail wire

14 At the switch box, connect the black circuit wire from the panel to one terminal on the light switch and one terminal on the fan switch (time-delay switch shown) with two pigtail wires. On the 3-wire cable from the vent unit, connect the black circuit wire from the fan to the fan switch's other terminal.Connect the red wire lead from the fan light to the other terminal on the light switch. Connect the two neutral wires. Connect the grounding wires and pigtail them to the box's grounding screw.

15 Tuck the wires into the switch box, then attach the switch and timer to the box. Attach the coverplate and timer dial. Turn on the power and test the fan and light.

Installing a Floor-warming System

Floor-warming systems require very little energy to run and are designed to heat ceramic tile floors only; they generally are not used as sole heat sources for rooms.

A typical floor-warming system consists of one or more thin mats containing electric resistance wires that heat up when energized, like an electric blanket. The mats are installed beneath the tile and are hardwired to a 120-volt GFCI circuit. A thermostat controls the temperature, and a timer turns the system off automatically.

The system shown in this project includes two plastic mesh mats, each with its own power lead that is wired directly to the thermostat. The mats are laid over a concrete floor and then covered with thin-set adhesive and ceramic tile. If you have a wood subfloor, install cementboard before laying the mats.

A crucial part of installing this system is to use a multimeter to perform several resistance checks to make sure the heating wires have not been damaged during shipping or installation.

Electrical service required for a floor-warming system is based on size. A smaller system may connect to an existing GFCI circuit, but a larger one will need a dedicated circuit; follow the manufacturer's requirements.

To order a floor-warming system, contact the manufacturer or dealer. In most cases, you can send them plans and they'll custom-fit a system for your project area.

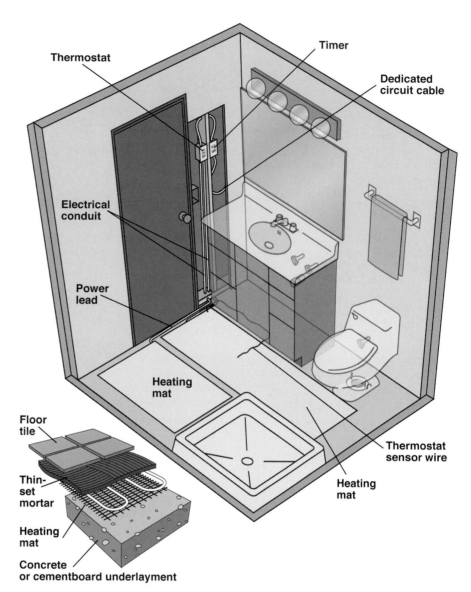

Thermostat · Timer · Dedicated circuit cable · Electrical conduit · Power lead · Floor tile · Thin-set mortar · Heating mat · Concrete or cementboard underlayment · Heating mat · Heating mat · Thermostat sensor wire

Everything You Need

Tools: Multimeter, drill, plumb bob, chisel, tubing cutter, combination tool, vacuum, chalk line, grinder, hot-glue gun, fish tape.

Materials: Floor-warming system, 2½" × 4" double-gang electrical box, single-gang electrical box, ½"-dia. thin-wall conduit, setscrew fittings, 12/2 NM cable, cable clamps, double-sided tape, electrical tape, insulated cable clamps, wire connectors.

Floor-warming systems must be installed on a circuit with adequate amperage and a GFCI breaker (pages 216 to 217). Smaller systems may tie into an existing circuit but larger ones need a dedicated circuit. Follow local building and electrical codes that apply to your project.

How to Install a Floor-warming System

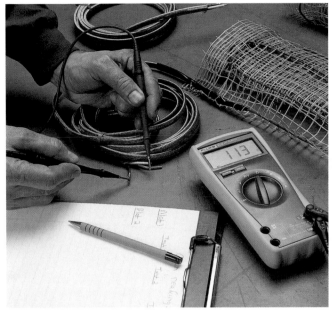

1 Check the resistance value (ohms) of each heating mat, using a digital multimeter. Record the reading. Compare your reading to the factory-tested reading noted by the manufacturer—your reading must fall within the acceptable range determined by the manufacturer. If it does not, the mat has been damaged and should not be installed; contact the manufacturer for assistance.

2 Install boxes for the thermostat and timer at an accessible location. Remove the wall surface to expose the framing, then locate the boxes approximately 60" from the floor, making sure the power leads of the heating mats will reach the double-gang box. Mount a 2½"-deep × 4"-wide double-gang box (for the thermostat) to the stud closest to the determined location, and a single-gang box (for the timer) on the other side of the stud.

3 Use a plumb bob to mark points on the bottom plate directly below the two knockouts on the thermostat box. At each mark, drill a ½" hole through the top of the plate, then drill two more holes as close as possible to the floor through the side of the plate, intersecting the top holes. (The holes will be used to route the power leads and thermostat sensor wire.) Clean up the holes with a chisel to ensure smooth routing.

Setscrew fittings

4 Cut two lengths of ½" thin-wall electrical conduit to fit between the thermostat box and the bottom plate. Place the bottom end of each length of conduit about ¼" into the holes in the bottom plate, and fasten the top end to the thermostat box, using a setscrew fitting. NOTE: If you are installing three or more mats, use ¾" conduit instead of ½".

(continued next page)

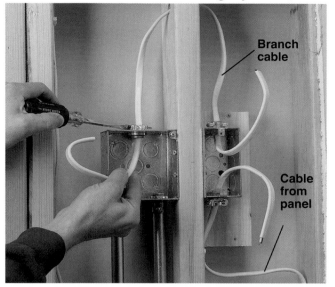

Branch cable

Cable from panel

5 Run 12/2 NM electrical cable from the panel to the timer box. Attach the cable to the box with a clamp. Drill a ⅝" hole through the center of the stud, about 12" above the boxes. Run a short branch cable from the timer box to the thermostat box, securing both ends with clamps. The branch cable should make a smooth curve where it passes through the stud. Protect the hole with a metal protector plate.

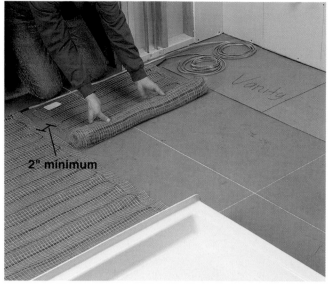

2" minimum

6 Vacuum the floor thoroughly. Plan the ceramic tile layout and snap reference lines for the tile installation. Spread the heating mats onto the floor with the power leads closest to the electrical boxes. Position the mats 3" to 6" away from walls, showers, bathtubs, and toilet flanges. You can lay the mats into the kick space of a vanity but not under the vanity cabinet or over expansion joints in the concrete slab. Set the edges of the mats close together, but do not overlap them: The heating wires in one mat must be at least 2" from the wires in the neighboring mat.

7 Confirm that the power leads still reach the thermostat box. Then, secure the mats to the floor using strips of double-sided tape spaced every 24". Make sure the mats are lying flat with no wrinkles or ripples. Press down firmly to secure the mats to the tape.

8 Create recesses in the floor for the connections between the power leads and the heating-mat wires, using a grinder or a cold chisel and hammer. These insulated connections are too thick to lay under the tile and must be recessed to within ⅛" of the floor. Clean away any debris, and secure the connections in the recesses with a bead of hot glue.

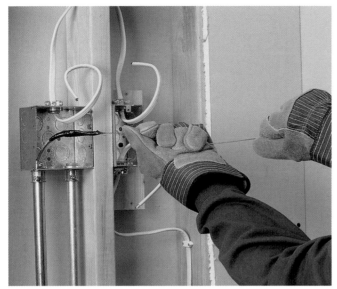

9 Thread a fish tape down one of the conduits, and attach the ends of the power leads to the fish tape, using electrical tape. Fish the leads up through the conduit. Secure the leads to the box with insulated cable clamps. Cut off the excess from the leads, leaving 8" extending from the clamps.

10 Feed the heat sensor wire down through the remaining conduit and weave it into the mesh of the nearest mat. Use dabs of hot glue to secure the sensor wire directly between two blue resistance wires, extending it 6" to 12" into the mat. Test the resistance of the heating mats with a multimeter (step 1, page 251) to make sure the resistance wires have not been damaged. Record the reading.

11 Install the ceramic floor tile. Use thin-set mortar as an adhesive, and spread it carefully over the floor and mats with a ⅜" × ¼" square-notched trowel. Check the resistance of the mats periodically during the tile installation. If a mat becomes damaged, clean up any exposed mortar and contact the manufacturer. When the installation is complete, check the resistance of the mats once again and record the reading.

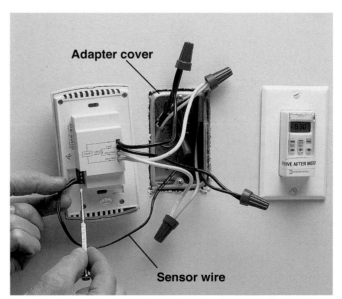

Adapter cover

Sensor wire

12 Install an adapter cover on the thermostat box, then patch the wall opening with drywall. Complete the wiring connections for the thermostat and timer, following the manufacturer's instructions. Attach the sensor wire to the thermostat setscrew connection. Apply the manufacturer's wiring labels to the thermostat box and service panel. Mount the thermostat and timer. Complete the circuit connection at the service panel. After the flooring materials have fully cured, test the system.

Baseboard heaters can provide primary or supplemental heat for existing rooms or additions.

Installing Baseboard Heaters

Baseboard heaters are a popular way to provide additional heating for an existing room or primary heat to a converted attic or basement.

Heaters are generally wired on a dedicated 240-volt circuit, controlled by a thermostat. Several heaters can be wired in parallel and controlled by a single thermostat (see circuit map 15, page 171).

Baseboard heaters are generally surface-mounted without boxes,so, in a remodeling situation, you only need to run cables before installing wallboard. Be sure to mark cable locations on the floor before installing drywall. Retrofit installations are also not difficult. You can remove existing baseboard and run new cable in the space behind (pages 200 to 201).

Everything You Need

Tools: Drill, combination tool, drywall saw.

Materials: Baseboard heaters, 240-volt thermostat, electrical box, 12/2 NM cable.

How to Connect 240-volt Baseboard Heaters

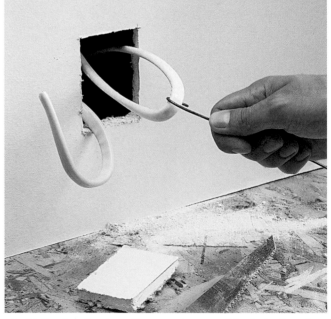

1 At the heater locations, cut a small hole in the drywall, 3" to 4" above the floor. Pull 12/2 NM cables through the first hole: one from the thermostat, the other to the next heater. Pull all the cables for subsequent heaters. Middle-of-run heaters will have two cables, while end-of-run heaters have only one cable. (See also circuit map 15, page 171.)

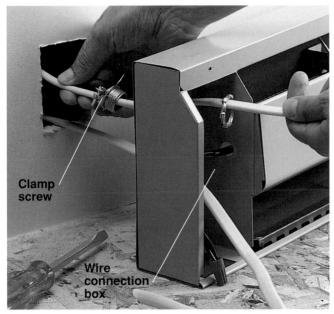

Clamp screw

Wire connection box

2 Remove the cover on the wire connection box. Open a knockout for each cable that will enter the box, then feed the cables through the cable clamps and into the wire connection box. Attach the clamps to the wire connection box, and tighten the clamp screws until the cables are gripped firmly.

3 Anchor heater against wall, about 1" off floor, by driving flat-head screws through back of housing and into studs. Strip away cable sheathing so at least ½" of sheathing extends into the heater. Strip ¾" of insulation from each wire, using a combination tool.

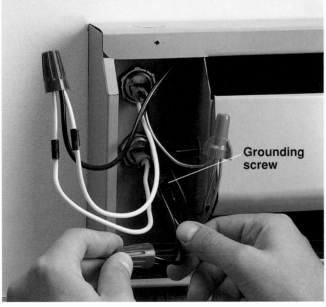

Grounding screw

4 Connect the white circuit wires to one of the wire leads on the heater. Tag white wires with black tape to indicate they are hot. Connect the black circuit wires to the other wire lead. Connect a grounding pigtail to the green grounding screw in the box, then join all grounding wires with a wire connector. Reattach cover.

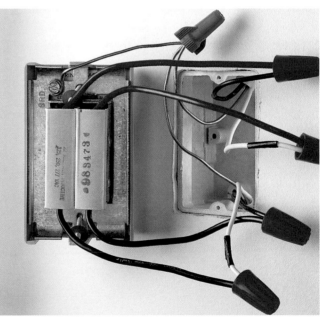

5 Run a 12/2 NM cable from the service panel to the thermostat box. Clamp the cable in the box. Connect the red wire leads on the thermostat to the circuit wires entering the box from the panel. Connect black wire leads to circuit wires leading to the baseboard heaters. Tag the white wires with black tape to indicate they are hot. Attach a grounding pigtail to the grounding screw on the thermostat; then connect all grounding wires. Tuck the wires into the box, and attach the thermostat and coverplate. Follow manufacturer's directions; the color coding for thermostats may vary.

Installing Wall Heaters

Installing a wall heater is an easy way to provide supplemental heat to a converted attic or basement without expanding an existing HVAC system.

Wall heaters are easy to install during a remodel (most have a separate can assembly that you attach to the framing before the drywall is installed). They can also be retrofitted.

Most models available at home centers use 120-volt current (shown below), but 240-volt models are also available.

Wall heaters are an easy-to-install way to provide supplemental heat. Some models have built-in thermostats, while others can be controlled by a remote thermostat.

Everything You Need
Tools: Drywall saw, drill, fishtape, combination tool, screwdrivers.
Materials: 12/2 NM cable, wire connectors, wall heater, thermostat (optional).

How to Install a Wall Heater in a Finished Wall

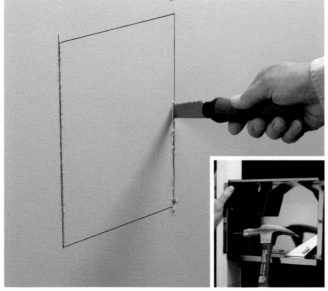

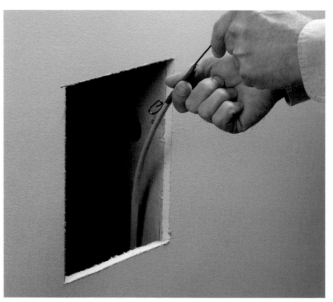

1 Make an opening in the wall for the heater. Use a stud finder to locate a stud in the area where you want to install the heater. Mark the opening for the heater according to the manufacturer's guidelines so that one side of the heater sits flush with a stud. Pay attention to clearance requirements. Cut the opening with a wallboard saw. If the wall is open, install the heater can before hanging drywall (inset).

2 Pull 12/2 NM cable from the main panel to the wall opening. If the heater is controlled by a separate thermostat, pull cable to the thermostat and then run another cable from the thermostat to the heater location.

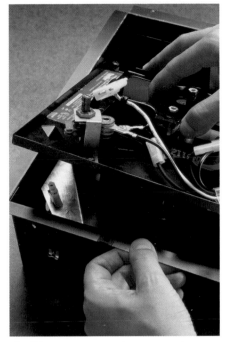

3 Disconnect and remove the motor unit from the heater can. Remove a knockout from the can, and route the cable into the can.

4 Install the can in the opening. Secure the cable with a clamp, leaving 8" to 12" of cable exposed. Attach the can to the framing as directed by the manufacturer.

5 Wire the heater. Connect the black circuit wire to one of the black heater leads. Connect the white circuit wire to the other lead. Connect the grounds.

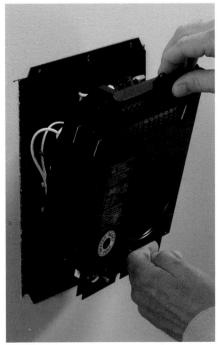

6 Secure the heater unit in the can as directed by the manufacturer. Reconnect the motor if necessary. Attach the grill and thermostat knob as directed. Connect the new circuit breaker at the main panel.

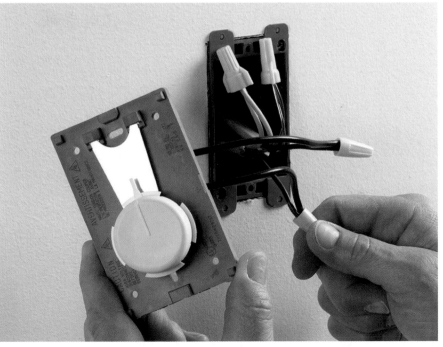

Variation: Connect a thermostat to control a wall heater. Some wall heaters do not use built-in thermostats. Install a thermostat in the heater circuit before the wall heater. Connect the black and white wires coming from the main panel to the red leads on the thermostat. Connect the wires going to the heater to the black leads on the thermostat. Connect the grounds.

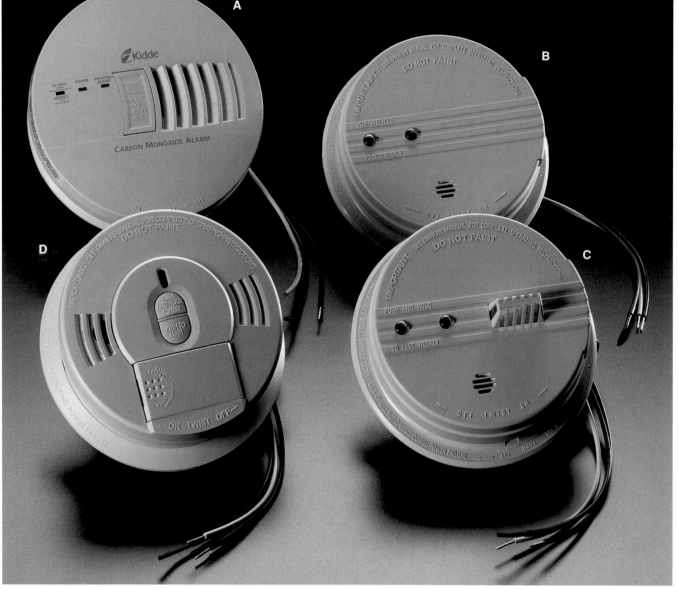

Hardwired carbon monoxide detectors (A) are triggered by the presence of carbon monoxide gas. Smoke detectors are available in photoelectric and ionizing models. In ionizing detectors (B), a small amount of current flows in an ionization chamber. When smoke enters the chamber, it interrupts the current, triggering the alarm. Photoelectric detectors (C) rely on a beam of light, which, when interrupted by smoke, triggers an alarm. Heat alarms (D) sound an alarm when they detect areas of high heat in the room.

Installing Hardwired Smoke, CO & Heat Alarms

Smoke and carbon monoxide (CO) alarms are an essential safety component of any living facility. All national fire protection codes require that new homes have a hard-wired smoke alarm in every sleeping room and on every level of a residence, including basements, attics, and attached garages. Smoke alarms must have their own 15-amp circuit.

Most authorities also recommend CO detectors on every level of the house and in every sleeping area.

Heat alarms, which detect heat instead of smoke, are often specified for locations like utility rooms, basements, or unfinished attics where conditions may cause nuisance tripping of smoke alarms.

Hard-wired alarms operate on your household electrical current, but have battery backups in case of a power outage. On new homes, all smoke alarms must be wired in a series so that every alarm sounds regardless of the fire's location. When wiring a series of alarms, be sure to use alarms of the same brand to ensure compatiility. Always check local codes before starting the job.

Ceiling-installed alarms should be four inches away from the nearest wall. Don't install smoke alarms near windows, doors, or ducts where drafts might interfere with their operation.

How to Connect a Series of Hardwired Smoke Alarms

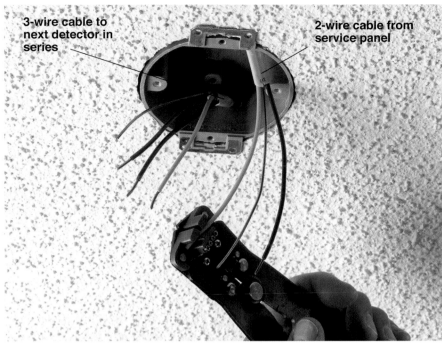

3-wire cable to next detector in series

2-wire cable from service panel

Everything You Need

Tools: Screwdriver, combination tool, fish tape, drywall saw.

Materials: Wall or ceiling outlet boxes, cable clamps (if boxes are not self-clamping), 2- and 3-wire 14-gauge NM cable, alarms, wire connectors, 15-amp single-pole breaker.

1 Pull 14/2 NM cable from the service panel into the first ceiling electrical box in the smoke alarm series. Pull 14/3 NM cable between the remaining alarm outlet boxes. Use cable clamps to secure the cable in each outlet box. Remove sheathing and strip insulation from wires.

2 Wire the first alarm in the series. Use a wire connector to connect the ground wires. Splice the black circuit wire with the alarm's black lead and the black wire going to the next alarm in the series. Splice the white circuit wire with the alarm's white wire and the white (neutral) wire going to the next alarm in the series. Splice the red traveler wire with the odd-colored alarm wire (in this case, the red wire).

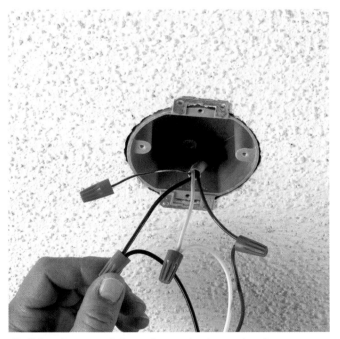

3 Wire the remaining alarms in the series by connecting the like-colored wires in each outlet box. Always connect the red traveler wire to the odd-colored (in this case, red) alarm wire. This red traveler wire connects all the alarms together so that when one alarm sounds, all the alarms sound. If the alarm doesn't have a grounding wire, cap the ground with a wire connector. When all alarms are wired, install and connect the new 15-amp breaker.

259

Installing a Whole-house Surge Arrestor

Surge arrestor unit

A whole-house surge arrestor is an inexpensive defense against expensive damage from high-voltage shocks caused by lightning strikes and power surges. Most models install next to the main panel.

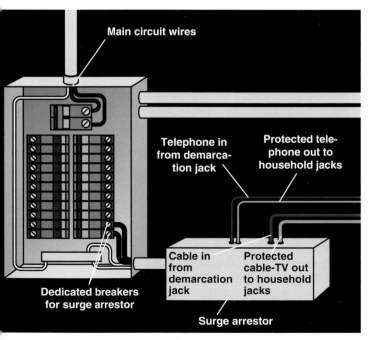

Main circuit wires

Telephone in from demarcation jack

Protected telephone out to household jacks

Cable in from demarcation jack

Protected cable-TV out to household jacks

Dedicated breakers for surge arrestor

Surge arrestor

A surge arrestor installed at the panel protects all downstream connected devices and wires.

Electrical surges caused by lighting or utility malfunctions can destroy or seriously damage sensitive electronics. Many homes contain tens of thousands of dollars worth of computers and home entertainment equipment protected by no more than a $10 plug-in surge suppressor. While these devices do afford a modest level of protection, they are no match for the voltage a lightning strike will push through a system. And they offer no protection for the wiring itself. Whole-house surge arrestors provide comprehensive protection for the wiring and devices attached to it.

Whole-house surge arrestors are available in two basic types. One type is wired on the utility side of the panel, normally at the meter. When installed by a licensed electrician, these devices provide the highest level of protection, shielding the panel and all electrical devices in the house. The other type wires directly into the panel and protects all circuits originating at that panel. Manufacturers offer units that are housed in separate boxes (these look like a small subpanel) as well as models that are designed to replace a double-pole breaker in the panel itself. These install like standard breakers. Both types provide protection for the whole house. Freestanding models are also available with separate protection for phone, data, and cable-television lines—a wise addition if you need to protect networked computers or cable-TV receivers.

Whatever style you choose, look for models with the Underwriters Laboratories 1449 rating and indicator lights showing that the system is protected. Most manufacturers also include a warranty against defect that covers a certain amount of property damage.

Everything You Need

Tools: Hammer, combination tool, screwdrivers, cable ripper, lineman's pliers, circuit tester, crimping tools.

Materials: Whole-house surge arrestor, conduit nipple and locknuts, two 15- or 20-amp single pole breakers, coaxial cable and terminators, UTP cable and terminators.

How to Install a Whole-house Surge Arrestor with Separate Data and Cable TV Protection

1 Turn off power at the main breaker. Remove the cover, and test to make sure the power is off. Mount the arrestor near the service panel, following the manufacturer's instructions. Typically, the arrestor mounts on one side of the panel so its knockout lines up with a lower knockout on the panel. Remove the knockout on the panel. Install a conduit nipple on the arrestor and thread the wires from the arrestor through the nipple and into the panel. Slip the other end of the nipple through the opening in the panel, and tighten the locknut. Secure the box to the wall with screws as directed.

2 Connect the two black wires to two dedicated 15-or 20-amp breakers. Trim the wires as short as possible without making sharp bends. Connect the white neutral wire to the neutral bar and green grounding wire to grounding bar. Keep wire lengths as short as possible. Snap the new breakers into the bus bar. Restore the power and carefully test that the voltage between the two black arrestor leads is 240 volts. Replace the panel cover and the arrestor cover. If the arrestor has indicator lights, they should glow, showing that the system is now protected.

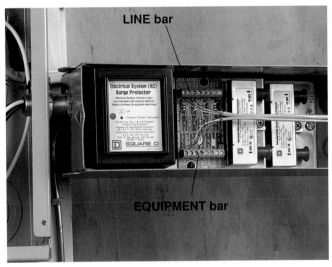

Variation: If the arrestor has separate protection for the telephone circuits, remove the cable that runs from the phone demarcation jack to the junction box. Then, remove a knockout in the arrestor and route a new UTP cable from the demarcation jack to the arrestor. Strip insulation from the wires and connect them to the terminals on the LINE bar (labeled IN on some models) on the phone protection module in the arrestor. Run a UTP cable from the EQUIPMENT bar (labeled OUT on some models) to the junction box. Strip and connect the wires from this cable to the appropriate terminals in the arrestor and the junction box.

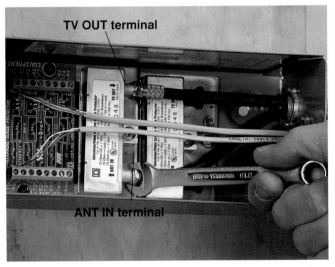

Variation: If the arrestor has separate protection for a cable television circuit, remove the appropriate knockout from the arrestor and run a coaxial cable to the arrestor from the cable-TV demarcation jack. Connect the coaxial cable to the ANT-IN terminal on the cable-TV protection module. Run another coaxial cable from the TV-OUT terminal to the cable TV junction box or the distribution panel. Do not overtighten the connections.

261

Generators have a range of uses. Large, hardwired models can provide instant emergency power for a whole house. Smaller models (inset) are convenient for occasional, short-term backup as well as job sites or camping trips.

Backup Generators

You don't have to be a survivalist to recognize the practicality of a plan for providing power. Installing a backup generator is an invaluable way to prepare your family for emergencies.

The simplest backup power system is a portable, gas-powered generator and an extension cord or two. A big benefit of this approach is that you can run a refrigerator and a few worklights during a power outage with a tool that can also be transported to remote jobsites or on camping trips when it's not doing emergency backup duty. This is also the least expensive way to provide some backup power for your home. You can purchase a generator at most home centers and be up and running in a matter of hours. If you take this approach, it is critically important that you make certain any loads being run by your generator are disconnected from the utility power source.

The next step up is to incorporate a manual transfer switch for your portable generator. Transfer switches are permanently hardwired to your service panel. They are mounted on either the interior or the exterior of your house between the generator and the service panel. You provide a power feed from a generator into the switch. The switch is wired to selected essential circuits in your house, allowing you to power lights, furnace blowers, and other loads that can't easily be run with an extension cord. But perhaps the most important job a transfer switch performs is to disconnect the utility power. If the inactive utility power line is attached to the service panel, "backfeed" of power from your generator to the utility line can occur when the generator kicks in. This condition could be fatal to lineworkers who are trying to restore power. The potential for backfeed is the main reason many municipalities insist that **only a licensed electrician hook up a transfer switch.** Using a transfer switch not installed by a professional may also void the warranty of the switch and the generator.

Automatic transfer switches turn on the generator and switch off the utility supply when they detect a significant drop in line voltage. They may be installed with portable generators, provided the generator is equipped with an electric starter.

Large standby generators that resemble central air conditioners are the top of the line in backup power supply systems. Often fueled by home natural gas lines or propane tanks, standby generators are made in sizes with as much as 20 to 40 kilowatts of output— enough to supply all of the power needs of a 5,000-sq.-ft. home. You can purchase smaller standby generators (4–5 kilowatts or so) for under $2,000, but the higher capacity models often top $10,000 in cost. If you're considering this option, also be aware that high-wattage standby generators require a transfer panel, not just a switch. Switches cost from $200 to $500, but transfer panels start at around $1,000.

Quality generators are expensive. For a well made basic model that has enough capacity to back up your essential systems (refrigerator, furnace, a few lights) expect to pay $1,000. A more sophisticated piece of equipment that has greater wattage and can run modern electronics safely will cost $3,000 to $4,000.

Options for Choosing a Backup Generator

A 2,000- to 5,000-watt gas-powered generator and a few extension cords can power lamps and an appliance or two during shorter-term power outages. Appliances must not be connected to household wiring and the generator simultaneously. Never plug a generator into an outlet. Never operate a generator indoors. Run extension cord through a garage door.

A permanent transfer switch patches electricity from a large portable generator through to selected household circuits via an inlet at your service panel (inset), allowing you to power hardwired fixtures and appliances with the generator. This installation is ideal for cabins or vacation homes where power may be unreliable.

For full, on-demand backup service, install a large standby generator wired through to an automatic transfer panel. In the event of a power outage, the household system instantly switches to the generator.

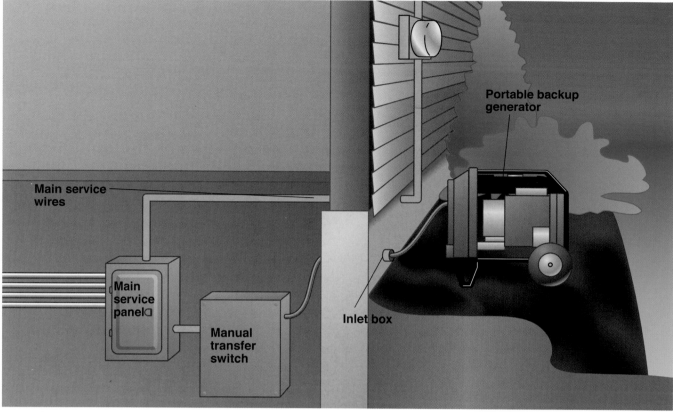

Main service wires

Main service panel

Manual transfer switch

Inlet box

Portable backup generator

Backup generators are usually installed to supply power to a manual transfer switch, which disconnects the house from the main service wires and routes power from the generator through selected household circuits.

Choosing a Generator

Choosing a generator for your home's needs requires a few calculations. The chart below gives an estimate of the size of generator typically recommended for a house of a certain size. You can get a more accurate number by adding up the power consumption (the watts) of all the circuits or devices to be powered by a generator. It's also important to keep in mind that, for most electrical appliances, the amount of power required at the moment you flip the ON switch is greater than the number of watts required to keep the device running. For instance, though an air conditioner may run on 15,000 watts of power, it will require a surge of 30,000 watts at startup (the power range required to operate an appliance is usually listed somewhere on the device itself). These two numbers are called run watts and surge watts. Generators are typically sold according to run watts (a 5,000-watt generator can sustain 5,000 watts). They are also rated for a certain number of surge watts (a 5,000-watt generator may be able to produce a surge of 10,000 watts). If the surge watts aren't listed, ask or check the manual. Some genera-

tors can't develop many more surge watts than run watts; others can produce twice as much surge as run wattage.

It's not necessary to buy a generator large enough to match the surge potential of all your circuits (you won't be turning everything on simultaneously), but surge watts should factor in your purchasing decision. If you will be operating the generator at or near capacity, it is also a wise practice to stagger startups for appliances.

Size of house (in square feet)	Recommended generator size (in kilowatts)
Up to 2,700	5–11
2,700–3,700	14–16
3,700–4,700	20
4,700–7,000	42–47

Types of Transfer Switches

Cord-connected transfer switches (shown above) are hardwired to the service panel (in some cases they're installed after the service panel and operate only selected circuits). These switches contain a female receptacle for a power supply cord connected to the generator. Automatic transfer switches (not shown) detect voltage drop-off in the main power line and switch over to the emergency power source.

When using a cord-connected switch, consider mounting an inlet box to the exterior wall. This will allow you to connect a generator without running a cord into the house.

Generator Tips

If you'll need to run sensitive electronics such as computers or home theater equipment, look for a generator with power inverter technology that dispenses "clean power" with a stable sine wave pattern.

A generator that will output 240-volt service is required to run most central air conditioners. If your generator has variable output (120/240) make sure the switch is set to the correct output voltage.

Running & Maintaining a Backup System

Even with a fully automatic standby generator system fueled by natural gas or propane, you will need to conduct some regular maintenance and testing to make sure all systems are ready in the event of power loss. If you're depending on a portable generator and extension cords or a standby generator with a manual transfer switch, you'll also need to know the correct sequence of steps to follow in a power emergency. Switches and panels also need to be tested on a regular basis, as directed in your owner's manual. And be sure that all switches (both interior and exterior) are housed in an approved enclosure box.

Pull-cord starter

Smaller portable generators often use pull-cords instead of electric starters

Anatomy of a Portable Backup Generator

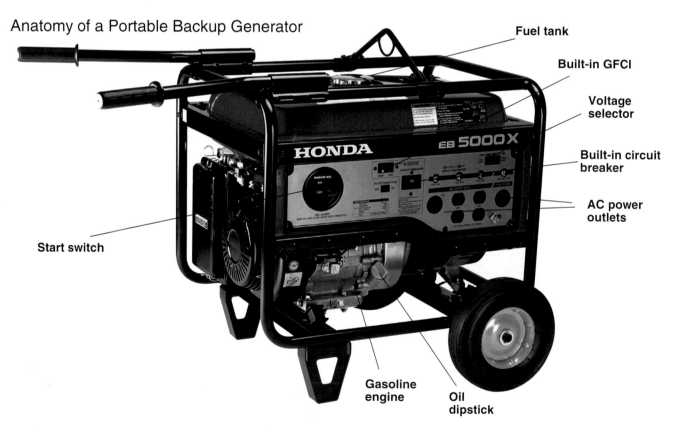

Fuel tank

Built-in GFCI

Voltage selector

Built-in circuit breaker

AC power outlets

Start switch

Gasoline engine

Oil dipstick

Portable generators use small gasoline engines to generate power. A built-in electronics panel sets current to AC or DC and the correct voltage. Most models will also include a built-in circuit breaker to protect the generator from damage in the event it is connected to too many loads. Bet-

ter models include features like built-in GFCI protection. Larger portable generators may also feature electric starter motors and batteries for push-button starts.

Operating a Manual System During an Outage

1 Plug the generator in at the inlet box. Make sure the other end of the generator's outlet cord is plugged into the appropriate outlet on the generator (120-volt or 120/240-volt AC) and the generator is switched to the appropriate voltage setting.

2 Start the generator with the pull cord or electric starter (if your generator has one). Let the generator run for several minutes before flipping the transfer switch.

3 Flip the manual transfer switch. Begin turning on loads one at a time by flipping breakers to ON, starting with the one that draws the most power. Do not overload the generator or the switch and do not run the generator at or near full capacity for more than 30 minutes at a time.

Maintaining and Operating an Automatic Standby Generator

If you choose to spend the money and install a dedicated standby generator of 10,000 watts or more and operate it through an automatic transfer switch or panel, you won't need to lift a hand when your utility power goes out. The system kicks in by itself. However, you should follow the manufacturer's suggestions for testing the system, changing the oil, and running the motor periodically.

Installing Outdoor Wiring

Adding an outdoor circuit improves the value of your property and lets you enjoy your yard more fully. Doing the work yourself is also a good way to save money. Most outdoor wiring projects require digging underground trenches, and an electrician may charge several hundred dollars for this simple but time-consuming work.

Do not install your own wiring for a hot tub, fountain, or swimming pool. These outdoor water fixtures require special grounding techniques that are best left to an electrician.

In this chapter you learn how to install the following fixtures:

Decorative light fixtures (A) can highlight attractive features of your home and yard, like a deck, ornamental shrubs and trees, and flower gardens. See pages 288 and 292.

A weatherproof switch (B) lets you control outdoor lights without going indoors. See page 284.

GFCI-protected receptacles (C) let you use electric lawn and garden tools, and provide a place to plug in radios, barbecue rotisseries, and other devices that help make your yard more enjoyable. See page 287.

A manual override switch (D) lets you control a motion-sensor light fixture from inside the house. See page 284.

Five Steps for Installing Outdoor Wiring:
1. Plan the Circuit (pages 274 to 275).
2. Dig Trenches (pages 276 to 277).
3. Install Boxes & Conduit (pages 278 to 281).
4. Install UF Cable (pages 282 to 283).
5. Make Final Connections (pages 284 to 288).

A motion-sensor light fixture (photos, right) provides inexpensive and effective protection against intruders. It has an infrared eye that triggers the light fixture when a moving object crosses its path. Choose a light fixture with a photo cell (E) that prevents the fixture from triggering in daylight. Look for an adjustable timer (F) that controls how long the light keeps shining after motion stops. Better models have range controls (G) to adjust the sensitivity of the motion-sensor eye. See pages 284 to 286.

Installing Outdoor Wiring:
Cutaway View

The outdoor circuit installation shown on the following pages gives step-by-step instructions for installing a simple outdoor circuit for light fixtures and receptacles. The materials and techniques also can be applied to other outdoor wiring projects, such as running a circuit to a garage workshop, or to a detached shed or gazebo.

Your outdoor wiring probably will be different from the circuit shown in this chapter. Refer to the circuit maps on pages 164 to 179 as a guide for designing and installing your own outdoor electrical circuit.

Learn These Techniques for Installing Outdoor Wiring

A: Install weatherproof decorative light fixtures with watertight threaded fittings (page 288).

B: Use rigid metal or intermediate metallic conduit (IMC) with threaded compression fittings (pages 280 to 281) to protect exposed wires and cables.

C: Install a cast-aluminum switch box (page 283) to hold an outdoor switch. The box has a watertight coverplate with toggle lever built into it.

D: Use weatherproof receptacle boxes made of cast aluminum with sealed coverplates and threaded fittings to hold outdoor receptacles (pages 280 to 281).

E: Install a retrofit light fixture box (page 279) to hold a motion-sensor security light. Retrofit boxes are used to install electrical fixtures that fit inside existing finished walls. The box is sealed with a foam gasket that fits between the light fixture and the box.

F: Run NM cable (pages 197 to 201, 279) through walls to provide power to electrical boxes that fit inside finished walls.

G: Install retrofit single-gang boxes (page 279) to hold a manual override switch for the motion-sensor light and the GFCI receptacle.

H: Attach a cast-aluminum extension ring to a retrofit receptacle box (page 280) to hold a GFCI receptacle.

I: Dig trenches (pages 276 to 277) to hold underground cables bringing power from the house to yard fixtures.

J: Install UF (underground feeder) cable (pages 282 to 283) to bring power from the house to the outdoor fixtures.

K: Run a feeder cable to connect the outdoor circuit to the circuit breaker panel (page 280).

Tools You Will Need

Tape measure, drill with masonry bits and twist bits, jig saw or reciprocating saw, shovel, hammer, screwdriver, caulk gun, ball-peen hammer or masonry hammer, masonry chisel, hacksaw, fish tape, cable ripper, combination tool, utility knife, needlenose pliers, circuit tester.

Installing Outdoor Wiring: Diagram View

This diagram view shows the layout of the outdoor wiring project featured on these pages. It includes the location of the switches, receptacles, light fixtures, and cable runs you will learn how to install in this chapter. The layout of your yard and the location of obstacles will determine the best locations for lights, receptacles, and underground cable runs. The wiring

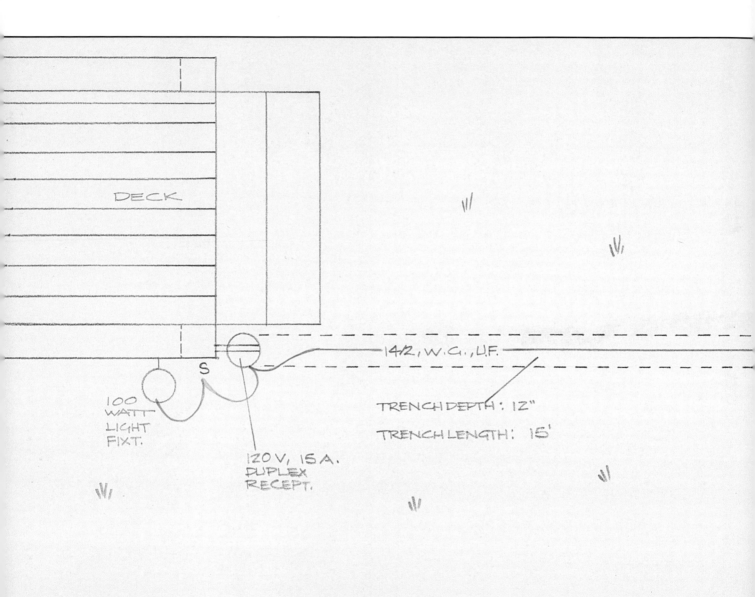

Yard is drawn to scale, with the lengths of trenches and cable runs clearly labeled.

Decorative light fixture is positioned to highlight the deck. Decorative fixtures should be used sparingly, to provide accent only to favorite features of your yard, such as flower beds, ornamental trees, or a patio.

Outdoor receptacle is positioned on the deck post, where it is accessible yet unobtrusive. Another good location for a receptacle is between shrubs.

diagram for your own project may differ greatly from the one shown here, but the techniques shown on the following pages will apply to any outdoor wiring project.

Note:

See page 155 for a key to the common electrical symbols used in this diagram, and to learn how to draw your own wiring diagrams.

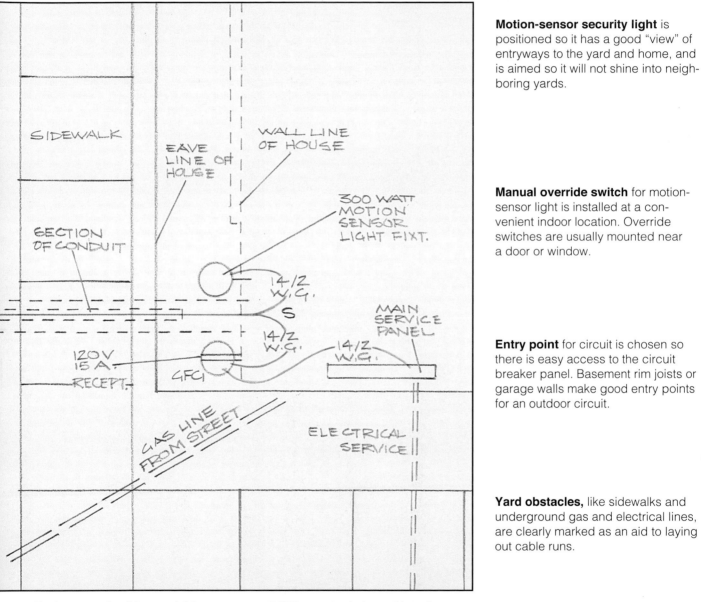

Motion-sensor security light is positioned so it has a good "view" of entryways to the yard and home, and is aimed so it will not shine into neighboring yards.

Manual override switch for motion-sensor light is installed at a convenient indoor location. Override switches are usually mounted near a door or window.

Entry point for circuit is chosen so there is easy access to the circuit breaker panel. Basement rim joists or garage walls make good entry points for an outdoor circuit.

Yard obstacles, like sidewalks and underground gas and electrical lines, are clearly marked as an aid to laying out cable runs.

Underground cables are laid out from the house to the outdoor fixtures by the shortest route possible to reduce the length of trenches.

GFCI receptacle is positioned near the start of the cable run and is wired to protect all wires to the end of the circuit.

Check for underground utilities when planning trenches for underground cable runs. Avoid lawn sprinkler pipes; and consult your electric utility office, phone company, gas and water department, and cable television vendor for the exact locations of underground utility lines. Many utility companies send field representatives to show homeowners how to avoid dangerous underground hazards.

Choosing Cable Sizes for an Outdoor Circuit

Circuit length		Circuit size
Less than 50 ft.	**50 ft. or more**	
14-gauge	12-gauge	15-amp
12-gauge	10-gauge	20-amp

Consider the circuit length when choosing cable sizes for an outdoor circuit. In very long circuits, normal wire resistance leads to a substantial drop in voltage. If your outdoor circuit extends more than 50 ft., use larger-gauge wire to reduce the voltage drop. For example, a 15-amp circuit that extends more than 50 ft. should be wired with 12-gauge wire instead of 14-gauge. A 20-amp circuit longer than 50 ft. should be wired with 10-gauge cable.

1: Plan the Circuit

As you begin planning an outdoor circuit, visit your electrical inspector to learn about local code requirements for outdoor wiring. The techniques for installing outdoor circuits are much the same as for installing indoor wiring. However, because outdoor wiring is exposed to the elements, it requires the use of special weatherproof materials, including UF cable (page 190), rigid metal or schedule 40 PVC plastic conduit (pages 204 to 205), and weatherproof electrical boxes and fittings (pages 182 to 183).

The National Electrical Code (NEC) gives minimum standards for outdoor wiring materials, but because climate and soil conditions vary from region to region, your local building and electrical codes may have more restrictive requirements. For example, some regions require that all underground cables be protected with conduit, even though the National Electrical Code allows UF cable to be buried without protection at the proper depths (next page).

For most homes, an outdoor circuit is a modest power user. Adding a new 15-amp, 120-volt circuit provides enough power for most outdoor electrical needs. However, if your circuit will include more than three large light fixtures (each rated for 300 watts or more) or more than four receptacles, plan to install a 20-amp, 120-volt circuit. Or, if your outdoor circuit will supply power to heating appliances or large workshop tools in a detached garage, you may require several 120-volt and 240-volt circuits.

Before drawing wiring plans and applying for a work permit, evaluate electrical loads (pages 150 to 153) to make sure the main service provides enough amps to support the added demand of the new wiring.

A typical outdoor circuit takes one or two weekends to install, but if your layout requires very long underground cables, allow yourself more time for digging trenches, or arrange to have extra help. Also make sure to allow time for the required inspection visits when planning your wiring project. See pages 140 to 155 for more information on planning a wiring project.

Tips for Planning an Outdoor Circuit

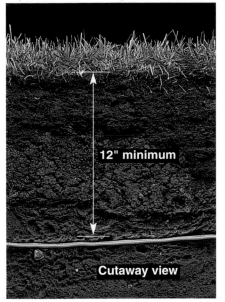

Bury UF cables 12" deep if the wires are protected by a GFCI and the circuit is no larger than 20 amps. Bury cable at least 18" deep if the circuit is not protected by a GFCI or if it is larger than 20 amps.

Protect cable entering conduit by attaching a plastic bushing to the open end of the conduit. The bushing prevents sharp metal edges from damaging the vinyl sheathing on the cable.

Protect exposed wiring above ground level with rigid conduit and weatherproof electrical boxes and coverplates. Check your local code restrictions: Some regions allow the use of either rigid metal conduit or schedule 40 PVC plastic conduit and electrical boxes, while other regions allow only metal.

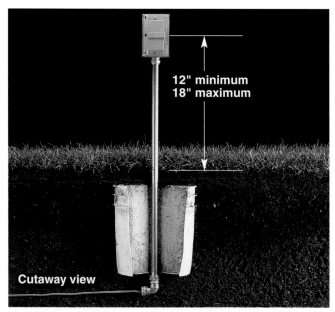

Prevent shock by making sure all outdoor receptacles are protected by GFCIs (page 74). A single GFCI receptacle can be wired to protect other fixtures on the circuit. Outdoor receptacles should be at least 1 ft. above ground level and enclosed in weatherproof electrical boxes with watertight covers.

Anchor freestanding receptacles that are not attached to a structure by embedding the rigid metal conduit or schedule 40 PVC plastic conduit in a concrete footing. One way to do this is by running conduit through a plastic bucket, then filling the bucket with concrete. Freestanding receptacles should be at least 12", but no more than 18", above ground level—requirements vary, so check with your local inspector.

2: Dig Trenches

When laying underground cables, save time and minimize lawn damage by digging trenches as narrow as possible. Plan the circuit to reduce the length of cable runs.

If your soil is sandy, or very hard and dry, water the ground thoroughly before you begin digging. Lawn sod can be removed, set on strips of plastic, and replaced after cables are laid. Keep the removed sod moist but not wet, and replace it within two or three days. Otherwise, the grass underneath the plastic may die.

If trenches must be left unattended, make sure to cover them with scrap pieces of plywood to prevent accidents and to keep water out.

Materials You Will Need

Stakes, string, scrap piece of conduit, compression fittings, plastic bushings.

How to Dig Trenches for Underground Cables

1 Mark the outline of trenches with wooden stakes and string.

2 Cut two 18"-wide strips of plastic, and place one strip on each side of the trench outline.

3 Remove blocks of sod from the trench outline, using a shovel. Cut sod 2" to 3" deep to keep roots intact. Place the sod on one of the plastic strips, and keep it moist.

4 Dig the trenches to the depth required by your local code. Heap the dirt onto the second strip of plastic.

5 To run cable under a sidewalk, cut a length of metal conduit about 1 foot longer than width of sidewalk, then flatten one end of the conduit to form a sharp tip.

6 Drive the conduit through the soil under the sidewalk, using a ball-peen or masonry hammer and a wood block to prevent damage to the pipe.

7 Cut off the ends of the conduit with a hacksaw, leaving about 2" of exposed conduit on each side. Underground cable will run through the conduit.

8 Attach a compression fitting and plastic bushing to each end of the conduit. The plastic fittings will prevent the sharp edges of the conduit from damaging the cable sheathing.

9 If trenches must be left unattended, temporarily cover them with scrap plywood to prevent accidents.

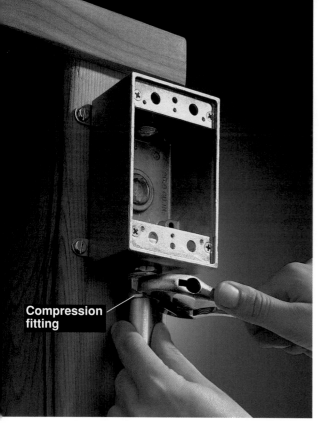

Compression fitting

Electrical boxes for an outdoor circuit must be weatherproof. This outdoor receptacle box made of cast aluminum has sealed seams and is attached to conduit with threaded, watertight compression fittings.

3: Install Boxes & Conduit

Use cast-aluminum or PVC plastic boxes for outdoor fixtures, and install approved conduit to protect exposed cables. Standard metal and plastic electrical boxes are not watertight, and should never be used outdoors. Some local codes require you to install conduit to protect all underground cables, but in most regions this is not necessary. Many local codes allow you to use boxes and conduit made with PVC plastic (page 205), while others allow only cast-aluminum boxes and metal conduit.

Begin work by installing the retrofit boxes and the cables that run between them inside finished walls. Then install the outdoor boxes and conduit.

Materials You Will Need

NM 2-wire cable, cable staples, plastic retrofit light fixture box with grounding clip, plastic single-gang retrofit boxes with internal clamps, extension ring, silicone caulk, IMC or rigid metal conduit, pipe straps, conduit sweep, compression fittings, plastic bushings, masonry anchors, single-gang outdoor boxes, galvanized screws, grounding pigtails, wire connectors.

How to Install Electrical Boxes & Conduit

1 Outline the GFCI receptacle box on the exterior wall. First drill pilot holes at the corners of the box outline, and use a piece of stiff wire to probe the wall for electrical wires or plumbing pipes. Complete the cutout with a jig saw or reciprocating saw.

Masonry variation: To make cutouts in masonry, drill a line of holes inside the box outline, using a masonry bit, then remove waste material with a masonry chisel and ball-peen hammer.

2 From inside house, make the cutout for the indoor switch in the same stud cavity that contains the GFCI cutout. Outline the box on the wall, then drill a pilot hole and complete the cutout with a wallboard saw or jig saw.

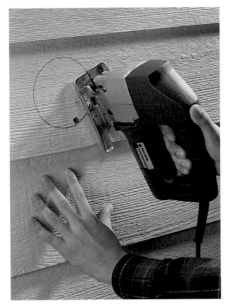

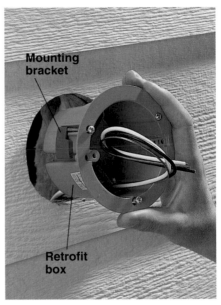

3 On outside of house, make the cutout for the motion-sensor light fixture in the same stud cavity with the GFCI cutout. Outline the light fixture box on the wall, then drill a pilot hole and complete the cutout with a wallboard saw or jig saw.

4 Estimate the distance between the indoor switch box and the outdoor motion-sensor box, and cut a length of NM cable about 2 ft. longer than this distance. Use a fish tape to pull the cable from the switch box to the motion-sensor box. See pages 197 to 201 for tips on running cable through finished walls.

5 Strip about 10" of outer insulation from the end of the cable, using a cable ripper. Open a knockout in the retrofit light fixture box with a screwdriver. Insert the cable into the box so that at least ¼" of outer sheathing reaches into the box.

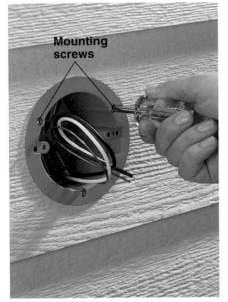

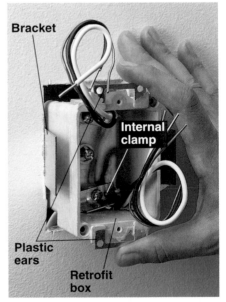

6 Insert the box into the cutout opening, and tighten the mounting screws until the brackets draw the outside flange firmly against the siding.

7 Estimate the distance between the outdoor GFCI cutout and the indoor switch cutout, and cut a length of NM cable about 2 ft. longer than this distance. Use a fish tape to pull the cable from the GFCI cutout to the switch cutout. Strip 10" of outer insulation from both ends of each cable.

8 Open one knockout for each cable that will enter the box. Insert the cables so at least ¼" of outer sheathing reaches inside box. Insert box into cutout, and tighten the mounting screw in the rear of the box until the bracket draws the plastic ears against the wall. Tighten internal cable clamps.

(continued next page)

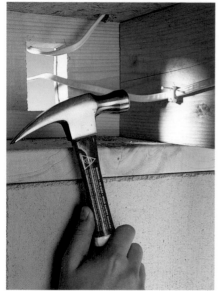

9 Install NM cable from circuit breaker panel to GFCI cutout. Allow an extra 2 ft. of cable at panel end and an extra foot at GFCI end. Attach cable to framing members with cable staples. Strip 10" of outer sheathing from the GFCI end of cable and ¾" of insulation from each wire.

10 Open one knockout for each cable that will enter the GFCI box. Insert the cables so at least ¼" of sheathing reaches into the box. Push the box into the cutout, and tighten the mounting screw until the bracket draws the plaster ears tight against the wall.

Foam gasket

Extension ring

11 Position a foam gasket over the GFCI box, then attach an extension ring to the box, using the mounting screws included with the extension ring. Seal any gaps around the extension ring with silicone caulk.

Extension ring

12 Measure and cut a length of IMC conduit to reach from the bottom of the extension ring to a point about 4" from the bottom of the trench. Attach the conduit to the extension ring using a compression fitting.

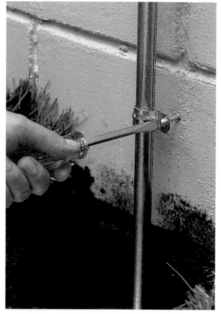

13 Anchor the conduit to the wall with a pipe strap and masonry screws. Or use masonry anchors and pan-head screws. Drill pilot holes for anchors, using a masonry drill bit.

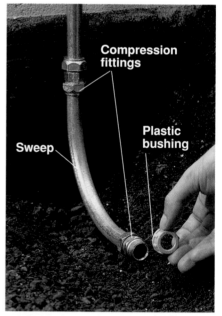

Compression fittings

Sweep

Plastic bushing

14 Attach compression fittings to the ends of metal sweep fitting, then attach the sweep fitting to the end of the conduit. Screw a plastic bushing onto the exposed fitting end of the sweep to keep the metal edges from damaging the cable.

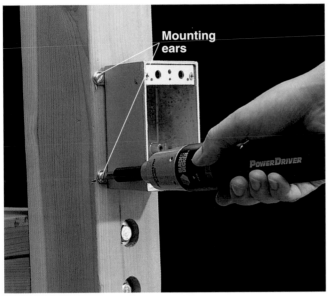

15 Attach mounting ears to the back of a weatherproof receptacle box, then attach the box to the deck frame by driving galvanized screws through the ears and into the post.

16 Measure and cut a length of IMC conduit to reach from the bottom of the receptacle box to a point about 4" from the bottom of the trench. Attach the conduit to the box with a compression fitting. Attach a sweep fitting and plastic bushing to the bottom of the conduit, using compression fittings (see step 14).

17 Cut a length of IMC conduit to reach from the top of the receptacle box to the switch box location. Attach the conduit to the receptacle box with a compression fitting. Anchor the conduit to the deck frame with pipe straps.

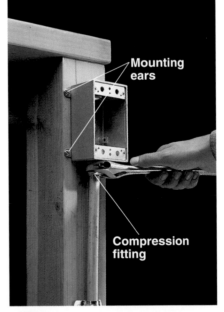

18 Attach mounting ears to the back of switch box, then loosely attach the box to the conduit with a compression fitting. Anchor the box to the deck frame by driving galvanized screws through the ears and into the wood. Then tighten the compression fitting with a wrench.

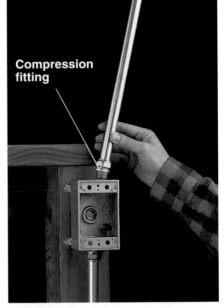

19 Measure and cut a short length of IMC conduit to reach from the top of the switch box to the deck light location. Attach the conduit with a compression fitting.

4: Install UF Cable

Use UF cable for outdoor wiring if the cable will come in direct contact with soil. UF cable has a solid-core vinyl sheathing and cannot be stripped with a cable ripper. Instead, use a utility knife and the method shown (steps 5 and 6, page 283). Never use NM cable for outdoor wiring. If your local code requires that underground wires be protected by conduit, use THHN/THWN wire (page 190) instead of UF cable.

After installing all cables, you are ready for the rough-in inspection. While waiting for the inspector, temporarily attach the weatherproof cover-plates to the boxes or cover them with plastic to prevent moisture from entering. After the inspector has approved the rough-in work, fill in all cable trenches and replace the sod before making the final connections.

Materials You Will Need

UF cable, electrical tape, grounding pigtails, wire connectors, weatherproof coverplates.

How to Install Outdoor Cable

1 Measure and cut all UF cables, allowing an extra 12" at each box. At each end of the cable, use a utility knife to pare away about 3" of outer sheathing, leaving the inner wires exposed.

2 Feed a fish tape down through the conduit from the GFCI box. Hook the wires at one end of the cable through the loop in the fish tape, then wrap electrical tape around the wires up to the sheathing. Carefully pull the cable through the conduit.

3 Lay the cable along the bottom of the trench, making sure it is not twisted. Where cable runs under a sidewalk, use the fish tape to pull it through the conduit.

4 Use the fish tape to pull the end of the cable up through the conduit to the deck receptacle box at the opposite end of the trench. Remove the cable from the fish tape.

5 Cut away the electrical tape at each end of the cable, then clip away the bent wires. Bend back one of the wires in the cable, and grip it with needlenose pliers. Grip the cable with another pliers.

6 Pull back on the wire, splitting the sheathing and exposing about 10" of wire. Repeat with the remaining wires, then cut off excess sheathing with a utility knife. Strip ¾" of insulation from the end of each wire, using a combination tool.

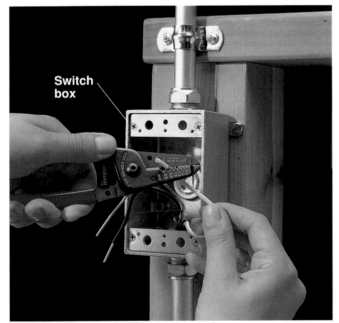

Switch box

7 Measure, cut, and install a cable from the deck receptacle box to the outdoor switch box, using the fish tape. Strip 10" of sheathing from each end of the cable, then strip ¾" of insulation from the end of each wire, using a combination tool.

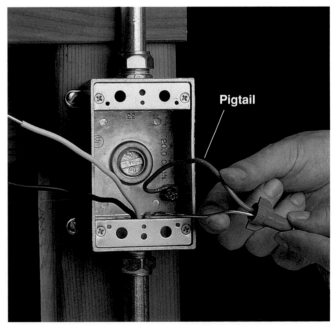

Pigtail

8 Attach a grounding pigtail to the back of each metal box and extension ring. Join all grounding wires with a wire connector. Tuck the wires inside the boxes, and temporarily attach the weatherproof coverplates until the inspector arrives for the rough-in inspection.

Foam gasket

Single-pole switch

Toggle lever

5: Make Final Connections

Make the final hookups for the switches, receptacles, and light fixtures after the rough-in cable installation has been reviewed and approved by your inspector, and after all trenches have been filled in. Install all the light fixtures, switches, and receptacles, then connect the circuit to the circuit breaker panel (pages 214 to 215).

Because outdoor wiring poses a greater shock hazard than indoor wiring, the GFCI receptacle (page 287) in this project is wired to provide shock protection for all fixtures controlled by the circuit.

When all work is completed and the outdoor circuit is connected at the service panel, your job is ready for final review by the inspector.

Switches for outdoor use have weatherproof coverplates with built-in toggle levers. The lever operates a single-pole switch mounted to the inside of the coverplate. Connect the black circuit wire to one of the screw terminals on the switch, and connect the black wire lead from the light fixture to the other screw terminal. Use wire connectors to join the white circuit wires and the grounding wires. To connect the manual override switch for the motion-sensor light fixture, see circuit map 4 on page 166.

Materials You Will Need
Motion-sensor light fixture, GFCI receptacle, 15-amp grounded receptacle, outdoor switch, decorative light fixture, wire connectors.

How to Connect a Motion-sensor Light Fixture

Sockets

Motion-sensor unit

1 Assemble fixture by threading the wire leads from the motion-sensor unit and the bulb sockets through the faceplate knockouts. Screw the motion-sensor unit and bulb sockets into the faceplate.

Locknut

2 Secure the motion-sensor unit and the bulb sockets by tightening the locknuts.

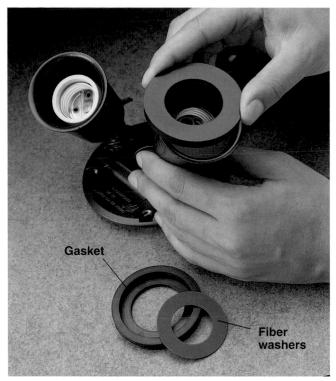

Gasket

Fiber washers

3 Insert the fiber washers into the sockets, and fit a rubber gasket over the end of each socket. The washers and gaskets ensure that the fixture will be watertight.

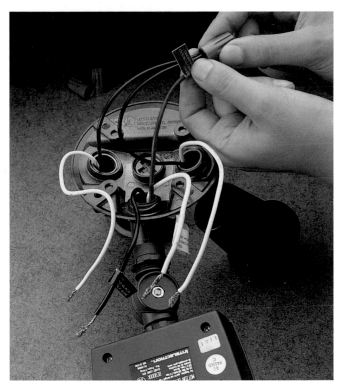

4 Connect the red wire lead from the motion-sensor unit to the black wire leads from the bulb sockets, using a wire connector. Some light fixtures have pre-tagged wire leads for easy installation.

Grounding clip

5 Attach the bare copper grounding wire to the grounding clip on the box.

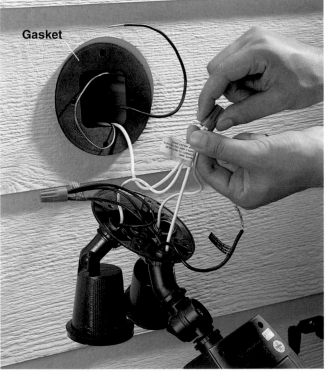

Gasket

6 Slide the foam gasket over the circuit wires at the electrical box. Connect the white circuit wire to the white wire leads on the light fixture, using a wire connector.

(continued next page)

How to Connect a Motion-sensor Light Fixture (continued)

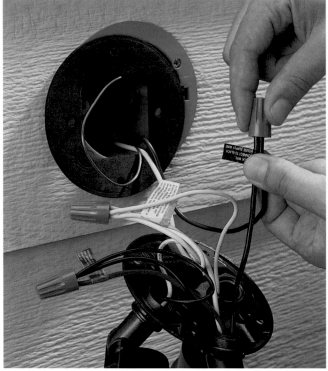

7 Connect the black circuit wire to the black wire lead on the light fixture, using a wire connector.

8 Carefully tuck the wires into the box, then position the light fixture and attach the faceplate to the box, using the mounting screws included with the light fixture. (See also circuit map 4, page 166.)

How to Add a Motion Sensor to an Existing Light Fixture

1 Retrofit an existing garage light with a motion sensor kit (available at most hardware stores and home centers). Remove the lightbulb and mount the sensor unit below the light fixture.

2 Screw the socket adapter into the bulb socket. Screw the lightbulb into the adapter.

3 Connect the socket adapter to the sensor unit. Test and adjust the sensor as directed by the manufacturer.

How to Connect the GFCI Receptacle

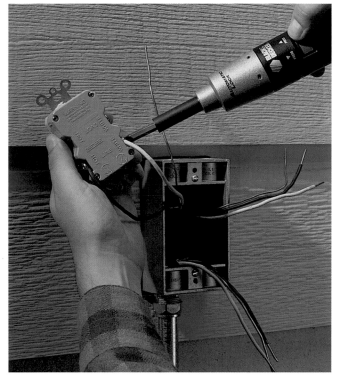

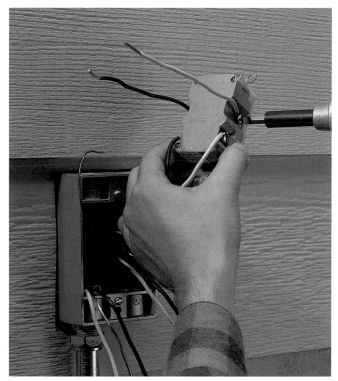

1 Connect the black feed wire from the power source to the brass terminal marked LINE. Connect the white feed wire from the power source to the silver screw terminal marked LINE.

2 Attach the short white pigtail wire to the silver screw terminal marked LOAD, and attach a short black pigtail wire to the brass screw terminal marked LOAD.

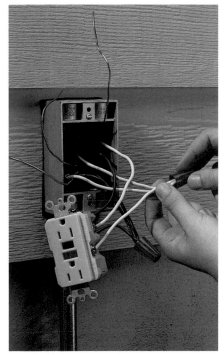

3 Connect the black pigtail wire to all the remaining black circuit wires, using a wire connector. Connect the white pigtail wire to the remaining white circuit wires.

4 Attach a grounding pigtail to the grounding screw on the GFCI. Join the grounding pigtail to the bare copper grounding wires, using a wire connector.

5 Carefully tuck the wires into box. Mount GFCI, then fit a foam gasket over the box and attach the weatherproof coverplate. (See also circuit map 3, page 165.)

How to Connect an Outdoor Receptacle

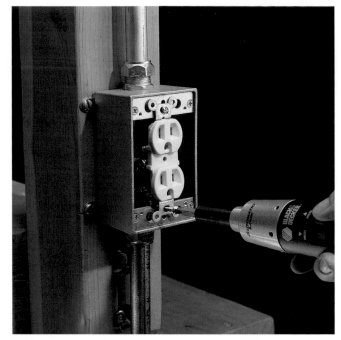

1 Connect the black circuit wires to the brass screw terminals on the receptacle. Connect the white circuit wires to the silver screw terminals on the receptacle. Attach a grounding pigtail to the grounding screw on the receptacle, then join all grounding wires with a wire connector.

2 Carefully tuck all wires into the box, and attach the receptacle to the box, using the mounting screws. Fit a foam gasket over the box, and attach the weatherproof coverplate.

How to Connect a Decorative Light Fixture

Compression fitting

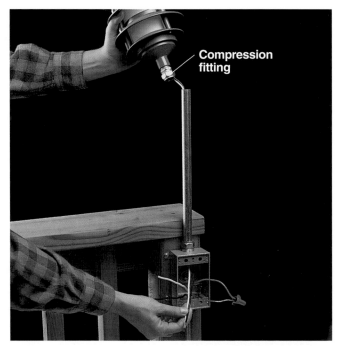

Compression fitting

1 Thread the wire leads of the light fixture through a threaded compression fitting. Screw the union onto the base of the light fixture.

2 Feed wire leads through conduit and into switch box. Slide light fixture onto conduit, and tighten compression fitting. Connect black wire lead to one screw terminal on switch, and connect white wire lead to white circuit wire. (See also circuit map 4, page 166.)

288

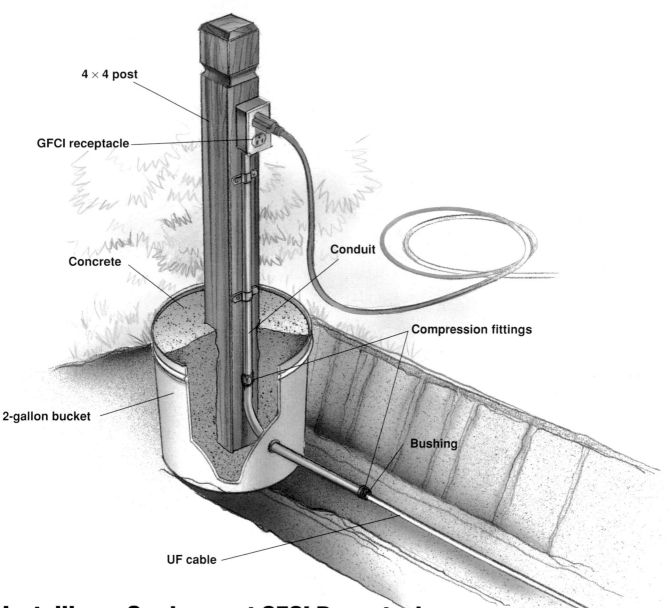

4 × 4 post

GFCI receptacle

Conduit

Concrete

Compression fittings

2-gallon bucket

Bushing

UF cable

Installing a Garden-post GFCI Receptacle

If exterior receptacles are in short supply or they're just too far from the landscaping you'd like to light, adding a garden-post GFCI may be the solution. Receptacles can be installed almost anywhere in a yard to power lighting or provide electricity for power tools.

The following sequence illustrates a basic method for creating a freestanding receptacle anchored to a wood post embedded in a bucket of concrete. The receptacle is wired with UF cable running through a trench from a junction box inside your house or garage. Sections of conduit protect the outdoor cable where it's exposed.

If you'd like to attach the outlet to an existing landscape structure, such as a deck, fence, or gazebo, you can modify the project by attaching the receptacle box and conduit to that structure. Keep in mind that freestanding receptacles

should be at least 12", but no more than 18", above ground level.

Before you begin this project, have your local inspector review your plans and issue a work permit. If local code requires that your work be inspected, schedule these visits at the appropriate points during the project.

Everything You Need

Tools: Shovel, drill, hack saw, combination tool, fish tape, screwdrivers, circuit tester.

Materials: LB connector, metal sweeps, 1" metal conduit, compression fittings, plastic bushings, pipe straps, 2-gallon bucket, concrete, 4-foot post, outdoor receptacle box, 12-gauge UF cable, GFCI receptacle.

How to Install a Garden-post GFCI Receptacle

1 Plan a convenient route from an accessible indoor junction to the location you've chosen for the receptacle. Drill a 1"-diameter hole through the exterior wall, near the junction box. Mark the underground cable run from the hole in the wall to the location for the receptacle. Carefully remove 8" to 12" of sod along the marked route, then dig a trench that's at least 12" deep.

2 Install the LB connector on the outside of the hole. Cut a length of conduit 4" shorter than the distance from the LB connector to the bottom of the trench. Attach the conduit to a sweep fitting, using a compression fitting. Fit a plastic bushing in the open end of the sweep to keep its edges from damaging the cable. Attach the conduit assembly to the bottom of the LB connector, then anchor the conduit to the wall with pipe straps. Cut a length of conduit to extend from the LB connector through the wall and into the house. Attach the conduit to the LB connector from the inside of the house, then attach a plastic bushing to the open end of the conduit.

3 Drill a 1½" hole through the side of a 2-gallon plastic bucket, near the bottom. Mount the receptacle box to the post with galvanized screws. Position the post in the bucket. Measure and cut a length of conduit to run from the receptacle box to a point 4" above the base of the bucket. Attach the conduit to the receptacle box and mount it to the post with pipe straps. Insert a conduit sweep through the hole in the bucket and attach it to the end of the conduit, using a compression fitting. Thread a plastic bushing onto the open end of the sweep. Dig a hole at the end of the trench. Place the bucket with the post into the hole, then fill the bucket with concrete and let it dry completely.

4 Measure the distance from the junction box in the house out to the receptacle box. Cut a length of UF cable 2 ft. longer than this measurement. At each end of the cable, use a utility knife to pare away 8" of the outer sheathing. Lay the cable along the bottom of the trench from the house to the receptacle location. Open the cover on the LB connector and feed a fish tape down through the conduit and out of the sweep. Feed the wires at the end of the UF cable through the loop in the fish tape, then wrap electrical tape around the wires up to the sheathing. Carefully fish the end of the cable up through the conduit to the LB connector.

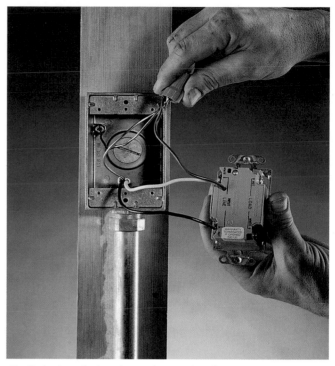

5 At the other end of the trench, feed the fish tape down through the conduit and out of the sweep. Attach the exposed wires to the loop in the fish tape, and secure them with electrical tape. Pull the cable through the conduit up into the receptacle box. About ½" of cable sheathing should extend into the box. Connect the cable with a cable clamp.

6 Strip insulation from the ends of the wires and connect the black wire to the brass LINE terminal on the GFCI. Connect the white wire to the silver LINE terminal. Connect the grouding wire and the grounding lead from the GFCI to grounding screw on the box. Carefully tuck all the wires into the receptacle box, then mount the receptacle. Install the coverplate.

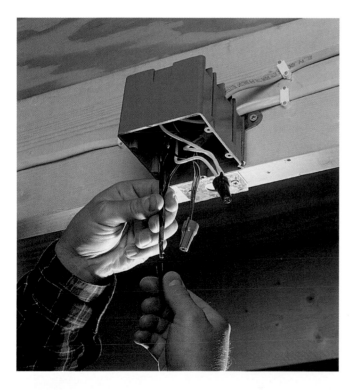

7 From inside the house, extend the fish tape through the conduit and LB connector. Attach the cable wires to the fish tape, then pull the cable into the house. Anchor the cable along framing members to the junction box, using cable staples. Turn off the power to the junction box, and remove the junction box cover. Test the circuit with a neon tester. Open a knockout in the side of the junction box, and then pull the end of the UF cable into the box through the knockout, and secure it with a cable clamp. Unscrew the wire connector attached to the bare copper grounding wires inside the box. Position the new grounding wire alongside the existing wires and re-place the wire connector. Using the same technique, connect the new black wire to the existing black wires, and connect the new white wire to the existing white wires. Replace the junction box cover and re-store the power to the circuit. Test the receptacle. Fill the trench and replace the sod.

Typical low-voltage outdoor lighting system consists of: lens cap (A), lens cap posts (B), upper reflector (C), lens (D), base/stake/cable connector assembly (contains lower reflector) (E), low-voltage cable (F), lens hood (G), 7-watt 12-volt bulbs (H), cable connector caps (I), control box containing transformer and timer (J), light sensor (K).

Low-voltage Landscape Lighting

Low-voltage outdoor lighting systems are the easiest way to bring lighting to a landscape. The basic system is simple: A transformer connected to an outdoor receptacle steps household voltage down to 12 volts. Cable then carries current to individual fixtures. Installation is easy, and you don't need a permit or an inspection. Home improvement centers carry a variety of fixtures, transformers, and controls, as well as all-in-one kits.

Kits are a quick and easy way to add a few lights, but you can also buy individual fixtures and transformers for a custom lighting array.

Determine what parts of your landscape you want to light. You'll need to know this to purchase fixtures and the right transformers. Make a sketch of your yard, including locations of re-

ceptacles. Mark locations for lights, including decks, arbors, patios, and other features. Light all pathways every 8 to 10 ft.

Once you've decided what you want to light, you can pick fixtures. All 12-volt fixtures will work together so you can mix and match manufacturers.

After you've decided on fixtures, note the wattage of all the lights you plan to use and add them to your diagram. Once you've filled in the wattages, you can begin mapping out circuits. The illustration on page 294 shows several common circuits. Draw cable paths onto your diagram, keeping in mind obstructions like sidewalks or driveways. Lengthy cable runs or too many fixtures on a single cable can result in dim lights, so plan multiple circuits and avoid long cable runs (see the chart on the next page).

If you will be lighting landscaping far from the main power source, consider installing a 120-volt GFCI receptacle near the area you want to light (page 289 to 291). This will minimize voltage drop on the low-voltage cables.

Some layouts may work better if you use several smaller circuits and transformers instead of one

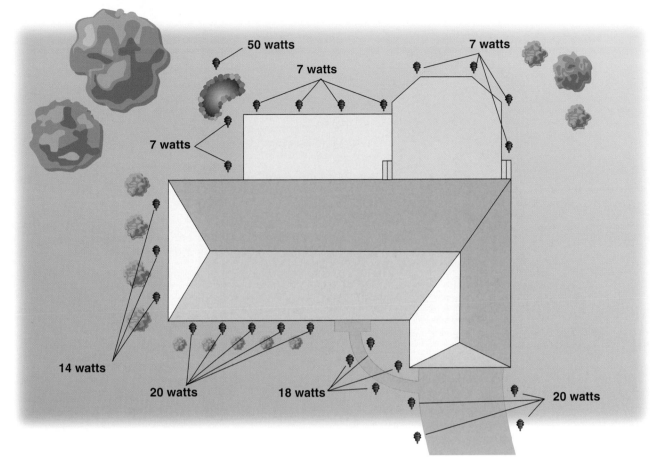

50 watts

7 watts

7 watts

7 watts

14 watts

20 watts

18 watts

20 watts

Make a diagram of your yard and mark the location of new fixtures. Note the wattages of the fixtures and use the diagram to select a transformer and plan the circuits.

high-wattage transformer and one large circuit. For example, if you want to light a back deck as well as front landscaping, install separate systems for greater control and ease of wiring.

Once you've mapped out the circuits and determined how many separate systems you want to use, add up the wattages on each system. Purchase transformers with enough capacity to handle the loads plus at least 25 watts. If you plan to use submersible lights, be sure to purchase a transformer rated for them.

Circuit length	Cable Gauge	Max Watts
up to 100 ft.	16	150 W
100–150 ft.	14	200 W
150–200 ft.	12	300 W

Recommended cable lengths and gauges.

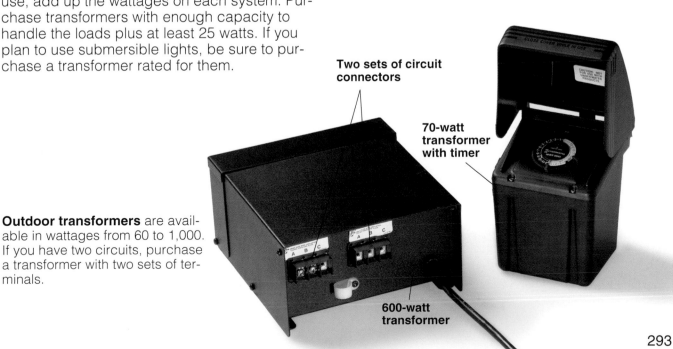

Two sets of circuit connectors

70-watt transformer with timer

Outdoor transformers are available in wattages from 60 to 1,000. If you have two circuits, purchase a transformer with two sets of terminals.

600-watt transformer

How to Install a Low-voltage Landscape Lighting Transformer

  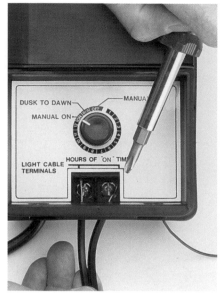

1 Install your transformer or transformers. If you are installing one in a garage, mount it on a wall within 24" of the GFCI receptacle and at least 12" off the floor. If you are using an outdoor receptacle on a wall or a post, mount the transformer on the same post or an adjacent post at least 12" off the ground and not more than 24" inches from the receptacle. Do not use an extension cord.

2 Drill a hole through the wall or rim joist for the low-voltage cable and any sensors to pass through (inset). If a circuit begins in a high-traffic area, it's a good idea to protect the cable by running it through a short piece of PVC pipe or conduit and then into the shallow trench.

3 Connect the cable to the transformer. Use the appropriate gauge cable for your circuit load (see page 293). Strip just enough insulation from the ends of the cable to make a good connection with the screw terminals. Make sure there is 10 ft. of cable between the transformer and the first fixture in the circuit. If you are running cable from a transformer on a post, staple the cable to the post an inch or two from the ground.

How to Install a Low-voltage Landscape Light Circuits and Fixtures

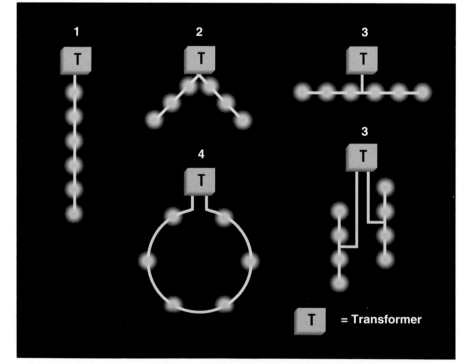

1 Select a circuit layout that avoids long runs of cable. This will minimize light-dimming voltage drop. Serial circuits (1) work best for simple designs with short cable runs. Split circuits (2) allow you to run two cables the maximum distance from the transformer. Tee circuits (3) distribute power evenly to lights that must be placed far from the transformer. You can also split the load over two tee circuits. For more compact designs, loop circuits (4) provide the most even power distribution. Use two transformers or a transformer with two sets of power outlets to create separate circuits that you can independently control (such as one circuit for path lights and another for landscape lights).

2 Lay the cables for each circuit. For routing around and under decks, use cable staples to hold the cable in place. Place the fixtures and connect their wires to the circuit cable. If drainpipes or irrigation systems are nearby, you may want to adjust the pipe or the fixture to minimize moisture contact. To create a branch circuit or to tie into an existing run, solder the wire connections or use plastic splice fittings (inset), which pierce insulation and provide a watertight connection. Use a multimeter to verify continuity on all splices.

3 Connect all the fixtures to the circuit cables. The fixture wires run from the fixture to the circuit cable and connect with special connectors that pierce the insulation on the cable and the wires to make a watertight connection. Most fixtures rest either in the ground or on a stake, but for fixtures mounted in trees, be sure any fasteners you use are stainless steel or cadmium-plated steel. Other materials may poison the tree.

4 Check to make sure the lights are working before you conceal the cable. You can use a multimeterr to make sure you are getting 10 to 12 volts at the point where you want to install your fixture. (Losing two volts to voltage drop on any one circuit is considered acceptable.)

Variation: It's not necessary to bury most low-voltage cable in a trench (in fact, it's easier to diagnose problems if you leave the cable exposed or cover it with wood chips). In high-traffic areas like next to footpaths, sidewalks, or driveways, however, dig a shallow trench to protect cable runs. To run a cable under a sidewalk, use the technique shown on page 277. Test all cable runs with a multimeter for proper current (10–12 volts) before burying.

Recessed Step Lights

Water-tight recessed lights are available for decks. Use them to provide safety lighting on stairs or near edges of raised decks.

Most fixtures are designed to be used on a low-voltage landscape lighting circuit.

The fixtures can be recessed in vertical or horizontal surfaces, but be aware that vertical mounting on stair risers may cause glare by putting bright lights at eye level.

Everything You Need

Tools: Multimeter, combination tool, drill, jig saw, hammer.

Materials: Recessed deck lighting kit, outdoor low-voltage cable, wire connectors, cable staples.

1 Use the template or trace the bottom of the fixture onto the treads to mark holes for each light. Center the fixture on the tread, 1" to 2" from the edge (the hole will center on the gap between the 2 × 6s on most deck stairs). Cut the holes with a jig saw. Test the fixtures to be sure they will fit (they should fit snugly), and adjust the holes as necessary.

2 Run cable from an existing low-voltage system or from a new transformer to the stairs. Drill a hole in the bottom riser if necessary, and snake the cable under the stairs along the inside edge. Pull a loop of cable through each of the holes for the fixtures and temporarily secure it to the tread with tape. Staple cable in place under the treads.

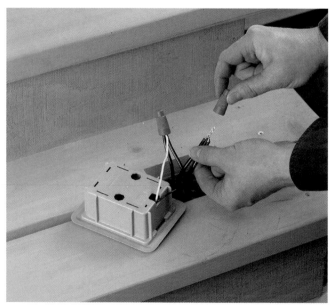

3 At the middle of the first loop of cable in the series, separate 3" to 4" of the two conductors in the cable by slicing down the center. Strip about 2" of insulation off of each wire. Cut the wire in the center of the stripped section, and twist the two ends and the end of one of the fixture wires into an outdoor wire connector. Secure the connection with electrical tape. Repeat with the other fixture wire and the other circuit wire. Tuck the wires back into the hole, and place the fixture into the hole. Test each fixture before installing the next one.

Deck Railing Lights

Rope light is thin, flexible, clear tubing with tiny lightbulbs embedded every few inches along its length. Most rope lights are meant to plug into a receptacle and use 120-volt current. While this is all right for indoor decorating, it limits their use outdoors. Low-voltage versions, however, are powered by transformers and can be connected inconspicuously to a low-voltage landscape lighting circuit. They are available from specialty lighting stores and catalogs.

Everything You Need

Tools: Multimeter, combination tool, hammer.

Materials: Rope lighting, U channel, low-voltage outdoor cable and connectors, cable staples.

1 Run a cable from a transformer or from a nearby low-voltage circuit using a T-connector. Route the cable up a post at the end of the rail, and secure it with cable staples. Leave enough length at the end of the cable to connect it to the rope light.

2 Secure the rope light to the underside of the railing with U channel. Cut the channel to length, and nail it to the bottom of the railing. Press the rope into the channel.

3 Connect the fixture cord to the end of the rope with the twist-on fitting. Connect the rope wires to the branch cable with a cable connector designed for low-voltage outdoor cable. Cap the end of the rope with a plastic cap.

Home Automation

An automated home can add security, peace of mind, and convenience to day-to-day activities like adjusting your home's lighting, temperature and security systems. Home automation components can also enable you to fully maximize the capabilities of your existing home's products and systems, and helps them run more efficiently together. Comprehensive systems have the capability to control lighting, HVAC, irrigation, entertainment components, video surveillance, and pool and spa equipment, just to mention a few. The applications are endless.

Most systems can be upgraded in segments. You can start off with a small, stand-alone system, that costs around $40, and will allow you to turn your lights on and off remotely. Or you can dive in and use your home computer as a command center where you monitor and control everything from your home's temperature and lighting. With some systems, you can configure alerts that call preprogrammed telephone numbers to warn you of a water leak or that an intruder has gained entry. These PC controllers can be software or hardware interfaces or a stand-alone PC-like device built for home automation.

All home-automation systems start with a backbone that carries commands, a main controller that issues commands, and device controllers that translate the command to a compatible device. The backbone of a system is the wiring that carries the commands. Many new homes are hard-wired with high-performance fiber optic, Category 5 (for telephone and data), and coaxial audio and video cable for the ultimate in home control and capability. With sufficient basement or attic access, remodeling a home network can be achieved by running new cables in walls and installing outputs for Internet, satellite, or digital TV data.

Wireless automation systems, like X10, use your home's existing electrical circuit wiring to carry bursts of RF (radio frequency) to command-compatible electric devices that understand the language. These "wireless" systems—sometimes called "powerline carrier systems"—allow ease of installation in places where hard-wiring is not practical.

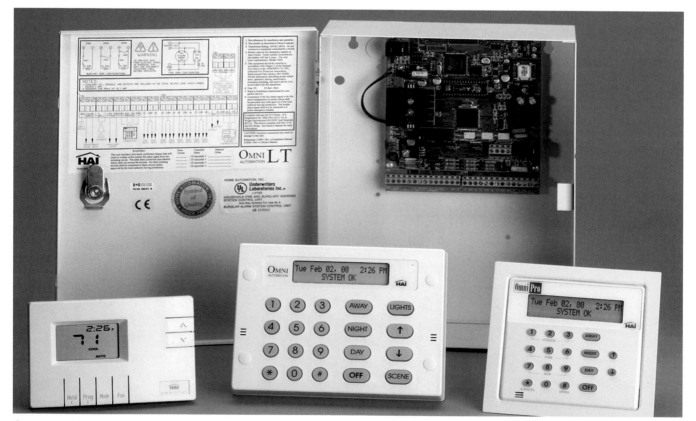

An automation system that uses a network wiring system to route signals throughout the home can be accessed through control panels or key pads mounted in convenient locations around your home.

Wireless home-automation systems all use a protocol—a common language—that all the devices in the automated home network understand to communicate with compatible remote devices. Today, X10 is the predominant protocol in home automation, but other common systems include CEBus, LonWorks, and Smart House. The main obstacle to any home automation is integration. When planning an automation system, take care to purchase components that are compatible with your data transmission system.

Many home automation components now offer two-way communication, meaning that they not only send out signals to control your home's lighting, heaters, home stereo equipment, or other electric devices, they also have the capability to receive information from external sensors, report on that information (by telephone), and intervene if necessary.

For example, sensors can be installed to shut off water in the event of a leak. When the sensor senses the leak, it will automatically shut off the water main and call several preprogrammed phone numbers to alert you to the situation. Other sensors can be programmed to report by phone on temperature and other indoor and outdoor home conditions to keep you informed while you

are away from home. These systems are especially useful for vacation homes or second homes.

Do-it-yourself home automation systems are readily available at home centers, retail outlets, and online retailers. Cost and complexity varies, depending on the scale, control, and complexity of the system. Almost all systems are upgradeable for future expansion. Command and control products have existed for years. To remain competitive, today's manufacturers are increasingly developing specifications for very low-cost command and control applications.

The market for automation devices is increasing as consumers become more technically savvy, and demand higher performance from their household devices. Many businesses now use a home-office as their main command center, and as such, they require high-speed data transmission and computer networking capabilities, not to mention increased security to protect their investment. Whether you are outfitting a single-family home, commercial property, or home office, home automation products increase the value of your property. They can also offer you increased home convenience, capability, safety, and energy efficiency that can save valuable time and money over time.

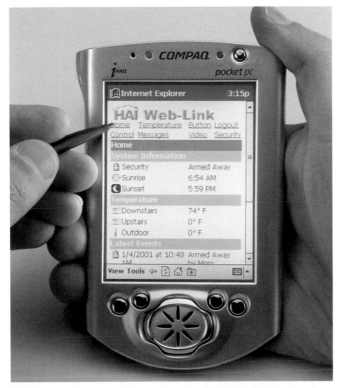

PDAs can be used to activate different features of your home automation system from outside the house via the Internet.

X10 is the simplest and most affordable retrofit automation system. It uses existing wiring to control everything from lighting to appliances from a variety of controllers.

X10 remote-control technology does not require additional wiring—so the chore and expense of cutting holes in wallboard and running new cable is eliminated. Devices can be switched on and off and dimmed from control panels or wireless remotes (inset).

Installing an X10 System

An X10 system uses your home's existing electric wiring to remotely control most electric devices in your home. Because X10 technology does not require cutting holes in drywall and running new wiring, the systems are popular additions to existing homes seeking home automation.

The X10 system works by using your home's existing electrical wiring as a communication conduit to transmit radio-frequency (RF) control signals to every outlet in your house, allowing you to plug in X10 modules (devices that receive and translate X10 signals) to turn individual lights, appliances, or other devices on and off.

Basic X10 modules understand six actions: on, off, all on, all off, dim, and brighten. More sophisticated modules can perform additional functions like controlling the speed of a ceiling fan or turning off a high-load appliance like a hot tub.

Because each X10 module in your home receives all the RF control signals sent from the X10 controller, the system is coded with addresses that identify which module is which. Otherwise it would be impossible to direct a command to only one light or one group of lights in a home full of X10 modules. For this reason, the X10 system identifies modules with 16 different house codes (letters A to P) and 16 different unit codes (numbers 1 to 16), for a total of 256 pieces of unique controllable equipment.

For example, program all your home's exterior lighting as house code "E." To turn all the exterior lights on at once, have your controller send a signal that commands all "E" lights to come on. If you would like only the front porch light to come on, then code that light as 1 of 16 possible outdoor lights on the "E" section of your home. Then send a signal that commands light "E-1" to come on.

Controllers vary from handheld models like TV remotes to key-fob remotes to desktop keypads. Most X10 modules are similar in size to a small, square AC adaptor. To minimize visibility of the system, you can install in-wall X10 receptacles that look similar to a typical 120-volt power outlet. X10 wall switches are a simple, discreet way to control hardwired lights, ceiling fans, heaters, and other devices.

Everything You Need

Tools: Screwdriver.

Materials: X10 starter kit.

How to Install an X10 System

1 Plug in the lamp or appliance receiver module into a standard 120-volt outlet.

2 Plug the lamp or appliances you would like to control into the receiver module.

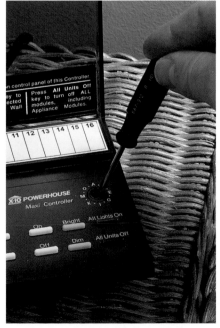

3 Program the unit. Some units program by pressing a reset button, after which they retain the first code received from a transmitter (shown). Others have dial for "house" and "unit" codes. Use a small screwdriver to turn the code dials to set a unique house and unit code that identifies the module's address.

4 Plug a system transmitter, such as the desktop controller (shown) or wireless remote transceiver, into another three-pin (grounded) or two-pin (nongrounded) outlet.

5 Set the system transmitter's code to match the house and unit codes you selected for your receiver modules. To test operation, use the controller to send a specific ON or OFF command to a specific lamp or appliance module address.

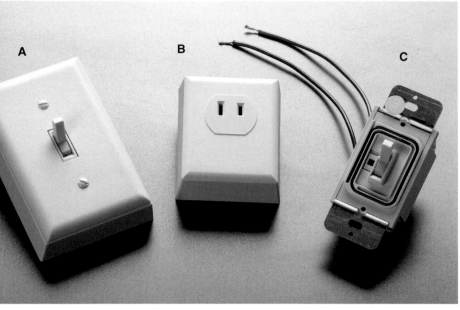

With a wireless wall switch kit, you can add a switch to control a hardwired light fixture in minutes, without any additional wiring. Kits include a transmitter switch (A) and a plug-in receiver (B) base or a receiver switch (C).

Everything You Need

Tools: Screwdriver, circuit tester.

Materials: Wireless switch kit.

Adding a Light Switch Without New Wiring

A wireless wall switch is a simple way to add an additional switch without the time and expense of cutting holes in wallboard and running new cable. Switches come in different configurations from basic toggle switches that control one light to X-10-based "scene" control panels with separate buttons that can turn on or off and dim several fixtures.

One easy and inexpensive configuration is to replace a standard light switch with a receiver light switch. The receiver switch operates like a normal switch, but it also can be turned on and off by a wireless transmitter switch, which can be mounted anywhere within a 50-ft. radius of the receiver switch. These systems can be found at hardware stores and home centers for under $20. Receivers that screw into bulb sockets are also available.

How to Add a Remote Switch to Control a Hardwired Fixture

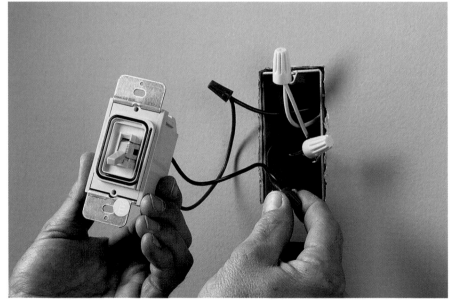

1 Turn off power to the circuit. Disconnect the old switch. If two cables enter the box, restore the power and use a tester to find the hot black wire (the "line" wire from the panel). Turn the power off. Connect the circuit wires to the new receiver switch. Connect the black line wire to the LINE lead. Connect the other black wire to the LOAD lead. Connect the two neutral wires, and pigtail ground wires together. Screw on the switch and replace the cover.

2 Install the battery in the wireless transmitter switch and mount it anywhere within a 50-ft. radius of the receiver switch. Most models mount with adhesive or Velcro.

Adding Keychain Remote Control to Home Lighting

A basic wireless keychain remote controller can be used to control two or more home lighting devices. More elaborate systems can control several devices and appliances. Keychain remotes allow you to turn on your home's interior or exterior lighting to brighten a dark sidewalk or entryway. Never walk into a dark house again.

Installation of the system is simple, just plug a receiver module into a 120-volt outlet and then plug a light or other device into the outlet on the bottom of the receiver module. Program the keychain remote to identify each individual transceiver's "address" (a house code and a unit code), and installation is complete.

Everything You Need

Tools: Screwdriver.

Materials: Keychain remote kit.

How to Add a Keychain Remote to Home Lighting

1 Select an address code on the receiver module. Lift the cover on the receiver module and use a screwdriver to choose a unique address for the lamp you wish to operate. If this is your only device, any address will do.

2 Plug the lamp you would like to control into the receiver module. Plug the module into a 120-volt receptacle. If the hardwired outlet you are utilizing is controlled by a wall switch, make sure the switch remains in the ON position.

3 To program the keychain remote with the address of the light you would like to control, hold the remote near the receiver module and press down one of the the remote's ON buttons for five to six seconds. The LED light will flash, signaling that the remote is programming itself with the address of the nearest module. Repeat this process to program the second ON button for another module. Programming methods may vary. Follow manufacturer's instructions.

Devices like the Cottage Sitter from Sensaphone can be programmed to dial up to eight phone numbers when abnormal conditions occur, such as temperature dips or spikes, water leaks, or forced entry/intrusions. The system will continue dialing your programmed alarm phone numbers in sequence, until the call is answered. It can also control a thermostat.

Installing a Remote Thermostat Control

Many thermostats that offer remote control from a computer or phone require professional installation. The Sensaphone Cottage Sitter is easy to install and allows you to use a telephone to monitor your home or cabin while you are away. The Cottage Sitter also allows telephone command of a thermostat, ensuring that your house is warm from the moment you walk in the door. And if you forget to turn the thermostat down before you leave, you can easily command that function by telephone. The thermostat can also be controlled locally, using the manual controls on the thermostat.

The Cottage Sitter is simple to install, program, and operate and requires no changes to your standard electrical or telephone service. The Cottage Sitter can work with an existing three- or four-wire, low-voltage thermostat, but you will need to install a secondary thermostat wired in parallel by passing the low-voltage supply through the Sensaphone. Set the primary thermostat to an "at-home" temperature. Set the secondary thermostat to an "away" temperature to keep your home at minimal heat when you are away. You can choose which thermostat will control your furnace from any touch-tone phone.

An easier option is to replace the existing thermostat with a Sensaphone-compatible setback thermostat that is preprogrammed with an "away" and a "home" temperature setting. The advantage of this option is that it requires only one thermostat for all heating and air conditioning tasks. One pair of wires connects the setback thermostat to the Cottage Sitter.

In addition to controlling thermostats, the Sensaphone will give you temperature updates, and depending on the sensors you install, it can alert you to water leaks, power failures, broken glass, and a host of others. The unit can be programmed to dial up to eight phone numbers until it gets an answer.

Everything You Need

Tools: Screwdriver, circuit tester.

Materials: Sensaphone Cottage Sitter, setback thermostat.

How to Install a Sensaphone Cottage Sitter with a Setback Thermostat

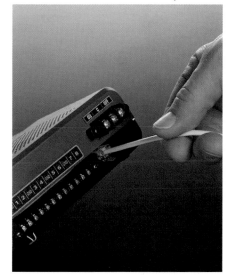

1 Open the battery compartment and install the recommended batteries for power backup (most units use six D-cell batteries). Use a phone cord to connect the transceiver to any standard phone jack. Plug the transceiver's electric cord into a 120-volt outlet.

2 At the main panel, shut off power to the furnace. Remove the cover plate on your existing thermostat and pull it out of the wall just enough to view wire connections. Write down the terminal location (R, W, G, Y) of each colored wire connected on the existing thermostat. Disconnect the wires on the old thermostat and remove.

3 Attach the base plate of the new thermostat to the wall. Connect each of the wires that were connected to the old thermostat to the same terminal labels on the new setback thermostat. Using the provided cable, connect the CLK1 wire to the remote terminal (in this case, labelled *X*); connect the CLK2 wire to the C (common) terminal. Snap the thermostat onto the base plate. Terminal labels may vary; consult manufacturer's instructions for exact wiring.

4 Connect the CLK1 wire from the setback thermostat to the ON terminal on the back of the Cottage Sitter. Connect the CLK2 wire to the C terminal. Turn on the power to the furnace and check the thermostat for proper operation.

5 Program the transceiver according to your needs and the manufacturer's specifications. Programming consists of setting high and low temperature limits, configuring any additional sensor inputs as normally open or normally closed (according to sensor type), and setting dial-out telephone numbers for emergency notification. Before programming, it is very important to check that the sensors you have wired to the unit are set in their normal, nonalarm positions. Mount the Cottage Sitter transceiver on a wall or set it on a table near the thermostat.

How to Install Automatic Water Shutoff Valves on a Washer

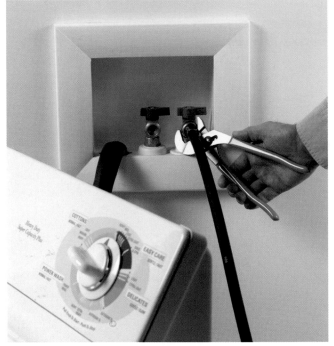

1 Turn your home's main water supply off. Locate the flexible supply hoses that supply the washer, and turn the shutoff valves off. Use a wrench or pliers to disconnect the water supply hoses from the existing shutoff valves.

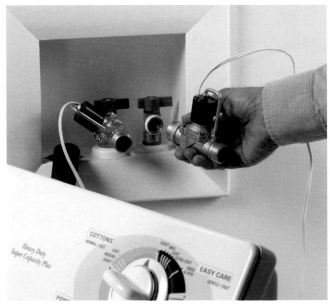

2 Connect one automatic shutoff valve to each of the existing hot and cold shutoff valves that serve the washer (wrap all threads with Teflon plumber's tape before installing). Reconnect the water supply hoses to the automatic shutoff valve outlets. Turn the water main on and check for leaks.

Installing Automatic Water Shutoff Valves

An automatic water shutoff valve can protect your home or vacation property from costly water damage caused by leaking washing machines, dishwashers, toilets, or refrigerator ice machines. The system uses a water sensor placed on the floor in the vicinity of the appliance. If a leak does occur, the sensor sends an electrical signal to a control unit, which then activates a magnetic shutoff valve that stops the flow of water to the appliance. Installation of the system is simple, requires no plumber or specialized tools, and typically can be up and running in under an hour.

More elaborate whole-house systems are also available. These install at the main shut off valve. Wireless sensors placed near appliances and pipes sense leaks and tell the valve to shut off water to the whole house.

Everything You Need

Tools: Drill, screwdriver, adjustable wrench or pliers.

Materials: Teflon tape, automatic shutoff valve kit.

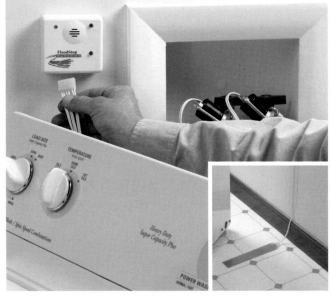

3 Mount the control unit in a location convenient for periodic testing. Plug the valve and sensor wiring harness into the control unit. Connect the water sensor by attaching the supplied two-conductor wire to the terminals on the back of the control unit. Place the water sensor on the floor immediately under the supply pipes (inset). Connect the transformer to the control unit and plug in the transformer. Look for an indicator light that signals the system is operational.

Installing a Wireless Phone Jack

A wireless phone jack system will allow you to quickly convert any 120-volt outlet into a working phone jack. A typical kit includes one base unit transmitter, one receiver module, and a six-foot phone cord. The system works by sending a signal from an existing phone jack (via 120-volt transmitter) to a 120-volt jack receiver module in another room. Change the location of the added phone jack at any time by moving it to a different 120-volt outlet. The entire system can be installed in minutes and requires no tools, drilling, or wiring.

Each wireless phone jack system can be used to add one phone jack anywhere in the house. This system is ideal for quickly installing a phone in a bathroom or guest room.

To prevent interference, locate the receiver module away from TV or radio equipment.

Everything You Need

Materials: Wireless switch kit, telephone.

How to Add a Wireless Phone Jack

1 Plug the telephone cable from an existing telephone jack into either jack on the right side of the base unit. (It is important to plug in the base unit before the receiver unit. In the event of a problem, unplug both units and start again.)

2 Plug the base unit transmitter into a nearby 120-volt outlet. To use a phone at the existing jack location, plug that phone into the extra jack on the side of the base unit transmitter.

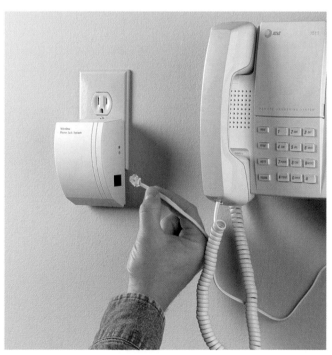

3 Plug the wireless phone jack receiver module into a 120-volt outlet near where you would like your new phone jack. Plug a telephone, modem, fax, or other telephone-operated equipment into the jack on the receiver unit. There should now be a dial tone on the added phone line.

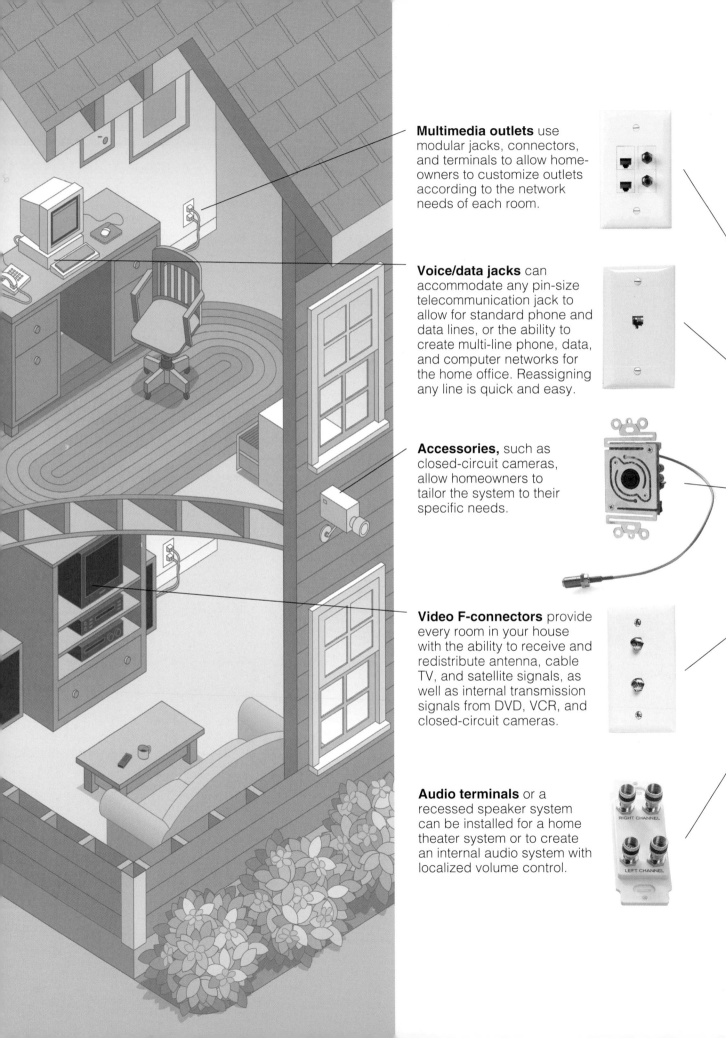

Multimedia outlets use modular jacks, connectors, and terminals to allow home-owners to customize outlets according to the network needs of each room.

Voice/data jacks can accommodate any pin-size telecommunication jack to allow for standard phone and data lines, or the ability to create multi-line phone, data, and computer networks for the home office. Reassigning any line is quick and easy.

Accessories, such as closed-circuit cameras, allow homeowners to tailor the system to their specific needs.

Video F-connectors provide every room in your house with the ability to receive and redistribute antenna, cable TV, and satellite signals, as well as internal transmission signals from DVD, VCR, and closed-circuit cameras.

Audio terminals or a recessed speaker system can be installed for a home theater system or to create an internal audio system with localized volume control.

RIGHT CHANNEL

LEFT CHANNEL

Home Network Wiring Systems

The ability to send and receive information electronically has become an important part of our lives. Internet access, multiple phone lines, cable television, satellites, wired and wireless home computer networks, and security systems are commonplace in many homes. And as our telecommunications needs grow, a better, faster, and more convenient way to manage these separate systems will be necessary.

A **home network system** brings all these single systems together at one central location. It provides a transmission path for **electronic information** rather than for electricity. Electronic information can be voice, video, audio, or computer data. Network wiring is about moving this electronic information to wherever you need it.

Older phone and cable TV wiring use a continuous loop wiring method. With this method, various jacks and connectors are installed along a single loop of cable or wire running throughout the house. Though easier to install, this method is unreliable, especially with the large demands placed upon the lines by computers and other electronic devices.

In this traditional method, the cable or wire that is split runs from the demarcation point, Network Interface Device (NID), or service entrance—the point where the service providers transfer ownership of the lines to the homeowner. The transmission signals are strongest at the point they enter the home. But repeatedly splitting cables and wires throughout the run degrades the strength of the signal. Also, if there is a problem in the line, all the jacks and connectors in the run are affected.

New home network wiring systems resolve this problem. The system employs a **star topology**, in which all cables and wires are distributed from a central point. All inputs are brought to a centralized distribution center that contains modules designed to maintain the strength of voice, data, and video (VDV) transmission signals. High-performance cable and wires are routed to any room in the house where VDV capability is necessary. Plug-and-play multimedia outlets provide easy access to a variety of signals.

The system can be used to create home computer networks, multiroom audio systems, multiple phone lines for home offices, and distribution for DVD, DVR, VCR, or closed-circuit television signals to any room of the house.

Installing a system is a project that any homeowner can accomplish. Many home centers carry all the components and materials necessary for installation.

It is much easier to run cables and wires in unfinished walls, but retrofit installations are quite manageable if you carefully plan the system needs, determine the optimal location for each unit, and map out the cable routes.

Though installation methods and techniques for network wiring systems are generally the same, there are some differences between the different manufacturers' systems. Always carefully read and follow both the instruction and operation manuals provided by the manufacturer of your specific network wiring system.

Installing a Home Network System

With the increasing need for networking capabilities in the home for work and entertainment, standards have been developed by the Telecommunications Industry Association (TIA) and the Electronic Industry Alliance (EIA) in accordance with the Federal Communications Commission (FCC). These standards are becoming the code requirements for home network wiring installation across the country. Make sure to check with your local building inspector for the current codes in this new and changing area of home wiring.

There are four components to a network wiring system: the **distribution center**, the **distribution modules, cables and wires,** and the **multimedia outlets.** Each component serves a particular function in the distribution of voice, data, and video signals throughout your home network system.

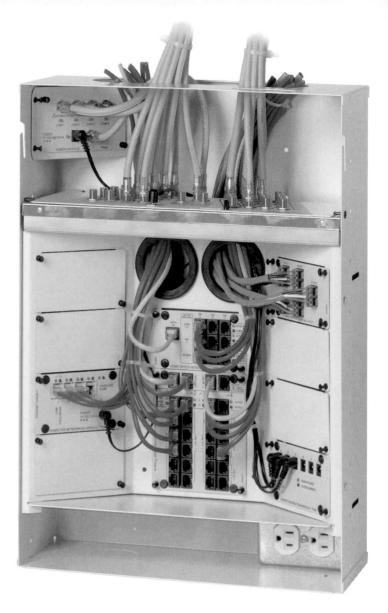

Installing a Home Network System

Distribution Center

The distribution center is the central hub of the network wiring system, housing the distribution modules and the cable and wire connections that link the entire network. All service cables from outside your home (antenna, cable TV, telecommunication lines, etc.) are routed from the service entrance to the distribution center, where their signals are then distributed to every room in your house. In addition, signals generated within your home (such as DVD, VCR, audio, or computer networks) can be routed back to the center and redistributed to the multimedia outlets in the rooms of your choice.

Distribution centers are designed to allow easy access to the modules and cable connections. This makes reconfiguring outlets in any room quick and simple. Most distribution centers are heavy-gauge steel boxes with plastic covers, sized to fit between standard stud spans of 16" on-center. These enclosure-style centers

have open tops or holes to accommodate the many cables and wires routed to and from the modules contained inside. Smaller distribution centers that hold only a few of the most basic modules are also available. These centers are generally not enclosed, so care must be taken to keep all cables and wires together.

Typically, the lower portion of the distribution center houses the electrical transformer that supplies power to the system. A dedicated 15-amp, 120-volt, nonswitchable duplex receptacle must be installed, either in the enclosure itself or within 60" of the distribution center.

The upper portion of the center is reserved for video distribution modules, while a mounting bracket or brackets are fastened at the middle section to hold various home network modules.

Installing a Home Network System
Distribution Modules

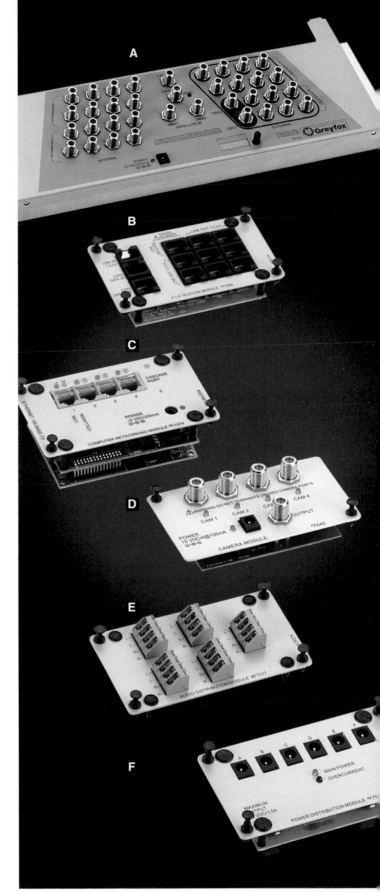

The distribution modules are the interface devices used to maintain and strengthen the signal for further routing throughout the system. Each module contains at least one INPUT port for receiving the incoming signal to be distributed (or redistributed), and a series of OUTPUT ports for routing the desired signal to the desired locations. Each module is designed to serve a particular function:

Video distribution modules receive and distribute cable, satellite, UHF, VHF, and other coaxial signals throughout the network. Video modules are also used to create internal video networks through the use of a modulator, a device that receives signals from a source (DVD, VCR, or video camera) and assigns those signals to the unused channels in the cable or satellite system.

Telecommunication modules distribute voice and data signals received from various RJ45 jacks throughout the home network and out to the world.

Computer network modules are used to create home computer networks when used with, and properly configured to, Ethernet network cards and software. Many **home office modules** are available that combine the best attributes of the telecommunication and computer network modules for convenient transference of information.

Camera modules distribute video and audio signals received from closed-circuit monitoring cameras to all external TV outlets for viewing. This module typically works in conjunction with a video distribution module.

Audio distribution modules route audio signals received from your stereo receiver or amplifier to speakers or terminals mounted in various locations.

Power distribution modules supply power for all internal DC power patch cords to the amplifier or panel, as well as to those modules requiring a source of electricity.

Manufacturers continually develop new interface modules to support a greater range of systems, from security to internal intercom. Modules compatible with home automation systems (pages 298 to 309) will receive and distribute the signals for lighting control or localized climate control options.

Video distribution modules (A), telecommunication modules (B), computer network modules (C), camera modules (D), audio distribution modules (E), power distribution modules (F).

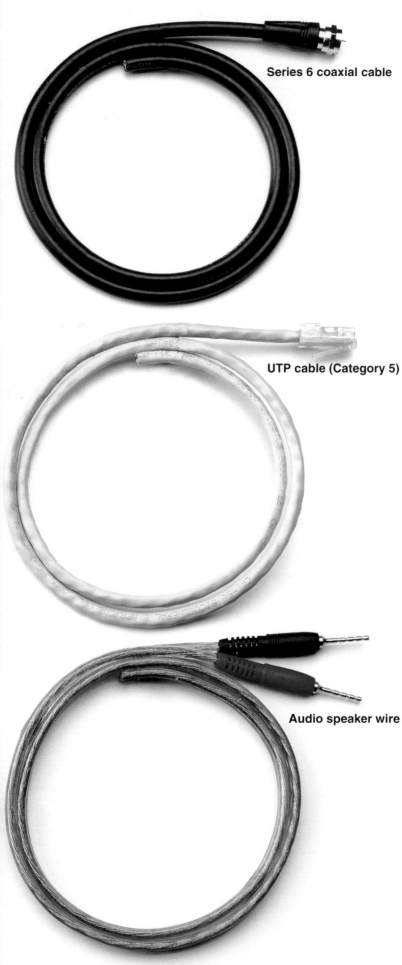

Series 6 coaxial cable

UTP cable (Category 5)

Audio speaker wire

Cables & Wires

Cables and wires carry signals dispatched from a source to their intended location. The growing need to transfer larger amounts of data faster requires that cables and wires be capable of carrying a high volume of data.

Cables and wires are rated based on their **bandwidth**, the amount of data that can flow through the cable or wire in a specified unit of time. The greater the bandwidth, the faster data can be transferred.

There are four basic types of cable:

Coaxial cable is used for the distribution of audio/video signals throughout the system. Series 6 cable (or RG-6) is a higher-grade coaxial cable and is preferred for home network systems.

Unshielded twisted-pair (UTP) cables are used to carry phone and data signals throughout the system. The most common UTP cable in use is category 5. It is a higher-grade cable with a large bandwidth and meets all standards requirements.

Audio speaker wire is used to route audio signals throughout the system to create a home theater or a multiroom audio system.

Fiber-optic cable (not pictured) uses a transducer that converts the electrical signal into light to pass through the glass or plastic optical fiber wires. At the other end, another transducer converts the light back to an electrical signal. It is less common in residential applications, but it holds tremendous potential for delivering massive amounts of data, video, and audio at unprecedented speeds. Some homeowners choose to "future-proof" their homes and run fiber optic cable even before they have devices to take advantage of it. That way, the cables will be in place when the technology becomes widely available.

Installing a Home Network System

Multimedia Outlets & Accessories

The network is accessed at various multimedia outlets installed throughout the home. Each outlet contains a series of jacks and connectors for plug-and-play connection of phones, computers, TVs, VCRs, DVDs, and stereo systems.

RJ45 jacks are the ports for connecting phone and data devices to the network system. RJ45 jacks are wired to a universal pin/pair assignment standard (standard T568A). This configuration allows any size telecommunication plug to be used with the jack. For example, your 4-pin phone plug can be inserted (and will fit) into the 8-pin RJ45 jack. That phone jack can then be removed and an 8-pin Ethernet data line plug can be inserted once the jack has been reconfigured at the distribution box.

F-connectors are threaded terminals for connecting video equipment to the system. F-connector fittings on coaxial cable ends simply screw onto the terminal.

Binding posts are the terminals for tying an audio system into the network. The posts are color coded for polarity. Red or "+" is used to signify positive terminals, and black or "–" for negative terminals. Crossing polarity may cause the speakers to be out of phase, in which case the sound will lack some of its bass.

Multimedia outlets can be tailored to the specific needs of the room in which they are located. Outlets in a home office could contain a dedicated RJ45 jack for each phone, fax, and modem line to allow each device to send and receive data more efficiently.

Accessory options are available with all network wiring systems, though most will require a specialized distribution module. The most common are video cameras sized to fit in 4" × 4" gang boxes for a closed-circuit television system and recess-mounted stereo speaker systems for multiroom audio systems with volume control in each room.

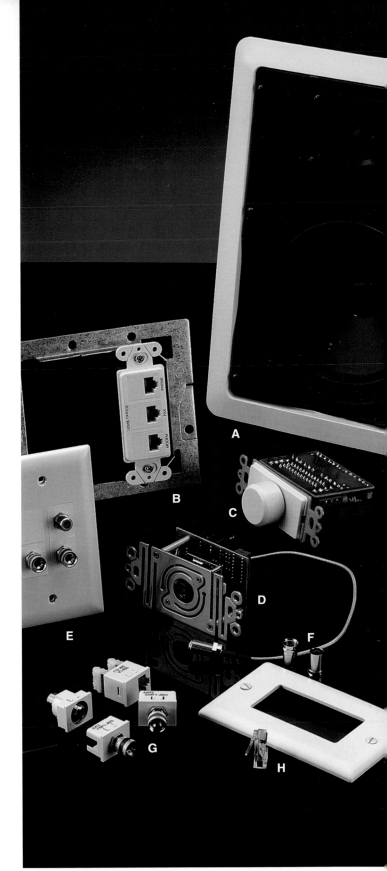

Audio speaker with bracket for recess mounting (A), multimedia outlet with bracket for mounting to electrical receptacles (B), audio system volume control (C), video camera (D), multimedia outlet with audio binding posts (E), F-connectors (F), module jacks and connectors for multimedia outlets (G), RJ45 jack plug (H).

313

A home office will greatly benefit from the many networking capabilities of a home network system. Installing Grade 2 multimedia outlets next to electrical receptacles will provide a centralized location for all your telecommunication connections.

Home entertainment systems also can use many of the networks in the system. Installing Grade 2 multimedia outlets on each wall of the room will help ease future remodeling or redecorating projects, or the addition of new components to the system.

Assessing Needs

When assessing your network system needs, it is always a good idea to install more than you currently think you will use. Routing extra cables and wires to large appliances, such as furnaces and refrigerators, will make it easier to add future home automation features. Extra outlets in rooms will let you connect new telecommunication devices to the network.

Two standard grades of residential cabling installation currently exist.

Grade 1 is a generic cabling system that meets only the minimum requirements for telecommunication services. Each multimedia outlet is provided with one 4-pair UTP cable (minimum category 3, category 5 recommended) as a voice/data line, and one 75-ohm coaxial cable as a video line.

Grade 2 installation meets the requirements for basic, advanced, and multimedia telecommunication services. Two 4-pair UTP cables (minimum category 5, category 5e recommended) are routed to outlets, for one voice line and one data line, as well as two 75-ohm coaxial cables (one input and one output) for video lines. Grade 2 installation standards also suggest two-fiber optical fiber cabling for future applications, though this is entirely optional.

Installing multiple Grade 2 outlets in various locations of a room is recommended, especially in entertainment areas and the home office.

314

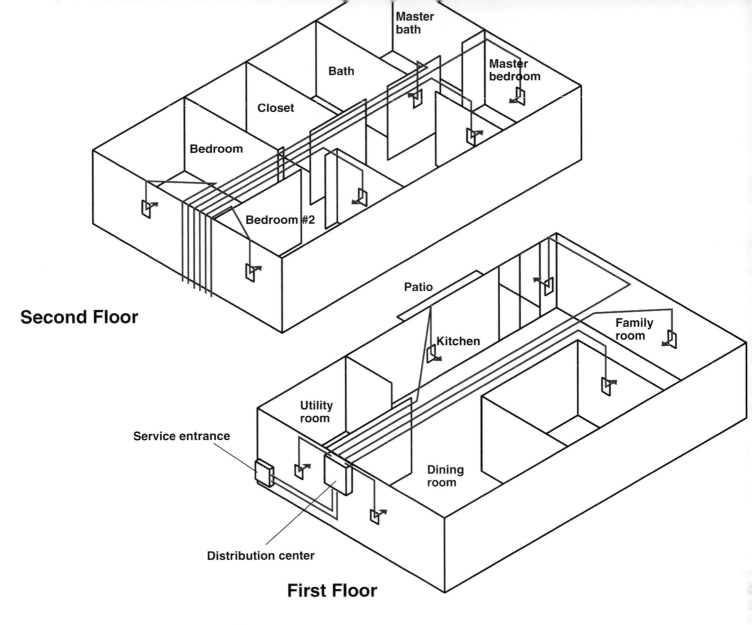

Second Floor

Master bath

Bath

Master bedroom

Closet

Bedroom

Bedroom #2

Patio

Kitchen

Family room

Utility room

Service entrance

Dining room

Distribution center

First Floor

Installing a Home Network System

Determining Locations

A home network system is designed to be installed in a **star topology,** where all cables and wires are distributed from one central point, the distribution center. The center should be installed in an accessible, central location (such as a basement or utility room) and near the demarcation point, NID, or service entrance. Easy access to the distribution center will not only simplify the current installation, but also simplify future alterations to the system. The central location will make cable lengths less likely to extend past their recommended routing length (295 ft.).

Low-voltage cable and wire routes should be carefully planned. Making sketches and routing maps will save time and help determine the best possible path with the least number of turns and bends. Refer to pages 322 to 323 for other cable and wire needs and restrictions.

The living room, home office, bedroom, entertainment room, recreation or game room, and den are all obvious places for multi-media outlets. But outlets in rooms such as the kitchen, bathroom, laundry and utility room, or at large appliances, will help ready your home for future conveniences.

When determining outlet locations within a room, consider the needs of that particular room. Home offices will benefit from multiple phone and data lines for Internet access on the computer. Plan for these outlets to be mounted alongside a 120-volt receptacle to centralize computer connections.

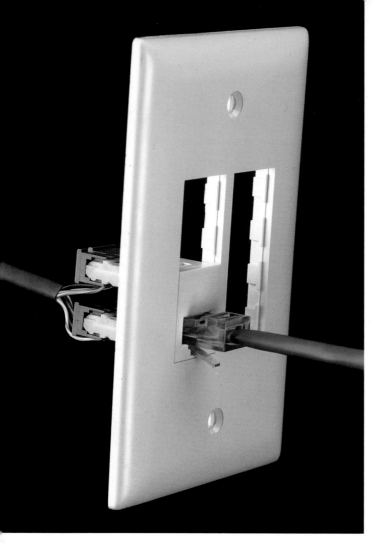

Preparing Multimedia Outlets

Multimedia outlets are installed much like electrical receptacles, though the connections do not need to be contained in a box. The outlets should be mounted at the same height as receptacles, according to local code.

Extension brackets allow multimedia outlets and electrical receptacles to be placed side by side. The location of the 120-volt receptacle/switch box will always determine the height and location of the bracket. Make sure to choose the correct bracket for the outlet type to be installed. Some manufacturers offer specialized alignment tools for lining up the extension brackets with the existing electrical boxes.

For retrofit installations, hollow-backed gang boxes or 4" × 4" gang boxes are used to prevent damage to cables and wires due to bending or twisting.

Everything You Need

Tools: Level, screwdriver, wallboard saw.

Materials: Extension brackets, hollow-back boxes, wallboard screws.

How to Mount a Multimedia Outlet Next to an Existing Electrical Receptacle

1 Fit the extension bracket over the existing electrical receptacle box. Align the bracket so that it is level and square, and properly spaced from the existing box. Use an aligning tool, if provided, or a faceplate as a guide.

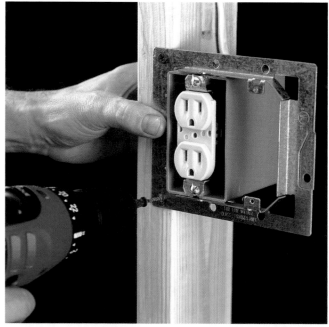

2 Fasten the bracket to the stud with two screws. The multimedia outlet box is then attached to the mounting ears on the extension bracket.

How to Retrofit a Single Multimedia Outlet

1 Use a wallboard saw to cut a hole at the outlet location that will accommodate the box size, a 4" x 4" gang box or hollow-back box, for a single outlet.

2 Route all the desired cables and wires to the distribution center location (pages 320 to 321, and 192 to 203). Leave 12" to 18" of slack at each outlet location.

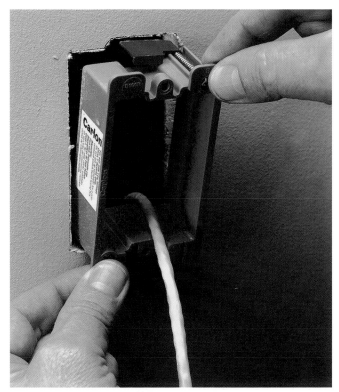

3 Thread all the cables into or through the gang box. Position the box in the hole.

4 Tighten the mounting screws until snug to the wall. Avoid over-tightening the screws to avoid damaging the wallboard.

Installing a Home Network System
Mounting the Distribution Center

Most distribution centers are designed to fit between standard stud spans of 16" on-center. For stud bays of different dimensions, you'll need to install blocking to support the distribution center. Retrofit installations will require that you remove a large portion of finished wall and then refinish it once installation of the entire system is complete.

The bottom of the enclosure should be installed at least 48" above the floor. Most models require a ¼" gap behind the enclosure to accommodate the modules and fastening hardware. The front should protrude $1^{11}/_{16}$" plus the thickness of the drywall from the studs to allow the cover to fit.

A dedicated 15-amp, 120-volt electrical receptacle is suggested, and may be required, depending on the grade of installation.

Everything You Need

Tools: Screwdriver, level.

Materials: Wood screws; distribution center; wood shims; cable clamp; 15-amp, 120-volt receptacle.

How to Recess Mount a Distribution Center

1 Install the distribution center at least 48" above the floor. Position between two studs with a standard span of 16" on-center.

2 Use wood screws, one for each of the mounting slots located on the sides of the distribution center, to fasten to the studs. Do not fully tighten the screws.

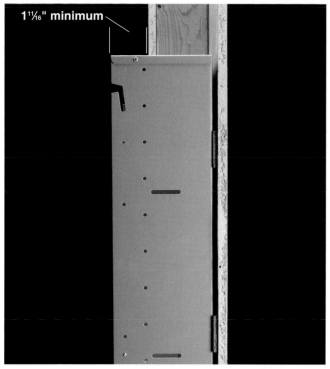

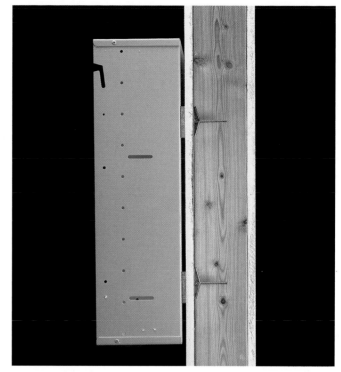

3 Use wood shims to create a minimum ¼" gap between the back of the distribution center and the wall. The front edge of the center should protrude at least 1¹¹⁄₁₆" from the finished wall face. Adjust the shims for proper spacing, check for level, and tighten the screws to secure the center in position.

Alternative Method: Surface-mount the distribution center. Leave a ¼" gap between the back of the center and the wall. Use wall anchors where needed, with spacers or shims as necessary.

How to Install the Power Supply

1 Run electrical NM cable in the bay next to the distribution center, using cable staples to affix the cable to the stud. Drill a 1" hole through the stud into the adjoining bay, 4" below the distribution center.

2 Feed the NM cable through the hole and into the gang box of the distribution center. Attach the cable with a cable clamp. Install a grounded 15-amp, 120-volt receptacle (page 64) before completing the rest of the installation.

Routing Cables & Wires

Routing cable and wire of any kind requires drilling holes through framing members throughout the home. Drill holes no closer than 2" from the top or bottom edge of joists. Use nail plates to protect holes in studs within 2" of the edge. Always check your local building codes for requirements in your area.

Low-voltage cable can run a maximum of 295 ft. from the distribution center without any significant signal loss. The cable cannot run within 6" of electrical wires and can cross only from a 90° angle, 6" from them.

To route cables and wires, begin at the outlet bracket or box locations, and feed to the distribution center. The maximum allowable pulling tension for UTP cable is 25 pounds. Use electrical tape to hold the tips of all cables and wires together as they are fed, and avoid knots and kinks. Leave at least 12" of slack at bracket or box locations for making connections.

If your service connections are outside the home, drill 1" holes through to the outside near the service entrance location. Insert a 1" PVC conduit, and feed cables and wires through it. Leave 36" of slack, and attach notice tags to the ends for utility workers.

At the distribution center, mark each cable and wire according to its routing location. Feed each through the top of the enclosure, and cut the lead ends so they hang even with the bottom of the distribution center. When routing is complete, tuck all cables and wires neatly inside the distribution center and finish wall construction. For tips on routing cables and wires in finished walls, refer to pages 192 to 203.

Everything You Need

Tools: Drill, RJ45 crimp tool, F-connector crimp tool.

Materials: Tape, cables, RJ45 plugs, F-connectors.

Drill 1" holes through the top plate above the distribution center. Drill holes in floor joists for running cable along the underside of house levels and from the service entrance to the distribution center.

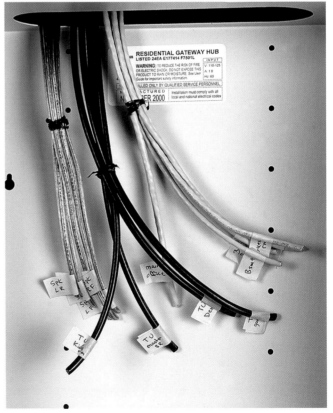

Label each run of cable and wire at the distribution center with the room and location within the room. All cables should hang even with the bottom of the distribution center.

How to Attach RJ45 Plugs to a UTP Cable

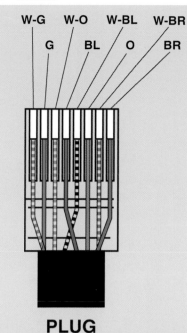

W-G W-O W-BL W-BR
G BL O BR

PLUG

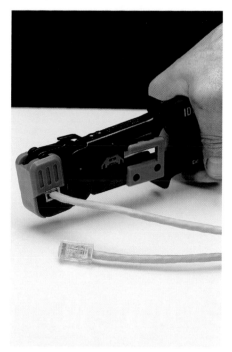

1 Strip 1" to 2" of outer insulation from the UTP cable. Separate the twisted pairs of individual wires.

2 Straighten and arrange each of the wires in order, according to the wiring assignment chart. Trim the ends evenly to ½" from the outer insulation. Insert the wires into the grooves of an RJ45 plug.

3 Make sure each wire is under the proper IDC (the conductor ends of the RJ45 plug) and that the outer insulation is ½" inside the plug. Crimp the plug with an RJ45 crimp tool.

How to Attach F-connectors to Coaxial Cable

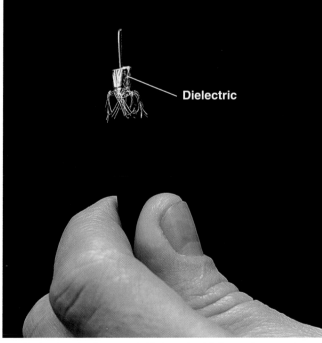

Dielectric

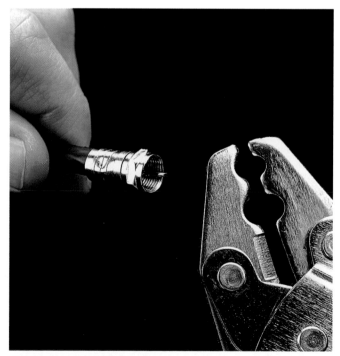

1 Strip the jacket and dielectric ⅜" from the center conductor. Strip the jacket ¼" from the foil and braid.

2 Slide the metal F-connector on until the dielectric is flush with center barrel. The center conductor should extend ¹⁄₁₆" past the end of the F-connector. Crimp the outer barrel of the connector to the cable jacket, using an F-connector crimp tool.

Installing an Audio System

How to Install a Recessed Speaker System

A home audio system routes speaker wire from a central receiver or amplifier, through the network distribution center, and back through to any room in the house. Each room can then be outfitted with either binding posts for an external speaker system or a recessed speaker system that is wired directly.

A volume control knob can be installed, typically at or near a light switch, to control the input level to the speakers in rooms wired to an external stereo system. Use a standard 4" × 4" gang box to house the module, and install as for an electrical switch.

1 Loosely fasten the speaker mounting brackets to the rails with the provided screws or ¼" sheet-metal screws. Attach the assembled brackets to the studs with 1½" screws. Align the loose bracket in the rails, so that the outer edge of the bracket will be flush with the outside face of the wallboard. Fully tighten the screws.

Everything You Need

Tools: Screwdriver.

Materials: Speaker mounting brackets, screws, volume control box, speakers.

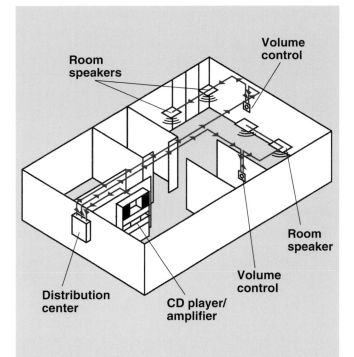

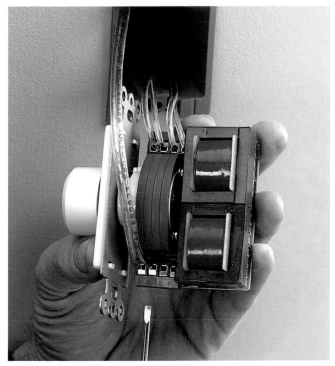

2 Run stereo speaker wire from each speaker location to the volume control box location. From the volume control box, run wire to the distribution center (page 320 to 321). Leave 8" to 12" of slack at each location.

3 Connect the wires at the volume control, with positive to positive (+ or red) and negative to negative (– or black). Position the module in the gang box, and screw into place. Attach the coverplate.

4 Connect the wires at each speaker. Keep positive to positive (+ or red) and negative to negative (– or black). Attach the speaker to the bracket. Some recessed speakers have plastic mounting arms that swing into place and clamp to the bracket when the front screws are tightened. Follow the manufacturer's directions.

Alternate Method: If not installing a recessed speaker system, install speaker binding posts. The network speaker wire is connected to the back of the binding posts. Run positive to positive (+ or red) and negative to negative (– or black).

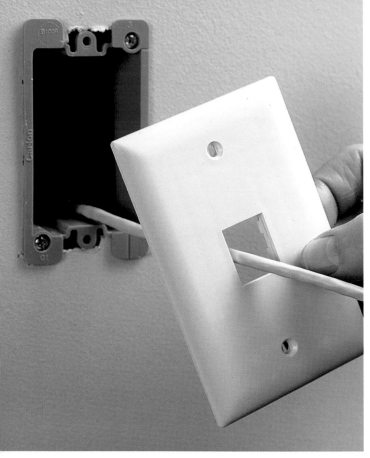

Before terminating a connector, pull all cables and wires for all multimedia outlets through the coverplate, leaving 8" to 12" of slack for termination. Attach the coverplate in place with the screws provided.

Terminating Connectors

With the distribution center and multimedia outlets placed, and all the cables and wires routed, finish the walls in each room before terminating the connectors. Most connectors and jacks are designed to snap into the coverplate.

Any style of telecommunication plug will fit in an RJ45 jack. UTP cable is terminated to the eight pins of the jack in an industry standard configuration, referred to as the T568A wiring standard. A 110-punchdown tool is used to terminate the wires to the corresponding terminals.

To terminate video connectors, crimp an F-connector to the coaxial cable end (page 321), and screw it to the backside of the self-terminating F-connector at the coverplate.

Everything You Need
Tools: Wire stripper, screwdriver, 110-punchdown tool.
Materials: RJ45 jacks, F-connector terminals.

How to Terminate an RJ45 Jack

1 Strip 2" of outer insulation from the UTP cable. Be careful not to cut through the twisted pairs within. Untwist each pair of individual wires.

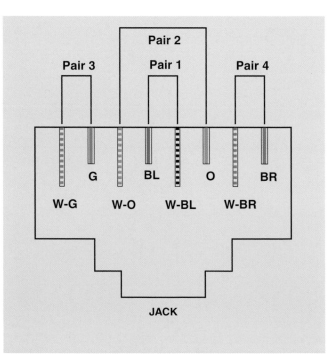

2 The backside of most RJ45 jacks are color-coded in the T568A wiring standard, so the proper colored wire from the UTP cable can be easily terminated to the proper terminal of the jack.

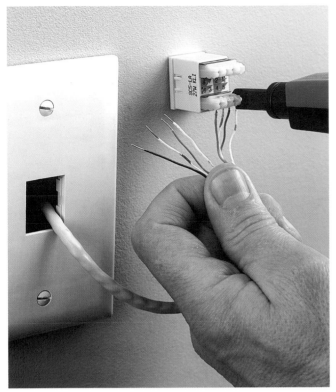

3 Place each wire into the groove of the appropriate terminal on the RJ45 jack, then use a 110-punchdown tool to seat the wire completely. The tool has a spring-tension head that forces the wire down and trims off the end. There should be no more than ½" of wire from the terminal to the outer cable insulation.

4 Fit a terminal cap over the ends of the jack terminals, then snap the jack into the coverplate.

How to Terminate Video Connectors

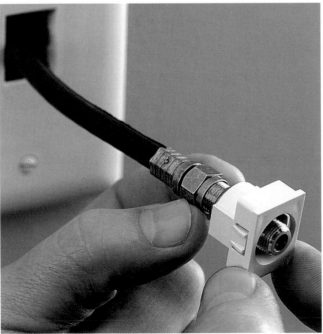

All coaxial video cables have plug-and-play connectors. The F-connector cable end is simply screwed to the back of the self-terminating F-connector terminal, and then snapped into the coverplate.

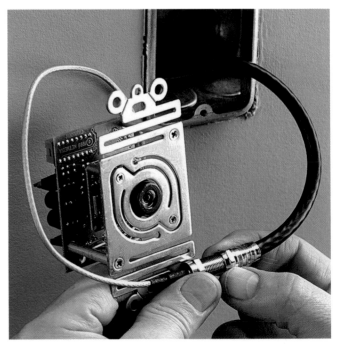

Video cameras also have plug-and-play, self-terminating F-connector connections. Consult the manufacturer's installation guide for setup and playback of your particular camera.

Making Final Connections

To house the distribution modules, mounting brackets are installed within the distribution center. Some brackets and modules will require screws for installation, while others use plastic push-pin grommets.

For easy connection to modules, RJ45 plugs are attached to UTP cable ends and F-connectors to coaxial cable ends (pages 324 to 326). All cables and wires should be clearly marked for easy identification and installation. It is best to keep all cables and wires routed to the same modules in neat, organized groupings. Bind the groupings with tie wraps where appropriate.

Once all the connections are made and the system is in working order, a cover is attached to protect the electronic modules and cable connections.

Everything You Need

Tools: Screwdriver.

Materials: Modules; RJ45 plugs; F-connectors; screws or push-pin grommets (as required).

How to Install Distribution Center Brackets

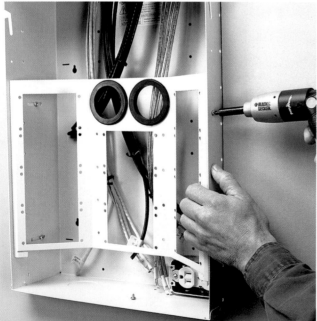

1 Attach the module mounting bracket to the distribution center. Align the mounting holes of the bracket panel with the prerouted holes in the sides of the distribution center and attach, using the screws provided.

2 Attach any additional single brackets that may be necessary for specialized modules or keeping power transformers separate. Some brackets require screws for installation, while others use push-pin grommets.

How to Mount & Connect Modules

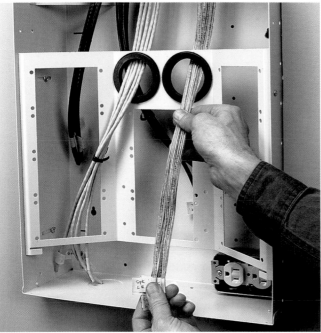

1 Determine where each module will be placed in the mounting brackets. Route any cables and wires through the mounting brackets to their corresponding module.

2 Plug the power transformer into the power distribution module, then snap the power module in place. The methods for module installation differ among network wiring manufacturers. Some require screws, while others use convenient push-pin grommets. Plug the power transformer into the 120-volt receptacle of the distribution center.

3 Use patch cords to connect the power module to those modules that require power, such as the video distribution, computer network, and video camera modules. Then, install the remaining modules in their chosen locations.

4 Trim the ends of all cables and wires, and attach the appropriate plugs or connectors (pages 320 to 321). Refer to the labels to connect the proper cable to the proper module OUTPUT port, in order to route the desired function to the desired location. Make sure all cables and wires from the service entrance are connected to an INPUT port.

Testing the System & Troubleshooting Problems

Before connecting to the home network system, do a quick recheck of the connections at the distribution center. Make sure that every module requiring power is patched to the power distribution module. Make sure the service lines from the service entrance are connected to the proper module INPUT port. Check that each cable and wire from the room outlets are hooked up to the proper module OUTPUT ports.

Cables and wires that are intended for future use should be gathered and loosely tied together. Run the grouping down one side of the distribution center, out of the way of the other connections. The system is now installed. Attach the cover and plug in the power distribution transformer to the receptacle for power.

To check the quality of signals at multimedia outlets, use a standard 2-way phone and phone

If an RJ45 jack does not work, remove the jack from the coverplate and check the pin/pair assignments on the back of the jack. If any wires are terminated to the wrong post, trim the wire ½" from the base and re-terminate the jack.

A variety of hand-held testers can be used to check cables and wires in the network system for continuity, network capabilities, and pin/pair assignments. If a cable or wire is bad, it will have to be replaced.

cord for RJ45 jacks, and a small television and short length of coaxial cable for F-connectors. The signals should be clear and strong.

Network system problems can be traced to one of a few simple causes: a bad connection, a bad cable or wire, a problem with a module, or a bad signal routed to the outlet.

Connectors: First, check that plugs and connection ends, and jack and connector terminations, are correct. A visual inspection of pin/pair alignment on an RJ45 jack or plug will quickly tell you whether it is in working order. If any of the wires of the UTP cable are terminated to the wrong posts, trim the cable ½" from the base and re-terminate the jack or plug. The center conductor of coaxial cables should be straight and extend ¹⁄₁₆" from the F-connector end. Coaxial cables should be tightly attached to the outlet F-connector. Recheck the connections at the distribution center to make sure the desired signal is routed to the proper outlet.

Cables and wires: Damage to cables and wires can easily occur during installation if the proper routing techniques are not observed (pages 320 to 321).

A variety of hand-held testers can be used to check cables and wires for continuity, network and performance capabilities, and pin/pair assignments. However, these testers are quite expensive and are not readily available at rental centers. For this reason, if a cable or wire is suspected to be faulty, it may be more economical to forgo testing and just replace the cable.

Modules: If none of the outlets in a particular network are functioning, check the power distribution module to see if there has been a power surge. The module contains a fuse that automatically resets, protecting the system against power trouble. If the LED light appears red, there has been an abnormal and significant electrical surge in the system. Disconnect all the modules from the power module. Begin reconnecting the modules one at a time, until the LED light on the power module appears red again, indicating the problem module. Disconnect the module,

and replace it. Modules for video distribution and computer networks are typically power surge-protected to keep your sensitive and expensive computer and entertainment equipment from damage.

Signals: If, after replacing any damaged modules, there still is no signal or only a very poor signal, test the incoming cables from the service entrance on the interior of the house only. If they are good and problems persist, contact your telecommunication and service providers to check the exterior lines and connections.

Another resource is the growing number of electrical contractors who work with and install network wiring systems. Call around or stop by a home center—many home centers that sell network wiring systems can also help you find a reputable contractor in your area.

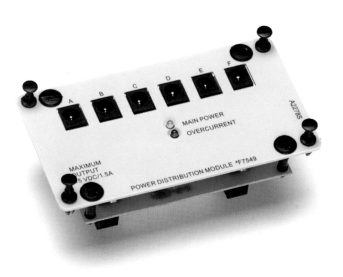

Most modules contain built-in surge protection to protect electronic equipment and devices connected to the network. An illuminated indicator light alerts that a power surge has occurred in the system, and the problem module will need to be identified and replaced.

An NID box is located on the outside of the home. It is where the service providers transfer the lines to the homeowner. Test the incoming cable lines on the interior of the house only. If they are good and problems persist, contact your telecommunication providers to have them check the exterior lines and connections from the NID back to the source.

Conversion Chart

Converting Measurements

To Convert:	To:	Multiply by:
Inches	Millimeters	25.4
Inches	Centimeters	2.54
Feet	Meters	0.305
Yards	Meters	0.914
Square inches	Square centimeters	6.45
Square feet	Square meters	0.093
Square yards	Square meters	0.836
Cubic inches	Cubic centimeters	16.4
Cubic feet	Cubic meters	0.0283
Cubic yards	Cubic meters	0.765
Ounces	Milliliters	30.0
Pints (U.S.)	Liters	0.473 (Imp. 0.568)
Quarts (U.S.)	Liters	0.946 (Imp. 1.136)
Gallons (U.S.)	Liters	3.785 (Imp. 4.546)
Ounces	Grams	28.4
Pounds	Kilograms	0.454

To Convert:	To:	Multiply by:
Millimeters	Inches	0.039
Centimeters	Inches	0.394
Meters	Feet	3.28
Meters	Yards	1.09
Square centimeters	Square inches	0.155
Square meters	Square feet	10.8
Square meters	Square yards	1.2
Cubic centimeters	Cubic inches	0.061
Cubic meters	Cubic feet	35.3
Cubic meters	Cubic yards	1.31
Milliliters	Ounces	.033
Liters	Pints (U.S.)	2.114 (Imp. 1.76)
Liters	Quarts (U.S.)	1.057 (Imp. 0.88)
Liters	Gallons (U.S.)	0.264 (Imp. 0.22)
Grams	Ounces	0.035
Kilograms	Pounds	2.2

Metric Equivalents

	1/64	1/32	1/25	1/16	1/8	1/4	3/8		1/2	5/8	3/4	7/8	1	2	3	4	5	6	7	8	9	10	11	12	36	39.4
Inches (in.)																										
Feet (ft.)																								1	3	3½
Yards (yd.)																									1	1½
Millimeters (mm)	0.40	0.79	1	1.59	3.18	6.35	9.53	10	12.7	15.9	19.1	22.2	25.4	50.8	76.2	101.6	127	152	178	203	229	254	279	305	914	1,000
Centimeters (cm)							0.95	1	1.27	1.59	1.91	2.22	2.54	5.08	7.62	10.16	12.7	15.2	17.8	20.3	22.9	25.4	27.9	30.5	91.4	100
Meters (m)																								.30	.91	1.00

Resources

Briggs and Stratton Power
   Products: pp. 262 (top), 263 (all),
   267 (all)
800-743-4115
www.briggsandstratton.com

Crossville, Inc.: p. 236 (top)
931-484-2110
www.crossvilleinc.com

Home Automation, Inc.: pp. 298-299
800-229-7256
www.homeauto.com

Honda Power Equipment
   American Honda Motor Company,
   Inc.: pp. 262 (bottom), 265 (all),
   266 (both)
678-339-2600
www.hondapowerequipment.com

Hubbardton Forge: p. 226 (top)
802-468-5516
www.vtforge.com

Ideal Industries, Inc.: p. 198
   (bottom right)
800-435-0705
www.idealindustries.com

Insinkerator: p. 241 (top)
800-558-5700
www.insinkerator.com

Pass and Seymour legrand:
   pp. 309, 310, 326
800-223-4185
www.passandseymour.com

Karen Melvin Architectural Stock
   Images, Inc.
©Karen Melvin: p. 322 for Lek
Design Group
www.karenmelvin.com

Index

Also from

CREATIVE PUBLISHING INTERNATIONAL

Complete Guide to Bathrooms
Complete Guide to Decks
Complete Guide to Ceramic & Stone Tile
Complete Guide to Creative Landscapes
Complete Guide to Easy Woodworking Projects
Complete Guide to Finishing Touches
  for Yards & Gardens
Complete Guide to Flooring
Complete Guide to Home Carpentry
Complete Guide to Home Masonry
Complete Guide to Home Plumbing
Complete Guide to Home Storage
Complete Guide to Home Wiring
Complete Guide to Kitchens
Complete Guide to Outdoor Wood Projects
Complete Guide to Painting & Decorating
Complete Guide to Roofing & Siding
Complete Guide to Windows & Doors
Complete Photo Guide to Home Repair
Complete Photo Guide to Home Improvement
Complete Photo Guide to Outdoor Home Repair

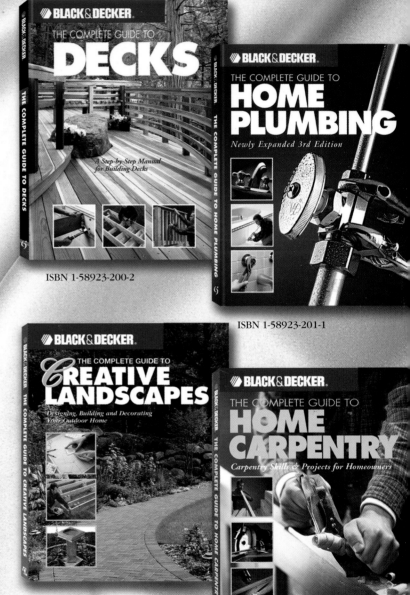

ISBN 1-58923-200-2

ISBN 1-58923-201-1

ISBN 0-86573-579-4

ISBN 0-86573-577-8

CREATIVE PUBLISHING INTERNATIONAL

18705 LAKE DRIVE EAST
CHANHASSEN, MN 55317

WWW.CREATIVEPUB.COM